Disruptive Technology and Business Continuity

Le Thanh Tung · Nguyen Hoang Sinh · Pham Ha
Editors

Disruptive Technology and Business Continuity

Proceedings of The 5th International Conference on Business (ICB 2023)

Springer

Editors
Le Thanh Tung
Faculty of Economics and Public Management
Ho Chi Minh City Open University
Ho Chi Minh City, Vietnam

Nguyen Hoang Sinh
Faculty of Business Administration
Ho Chi Minh City Open University
Ho Chi Minh City, Vietnam

Pham Ha
Faculty of Banking and Finance
Ho Chi Minh City Open University
Ho Chi Minh City, Vietnam

ISBN 978-981-97-5451-9 ISBN 978-981-97-5452-6 (eBook)
https://doi.org/10.1007/978-981-97-5452-6

This Springer imprint is published by the registered company Springer Nature Singapore Pte Ltd.
The registered company address is: 152 Beach Road, #21-01/04 Gateway East, Singapore 189721, Singapore

Preface

Welcome to the Springer proceedings entitled "Disruptive Technology and Business Continuity: Proceedings of The 5th International Conference on Business (ICB 2023)." This volume delves into the profound impacts of disruptive technologies on business operations, with a keen focus on management, finance, economics, and sustainability within an evolving business environment.

In today's dynamic marketplace, businesses face unprecedented challenges and opportunities arising from disruptive technologies. From artificial intelligence to blockchain, these innovations reshape industries, redefine competition, and compel organizations to adapt swiftly to ensure continuity and sustainable growth. Understanding the intricacies of managing disruptive technologies and their implications on business continuity is paramount for researchers, practitioners, students, policymakers, and managers alike.

This collection of conference proceedings aims to shed light on various facets of this complex landscape. Through a diverse array of topics, including emerging trends, best practices, and illuminating case studies, readers will gain valuable insights into mitigating risks, seizing opportunities, and fostering sustainability amidst technological disruption. The interdisciplinary nature of this work, spanning business, management, finance, and economics, underscores the holistic approach required to navigate today's business challenges effectively.

What sets this volume apart are its practicality and depth of analysis. It offers not only theoretical frameworks but also actionable strategies drawn from real-world experiences. Through a didactic approach enhanced by illustrations, tables, and innovative presentation styles, readers will find the material both accessible and applicable to their own professional endeavors.

Key themes explored include strategies for managing risks and uncertainties in the face of technological disruption, the pivotal role of financial management in ensuring business continuity and growth, and best practices for fostering sustainable business operations. Moreover, through engaging case studies, readers will glean valuable lessons from successful businesses that have adeptly navigated disruptive technologies to achieve sustainable growth and continuity.

As you embark on this journey through the intersection of disruptive technology and business continuity, we trust that these proceedings will equip you with the knowledge, tools, and inspiration to thrive in an ever-changing business landscape. Whether you are a seasoned practitioner, a budding researcher, or a policymaker shaping the future of industries, we invite you to delve into these pages and discover the keys to sustainable success amidst technological disruption.

We extend our sincere gratitude to the contributors, reviewers, and organizers whose dedication and expertise have made this publication possible. May these proceedings serve as a beacon of insight and innovation, guiding businesses toward resilience, agility, and enduring prosperity in the face of disruptive technologies.

Ho Chi Minh City, Vietnam

Le Thanh Tung
Nguyen Hoang Sinh
Pham Ha

Contents

Path to Sustainability: Technological Innovation and Digital Economy as Main Drivers of Green Economic Development 1
Nguyen Van It, Nguyen Gia Khuong, and Nguyen Thanh Tuan

Corporate Social Responsibility in the Supermarket Sector: Evidence from Vietnam 15
Loan Thi-Hong Van and Thao Hoang-Minh Nguyen

Factors Affecting Electronic Word of Mouth on the Acceptance of Digital Banking: An Evidence in Vietnam 31
Nguyen Hoang Sinh, Lam Quoc Bao, and Nguyen Huu Long

The Impact of Mobile Trust and Mobile Satisfaction to Electronic Word-of-Mouth and Intention to Use E-Wallet 45
Nguyen Tran Cam Linh and Nguyen Hoang Chau

Analyzing the Influence of Artificial Intelligence on Consumers' Online Purchase Intentions 67
Chi Thi Kim Nguyen, Y Thi Nhu Nguyen, and Anh Ngoc Tuan Bui

How Interactivity Has Effects on Satisfaction and Vising Intention: Non-immersive Virtual Reality Technology 79
Dinh Tien Minh, Nguyen Thi My Xuyen, Thai Hong Son, and Nguyen Thi Lien

Factors Influencing the Intention and Behavior to Use E-Wallets of Customers in Ho Chi Minh City 91
Nguyen Khanh Ngan and Le Dinh Nghi

Virtual Reality as a Tool for Destination Marketing of Sustainable Tourism During the COVID-19 Pandemic 103
Sinh Duc Hoang, Diep T. N. Nguyen, and Minh Pham

Intention to Accept Smart Contracts Based on Blockchain Technology in Vietnamese Businesses 119
Thi Hong Nhung Vo, The Huu Chau, and Quan Tri Dang

Do the Uses of Technology Increase Firm Performance? Evidence from the WBES Dataset 135
Thuy An Chung and Quynh Trang Phan

Impact of Work-Life Balance on Employee Work Performance: The Mediating Role of Employee Creativity 151
Nguyen Minh Ha, Nguyen Thanh Phuong Thuy, and Ngo Thanh Trung

Impact of the Authentic Leadership on Employee's Creativity: The Intermediate Role of Well-Being, Person-Job Fit, Person-Organization Fit 165
Anh Thuy Trinh, Tram Thi Bich Nguyen, and Nuong Thi Xuan Nguyen

Knowledge Sharing for Enhanced Job Engagement of Public Servants in Ho Chi Minh City 177
Le Quang Thang and Mai Ngoc Khuong

Factors Affecting Meaningful Work and Employee Engagement in the Information Technology Industry: Evidence in Ho Chi Minh City 189
Nong Quy Ngoc An and Le Dinh Nghi

Linking Green Organizational Identity and Employee Pro-Environmental Behaviors: The Role of Green Shared Vision 201
Nguyen The Khai, Tran Quoc Cuong, Nguyen Ngoc Duy Phuong, and Do Thi Thanh Truc

The Role of External Stimulation on the Relationship between Mental Imagery and Purchase Intentions: Case Study of Vietnamese Gen Z 213
Ha Nguyen Le Khanh and Linh Huynh Thi My

How Does Knowledge Shape the Student's Entrepreneurial Intention? the S-O-R Theory Perspective 225
Tuyen Kim Thi Dinh, Trang Thuy Duong Mai, and Linh Thuy Thi Ly

How Do Emotional Support and Emotional Exhaustion Affect the Relationship Between Incivility and Students' Subjective Well-Being? 237
Uyen Phuong Nguyen Le, Anh Tram Tuong Nguyen, Anh Van Nguyen, Van Khanh Huynh, Chi Thao Le Bui, and Anh Lan Thuy Nguyen

How Does Acculturation Affect International Students' Choice to Study Abroad? Explanation and Comparison Based on a Relationship with Destination Country Image and Cross-Cultural Awareness 249
Tri Minh Cao, Anh Lan Thuy Nguyen, and Anh Quynh Duong Nguyen

Enhancing Student Satisfaction in Online Learning: An Empirical Study During the COVID-19 Pandemic 259
Nguyen Hoang Sinh and Hoang Thi Hoa

The Relationship Between Public Debt and Economic Growth: A Note from Developing Countries 271
Le Thanh Tung and Tran Le Nguyen

Diversity and Bank Performance in Transition Economies: The Mediating Role of State Ownership 285
Doan Ngan Ha, Duong Dang Khoa, and Pham Ha

Trading Strategies in the Ho Chi Minh Stock Exchange 297
Thach H. Pham and Thi Minh Hue Phan

About the Editors

Assoc. Prof. Dr. Le Thanh Tung is an Associate Professor in Economics and the Dean at the Faculty of Economics and Public Management, Ho Chi Minh City Open University, Vietnam. Le Thanh Tung is also the head of the Policy and Applied Economics Research Group. His research interests are socio-economic policy analysis, public policy assessment, managerial economics, and solutions for social issues. He published numerous articles in peer-reviewed journals such as *Eurasian Geography and Economics, Applied Economics Letters, Asia Pacific Journal of Social Work and Development, Post-Communist Economies, Asian Journal of Technology Innovation, Behaviour & Information Technology and Journal of Product & Brand Management*. In the academic system, Le Thanh Tung serves as a reviewer for international journals such as the *Journal of Economic Structures, Current Issue in Tourism, Organizations and Markets in Emerging Economies,* and *Transforming Government: People, Process and Policy*. Besides, Tung has joined many international conferences and has published several peer-reviewed book chapters in recent years.

Dr. Nguyen Hoang Sinh is the Acting Dean of the Faculty of Business Administration at Ho Chi Minh City Open University in Vietnam. He earned a Ph.D. in Marketing as a recipient of the New Zealand ASEAN Scholars Awards in 2013 and a Master's degree in Australia as an Australian Development Scholarships recipient in 2004. Sinh's research has been published in various peer-reviewed journals such as *Sage Open, Australasian Marketing Journal, Journal of International Business and Economy, Journal of Asian Business and Economic Studies, Journal of Asian Finance, Economics and Business,* and *Ho Chi Minh City Open University Journal of Science—Economics and Business Administration*. His research interests center around marketing communications that use emotional appeals in health and pro-social behavior, with a focus on persuasive messages that utilize self-conscious emotions in public health. He has served as a peer reviewer for the Journal of International Business and Economy since 2013, as well as for the 2017 AMA Marketing and Public Policy Conference and the 2017 ANZMAC Conference. With over 15 years of experience in marketing, corporate communications, and public relations,

Sinh has previously managed accounts for major clients, including Abbott, Coca-Cola, PepsiCo, Samsung, Ariston, Microsoft, GuocoLand, ACCA, ACE Life, HSBC Bank, PG Bank, among others.

Assoc. Prof. Dr. Pham Ha has completed his Ph.D. in the Economic Sciences (Université de Limoges, France). He is currently Dean of the Faculty of Banking and Finance at Ho Chi Minh City Open University. His research interests are in the field of corporate governance, prudential regulation, bank risk and performance, and the behavioral finance. His research has been published in peer-reviewed journals such as *International Review of Economics and Finance, Managerial and Decision Economics, Cogent of Economics and Finance, Risk, Financial Research Letters, Economic Research, Economics & Sociology, Journal of Risk and Financial Management.* He also serves as a reviewer and the editorial advisory board member of *Journal of Global Business Insight*; a referee for various journals: *Global Finance, International Financial Markets, Institutions & Money, Emerging Markets, Finance and Trade, International Journal of Managerial Finance, Economic Research.*

Path to Sustainability: Technological Innovation and Digital Economy as Main Drivers of Green Economic Development

Nguyen Van It, Nguyen Gia Khuong, and Nguyen Thanh Tuan

Abstract Nowadays, the majority of nations worldwide aim to achieve green economic development (GED). Given the industrial revolution's backdrop 4.0, the digital economy (DE) and technological innovation (TI) play an important role as the main drivers of the development of the green economy. This study was conducted to assess the impact of TI and DE on GED. In particular, the GED indicator was built from three components with the weight of each component evaluated by 9 experts in the field of economic development, digital technology, and innovation, then measured by the Analytic Hierarchy Process (AHP) method. Using panel data from 32 countries within 2015–2020 and the Generalized method of moments (GMM) estimation method through employing STATA software version 16.0, the research results show evidence to confirm the significant positive impact of TI and DE on GED of countries. At the same time, this study also assesses the impact of these factors on GED between two groups of middle-income (MI) and high-income (HI) countries to see what the different impacts are. The results of this study lead to recommendations on policy implications for GED and toward sustainable development of countries, including Vietnam.

Keywords Sustainability · Innovation · Digital economy · Green economic development · Impact

1 Introduction

Sustainable development is always the goal of countries, especially developing countries as they must balance resources and economic development priorities while still ensuring environmental and social factors [1]. In fact, some countries focusing solely

N. Van It · N. G. Khuong (✉)
Ho Chi Minh City University of Industry and Trade, Ho Chi Minh, Vietnam
e-mail: nguyengiakhuong2606@gmail.com

N. T. Tuan
LAMIH, UMR CNRS 8201, Université Polytechnique Hauts-de-France, Valenciennes, France

L. T. Tung et al. (eds.), *Disruptive Technology and Business Continuity*,
https://doi.org/10.1007/978-981-97-5452-6_1

on economic growth harm the environment. Hence, the urgent problem posed is how to promote coordinated and balanced economic development and environment [2]. Economic efficiency is emphasized by Industry 4.0, and green total factor productivity is a crucial indicator in this regard. The green development trend, including green economy, finance, logistics, and technology, has gained momentum, particularly following the COVID-19 pandemic. In which, GED has been widely agreed as the objective of all global economies [3], and one of the keys to attaining sustainable development is GED [4]. The measurement of GED level is the primary focus of the academic research on GED that is currently available [5].

In both developed and developing countries, the green economy has become a crucial framework for sustainable development policy [6]. However, studies on GED measurements do not have a unified analytical framework. At the same time, due to limited access to necessary data, most studies use common environmental and economic indicators and development research without going deeper. This research topic has representative research by Yang et al. [3] for the case of China. There have been no studies evaluating the effects of DE and TI on GED for groups of HI and MI countries. Therefore, this study was conducted with three main goals: (i) provide an analytical framework to measure GED, TI, and DE indicators; (ii) evaluate the impact of TI and DE on GED, and moreover, interaction variables are also used to evaluate the difference in the impact of TI and DE on GED between two groups of HI and MI countries; and (iii) based on the results, policy implications for governments and businesses are proposed to promote green and sustainable economic development.

2 Literature Review

2.1 *Basic Concept*

The economist Pearce introduced the idea of a "green economy," arguing that there is an indispensable relationship between the environment and the economy [7]. It also emphasized on the improvement of human well-being and social equity, while reducing environmental risks and ecological scarcities significantly [8]. Although it is acknowledged that environmental preservation is crucial to GED, Wang et al. [9] supposed that GED refers to the enhancement of quality and efficiency in an economy through TI, industrial development, and resource allocation while simultaneously conserving the environment and preserving resources. Thereby, GED is considered an effective way to achieve sustainable development [10]. Added to that, Zhao et al. [11] verified that GED is an economic form built on the preservation of the environment, the responsible use of resources, and the development of those resources in a way that results in sustainable development. Obviously, there are many concepts of GED, and they cover different components, but in general, the concept of GED mentions these main components: environment protection, economic development, and human well-being.

2.2 Previous Related Studies

Absolutely, GED is an important proposition of today's world development. There are many studies related to GED, including the methodology for GED's measurement, GED's impacts, and also its influencing factors. Actually, there is no agreement on how to measure the GED indicator, despite an increasing number of academics assessing the degree of GED using a multidimensional index system [3]. Studies on GED and its influencing factors and also the impacts of TI and DE on GED were summarized as follows:

The impact of Innovation-Driven Strategy on GED in China was examined by Cao et al. [12]. The authors used panel data from 47 Chinese pilot smart city projects between 2009 and 2017. The relationship between innovation-driven strategy and GED was estimated using the individual fixed effect model. Additionally, the heteroscedasticity was decreased by applying the cross-section weighting method. In the study, dust, water, and SO2 are used to measure GED. The results show that although different innovation-driven indicators play different roles in GED promotion, the innovation-driven strategy positively affects GED. In order to deal with data classification effectively for the purpose of removing redundant information, Peng and Fan [13] implemented an evaluation of GED based on a rough set calculation method. The authors confirmed that the green economy should not pursue the growth of economic targets blindly, but should instead pay attention to the development of the environment and society in accordance with those goals. In terms of the degree of renewable energy consumption, according to Xie et al. [14], GED can only be promoted by a certain amount of renewable energy consumption within the range of 0.67–10.87. If it is outside this range, it is not beneficial for GED.

Yang et al. [3] studied the interrelationship and degree of influence of digitalization, TI, and GED. By building a PVAR model and applying the entropy method, the authors were able to test their relationships empirically using panel data from 30 Chinese provinces between 2011 and 2019. Then authors concluded that digitization positively impacts GED, while TI has a negative coefficient and not significantly. Related to this field of study, Lin and Zhou [15] constructed a comprehensive system for measuring the green economy. The authors then used the entropy weighted TOPSIS method to investigate China's growth in the green economy between 2000 and 2017. The authors came to the conclusion that TI hasn't yet played a big part in the growth of the green economy. Another typical study was conducted by Guo and Diao [16] on the relationship between urban spatial functional division (USFD) and GED. From 2009 to 2019, the authors computed the USFD and GED indicators for 108 cities within the Yangtze River Economic Belt. The results showed that TI has a positive significant impact on the coupling between USFD and GED.

Moreover, related to the impact of technologies on GED, Wang et al. [9] utilized panel data from 30 Chinese provinces between 2011 and 2018. They concluded that big data and big data sub-indicators (*cloud computing, Internet of things, and artificial intelligence*) have different implications on the growth of the green economy.

3 Theoretical Framework, Data, and Methodology

3.1 Theoretical Framework

Basically, the measurement of GED is based on GED's concepts and its first components including environment, economic development, and social development as mentioned by Peng and Fan [13]. While TI was designed with Input and Output as Yang et al. [3] and Han et al. [17]. Also, DE was developed with the first components of DE infrastructure and DE openness as Zhang et al. [18] and Han et al. [17]. These first components of GED, TI, and DE have different levels of importance in the aggregate indicators, so AHP method will be employed to determine the respective weights of these components (Fig. 1).

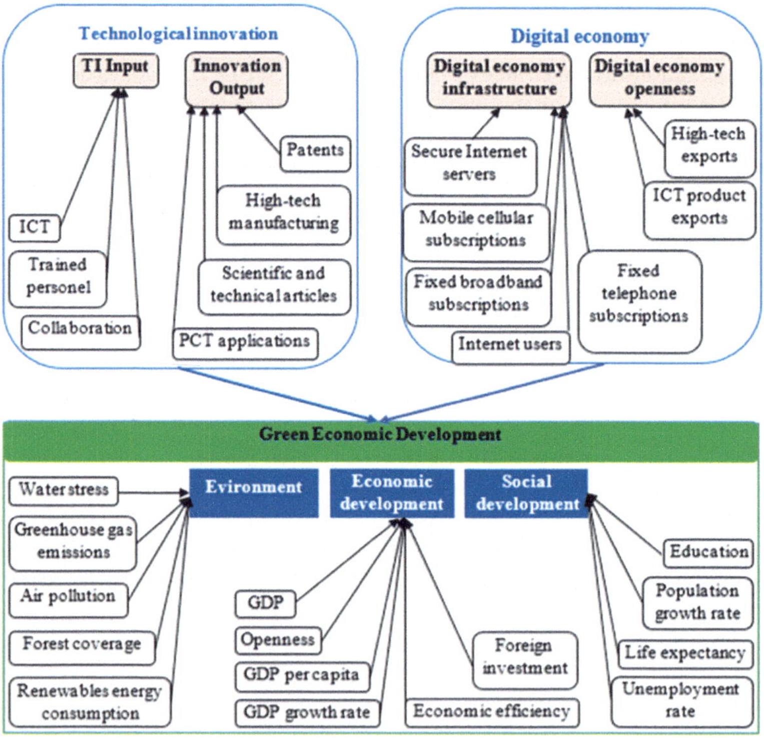

Fig. 1 Framework of the study

3.2 Data and Variables

The study used a strong balanced panel dataset, and Table 1 describes variables to calculate GED, TI, and DE indicators; meanwhile, all variables used for the study are collected from 32 economies over the period 2015–2020.

3.3 Research Methodology

The study uses rigorous quantitative methods with software support the tool of Stata 16.0. Following Nguyen et al. [23], generally data in different ranges $x_i \in [a; b]$ will be normalized to $y_i \in [c; d]$ based on this formula: $y_i = f_{(x)} = c + \frac{(x_i-a)(d-c)}{(b-a)}$. In the study, this formula will be employed to normalize all values of variables into the same range of the interval [0; 1]. For the second components, which have negative expected signs in their respective aggregate indicators, values will be transformed by the adjusted formula $1 - \frac{(x_i-a)}{(b-a)}$, , to make sure that 0 and 1 still correspond to the worst and best possible outcomes, respectively. Values of the level 1 component indicators (a_i) are the average of the corresponding level 2 component indicators, and values of the aggregate GED, TI, and DE indicators follow this formula: $\sum_{i=1}^{192} (x_i * w_i)$, in which w_i is the relative weight of each first component in the aggregate indicators.

To measure the weights of the first components of GED, TI, and DE, the AHP method six steps were applied by Trinh et al. [24]. To evaluate the weights for first components, an AHP survey was designed and sent to 15 experts in the fields of development economics, international economics, technology, and innovation. Then, there were 9 responses collected. To check the consistency, the upper limit of CR was employed at 9% [25].

3.4 Econometrics Model

Relating to TI and DE, Yang et al. [3] used digitalization and TI to see the impacts on GED. Moreover, Lin and Zhou [15] conjectured that the GED of developed countries is unquestionably superior to that of developing countries. In today's world, urbanization also become a concerned issue for many countries. However, Chen et al. [26] claimed that increased urbanization contributes positively to regional green development; hence, the model was updated to include the urban population rate. Finally, our model was derived as follows:

$$\mathrm{Log}(\mathrm{GED}_{it}) = \alpha_0 + \sum_{i=1}^{k} \beta_i \mathrm{Log}(X_{it}) + \mathrm{DGNI}_{it} + \mathrm{Log}(\mathrm{UrPop}_{it}) + \vartheta_{it}$$

Table 1 Components of GED, TI, and DE indicators

	Sub-dimensions	Variables	Explanations	Sign	Source
Green economic development					
Environment Cato [20], Cao et al. [12], Xie et al. [14]	Water stress	GWS	Level of water stress	(−)	UNEP. [19]
	Greenhouse gas emissions	GCO2	Annual CO_2, emissions	(−)	Yang et al. [3]
	Air pollution	GNO2	Nitrous oxide emissions	(−)	
	Renewables energy consumption	GREC	Renewable energy consumption	(+) if $0.67 \leq$ GREC ≤ 10.87; (−) if other	Xie et al. [14]
	Forest coverage	GFA	Forest area	(+)	Peng and Fan [13]
Economic development Wang et al. [13], Peng and Fan [13], Lin and Zhou [15]	Economic efficiency	GLD	Labor productivity	(+)	Lin and Zhou [15]
	GDP growth rate	GGrowth	Measured by $= \frac{GDP_t - GDP_{t-1}}{GDP_{t-1}}$	(+)	Wang et al. [22], Yang et al. [3]
	Openness	GTrade	Openness $= \frac{Export_t + Import_t}{GDP_t}$	(+)	OECD [21], Wang et al. [22]
	GDP	GGDP	Total GDP	(+)	Peng and Fan [13], Lin and Zhou [15]
	GDP per capita	GGPDcap	GDP per capita	(+)	Wang et al. [22], Guo and Diao [16]

(continued)

Table 1 (continued)

	Sub-dimensions	Variables	Explanations	Sign	Source
	Proportion of foreign investment	GFDI	FDI (Net inflows, US)	(+)	Yang et al. [3]
Social development Peng and Fan [13], Lin and Zhou [15], Guo and Diao [16]	Education	GEdu	Government expenditure on education, total (% of GDP)	(+)	Lin and Zhou [15]
	Life expectancy	GLE	The average number of years that a person may expect to live	(+)	Peng and Fan [13]
	Population growth rate	GPG	Population growth rate = $\frac{\text{Population}_t - \text{Population}_{t-1}}{\text{Population}_{t-1}}$	(−)	
	Unemployment rate	GUnemp	Unemployment rate	(−)	Peng and Fan [13], Guo and Diao [16]
Technological innovation development					
TI Input Yang et al. [3], Han et al. [17], Zhang et al. [18]	ICT	TICT	Information and communication technologies	(+)	By authors
	Trained personnel	TTrained	Graduates in science and engineering, %	(+)	Zhang et al. [18]
	Collaboration	TColla	University-industry Research collaboration	(+)	By authors
Innovation Output Yang et al. [3], Han et al. [17]	Patents by origin/bn	TPBO	Number of resident patent applications filed at a given national or regional patent office	(+)	Han et al. [17]
	High-tech manufacturing	THT	High-tech and medium–high-tech manufacturing	(+)	By authors
	Scientific and technical articles/bn	TSATA	Number of scientific and technical journal articles	(+)	Han et al. [17]
	PCT patents by origin/bn	TPCT	Number of Patent Cooperation Treaty (PCT) applications	(+)	Yang et al. [3]

(continued)

Table 1 (continued)

	Sub-dimensions	Variables	Explanations	Sign	Source
Digital economy indicator					
DE infrastructure Zhang et al. [18]	Mobile cellular subscriptions	DMCS	Mobile cellular subscriptions	(+)	Zhang et al. [18]
	Secure Internet servers	DSIS	Secure Internet servers	(+)	Zhang et al. [18]
	Fixed broadband subscriptions	DFBS	Fixed broadband subscriptions	(+)	Zhang et al. [18]
	Fixed telephone subscriptions	DFTS	Fixed telephone subscriptions	(+)	Zhang et al. [18]
	Individuals using internet	DIUTI	Individuals using the Internet	(+)	Zhang et al. [18]
Zhang et al. [18]	High-tech exports	DHT	High-technology exports	(+)	Zhang et al. [18]
	ICT product exports	DICTge	ICT goods exports	(+)	Zhang et al. [18]

where X_{it} are target variables, comprised of variables (TI, DE) and interaction terms (TI*DGNI, DE*DGNI); $DGNI_{it}$ is dummy variable, which was created in the way that if Gross national income (GNI) per capita of a country is more than $12,695, DGNI takes value of 1 and takes value of "0" otherwise. According to the United Nations [27], if a country has a GNI per capita over $12,695; it is classified in the group of HI countries. This variable was included in the model in order to find out the difference in impacts of TI and DE between the groups of MI countries and HI countries. $UrPop_{it}$ is the urban population of country i in the year t. Lastly, ϑ_{it} is the white noise. This model is regressed using the GMM method.

4 Results and Discussion

4.1 Descriptive Analysis

This study utilized a dataset including 41 variables, collected from 32 countries during 2015–2020. There are 66.67% of countries in HI group, which leaves a proportion of 33.33% that are MI economies. Figure 2 shows that the level of GED, TI, and DE of the group of HI countries is often larger than that of the group of MI countries. The biggest difference between the two groups belongs to TI, followed by DE and GED.

Table 2 presents the correlations between variables used in the regression model according to the Bonferroni method. This shows that the variables TI, DE, DGNI, and UrPop are all statistically significantly positively correlated with GED at the 5% significance level. The remaining correlation coefficients are all at a moderate level, so according to the rule of thumb, the model is not seriously affected by multicollinearity.

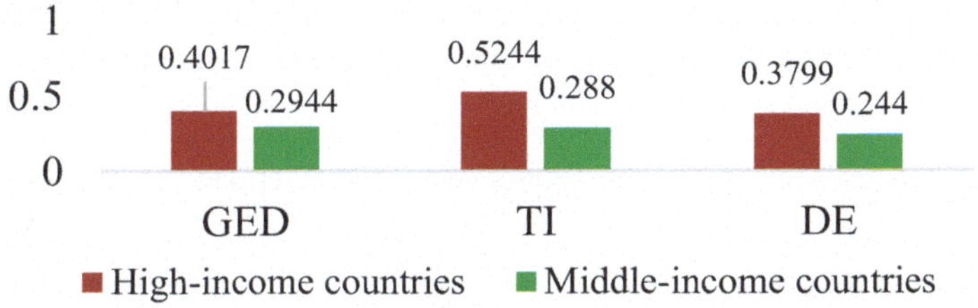

Fig. 2 A comparison of GED, TI, and DE between groups of MI countries and HI countries

Table 2 Summarization of the correlation of variables

Variables	GED	TI	DE	DGNI	UrPop
GED	1				
TI	0.6758[a]	1			
DE	0.5625[a]	0.6429[a]	1		
DGNI	0.6568[a]	0.6732[a]	0.6276[a]	1	
UrPop	0.6679[a]	0.4788[a]	0.3418[a]	0.4387[a]	1

Note [a] indicates the significance of 5%

4.2 Results and Discussion

Table 3 presents the weights of the first-level components of GED, TI, and DE based on the AHP method. Accordingly, the "environment" component is considered as the most important with a weight of 0.4242, and it shows that while focusing on economic development, environmental factors are the top priority for GED, followed by social and welfare issues. Peng and Fan [13] reaffirm the significance of the environment and society, arguing that an assessment of the green economy should take into account social and environmental data in addition to economic data. For TI, the expert evaluation results show that Innovation Input such as "information and communication technologies", "graduates in science and engineering", and "university-industry research collaboration" plays a highly important role in developing a country's TI with a weight of 0.6052. Similarly, for DE development, the important role of DE infrastructure is also confirmed with a weight of 0.6885, while the weight of DE openness is 0.3115.

Model regression results evaluating the impact of TI and DE on GED using the GMM method are presented in Table 4. All regression models have statistically significant regression coefficients at the level of 10%.

In particular, the regression coefficients of model 1 are all positive and statistically significant at the level of 5%. The regression coefficient of the TI variable is 0.1853 which is the largest one. This is evidence that TI has the greatest impact on countries'

Table 3 Summarization of weights of first components of GED, TI, and DE indicators

Variables	Components	Weights
Green economic development	Environment	0.4242
	Economic development	0.1804
	Social development	0.3954
Technological innovation development	Innovation input	0.6052
	Technological innovation output	0.3948
Digital economy indicator	Digital economy infrastructure	0.6885
	Digital economy openness	0.3115

Table 4 Summarization on results of model regressions

Variables	Model 1	Model 2	Model 3
Log(TI)	0.1853[c] (0.0428)		0.2142[c] (0.0359)
DGNI*Log(TI)		0.2958[c] (0.0475)	
Log(DE)	0.1281[c] (0.0461)	0.1482[c] (0.0390)	
DGNI*Log(DE)			0.1375[a] (0.0819)
DGNI	0.0985[b] (0.0446)	0.3968[c] (0.0410)	0.2903[c] (0.0813)
Log(UrPop)	0.0758[b] (0.0322)	0.0837[c] (0.0287)	0.0594[a] (0.0345)
Cons	−0.7397[c] (0.0833)	−0.9397[c] (0.0625)	−0.9098[c] (0.0509)

Note "a", "b", and "c" denoted the significance levels at 10%, 5%, and 1%, respectively; the standard errors are in parentheses

GED. Accordingly, each percentage increase in TI tends to increase GED by 0.1853% *(ceteris paribus).* The results of this study are supported by Cao et al. [12]; but Yang et al. [3] showed the evidence that the impact of TI on GED is not significant. Next, DE also has a significant impact on GED, as a 1% increase in DE tends to increase GED by 0.1281% *(ceteris paribus).* Yang et al. [3] also concluded that there was a positive impact of digitalization on GED.

Besides, the study results also show that urbanization leading to dense population concentration in urban areas does not lead to negative environmental impacts as many people are concerned about. On the contrary, the model regression confirmed that the higher the level of urbanization, the higher the GED. Zhao et al. [28] also supposed that urban population impact on green economic efficiency. This is explained by the fact that people expect the quality of the environment to improve when they live in densely populated cities. Local businesses are compelled to make modifications and employ new technology in order to lower energy consumption and pollution emissions as a result of the local government starting to pay attention to environmental protection efforts and improve environmental monitoring. The regression coefficient of the DGNI variable is 0.0985, which means that in general, the GED level of the HI country group is different from the GED level of the MI group, and this difference is statistically significant at the level of 5%. Lin and Zhou [15] also confirmed that developed countries' GEDs outperform those of developing countries.

Furthermore, model 2 regression results show that the regression coefficient of the interaction variable (DGNI*TI) is 0.2958, which is statistically significant at the 1% level. This is evidence that when TI is improved by 1%, it tends to increase GED in HI countries by about 0.2958% higher than GED in MI countries.

In similarity to model 3, the regression coefficient of the interaction variable (DGNI*DE) is 0.1375% and is statistically significant at the 1% significance level. This means that for the same 1% improvement in DE, there tends to be a higher GED increase in HI countries than in MI countries.

5 Conclusion and Recommendations

5.1 Conclusion

The study built a novel theoretical framework for measuring GED, TI, and DE indicators. The results reveal that environment is the most important component regarding GED, followed by social development. Additionally, for TI and DE, input factors such as infrastructure and human resources play a significantly important role. Moreover, the results of model regression confirmed that: (i) There is a significant difference in GED between two groups of HI and MI countries; (ii) TI and DE both have significant positive impacts on GED at 1% level, in which the impact of TI is greater than that of DE; (iii) Furthermore, the same 1% improvement in TI and DE tends to lead to higher GED gains in HI countries than in MI countries. These conclusions are the basis for research to provide policy implications to promote GED in countries.

5.2 Recommendations

To the government: (i) It is necessary to have GED policies and suitable strategies for the country as an important part of sustainable development. (ii) Promote and enhance the application of technology, especially green technologies to reduce negative impacts on environment, creating a favorable environment for the development of innovation. (iii) Focus on training human resources to respond to the new development of the green economy. (iv) Besides pursuing economic growth goals, countries should pay more attention to environmental protection, developing renewable energy, exploiting new environmentally friendly energy sources, protecting forests, and inclusive growth. (v) For developing countries like Vietnam, it is necessary to focus on investing and building information and communications technology infrastructure.

To enterprises: (i) Strengthen cooperation with educational institutions in exchanging and collaborating on scientific research, enhancing the application of science and technology, and implementing innovation in business operations. (ii) Implement digital transformation according to an appropriate roadmap. Enhance the application of technology in production and business activities with the goal of increasing the effective use and exploitation of enterprise resources. Additionally, focus on new technology to help reduce carbon emissions and energy consumption.

Limitations and further study: The study has a limitation on analyzing in depth the motivations and obstacles of businesses when implementing technology applications and solutions for GED goals. This should be the next research direction.

References

1. Nguyen, T.T., Nguyen, T.Q., Trinh, T.T.H.: Determinants of sustainable and socially responsible economy: the analysis on developing countries. In: The International Conference on "Business and economics issues for building a more sustainable and socially responsible economy" was held by Foreign Trade University (Vietnam) and Nantes Université (France) (2022)
2. Rao, C., Yan, B.: Study on the interactive influence between economic growth and environmental pollution. Environ. Sci. Pollut. Res. **27**(31), 39442–39465 (2020)
3. Yang, W., Chen, Q., Guo, Q., Huang, X.: Towards sustainable development: how digitalization, technological innovation, and green economic development interact with each other. Int. J. Environ. Res. Public Health **19**(19), 12273 (2022)
4. Van Der Ploeg, R., Withagen, C.: Green growth, green paradox and the global economic crisis. Environ. Innov. Soc. Trans. **6**, 116–119 (2013)
5. Li, C., Ji, J.: Retracted article: spatial–temporal characteristics and driving factors of green economic efficiency in China. Ann. Oper. Res. **326**(1), 93–93 (2023)
6. Georgeson, L., Maslin, M., Poessinouw, M.: The global green economy: a review of concepts, definitions, measurement methodologies and their interactions. Geo: Geogr. Environ. **4**(1), e00036 (2017)
7. Pearce, D., Markandya, A., Barbier, B.: Blueprint for a Green Economy, vol. 1. Earthscan (1989)
8. United Nations Environment Programme-UNEP: Towards a Green Economy: Pathways to Sustainable Development and Poverty Eradication (2011)
9. Wang, L., Wu, Y., Huang, Z., Wang, Y.: How big data drives green economic development: evidence from China. Front. Environ. Sci. **10**, 1055162 (2022)
10. Yi, H., Liu, Y.: Green economy in China: regional variations and policy drivers. Glob. Environ. Change. **31**, 11–19 (2015)
11. Zhao, X., Mahendru, M., Ma, X., Rao, A., Shang, Y.: Impacts of environmental regulations on green economic growth in China: new guidelines regarding renewable energy and energy efficiency. Renewable Energy **187**, 728–742 (2022)
12. Cao, W., Zhang, Y., Qian, P.: The effect of innovation-driven strategy on green economic development in china—an empirical study of smart cities. Int. J. Environ. Res. Public Health **16**(9), Article 9 (2019)
13. Peng, M., Fan, J.: Statistical evaluation of green economic development based on rough set calculation method. J. Phys: Conf. Ser. **1994**(1), 012042 (2021)
14. Xie, F., Liu, Y., Guan, F., Wang, N.: How to coordinate the relationship between renewable energy consumption and green economic development: from the perspective of technological advancement. Environ. Sci. Eur. **32**(1), 71 (2020)
15. Lin, B., Zhou, Y.: Measuring the green economic growth in China: influencing factors and policy perspectives. Energy **241**, 122518 (2022)
16. Guo, S., Diao, Y.: Spatial-temporal evolution and driving factors of coupling between urban spatial functional division and green economic development: evidence from the Yangtze River Economic Belt. Front. Environ. Sci. **10** (2022)
17. Han, X., Fu, L., Lv, C., Peng, J.: Measurement and spatio-temporal heterogeneity analysis of the coupling coordinated development among the digital economy, technological innovation and ecological environment. Ecol. Ind. **151**, 110325 (2023)
18. Zhang, J., Zhao, W., Cheng, B., Li, A., Wang, Y., Yang, N., Tian, Y.: The impact of digital economy on the economic growth and the development strategies in the post-COVID-19 era: evidence from countries along the "Belt and Road." Front. Public Health **10**, 856142 (2022)
19. United Nations Environment Programme-UNEP: Measuring Progress towards an Inclusive Green economy (2012)
20. Cato, M.S.: Green Economics: An Introduction to Theory. Routledge, Policy and Practice (2008)
21. OECD.: Green Growth Indicators 2017. Paris: OECD Publishing (2017)

22. Wang, M., Zhao, X., Gong, Q., Ji, Z.: Measurement of regional green economy sustainable development ability based on entropy weight-topsis-coupling coordination degree—a case study in shandong province, China. Sustainability **11**(1), Article 1 (2019)
23. Nguyen, T.T., Luong, T., Trinh, T.T.H., Nguyen, G.K., Dang, T.K.T.: The impact of the customs environment on Vietnam's exports. Asian Econ. Financial Rev. **13**(5), Article 5 (2023)
24. Trinh, T.T.H., Nguyen, T.T., Le, H.: The impacts of trade facilitation on Vietnam's imports and exports: evidence from a gravity model. The J. Soc., Polit., and Econ. Stud. **47**, 269–307 (2023)
25. Ordoobadi, S.M.: Application of AHP and Taguchi loss functions in supply chain. Ind. Manage. Data Syst. **110**(8), 1251–1269 (2010)
26. Chen, L.L., Zhang, X.D., He, F., Yuan, R.S.: Regional green development level and its spatial relationship under the constraints of haze in China. J. Clean. Prod. **210**, 376–387 (2019)
27. United Nations: World Economic Situation and Prospects 2022. New York (2022)
28. Zhao, P., Zeng, L., Lu, H., Zhou, Y., Hu, H., Wei, X.-Y.: Green economic efficiency and its influencing factors in China from 2008 to 2017: based on the super-SBM model with undesirable outputs and spatial Dubin model. Sci. Total Environ. **741**, 140026 (2020)

Corporate Social Responsibility in the Supermarket Sector: Evidence from Vietnam

Loan Thi-Hong Van and Thao Hoang-Minh Nguyen

Abstract This research is to identify the relationship amongst corporate social responsibility (CSR), satisfaction and loyalty of customers in the Vietnamese supermarket industry. The methods utilized are qualitative and quantitative ones. The authors used in-depth interviews of 10 managers in supermarkets to correct the research scales and model. Online surveys were used through asking 330 customers who often go to supermarkets in Vietnam. The data was analyzed and interpreted by using SPSS and AMOS software. The results of study indicate that CSR positively influences customer satisfaction and loyalty. However, factors of community and ethical responsibility do not impact them—this is different compared to other research, and can be explained as because of customers' awareness and understanding of CSR. This research contributes to understanding the CSR of Vietnam especially in supermarkets where knowledge is little. This also helps to strengthen the stakeholder theory and provides knowledge of CSR in developing countries.

Keywords Corporate social responsibility (CSR) · Customer loyalty · Customer satisfaction · Supermarket · Vietnam

1 Introduction

In 2015, many supermarkets in Hanoi such as BigC, Metro, Lotte Mart got scandals when journalists found out that greenwashed vegetables in traditional markets were labeled "green" and then put into the supermarkets [1]. Recently, Vietnamese people were shocked by the fraud of vegetables taken from traditional markets labeled VietGap clean and safe vegetables, Chinese mushrooms stripped of packaging and labeled with Vietnamese origin, and then these goods were put into the Bach Hoa Xanh supermarket system [2, 3]. Consumers' trust in the supermarket system was therefore seriously broken. Customers said to the media that supermarkets' owners

L. T.-H. Van (✉) · T. H.-M. Nguyen
Ho Chi Minh City Open University, 35-37 Ho Hao Hon Street, District 1, Ho Chi Minh City 700000, Vietnam
e-mail: loan.vth@ou.edu.vn

L. T. Tung et al. (eds.), *Disruptive Technology and Business Continuity*,
https://doi.org/10.1007/978-981-97-5452-6_2

must be responsible for the origin of the goods in their supermarkets [2]. After this problem, many other supermarkets were also influenced, many customers no longer trust and are loyal to the supermarket system that they usually bought goods from. In order to persuade customers to be loyal to the supermarket system, protect and improve its reputation, it needs to practice responsibilities of the transparency of the goods' origins, has food inspection systems, and ensures the safety and quality of goods for consumers' health.

The benefits of corporate social responsibility (CSR) implementation in organizations have been studied in many countries. The results of research by Chung et al. [4] in China show that CSR positively affects customers' satisfaction and loyalty. The study by Balqiah et al. [5] concludes that CSR implementation is not only a cost but also creates a reputation for organizations. Pérez and Rodríguez [6] said that loyalty is influenced indirectly by CSR, through the mediation of trust, customer identity and satisfaction. Hotels such as Wyndham Hotels and Resorts and Hyatt have put CSR as an essential element of their strategic marketing plans [7]. However, recent studies show that customers want business companies to be more transparent and put CSR in practice more [8, 9]. In addition, business companies should implement CSR according to a specific context and customers' beliefs [10]. This means that CSR implementation depends on the social and cultural context—where business companies conduct sales activities. Moreover, depending on the characteristics of different fields such as education, banking and tourism, the implementation of CSR in practice is also different. Conducting CSR in the supermarket sector thus may be different compared to other business sectors.

CSR has been undertaken differently in different countries because of economic and social differences and stakeholder expectations [10]. This means that stakeholders including customers in Asian countries may have different perceptions of CSR compared with in Western countries. The theory of CSR, which has been developed in the West, may not work well in Asian countries, such as Vietnam. CSR in Asian countries, including Vietnam, needs to be researched more [10, 12], especially CSR studies related to customers— how business companies use CSR to affect customer trust and loyalty to them. Several studies have shown that CSR implementation provides benefits such as worker trust and customer trust [11, 12]. However, the benefits of CSR to organizations have not been studied much in the supermarket sector, especially in the current context of Vietnam—the control of supermarkets on goods quality, hygiene and food safety has not been effective; customers have not fully trusted supermarket systems [3]. So, this study will look at this. The objective of the study is to identify CSR factors that influence customers' loyalty in current supermarkets in Vietnam. The research can help to improve customers' loyalty through CSR activities. The results of the study may contribute to strengthening the stakeholder theory if it demonstrates that CSR increases their customer satisfaction and loyalty to their organization, especially in the supermarket sector in Vietnam when there is not much research in this area.

2 Literature Review

Considered as one of the pioneers of the concept of CSR, Bowen [13] argues that business companies should develop and implement strategies, policies and actions that bring values to the whole society. Carroll [14] offers a CSR model that includes economic, ethical, legal and philanthropic aspects. According to Aguinis [15], CSR is defined as an organization's actions and policies in a specific context, in which stakeholder expectations, and three economic, social, and environmental factors are emphasized. Therefore, organizations need to minimize negative impacts and increase benefits for stakeholders, communities and society in order to meet their expectations.

Freeman and Reed [16] argue that stakeholders include individuals and groups who have benefits or damages from organizational activities. Customers are the most important stakeholders of business companies so their interests must be focused [17]. Ensuring the benefits of customers will increase companies' prestige and reputation, then their goods will be sold more, their profits will be increased, their success will be therefore achieved [18]. This study examines the relationship between business companies and their customers—one of their key stakeholders. The theory of stakeholders will be used in this research to study customer satisfaction and loyalty towards businesses because of their social responsibilities.

Boshoff and Grey [19] emphasize that satisfaction is not a product or service. Satisfaction mainly consists in customers' perception of the attributes of products or services as relating to individuals. So, different customers will show different levels of satisfaction to experience the same product or service. In the field of marketing, customer satisfaction has been known as an important part of the business strategy of companies, and a main driver of the organization in terms of long-term profitability and market value. Satisfaction is customers' overall assessment based on their experiences of consuming and purchasing goods and services over time, compared to their few initial standards and met their expectations [20].

Customer loyalty is a fundamental goal of every company, especially in competitive environments, economic crises and international scandals. It is considered an important objective for organizations' survival and growth, as well as an important basis for the development of sustainable competitive advantage [21]. Loyalty can be considered as unconditional commitment of customers to organizations, and it has a close relationship with their brand [22]. Customer loyalty refers to a range of their behavior to maintain a relationship with an organization, including purchase that contributes to an increase of selling goods, positive word of mouth, and repeat purchases [23]. Customers are limited and the most valuable resource of business organizations, and have a direct impact on their profitability. Research by Kandampully and Suhartanto [24] has shown that a 5% increase of customer loyalty can improve profits by 25–85%.

In addition, loyalty is very important to the success of business organizations. Kotler [25] argues that it is often more expensive to attract new customers than to retain old ones. Businesses often have an illusion that they always look for a new market and forget the existing market. Meanwhile, profit brought to the business from the existing market is often much higher than from the new market because of less expensive marketing costs. Loyalty is considered as a solid "stronghold" against any attack by competitors. Competitors will be discouraged because they pay a lot of costs to attract customers who are loyal to a certain business.

Research by Pérez and Rodríguez [6] found that loyalty is indirectly impacted by CSR, mediated by trust, customer identification and satisfaction; however, this focuses on the banking sector, not the supermarket sector. Mai and Thao [26] studied the impact of CSR on brand image and brand loyalty by customers at Vinamilk Joint Stock Company—the largest dairy company in Vietnam. The research concluded that CSR factors such as economic, ethical and charitable responsibilities, ethics in marketing have impacts on brand image and brand loyalty. Therefore, when this company focuses on social responsibility, especially ethical responsibility, its brand image has been enhanced in the market, and customer loyalty to it has increased. Chung et al. [4] also studied the effects of CSR on customer satisfaction and loyalty. The research showed that CSR positively affects satisfaction and loyalty, and satisfaction positively affects loyalty. The research suggested that executives should put CSR into practice from the customers' perspectives, rather than from businesses' perspectives—this will help customers to have a more positive look towards organizations. Moisescu [27] surveyed 1449 customers of retail banks in Romania about their perception of CSR. The results of the study showed that customer loyalty is positively and significantly affected by the way customers feel about the implementation of CSR by banks. Responsibility to customers is the element of CSR that has the strongest impact on customer loyalty. The second factor is community responsibility: the more responsible the bank is for the community, the more it has customers. A study by Vo et al. [12] also showed that CSR has an impact on customer loyalty; however, this is in the banking sector, not in the supermarket sector. Tran's research was also about the influence of CSR on customer loyalty in Vietnam but it is in the jewelry sector [9]. Thus, it can be seen that research on the link between CSR and loyalty in the supermarket sector has not been studied much.

Research Hypotheses

Based on our review of literature, we found that factors such as Customer Responsibility, Community Responsibility, Ethical Responsibility, Philanthropic Responsibility are usually factors that are used to study CSR. However, as mentioned above, previous studies mostly conducted in other sectors such as banking, not supermarkets. In addition, Chang and Yeh' research showed that customers are more likely to develop a sustainable relationship with a business due to its CSR activities, so they are more aware and satisfied with its products or services provided [28]. Research by Pérez & Rodríguez [6] and Chung et al. [4] confirmed that when customers see a company's practice of social responsibility, they will feel more satisfied with its activities, including sales activities, so they will be more loyal to it. Research by McDonald and Lai [29] and Pérez and Rodríguez [6] showed that CSR has a positive link with satisfaction. When customers are satisfied because a business has CSR activities, customers tend to be more loyal to it. Therefore, this study expects that customer satisfaction will increase when businesses implement CSR and will impact on customer loyalty. Research hypotheses between distinct attributes of the CSR and customer satisfaction, and between customer satisfaction and customer loyalty are thus developed: H1: Supermarket's implementation of social responsibility to customers has a positive impact on Customer Satisfaction. H2: Supermarket's implementation of social responsibility to the community has a positive impact on Customer Satisfaction. H3: Supermarket's implementation of ethical responsibility has a positive impact on Customer Satisfaction. H4: Supermarket's implementation of philanthropic responsibility has a positive impact on Customer Satisfaction. H5: Supermarket's implementation of environmental responsibility has a positive impact on Customer Satisfaction. H6: Customer satisfaction has a positive impact on customer loyalty.

3 Methodology

3.1 Qualitative Research

The qualitative study was conducted by face-to-face interviews of 10 managers who were working at supermarkets in Ho Chi Minh City, Vietnam. The content of interviews focuses on the factors in the proposed research model, and the observed variables. An interview was conducted from 30 to 45 min at a book cafe with a quiet space. The interview consists of 04 steps as follows: (1) Introduce the purpose of the interview; (2) Introduce the factors in the research model and explain in details; (3) Ask the respondents for comments on CSR factors which affect customer loyalty, suitability of the model, scales of the study, and their suggestion; (4) Summarize the comments. The interview process is carried out on the principle of saturation when the number of respondents increases but the answers do not change, so the interview is stopped. The interview results will be synthesized, selected and edited for opinions with the same views. Then, a pilot interview of 30 persons is conducted in order to check the clarity of words or duplicate content before starting the next step.

Qualitative Results

The qualitative research results show that the hypotheses are not sufficient to reflect the relationship between the dependent and independent variables. The research model was therefore rebuilt. Independent variables remain the same, however, both dependent variables, not one as initially proposed, in the model as customer loyalty and satisfaction are directly affected by CSR factors. So, hypotheses are restated more precisely: H1a Supermarket's implementation of social responsibility to customers has a positive impact on Customer Loyalty. H1b Supermarket's implementation of social responsibility to the community has a positive impact on Customer Loyalty. H1c Supermarket's implementation of ethical responsibility has a positive impact on Customer Loyalty. H1d Supermarket's implementation of philanthropic responsibility has a positive impact on Customer Loyalty. H1e Supermarket's implementation of environmental responsibility has a positive impact on Customer Loyalty. H2a Supermarket's implementation of social responsibility to customers has a positive impact on Customer Satisfaction. H2b Supermarket's implementation of social responsibility to the community has a positive impact on Customer Satisfaction. H2c Supermarket's implementation of ethical responsibility has a positive impact on Customer Satisfaction. H2d Supermarket's implementation of philanthropic responsibility has a positive impact on Customer Satisfaction. H2e Supermarket's implementation of environmental responsibility has a positive impact on Customer Satisfaction. H3: Customer satisfaction has a positive impact on customer loyalty.

After synthesizing comments from the respondents, the authors revised the scales. Some variables are also adjusted to understand and match the actual research context. The scales of customer responsibility proposed to add two new variables is KH5: Supermarket's effectively ensure customer benefits (promotions, convenient shopping space, etc.), and KH6: I think that supermarkets always attempt to improve product/service quality. In addition, some respondents said that CSR promotes businesses to be responsible to the community in different aspects such as human rights, non-discrimination, and workers' treatment equally. Therefore, after our discussion, the study adds a variable CD3: Supermarkets follow the policies and regulations of the state (treatment of employees without gender discrimination, protecting child labor, equal payment, etc.). The final one is the environmental responsibility scale. Because of the harmful effects of plastic bags on the environment, supermarkets are interested in changing plastic bags into green bags. So, we have a variable MT5: Supermarket has a use of green packaging. In sum, the total number of observed variables has increased to 31 variables (see also Table 1).

The pilot research results of the 30 respondents showed that the questionnaire is clear and has no duplicate content, so the authors did not make any further adjustment.

3.2 *Quantitative Research*

330 questionnaires were distributed via online surveys from May to August 2022. Respondents chosen were ones who answered a question of whether they shop at supermarkets such as Coop mart, Citi mart, Lotte mart, etc. at least 2 times in 3 months or more. The authors collected 306 valid surveys. The collected data was processed by SPSS 22 and AMOS 22 software in the following steps: descriptive statistics, test for internal consistency using Cronbach's Alpha, exploratory factor analysis (EFA), confirmatory factor analysis (CFA) and structural equation modeling (SEM).

Table 1 Cronbach's alpha

No	Factor	Variable	Cronbach's alpha	Corrected Item-total correlation	Cronbach's alpha if Item deleted
1	Customer responsibility	KH1	0.876	0.648	862
		KH2		0.716	849
		KH3		0.692	854
		KH4		0.744	0.845
		KH5		0.710	0.850
		KH6		0.586	0.871
2	Community responsibility	CD1	0.806	0.626	0.764
		CD2		0.757	0.624
		CD3		0.585	0.804
3	Ethical responsibility	DD1	0.847	0.657	0.818
		DD2		0.760	0.772
		DD3		0.743	0.781
		DD4		0.584	0.847
4	Philanthropic responsibility	TT1	0.849	0.597	0.846
		TT2		0.751	0.781
		TT3		0.749	0.782
		TT4		0.661	0.820
5	Environmental responsibility	MT1	0.881	0.658	0.868
		MT2		0.757	0.845
		MT3		766.0	0.843
		MT4		0.766	0.843
		MT5		0.627	0.875
6	Customer satisfaction	HL1	0.841	0.668	0.816
		HL2		0.743	0.742
		HL3		0.708	0.778
7	Customer loyalty	LT1	0.876	0.610	0.866
		LT2		0.700	0.851
		LT3		0.726	0.847
		LT4		0.705	0.851
		LT5		0.698	0.852
		LT6		*0.641*	*0.861*

Source Results from SPSS 22

4 Research Results

23.5% of the respondents are male and 76.5% are female. People aged under 30 account for 35.6%—the highest proportion of any aged group, in terms of comparison with the group aged between 31 and 40 (29.7%), between 40 and 55 (16.3%) and over 55 (18.3%). The income of customers per month are approximately the same, but the highest proportion is the group with an income between 5 and 10 million VND (33.7%). Office workers account for 27.1%; the highest proportion of any occupation group, in contrast, the lowest proportion is retired people (6.9%).

All factors in the model, including Customer responsibility, Community responsibility, Ethical responsibility, Philanthropic responsibility, Environmental responsibility, Customer satisfaction and Customer loyalty were surveyed on a 5- point Likert scale (1 = Strongly disagree, 5 = Strongly agree). The average of all variables is more than 3 (between 3.206 and 3.614), so they were acceptable. The standard deviation is almost similar; and there is no big change so this indicates that the data tends to be close to the mean. Table 1 shows that in general, the scales have Cronbach's Alpha coefficient > = 0.6. Corrected Item – Total Correlation > = 0.3. Therefore, all 31 variables were satisfactory and included in the EFA factor analysis.

The results of EFA show that $0.5 \leq KMO = 0.877 \leq 1$, Sig. $= 0.000 < 0.05$; eigenvalue $= 1.115 > 1$; cumulative percentage of Eigenvalue = 69.835%, so the scales are suitable. However, some items have two factors at the same time, and the gap between the two factors is lower than 0.3—this means there is not a distinguished value. So, these items must be deleted. These are KH1, KH6 (responsibility to customers), CD3 (responsibility to the community), DD1, DD4 (ethical responsibility), TT1 (philanthropic responsibility), and LT1 (customer loyalty). Thus, the authors must analyze the EFA for the second time. The results of the second EFA show that $0.5 \leq KMO = 0.863 \leq 1$; Sig. $= 0.000 < 0.05$; eigenvalue $= 1.008 > 1$; cumulative percentage of Eigenvalue = 74.67%; all loading factors are more than 0.5 and there is not two factors appeared for the same item. This means that since factor loadings can be interpreted as standardized regression coefficients, there exists a very strong correlation between factors and latent variables.

In addition, results from the confirmatory factor analysis (CFA) confirm the consistency and validity of the factors in the model (Fig. 1). In particular, all of the critical statistics, including Chi-square (3.162), P-value (0.000), RMSEA (0.084), CFI (0.882), TLI (0.859), have satisfied the conditions.

Moreover, the standardized weights being greater than 0.5 and statistically significant at the 95% level confirm the convergent criterion. The estimates are statistically different from 1, implying no correlation between the factors.

Furthermore, the composite reliability (CR) value is greater than 0.7 and convergent validity with average variance extracted (AVE) is greater than 0.5 (Table 2). The structural equation modeling (SEM) was used to test the proposed hypotheses. The results of model testing show that all of the critical statistics have satisfied the prerequisites: df = 241, Chi-square/df $= 4.595 < 5$, P-value $= 0.000 < 0.05$ (5%), RMSEA $= 0.109 < 0.08$, CFI $= 0.795 > 0.9$, TLI $= 0.765 > 0.9$ (Fig. 2).

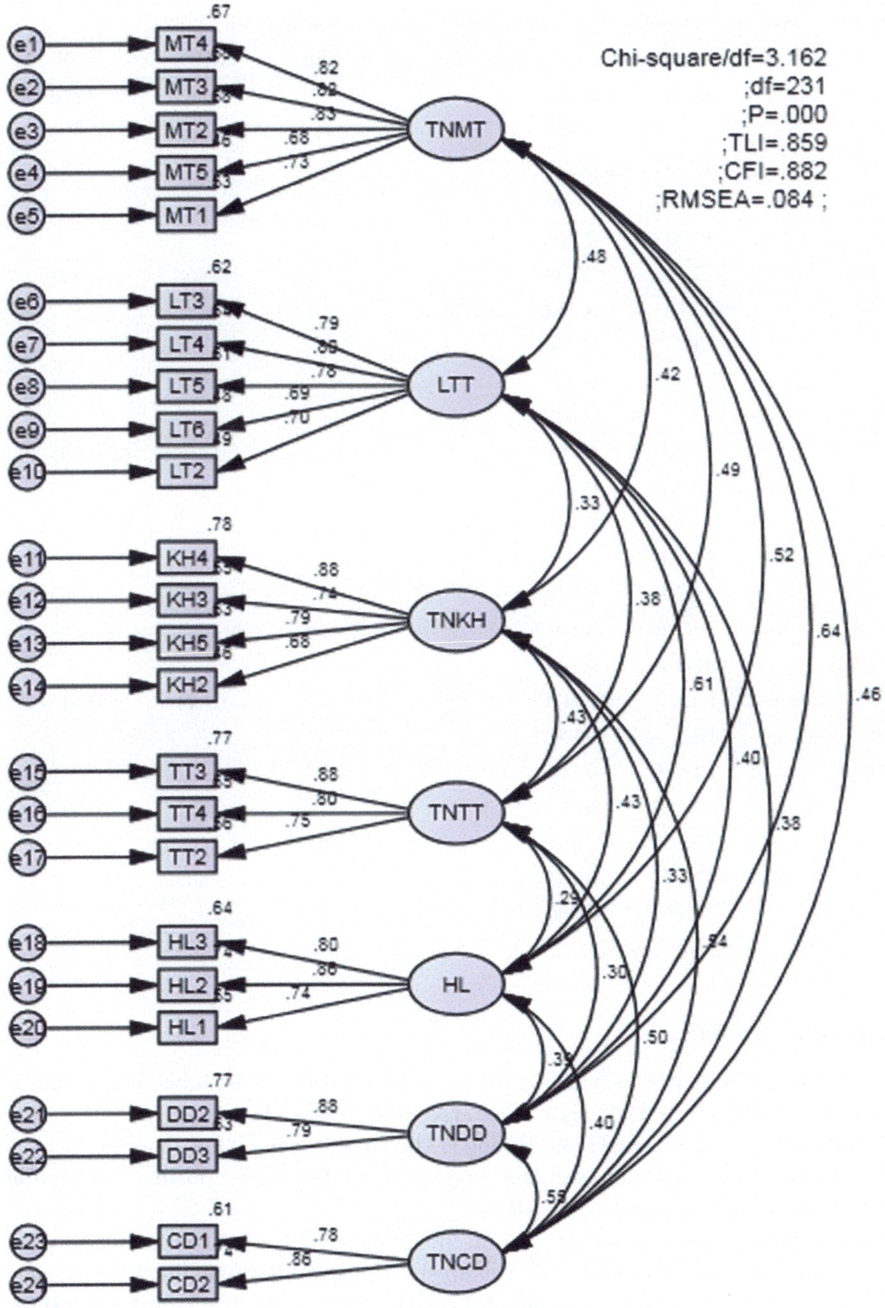

Fig. 1 Confirmatory factor analysis (CFA) results

Table 2 Composite reliability (CR) and average variance extracted (AVE)

			Standardized regression weights	CR	AVE
MT4	<–	TNMT	0.816	0.883	0.604
MT3	<–	TNMT	0.823		
MT2	<–	TNMT	0.826		
MT5	<–	TNMT	0.680		
MT1	<–	TNMT	0.729		
LT3	<–	LTT	0.790	0.868	0.568
LT4	<–	LTT	0.798		
LT5	<–	LTT	0.778		
LT6	<–	LTT	0.693		
LT2	<–	LTT	0.703		
KH4	<–	TNKH	0.881	0.858	0.605
KH3	<–	TNKH	0.741		
KH5	<–	TNKH	0.794		
KH2	<–	TNKH	0.681		
TT3	<–	TNTT	0.879	0.853	0.660
TT4	<–	TNTT	0.804		
TT2	<–	TNTT	0.748		
HL3	<–	HL	0.800	0.844	0.643
HL2	<–	HL	0.858		
HL1	<–	HL	0.744		
DD2	<–	TNDD	0.877	0.821	0.697
DD3	<–	TNDD	0.791		
CD1	<–	TNCD	0.781	0.806	0.675
CD2	<–	TNCD	0.860		

Source Results from SPSS 22

Hypothesis Testing

The results of the hypothesis testing are presented in Table 3. In Table 3, hypotheses are rejected: H1a, H1b, H1c, H1e, H2b, H2c, H2d because P-value is more than 5%. Hypotheses accepted: H1d, H2a, H2e and H3 because P-value is less than 5%. Table 3 also shows that H3 with an estimated impact of 0.479 means a positive correlation between customer satisfaction and loyalty.

Two of the four scales obtained from the qualitative study, KH6 and CD3, were rejected from the results of the EFA analysis. However, the remaining two scales, KH5 and MT5, are accepted because H2a (KH2, KH3, KH4, KH5) and H2e (MT1, MT2, MT3, MT4, MT5) are accepted. KH5 and MT5 are new in this study (Table 3).

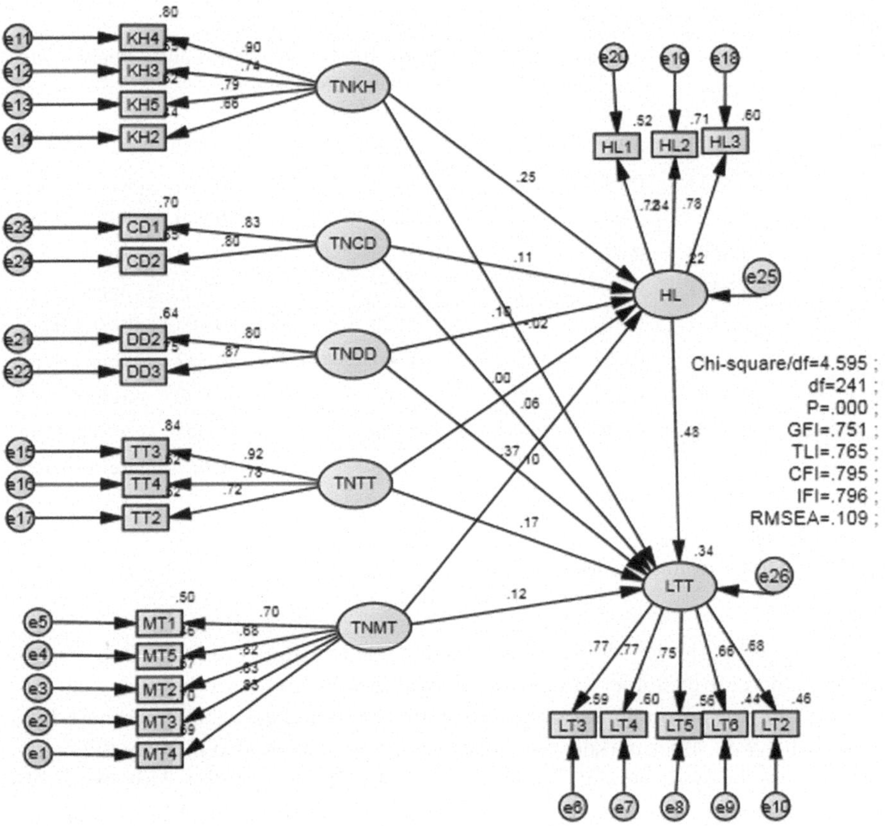

Fig. 2 Structural equation modeling

5 Discussion

The research results show that four hypotheses are accepted. These are H1d, H2a, H2e and H3. This means that supermarket's implementation of philanthropic responsibility has a positive impact on customer loyalty. This result is similar to the study by Chung et al. [4], Mai and Thao [26], Balqiah et al. [5] and Vo et al. [12]. Philanthropic activities may create sympathy for customers towards the organization, thus these may create their motivation to continue using its products and services. At the same time, customers can recommend and encourage others to use the products and services. Our study also shows that supermarket's implementation of social responsibility to customers and of environmental responsibility have positive influences on customer satisfaction. The more responsible supermarkets do for customers and the environment, the more satisfied their customers feel. These results are similar to the study by Chung et al. [4], Pérez and Rodríguez [6], Tengku et al. [5] and Vo et al. [12]. Socially responsible businesses often build good relationships with their customers

Table 3 Hypothesis testing results

Correlation			Unstandardized estimation coefficient	Normalized estimated coefficient (β)	P-value	Study results
HL	<–	TNKH	0.176	0.251	***	Accept H2a
HL	<–	TNCD	0.090	0.114	0.102	Reject H2b
HL	<–	TNTT	−0.004	−0.005	0.940	Reject H2d
HL	<–	TNDD	0.082	0.098	0.129	Reject H2c
HL	<–	TNMT	0.310	0.371	***	Accept H2e
LTT	<–	TNKH	−0.017	−0.023	0.706	Reject H1a
LTT	<–	TNCD	0.052	0.061	0.332	Reject H1b
LTT	<–	TNDD	0.095	0.104	0.090	Reject H1c
LTT	<–	TNTT	0.140	0.166	0.004	Accept H1d
LTT	<–-	TNMT	0.106	0.118	0.067	Reject H1e
LTT	<–	HL	0.517	0.479	***	Accept H3

Source Results from SPSS 22
Note *** is a 0.001 significance level

and have good customer service programs that meet customer requirements. So, this may help increase customer satisfaction. In addition, customers today may want businesses to have environmental programs. Our results indicate that customers focus not only the way supermarkets meet their requirements but also the way the organizations treat the environment. Table 3 also shows H3 is accepted. This means that the satisfaction of supermarket's customers has a positive impact on its customer loyalty. The result is similar to the study by Balqiah et al. [5] and Chung et al. [4]. Satisfaction is considered one of the important criteria to improve customer loyalty.

Hypotheses named H1a, H1b, H1c, and H1e are rejected (Table 3). This means that supermarket's implementation of ethical and environmental responsibility, and of social responsibility to customers and to the community have no impact on customer loyalty. These results are different from the studies of Chung et al. [4], Pérez and Rodríguez [6], Balqiah et al. [5], Moisescu [27] and Vo et al. [12]. The differences may be because customers have no information about the supermarket's social responsibility activities, or the level of the supermarket's CSR implementation may be little. According to Singh et al. [31], customers often feel uncertain about the implementation of CSR by enterprises because they lack understanding of real community actions, or have doubts about the motivation of enterprises when practicing such activities. Research by Pérez and Rodríguez [6] concludes that young customers seem to be subjective in their assessment of CSR. More than 35% of our research sample are customers under 30 years old. Furthermore, in our questionnaire, we forgot to ask the educational level of the research participants. The rejection of these hypotheses thus may be partly due to the sample and the problem.

Hypotheses named H2b, H2c, H2d are rejected. This means that supermarket's implementation of social responsibility to the community, and of ethical and philanthropic responsibility have no impact on customer satisfaction. This is different compared to research by Chung et al. [4] and Balqiah et al. [5] when their studies show that these factors have influences on customer satisfaction. Pomering and Dolnicar [30] also said that businesses will be seriously difficult in competing and recovering from the crisis if CSR is not implemented. This result of our research is different from other research because customers may not be interested in CSR activities in organizations [6].

Our research result analysis showed that KH5 and MT5–new variables from our qualitative research–are accepted. So these are new points of this study. This means that if the supermarket effectively ensures customer benefits through promotions, convenient shopping space, etc. and has a use of green packaging, it will increase customer satisfaction and loyalty to the supermarket.

From the above analysis, it can be seen that supermarkets' customers in Vietnam are still not aware of the CSR activities of the organizations. The reason can be that supermarkets still do not have specific and convincing social responsibility programs in order to be easily recognized by customers. Supermarkets may not have effective communication programs of CSR for customers to understand what CSR activities really conduct in the organizations. Our results also indicate that the lack of understanding of CSR by customers may lead them to consider that community activities and ethical acts in supermarkets are not social responsibility activities. Nevertheless, customers consider volunteering, environmental and customer protection activities as CSR ones.

6 Conclusion

The results of our research show that three components of CSR such as customer responsibility, philanthropic responsibility and environmental responsibility affect the satisfaction and loyalty of customers at supermarkets. Community responsibility and ethical responsibility do not have an impact on customer satisfaction and loyalty–this may be related to customer awareness and understanding of CSR. On the other hand, customer responsibility and environmental responsibility positively affect customer satisfaction. Philanthropic responsibility has an impact but not much on customer loyalty. Customer satisfaction has the most positive impact on customer loyalty. Our research results also indicate that supermarkets' customers in Vietnam have a little understanding and awareness of CSR activities in the organizations. So, supermarkets can build communication strategies in order to communicate effectively CSR activities and programs of supermarkets for customers and improve their awareness of CSR.

Our research contributes to theory and practice. Firstly, the research conducted in Vietnam where the field of CSR in supermarkets has not been studied much. The research thus contributes to providing knowledge about CSR in a developing

Asian country as Vietnam. Secondly, the study contributes two variables of CSR for supporting future studies in contexts similar to Vietnam. Thirdly, this study is one of the empirical studies investigating the relationship between CSR, satisfaction and loyalty in supermarkets in Vietnam. This helps to strengthen the stakeholder theory that organizations should consider the interests and needs of customers—one of stakeholders, through philanthropic and environmental responsibility programs, for example.

The study has some limitations. The first limitation relates to the study sample. More than 35% of respondents are under 30 years old—this sample may not represent supermarkets' customers. Also, the study had not yet collected the educational information of the research sample—this may not help to explain reasons regarding customers' lack of understanding of CSR. So, their awareness of social responsibility revolves around philanthropic and environmental activities, and considers that the community activities and ethical acts of supermarkets are not CSR factors. Future research should collect more balanced samples and educational information of respondents. The second limitation relates to the supermarket sector. Future research should explore other business areas to find out similarities and differences of CSR amongst them.

References

1. Chu, K.: Hàng loạt siêu thị Hà Nội dính scandal rau sạch (A series of supermarkets in Hanoi got scandals). VNEconomy (2015). https://vneconomy.vn/hang-loat-sieu-thi-ha-noi-dinh-scandal-rau-sach.htm
2. Bong, M., Nguyen, T., Thao, T.: Braking fake VietGAP vegetables: Chinese goods' VietGAP 'into Bach Hoa Xanh. Tuoi Tre online (2022). https://tuoitre.vn/phanh-phui-rau-vietgap-dom-hang-trung-quoc-vietgap-vao-bach-hoa-xanh-2022092109081867.htm
3. Le, H.: How does the supermarket 'guarantee' the trust of consumers. Saigon Economics online (2022). https://thesaigontimes.vn/sieu-thi-bao-chung-ra-sao-truoc-niem-tin-cua-nguoi-tieu-dung/
4. Chung, K.H., Yu, J.E., Choi, M.G., Shin, J.I.: The effects of corporate social responsibility on customer satisfaction and loyalty in China: the moderating role of corporate image. J. Econ., Bus. Manage. **3**(5), 542–547 (2015)
5. Balqiah, T.E., Hapsari, S., Khairani, K.: The influence of CSR activity toward customer loyalty through improvement of quality of life in urban area. The South East Asian J. Manage. **5**(1), 73–83 (2011)
6. Pérez, A., Rodríguez del Bosque, I.: How customer support for corporate social responsibility influences the image of companies: evidence from the banking industry. Corporate Soc. Responsibility Environ. Manage. **22**(3), 155–168 (2013)
7. Kucukusta, D., Mak, A., Chan, X.: Corporate social responsibility practices in four and five-star hotels: perspectives from Hong Kong visitors. Int. J. Hosp. Manage. **34**, 19–30 (2013)
8. Saeidi, S.P., Saudah, S., Saeidi, P., Saeidi, S.: How does corporate social responsibility contribute to firm financial performance? The mediating role of competitive advantage, reputation, and customer satisfaction. J. Bus. Res. **68**(2), 341–350 (2015)
9. Tran, N.T.: Impact of corporate social responsibility on customer loyalty: evidence from the Vietnamese jewelry industry". Cogen Bus. Manage. (2022). https://doi.org/10.1080/23311975.2022.2025675

10. Van, T.L., Nguyen, H.H., Vo, D.H.: Corporate social responsibility: a study on consumer awareness in Vietnam. Rev. Pacific Basin Financial Markets and Policies **23**(3) (2020)
11. Van, T.-H., Ngo, T.-P., Pham, L.-T.: The impact of internal corporate social responsibility (iCSR) on employee commitment: a study in Southern regional retail chains. Sci. J. Ho Chi Minh City Open Univ. **17**(1), 43–58 (2022)
12. Vo, H.D., Van, L.T., Dinh, L.T., Ho, C.M.: Financial inclusion, corporate social responsibility and customer loyalty in the banking sector in Vietnam. J. Int. Stud. **13**(4) (2020)
13. Bowen, H.R.: Social Responsibility of Businessman. Harper & Row. New York (1953)
14. Carroll, A.: The pyramid of corporate social responsibility: toward the moral management of organizational stakeholders. Bus. Horiz. **3**(4), 39–49 (1991)
15. Aguinis, H.: . Organizational responsibility: doing good and doing well. In: APA Handbook of Industrial and Organizational Psychology, pp. 855–879 (2011)
16. Freeman, E., Reed, D.: Stockholders and stakeholders: a new perspective on corporate governance. Calif. Manage. Rev. **25**(3), 88–106 (1983)
17. Clarkson, M.: A stakeholder framework for analyzing and evaluating corporate social performance. Acad. Manage. Rev. **20**(1), 92–118 (1995)
18. Brennan, C.: Being a Good Corporate Citizen Pays Dividends. The Irish Times, January 4 (2002)
19. Boshoff, C., Gray, B.: The relationships between service quality, customer satisfaction and buying intentions in the private hospital industry. South Afr. J. Bus. Manage. **35**(4), 27–37 (2004)
20. Swaen, V., Chumpitaz, R.C.: Impact of corporate social responsibility on consumer trust. Rech. Appl. Mark. **23**(4), 7–14 (2008)
21. Chung, K.H., Yu, J.E., Choi, M.G., Shin, J.I.: The effect of CSR on customer satisfaction and loyalty in China: the moderating role of corporate image. J. Econ., Bus. Manage. **3**(5), 542–547 (2015)
22. Maheshwari, V., Lodorfos, G., Jacobsen, S.: Determinants of brand loyalty: a study of the experience–commitment–loyalty constructs. Int. J. Bus. Adm. **5**(6), 13–23 (2014)
23. Sirdeshmukh, D., Japdig, S., Berry, S.: Customer trust, value, and loyalty in relational exchanges. J. Mark. **66**(1), 15–37 (2002)
24. Kandampully, J., Suhartanto, D.: Customer loyalty in the hotel industry: the role of customer satisfaction and image. Int. J. Contemp. Hosp. Manag. **12**(6), 346–351 (2000)
25. Kotler, P.: Marketing Management, 11th edn. Prentice-Hall, Upper Saddle River (2003)
26. Mai, N.K., Thao, D.T.: The impact of corporate social responsibility on brand image and customer brand loyalty—a case study of Vinamilk. In 5th International Conference On Business And Economic Research. International University, Vietnam, pp. 327–338 (2014)
27. Moisescu, O.: From CSR to customer loyalty: an empirical investigation in the retail banking industry of a developing country. Sci. Ann. Econ. Bus. **64**(3), 307–323 (2017)
28. Chang, Y.H., Yeh, C.H.: Corporate social responsibility and customer loyalty in intercity bus services. Transp. Policy **59**, 38–45 (2017)
29. McDonald, L., Lai, C.: Impact of corporate social responsibility initiatives on Taiwanese banking customers. Int. J. Bank Market. **29**(1), 50–63 (2011)
30. Pomering, A., Dolnicar, S.: Assessing the prerequisite of successful CSR implementation: are consumers aware of CSR initiatives? J. Bus. Ethics **85**, 285–301 (2009)
31. Singh, S., Kristensen, L., Villasenor, E.: Overcoming skepticism towards cause related claims: the case of Norway. Int. Mark. Rev. **26**(3), 312–326 (2009)

Factors Affecting Electronic Word of Mouth on the Acceptance of Digital Banking: An Evidence in Vietnam

Nguyen Hoang Sinh, Lam Quoc Bao, and Nguyen Huu Long

Abstract This research investigates the impact of electronic word of mouth (eWOM) on customer acceptance and usage intentions of digital banking applications in Vietnam, aiming to provide nuanced insights within the unique cultural context of the country. Key factors influencing eWOM acceptance, such as attitude toward eWOM, reliability, quality, quantity, information need, and user proficiency, are identified. The study establishes a positive relationship between attitude toward eWOM and the intention to use digital banking, emphasizing the pivotal role of eWOM in shaping consumer perceptions and driving widespread adoption. Data collection involved direct qualitative interviews and adjusted quantitative survey questionnaires. Although the non-probability convenient sampling method was selected primarily for its efficiency, the study managed to obtain 368 valid responses through an online survey distributed via email to bank customers in Ho Chi Minh City. The utilization of SME for meticulous data entry and validation procedures significantly enhanced response validity, thus satisfying the scientific significance criteria necessary for subsequent analysis, including the examination of the measurement model and hypotheses. From a practical standpoint, the findings have substantial implications for practitioners, managers, and electronic marketers, offering a deeper understanding of the impact of eWOM on consumer behavioral intentions in the digital banking realm. The identification of critical factors empowers marketers to develop more effective strategies for leveraging eWOM within the specific context of digital banking in Vietnam.

Keywords Digital banking · Electronic word of mouth · Customer acceptance · Usage intentions · Vietnam

---

N. H. Sinh (✉) · L. Q. Bao · N. H. Long
Ho Chi Minh City Open University, 97 Vo Van Tan, District 3, Ho Chi Minh City, Vietnam
e-mail: sinh.nh@ou.edu.vn

L. T. Tung et al. (eds.), *Disruptive Technology and Business Continuity*,
https://doi.org/10.1007/978-981-97-5452-6_3

1 Introduction

The banking landscape in Vietnam has rapidly transformed due to the COVID-19 pandemic, leading to increased adoption of digital solutions such as mobile banking and electronic wallets. By 2021, over 68.17 million individuals in Vietnam embraced Internet services, with mobile banking experiencing a 200% growth rate and engaging nearly 30 million users in daily transactions [1, 2]. In this era of digital banking, intensified competition among financial institutions necessitates strategic development for continued relevance.

However, findings from a Mibrand [2] report indicate that despite the remarkable growth in mobile banking, users primarily utilize basic services like fund transfers. Advanced features such as savings deposits, international fund transfers, credit card payments, insurance purchases, and card locking/unlocking are relatively underutilized, with recognition rates ranging from 30 tp 60% and usage rates around 20%. Surveys on digital banking literacy reveal notable gaps in understanding, particularly in areas like online transactions (74.8%), distinctions between digital banks and Internet or mobile banking (77.9%), and the misconception that digital banks do not issue credit or debit cards (39.7%).

Online banking has revolutionized business practices and consumer lifestyles, emphasizing convenience and time-saving attributes. Financial institutions have introduced various digital banking applications to meet evolving consumer needs, yet challenges in user adoption persist, influenced by factors such as brand perception and the completeness of application features.

With multiple Vietnamese banks rolling out digital banking applications, consumers face diverse choices. Marketing strategies, including television commercials, online newspapers, and presence on social media platforms like Zalo, Facebook, and YouTube, are employed to promote these solutions. However, managing information on social media platforms, particularly through blog posts, presents a formidable challenge.

The effectiveness of word of mouth marketing is evident in shaping consumer perceptions, as seen in diverse opinions found in digital banking reviews. Positive endorsements and critical viewpoints significantly contribute to shaping the reputation of these services. This research aims to investigate the impact of eWOM on consumer acceptance and usage intentions of digital banking applications, recognizing the need for a nuanced understanding within the Vietnamese cultural context.

The primary objectives of this research are to identify factors influencing eWOM acceptance and usage intentions for a digital banking application in Ho Chi Minh City, evaluate the magnitude and significance of these factors, and propose managerial implications to enhance consumer engagement and adoption of the digital banking application.

This study then provides valuable insights for banking sector managers and marketing professionals to formulate strategies based on eWOM to impact consumer intentions and enhance the adoption of digital banking applications.

2 Literature Review

2.1 Definitions

Digital Banking, defined by scholars in diverse ways, encompasses services allowing customers to access information and conduct transactions through devices such as phones, computers, and digital televisions. Daniel [3] characterizes it as information and service distribution through channels accessible via personal computers or smart devices. Allen et al. [4] describe it as banks providing services or information through computers or televisions. Keivani et al. [5] term it as a process enabling electronic banking transactions without traditional organizational structures. Notably, digital banking ensures round-the-clock access through advanced information systems.

Crucial for banks in fiercely competitive industries, digital banking products and services like ATMs and electronic fund transfers differentiate their offerings [6]. To maintain market presence, banks must adapt strategies to evolving customer needs and technological advancements.

Mobile banking, emerging in the late 1990s, enables customers to access banking services via mobile devices, driven by the convenience of accessing services anywhere, anytime. This mode of banking is referred to by various terms including mobile branch banking, mobile payment, mobile transfer, and mobile finance. Scholars commonly define it as a subset of mobile commerce, facilitating bank account access for various transactions.

Globally, retail and microfinance banks offer mobile banking through four access points: smartphone apps, mobile browser compatibility, tablet apps, and SMS notifications for account updates. Mobile banking has revolutionized the financial landscape, leveraging diverse applications to provide an array of services and products to consumers.

Word of Mouth (WOM) entails individuals directly conveying non-commercial perceptions of brands, products, or services, often recommending them to others in future purchases [23]. It is essentially free advertising shaped by customer perceptions. Addressing customer complaints promptly can mitigate negative WOM, turning them into positive experiences. WOM is classified into sender and receiver categories, with senders often engaging in positive WOM to appear knowledgeable, while competitiveness may drive negative WOM. Receivers are more susceptible to negative WOM's influence.

Encouraging positive WOM is vital for retailers in competitive markets, as it enhances revenue. **Electronic WOM** (eWOM) occurs through Internet platforms like social media, allowing users to share reviews and opinions, overshadowing traditional WOM channels. It significantly influences consumer decisions, aiding informed purchasing choices, with approximately 90% of people directly influenced by eWOM.

Behavioral Intention refers to the likelihood that a customer will purchase a specific product or use a particular service. It is a predictive factor for actual behavior, and this relationship has been experimentally tested in various studies.

Parasuraman et al. [7] propose factors such as positive WOM, recommending the company to others, considering the company as the first choice for services, and doing more business with the company in the coming years as indicators of favorable behavioral intentions.

2.2 Theoretical Framework

The **Information Adoption Model** (IAM), developed by Sussman and Siegal [28], explores how individuals are influenced by messages through two pathways: central and peripheral. The central route involves the core content of the message, while the peripheral route involves indirectly related factors. IAM consists of four key components including message quality, source credibility, information utility, and information acceptance.

IAM elucidates how information impacts individual behavior, particularly on computer-mediated communication platforms. Due to its emphasis on the influence of information in these settings, IAM has been extensively utilized in studies on eWOM.

To address the limitations of assessing eWOM's impact on consumer purchasing intentions based solely on eWOM characteristics, researchers have proposed the **Information Acceptance Model** (IACM). This model integrates IAM with the Theory of Reasoned Action (TRA) [8].

TRA posits that individual behavior is driven by their intention to perform that behavior, which is influenced by their attitudes toward it and subjective norms surrounding it. IACM incorporates TRA's components—attitude and behavioral intention—alongside IAM elements to evaluate user's attitude toward eWOM information.

The IACM model includes factors such as information quality, information credibility, information needs, attitude toward information, perceived usefulness of information, information acceptance, and behavioral intention to measure the effect of eWOM on consumer purchasing intentions.

The **Technology Acceptance Model** (TAM), introduced by Davis [9], examines how technology influences user behavior. TAM emphasizes two main factors: perceived usefulness and perceived ease of use, which significantly affect users' intention to use technology.

TAM has been widely applied to study technology acceptance using various methodologies. It suggests that a user's beliefs about the technology's usefulness and ease of use shape their intention to use it. This model has been employed to evaluate technology acceptance across different contexts.

In e-banking, TAM has been utilized to understand user acceptance of mobile banking services. Researchers have analyzed factors like perceived ease of use, perceived usefulness, and users' attitudes toward mobile banking to determine their impact on behavioral intentions.

2.3 Research Model and Hypotheses

In Vietnam, WOM stands as a crucial source of information for consumers, with up to 89% considering information and recommendations from family and friends as the most reliable [1, 2]. Additionally, 75% of users express trust in consumer opinions posted online, indicating the significant influence of eWOM on Vietnamese consumer behavior. Global studies by Nielsen [1] also highlight that 66% of consumers globally trust the opinions of other consumers in the form of online or eWOM. This underscores the considerable impact of eWOM on online consumer perceptions and behaviors, including initial brand trust and purchase intentions [16]. Furthermore, research by Nieto et al. [10] suggests that customers trust reviews from fellow consumers more than information provided by sellers or manufacturers about products or services. Consequently, trust in online product reviews significantly affects consumer purchasing decisions and intentions [11, 12].

In response to this, the present study focuses on investigating the factors of trust in eWOM and eWOM quality within its proposed research model, specifically in the context of digital banking services. Researchers have utilized IAM to understand user information adoption patterns [13]. IAM aligns well with eWOM as it provides explanations for information on online platforms [14, 15]. In this context, IACM extends IAM by introducing intention-behavior factors. Traditionally, TRA has been employed to establish the relationship between eWOM and consumer purchase intentions [16, 17]. Thus, IACM integrates two factors from TRA, attitude, and behavioral intention, which will also be employed in this study. With the evolution of social media and digital communication, eWOM has emerged as a crucial information source influencing purchasing decisions [18]. Consumers can continuously access online product reviews from third-party review platforms, brand community blogs, brand websites, and online retailers, engaging in discussions and sharing their consumption experiences. The robust development of the Internet has facilitated consumers' ability to seek information and advice related to consumer behavior from other consumers through eWOM [18, 19]. This study proposes that the information need is a variable influencing the acceptance of eWOM and the intention to use digital banking services.

Consumers are empowered to share their opinions and perspectives on digital banking services across social media and various online platforms [20, 21]. Social media somehow diminishes user anonymity, making online reviews and opinions more authentic and trustworthy [15, 21]. Most online discussions are brand-related [22], significantly impacting consumer purchase intentions [23]. Consumers face the challenge of information overload and must select authentic information before usage, filtering out misinformation [8]. Moreover, this research model implies assessing perceived information relevance [24]. Consequently, the factors of eWOM quantity and consumer expertise are added to the model to yield meaningful results [25].

Based on the relevant theoretical framework, a review of previous related studies, and qualitative research findings, this study proposes a model comprising attitudes

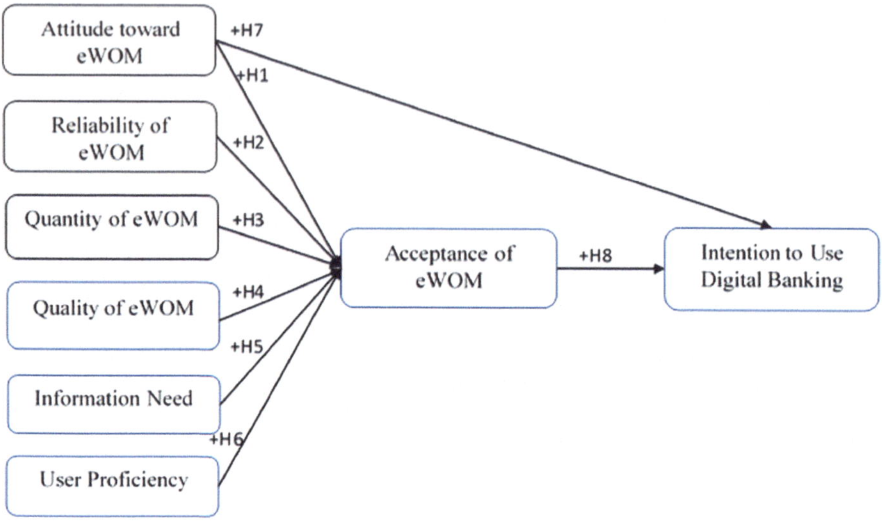

Fig. 1 Research model

toward eWOM, source trustworthiness of eWOM, eWOM quantity, eWOM quality, information need, and user expertise affecting the intention to use digital banking services through eWOM acceptance. Additionally, the study examines the direct impact of attitudes toward eWOM on the intention to use digital banking services (Fig. 1).

In the context of digital banking services, if consumers have a more positive attitude toward eWOM information on social media, they are more likely to accept such information [25].

H1. Attitude toward eWOM positively influences the acceptance of eWOM.

The reliability of eWOM, defined as the extent to which a person agrees that a statement is reliable, promising, and truthful, impacts the acceptance of eWOM information in the realm of digital banking services. The quantity of eWOM, representing the number of reviews or comments about a product across all websites, has a positive impact on the acceptance of eWOM information, making it more observable and influencing the perception of digital banking services The credibility of the source of eWOM, defined as the extent to which a person agrees that a statement is reliable, promising, and truthful, impacts the acceptance of eWOM information in the realm of digital banking services. High-quality eWOM, characterized by logical, detailed, and persuasive content that explains the merits based on the truth about a product or service, positively influences the acceptance of eWOM information, particularly in the context of digital banking services. The information need, defined as the user's demand for advice or experiences from knowledgeable individuals, influences the acceptance of eWOM information in the realm of digital banking services. User proficiency, reflecting the user's experiential knowledge related to the processing of information, positively influences the acceptance of eWOM information in the context of digital banking services [18, 24].

H2. Reliability of eWOM; H3. Quantity of eWOM; H4. Quality of eWOM; H5. Information need; and H6. User proficiency positively influence the acceptance of eWOM.

A positive attitude toward eWOM information on social media positively influences the intention to use digital banking services [18, 24].

H7. Attitude toward eWOM Positively influences the intention to use digital banking.

The acceptance of eWOM information received by consumers positively influences their intention to use digital banking services [26].

H8. Acceptance of eWOM positively influences the intention to use digital banking.

3 Research Methodology

3.1 Methods

After proposing the research model based on the theoretical framework, a preliminary set of study questions was developed through group discussions involving two IT experts and seven consumers with prior electronic banking experience. The aim was to explore new factors and refine the research scale.

The preliminary study questions, aligned with the research purpose, were designed to validate participants' assessments during group discussions. Interviews were divided into two parts: (1) General awareness of eWOM information and factors influencing eWOM acceptance, and (2) Evaluation and adjustment of scale statements.

Prior to the formal study, research concepts and scales underwent preliminary validation to identify errors in the survey questionnaire and ensure accurate measurement without systematic or random errors. Data for this validation were collected through direct interviews using adjusted and supplemented survey questionnaires from the earlier qualitative research.

3.2 Sampling

Following Nguyen [27], considering approximately 35 variables, a sample size of 400 was determined, allowing for the removal of non-compliant observations and ensuring a minimum of 350 for reliable estimates. The survey targeted bank customers in Ho Chi Minh City who had prior experience with banking applications.

A non-probability convenient sampling method was chosen due to time and cost constraints, enabling efficient collection of numerous responses despite limitations such as potential bias, sampling errors, and reduced generalizability.

Quantitative research involved distributing an online survey via email to bank customers in Ho Chi Minh City, using a customer list obtained from the Customer Relations Departments. Screening questions were employed to filter respondents based on prior digital banking usage. Data entry and validation procedures were conducted to ensure response validity, with invalid responses primarily due to incompleteness or failure to meet screening criteria.

4 Results and Discussion

4.1 Descriptive Statistics

After synthesis and classification, 368 valid responses were obtained, meeting scientific significance criteria for analysis. Sample demographics are as follows:

Gender: 183 males (49.65%) and 185 females (50.35%). Age: 123 respondents (33.34%) aged 18–35, 154 (41.85%) aged 36–55, and 91 (24.81%) aged over 55. Education: 79 respondents (21.37%) with education below university, 216 (58.85%) with university education, and 73 (19.78%) with postgraduate education. Income: 85 respondents (22.98%) with an income of 5–10 million VND, 189 (51.27%) with an income of 11–15 million VND, and 94 (25.75%) with an income above 15 million VND.

The descriptive table compares the mean values of observed variables within the same group, revealing which variables are most and least agreed upon by the surveyed individuals. The results indicate that, on a scale of 1–5, the majority of observations have mean values ranging from 3.30 to 3.75. This suggests a consensus or positive evaluation from the participants toward the points investigated in the study.

4.2 Measurement Testing

Cronbach's Alpha Reliability. The study explored the reliability of the measurement scale using Cronbach's alpha for the 8 factors and 35 observed variables related to the intention to use the Digimi application. Considering the diverse sources of these variables, a reliability check was crucial before applying them to the customer base in Ho Chi Minh City. The Cronbach's alpha coefficient, a statistical measure of the correlation between observed variables within the same factor, was employed for this purpose. Variables with correlation coefficients below 0.3 were eliminated, and a Cronbach's alpha greater than or equal to 0.7 was considered reliable [27]. The reliability test results are summarized in Table 1.

Table 1 Mean and coefficient analysis

No.	Factors	Mean	Cronbach's alpha
1	Attitude toward eWOM	3.30	0.893
2	Reliability of eWOM	3.66	0.836
3	Quantity of eWOM	3.56	0.818
4	Quality of eWOM	3.73	0.806
5	Information need	3.54	0.805
6	User proficiency	3.66	0.806
7	Acceptance of eWOM	3.75	0.808
8	Intention to use digital banking	3.74	0.878

The analysis revealed that all observations had correlation coefficients above 0.3, and Cronbach's alpha coefficients for each factor exceeded 0.7. Thus, all measurement scales exhibited good reliability, ensuring a basis for the subsequent exploratory factor analysis (EFA).

Exploratory Factor Analysis (EFA). EFA was conducted to assess the internal consistency and coherence of the concepts in the theoretical research model. Additionally, EFA aids in data reduction and the discovery of new factors if present. The principal axis factoring method combined with promax rotation was used for a more accurate reflection of the data structure. Criteria were applied to evaluate the suitability of EFA, including a KMO value greater than 0.5, significant Bartlett's test ($p < 0.05$), total variance extracted greater than 50%, Eigenvalues exceeding 1, and factor loadings above 0.5. The results indicated EFA suitability (KMO = 0.858) and a satisfactory explanation of 55.23% of the dataset's variance by the eight factors.

All measurement scales demonstrated good reliability and validity, as observed variables converged within each factor. The next step involved subjecting these 35 observed variables from the eight factors to confirmatory factor analysis.

Confirmatory Factor Analysis (CFA). CFA was employed to assess the theoretical model's overall fit, reliability, convergent validity, and discriminant validity. The results are presented in Table 2.

The structural validity was considered appropriate with a Chi-square/df ratio of 1.180 ($p = 0.003$), RMSEA = 0.022 (< 0.08), GFI = 0.914 (> 0.9), CFI = 0.981 (> 0.9), and TLI = 0.979 (> 0.9). These results confirmed that the model was a good fit for the research data.

Following the assessment of model fit, the study computed composite reliability (CR), average variance extracted (AVE), maximum shared squared variance (MSV), and average squared variance (ASV). CR values were all above 0.8, AVE values exceeded 0.5, and MSV and ASV were less than AVE, indicating good reliability, convergent validity, and discriminant validity for all measurement scales.

Table 2 Composite reliability coefficient and extracted variance

Factors	CR	AVE	MSV	ASV
Attitude toward eWOM	0.808	0.513	0.006	0.003
Reliability of eWOM	0.808	0.514	0.353	0.127
Quantity of eWOM	0.818	0.530	0.194	0.085
Quality of eWOM	0.807	0.457	0.021	0.011
Information need	0.836	0.561	0.307	0.106
User proficiency	0.893	0.583	0.353	0.135
Acceptance of eWOM	0.808	0.514	0.181	0.070
Intention to use digital banking	0.878	0.643	0.013	0.003

Table 3 Hypothesis testing results

Correlation			Standardized estimate	Unstandardized estimate	S.E	C.R	p
CN	<–	TT	0.505	0.453	0.069	3.692	0.000
CN	<–	TC	0.202	0.202	0.072	0.028	0.000
CN	<–	NC	0.297	0.284	0.067	1.261	0.007
CN	<–	SL	0.361	0.345	0.064	2.276	0.023
CN	<–	TD	0.287	0.283	0.057	1.462	0.044
CN	<–	CL	0.266	0.261	0.055	1.109	0.000
YD	<–	CN	0.262	0.280	0.079	1.011	0.012
YD	<–	TD	0.218	0.222	0.076	0.295	0.000

4.3 Hypothesis Testing

Structural Equation Modeling (SEM). SEM was employed to analyze the theoretical model comprehensively. The results indicated a well-fitting model with Chi-square/df = 1.177 ($p = 0.003$), RMSEA = 0.022 (< 0.08), GFI = 0.913 (> 0.8), CFI = 0.982 (> 0.9), and TLI = 0.980 (> 0.9). These findings confirmed that the research model was well-suited to the collected data.

Hypothesis Testing. Following the examination of measurement scales and SEM, the study tested eight hypotheses (H1–H8), and the results are presented in Table 3.

4.4 Discussion

The study unveils key insights into eWOM acceptance and the intention to use digital banking services. Results support H1, revealing a significant positive impact of attitude toward eWOM on eWOM acceptance. This aligns with prior research by Cheung et al. [14] and Fan et al. [24], emphasizing the positive influence of perceiving eWOM from friends as useful. H2 is confirmed, indicating a significant positive impact of source credibility on eWOM acceptance. This aligns with Cheung et al. [14] and Fan et al. [24], underlining the crucial role of credibility from familiar sources on mobile social media platforms. Support for H3 shows a positive impact of the quantity of eWOM on acceptance, consistent with prior studies. In the realm of social media, a higher quantity fosters information exchange, influencing perceptions of usefulness. H4 is supported, indicating the positive impact of eWOM quality on acceptance. High-quality information from friends on platforms like Telegram and Instagram contributes to positive acceptance. H5 is confirmed, revealing the positive impact of information need on eWOM acceptance. Consumers with information needs evaluate and accept or reject information based on perceived usefulness in decision-making. H6 is supported, demonstrating the positive impact of user expertise on eWOM acceptance. Consumers with high online expertise selectively accept information aligning with their needs. H7 reveals the positive impact of attitude toward eWOM on the intention to use digital banking services, contributing to TRA. H8 underscores the direct positive influence of eWOM acceptance on the intention to use digital banking services, emphasizing its relevance in the decision-making process.

Considering the COVID-19 pandemic, the study acknowledges evolving consumer perceptions and habits related to digital banking services in Vietnam, driven by the digital transformation strategies adopted by Vietnamese banks and the increased use of the Internet, shaping consumer behavior toward seeking information on social media platforms.

5 Conclusion and Implications

5.1 Conclusion

In summary, this study investigated the factors influencing eWOM acceptance and the intention to use digital banking services in Vietnam. Key factors identified include attitude toward eWOM, reliability, eWOM quality, quantity, information need, and user proficiency. The research assessed the impact of each factor on eWOM acceptance, ranking them in descending order of strength: user proficiency (0.505), eWOM quantity (0.361), information need (0.297), attitude toward eWOM (0.287), eWOM quality (0.266), and reliability of eWOM (0.202). Positive relationships were established between attitude toward eWOM and usage intention (0.218) and eWOM acceptance and usage intention (0.262), resulting in the acceptance of all initially hypothesized hypotheses.

Previous research underscores the impact of eWOM on consumer decision-making, particularly in the context of intangible services like digital banking. Companies actively engage in managing eWOM activities, especially when service evaluation is challenging before consumption. Practically, this research provides valuable insights for practitioners, managers, and electronic marketers regarding the influence of eWOM on consumer behavioral intentions on social networking sites. Given the substantial user base on these platforms, they serve as ideal channels for WOM information. Thus, the critical factors identified in this study for applying eWOM information empower marketers to develop more effective strategies and enhance their understanding of eWOM on digital banking.

5.2 Implications

This study highlights user familiarity's significant impact on eWOM acceptance in digital banking. With Vietnam's e-banking sector growing rapidly due to the Fourth Industrial Revolution, commercial banks are leading the shift toward convenient, secure, and accessible financial services.

To maintain competitiveness, banks must actively monitor user feedback to prevent negative eWOM from tarnishing their digital banking reputation. Tech-savvy users, adept at filtering information, necessitate transparent grievance handling and continuous digital service improvement.

The study identifies the considerable influence of eWOM quantity, suggesting banks offer free trials, simplify interfaces, and promote user-generated content to capture consumer attention. Strategic partnerships and utility payment service integration can enhance digital banking utility, fostering positive eWOM.

Furthermore, the research underscores information needs' impact on eWOM acceptance, suggesting banks create and manage online discussion groups to monitor user experiences and tailor content accordingly.

User attitudes toward information significantly influence eWOM acceptance. Banks can build customer trust by providing informative, engaging social media content rather than solely focusing on product advertising.

Quality eWOM positively impacts acceptance, incentivizing high-quality reviews to foster trust in digital banking applications.

Although source credibility's impact on eWOM acceptance is relatively lower, banks can enhance credibility by providing tools for users to assess source reliability.

The study acknowledges limitations, including sample size constraints and cultural contexts, suggesting future research delve into demographics and previous application experiences for deeper insights.

References

1. Nielsen: Global Trust in Advertising: Winning Strategies for an Evolving Media Landscape (2019). https://www.nielsen.com/content/dam/nielsenglobal/apac/docs/reports/2015/nielsenglobaltrustin-advertising-report-september-2015.pdf
2. Mibrand: Banking Brand Beat Score 2021 (2021). https://mibrand.vn/bao-cao/banking-brand-beat-score-2021
3. Daniel, E.: Provision of electronic banking in the UK and the Republic of Ireland. Int. J. Bank Market. **17**(2), 72–82 (1999)
4. Allen, F., McAndrews, J., Strahan, P.: E-finance: An Introduction, Working Paper No. 01-36. Financial Institutions Center, Wharton University, Philadelphia, PA (2001)
5. Keivani, F.S., Jouzbarkand, M., Khodadadi, M., Sourkouhi, Z.K.: A general view on the e-banking. Int. Proc. Econ. Dev. Res. **43**, 62–65 (2012)
6. Mobarek, A.: E-banking practices and customer satisfaction: a case study in Botswana. SSRN Electron. J. 1–15 (2007)
7. Parasuraman, A., Zeithaml, V.A., Berry, L.L.: The behavioral consequences of service quality. J. Market. **60**, 31–46 (1996)
8. Erkan, I., Evan, C.: The influence of eWOM in social media on consumers purchase intension: an extended approach to information adoption. Comput. Human Behav. **61**, 47–55 (2016)
9. Davis, F.D.: Perceived usefulness, perceived ease of use, and user acceptance of information technology. MIS Q. 319–340 (1989)
10. Nieto, J., Hernández-Maestro, R.M., Muñoz-Gallego, P.A.: Marketing decisions, customer reviews, and business performance: the use of the Toprural website by Spanish rural lodging establishments. Tour. Manage. **45**, 115–123 (2014)
11. Tham, A., Croy, G., Mair, J.: Social media in destination choice: distinctive electronic word-of-mouth dimensions. J. Travel Tour. Mark. **30**(1–2), 144–155 (2013)
12. Lee, M., Youn, S.: Electronic word of mouth: how eWOM platforms influence consumer product judgement. Int. J. Advert. **28**(3), 473–499 (2009)
13. Nonaka, I.: A dynamic theory knowledge of organizational creation. Organ. Sci. **5**(1), 14–37 (1994)
14. Cheung, C.K., Lee, M.O., Rabjohn, N.: The impact of electronic word of mouth: the adoption of online opinions in online consumer communities. Internet Res. **18**(3), 229–247 (2008)
15. Shu, M.L., Scott, N.: Influence of social media on Chinese students' choice of an overseas study destination: an information adoption model perspective. J. Travel Tour. Mark. **31**(2), 286–302 (2014)
16. Cheung, C.K., Thandani, D.R.: The impact of electronic word of mouth communication: a literature analysis and integrative model. Dec. Support Syst. **54**(1), 461–470 (2012)
17. Reichelt, J., Sievert, J., Jacob, F.: How credibility affects eWOM reading: the influences of expertise, trustworthiness, and similarity on utilitarian and social functions. J. Market. Commun. **20**(1e2), 65e81 (2014)
18. Hennig-Thurau, T., Gwinner, K.P., Walsh, G., Gremler, D.D.: Electronic word-of-mouth via consumer-opinion platforms: what motivates consumers to articulate themselves on the internet? J. Interact. Mark. **18**(1), 38–52 (2004)
19. Chu, S., Kim, Y.: Determinants of consumer engagement in electronic word of-mouth in social Networking sites. Int. J. Advert. **30**(1), 47–75 (2011)
20. Kozinets, R.V., de Valck, K., Wojnicki, A.C., Wilner, S.J.: Networked narratives: understanding word-of-mouth marketing in online communities. J. Mark. **74**(2), 71–89 (2010)
21. Akturan, U., Tezcan, N.: Mobile banking adoption of the youth market Perceptions and intentions. Mark. Intell. Plan. **30**(4), 444–459 (2012)
22. Andy, S.: Word of mouth marketing: how smart companies get people talking. Kaplan Publishing, New York (2013)
23. Bansal, H.S., Voyer, P.A.: Word-of-mouth processes within a services purchase decision context. J. Serv. Res. **3**(2), 166–177 (2000)

24. Fan, Y.W., Miao, Y.F., Fang, Y.H., Lin, R.Y.: Establishing the adoption of electronic word-of-mouth through consumers' perceived credibility. Int. Bus. Res. **6**(3), 58–65 (2013)
25. Wang, X., Yu, C., Wei, Y.: Social media peer communication and impacts on purchase intentions: a consumer socialization framework. J. Interact. Mark. **26**(4), 198–208 (2012)
26. Wolny, J., Mueller, C.: Analysis of fashion consumers' motives to engage in electronic word-of-mouth communication through social media platforms. J. Mark. Manage. **29**(5–6), 562–583 (2013)
27. Nguyen, S.H.: Using an Experiment and a Survey to Examine Guilt and Shame Separately via the Distinct Emotional Arousals of Guilt versus Shame under Moderating Effects, Part II: The Case of Personal Cultural Orientation. Business. Sage Publications, Sage Research Methods (2024)
28. Sussman, S.W., Siegal, W.S.: Informational influence in organizations: an integrated approach to knowledge adoption. Inf. Syst. Res. **14**(1), 47–65 (2003)

The Impact of Mobile Trust and Mobile Satisfaction to Electronic Word-of-Mouth and Intention to Use E-Wallet

Nguyen Tran Cam Linh and Nguyen Hoang Chau

Abstract Electronic Word-of-Mouth plays a crucial role in communication, and this factor has been demonstrated in previous studies. This research proposes suggestions to enhance the intention to use e-wallets and address consumer concerns when using electronic wallets. The objectives of this study are: First, to understand and determine the factors of Mobile Trust and Mobile Satisfaction to eWOM and the Intention to Use E-wallets by consumers. Second, to evaluate the level of impact of eWOM and examine the impact factor on Intention To Use E-Wallets. Third, based on the research findings, propose managerial implications to identify the factors influencing the intention to use e-wallets. This supports new businesses in the electronic payment industry to improve revenue and increase market share. Businesses can implement strategies that provide convenient and secure services for Vietnamese consumers. Primary data collection was conducted through the use of an online questionnaire. A mixed-method approach combining qualitative and quantitative analysis techniques will be employed, and the questionnaire will be constructed based on a 5-point Likert scale. Survey results will be processed using SPSS 25, and AMOS 24 software. The novel aspect of this study lies in examining the two factors of Mobile Trust and Mobile Satisfaction. The research results indicate that Satisfaction and Trust factors on mobile platforms, security, and perceived risk have an impact on electronic word-of-mouth intermediaries. Furthermore, electronic word-of-mouth on social media also affects customers' intentions to use electronic wallets. However, risk perception hurts consumers' intention to adopt digital wallets.

Keywords Mobile trust · Mobile satisfaction · Intention to use E-wallet

---

N. T. C. Linh (✉) · N. H. Chau
Ho Chi Minh City Open University, 97 Vo Van Tan, Ward 6, District 3, Ho Chi Minh City 700000, Vietnam
e-mail: linh.ntc@ou.edu.vn

N. H. Chau
e-mail: 2054010079chau@ou.edu.vn

L. T. Tung et al. (eds.), *Disruptive Technology and Business Continuity*,
https://doi.org/10.1007/978-981-97-5452-6_4

1 Introduction

Non-cash payments and transactions through electronic wallets are an inevitable trend in the future, with significant implications in the modern economy. It is a natural outcome of technological advancement and international economic integration. Electronic Wallets enable payments without the need for physical cash or equivalent assets. Therefore, they play a crucial role in today's commerce, replacing physical cash and traditional wallets in a digital form. They store personal information, such as payment cards, on mobile devices, offering benefits such as convenience, low costs, fast transactions, and security [49]. According to the report by the State Bank of Vietnam, in 2021, non-cash transactions witnessed an increase both in quantity and value. Specifically, the number of transactions surged by 30%, and the transaction value rose by 18%. Currently, more than 150 fintech companies are operating in Vietnam, with a major focus on electronic payment, accounting for over 40% of the industry. In 2021, Vietnam ranked among the top three countries in Asia with a mobile payment user rate of 29.1%. The latest data from the State Bank of Vietnam revealed that in the early months of 2021, there were over 200 million transactions carried out through electronic wallets, amounting to approximately 77.7 trillion Vietnamese dong in value.

Vietnam is experiencing rapid development, with advancements in technology, particularly in the realm of cashless online payments. Following the occurrence of the Covid-19 pandemic, the use of electronic wallets has seen further growth. According to [35], more than half of Vietnam's population owns a mobile phone. As of March 2022, the Ministry of Information and Communications reported that 75.3% of Vietnamese adults use smartphones, equivalent to 93.5 million people out of the current population of 99 million. Statistics from 2019 to 2022 demonstrate the remarkable evolution of the digital age, transitioning from traditional phones to smartphones, emphasizing the significant role of mobile phones in daily life. Visa's research indicates that 57% of Vietnam's users own more than 3 e-wallet applications on their phones, with 55% utilizing apps that support various transactions. The latest data from the State Bank of Vietnam, as of early 2021, reveals over 200 million transactions through e-wallet platforms. Looking ahead to 2023, the State Bank's statistics indicate widespread and favored use of e-wallet applications among three generations: Gen X, Y, and Z, accounting for 38%, a 2% increase from Q2 2022, signifying a substantial rise in consumer acceptance of e-wallet payments. Moreover, the data illustrates that over 85% of individuals use at least one e-wallet, indicating a high level of acceptance, and 75% of e-wallet users make payments at least once a week, showcasing the convenience and preference for weekly e-wallet transactions. The diversity in user demographics across generations signals a positive trend toward modernization and establishes a robust foundation for the cashless payment industry through electronic wallets.

Previously, all financial transactions were mainly conducted using cash or cards, which required consumers to make direct payments at the stores. This method was time-consuming, inconvenient, and inflexible. In recent years, with the development of technology, the number of payment methods has been improved and expanded, such as Internet Banking, Mobile Money, and Mobile E-Wallets. Instead of making direct payments at physical retail points, consumers mostly opt for online payment methods, which in turn has promoted the acceptance of electronic wallets, mobile payments, and convenient payment options as the norm. The increasing presence of electronic wallets in the market, along with attractive incentives to attract customers, has intensified the competition in the electronic wallet race. Thanks to the benefits of minimizing risks associated with direct contact, electronic wallets have successfully expanded their customer base.

Nowadays, the Internet enables consumers to share their experiences and opinions about a product through electronic word-of-mouth (eWOM) activities. Consumers tend to share information or consumption outcomes with other consumers through online platforms, also known as electronic word-of-mouth (eWOM) [23]. Electronic word-of-mouth is an adaptation or adjustment to the current changes and developments [12]. The Internet plays a crucial role in transforming traditional word-of-mouth into electronic word-of-mouth, where consumers share information through digital media or the Internet [31]. Previous research has focused on studying individual factors such as Mobile Trust, Mobile Satisfaction, Perceived Risk, and Security, rather than examining their combined effects on electronic word-of-mouth (eWOM) and the Intention to use Electronic wallets (E-Wallets). For instance, [45] investigated the impact of trust on mobile wallets, while [39] demonstrated how satisfaction affects e-wallet continuance intention. Similarly, [51] study revealed that individual factors like perceived risk and perceived security influence the intention to use mobile payment.

Although many studies have highlighted the significance of eWOM in consumer purchasing intentions, such as those conducted by [8, 12] and [30], it may be challenging to directly apply the findings of these studies to the Vietnamese market due to differences in cultural environments and consumer behaviors among different countries. Moreover, both domestic and international studies have rarely addressed the factors of trust and satisfaction concerning users' utilization of mobile devices for online transactions through e-wallets. [36] focused on E-Trust and E-Satisfaction to eWOM when using mobile services (MSQ). In this study, the authors proposed further exploration for subsequent research on how the factors of M-Trust and M-Satisfaction influence eWOM when using mobile services. This would help shed more light on the impact of trust and satisfaction when consumers use their mobile phones to engage with mobile services.

This article conducts an in-depth study on the two factors of Trust and Satisfaction of consumers when using their mobile phones for Electronic Wallet payments and their impact on electronic word-of-mouth (eWOM). It means that before using an electronic wallet for payment, consumers would preview comments on websites and social media, seeking information from previous users to consider factors such as transaction fees, security, and potential risks associated with the electronic wallet. Therefore, this research paper studies the topic: "The impact of Mobile Trust and Mobile Satisfaction to Electronic Word-of-Mouth and Intention to Use E-wallet."

Based on this, the study offers suggestions to enhance the intention to use electronic wallets and address consumer concerns when using various types of electronic wallets. The topic hopes to be a reference source for administrators in the electronic payment industry in the future. The research specifically measures the impact of factors that influence the intention to use e-wallets. At the same time, it helps administrators improve revenue and expand the market share of businesses. In addition, research also helps administrators save time, effort, and costs. From there, administrators can rely on the research and develop their strategies and measures to promote consumer adoption of e-wallets as well as improve services and understand more about consumers' intention to use e-wallets.

2 Grounded Theory

The Technology Acceptance Model (TAM), introduced by [9], posits that behavior is influenced by two factors: perceived ease of use and perceived usefulness. Furthermore, it suggests that behavior also impacts the intention to use technology. Building upon the TAM, [1] specifically identified additional factors such as usefulness, perceived risk, and ease of use, as well as their impact on consumer acceptance of mobile banking services. They also introduced two additional factors: trust and satisfaction in mobile payment adoption.

In 2019, the Theory of Planned Behavior (TPB) demonstrated the impact of perceived risk through their analysis. To gain a comprehensive understanding of perceived risk, [27] integrated both the Technology Acceptance Model (TAM) and TPB to investigate five types of risks, including performance risk, time risk, social risk, financial risk, and security risk. As analyzed above, positive or negative beliefs can alter the direction of behavior, thereby influencing the online payment intention of users.

The Information Acceptance Model (IAM) proposed [50] suggests that the quality and reliability of information will impact the usefulness of the information in meeting users' information needs. Several authors have acknowledged the applicability of the Information Acceptance Model in their research, especially when studying electronic word-of-mouth (eWOM) [8, 46]. In the context of this research focusing on electronic word-of-mouth (eWOM), the application of the IAM is deemed appropriate. The IAM factors are compared to the original model of [50], demonstrating the similarities of both models in studying electronic word-of-mouth and its potential to yield positive outcomes and provide crucial insights into information acceptance and usage from various online media sources.

Based on this foundation, the research model on consumers' intention to use electronic wallets in Ho Chi Minh City comprises six factors: Mobile Trust, Mobile Satisfaction, Perceived Risk, Security, Electronic Word-of-Mouth (eWOM), and Intention to Use E-wallet.

2.1 Mobile Satisfaction (M-Satisfaction)

Further investigated the importance of mobile satisfaction by stating that "Customer satisfaction with mobile services (Mobile Satisfaction) is equally significant as Electronic Satisfaction (E-Satisfaction)" [3]. They argued that the success of electronic banking and the prevalence of smartphones have led companies to adopt more user-centric approaches. Accordingly, they defined Mobile Satisfaction (M-Satisfaction) as the satisfaction customers perceive when using mobile services through applications installed on mobile devices. Previous studies have indicated that electronic word-of-mouth (eWOM) can influence customers' decision-making in online environments [5, 11, 21]. As eWOM can impact customers' online shopping behavior on mobile applications, mobile satisfaction may affect customers' choices when making purchases through mobile platforms.

Drawing from the concepts of [3] regarding Mobile Satisfaction (M-Satisfaction), which is a crucial factor in determining consumers' intention to use electronic wallets, and [54], who studied how electronic word-of-mouth can positively influence consumers' intentions to use online payment services, the present study proposes the following hypothesis:

H1: Mobile Satisfaction positively impacts Electronic Word-of-Mouth.

2.2 Mobile Trust (M-Trust)

Proposed that online trust can also translate into mobile trust. Additionally, the author mentioned, "Online Trust also influences performance expectations" [55]. This means that trust in online payments will impact consumers' trust in the reliability of mobile payments. Subsequently, once users have placed their trust in the online payment system, they will expect mobile payment systems to provide better and higher quality services.

How electronic word-of-mouth can positively influence consumers' intentions to use online payment services through banks [54]. When combining these two concepts, it can be observed that trust generates strong confidence from consumers toward the mobile payment system. When consumers have trust in the security of mobile payments, they are likely to share their positive experiences with others through social media channels, thereby creating positive electronic word-of-mouth. Therefore, a hypothesis related to Mobile Trust (M-Trust) and Electronic Word-of-Mouth (eWOM) is proposed as follows:

H2: Mobile Trust positively impacts Electronic Word-of-Mouth.

2.3 Perceived Risk (PR)

Perceived risk is defined as a crucial factor in the adoption of the latest mobile wallet technologies, which leads to consumer acceptance of mobile wallets [33]. Therefore, the reliability and security of the system will enhance users' interest in using mobile payments. Combining this definition [54] concept of electronic word-of-mouth, it can be explained that consumers, being highly aware of potential risks, tend to seek more information about the technology's implementation. The level of perceived risk will influence how consumers understand, interpret, and utilize electronic word-of-mouth based on their strong emotional response and trust in the information source. Despite the perceived benefits and usefulness of using mobile wallets, consumers are still aware of potential risks that may arise, which can impede their intention to use such wallets. Therefore, this study proposes the following two hypotheses:

H3: Perceived Risk positively impacts Electronic Word-of-Mouth.

H4: Perceived Risk positively impacts Intention to use E-Wallet.

2.4 Security (SE)

Security is defined as the protection and safety of transactions against potential harm to devices. Consumers' intention to use electronic payments increases and providers must pay special attention to security as it is considered a crucial factor influencing consumers [25]. To gain more trust and willingness to use mobile wallets as a means of online payment (as analyzed [54] in the context of electronic word-of-mouth), providers need to prioritize information security in online transactions. When consumers are concerned about the security of their transactions, they tend to use online payment services with high-security measures and positively evaluate them on social media, creating positive electronic word-of-mouth. When users perceive a high level of security in mobile wallets, their intention to use these wallets also significantly increases. Therefore, the following hypotheses are proposed:

H5: Security positively impacts Electronic Word-of-Mouth.

H6: Security positively impacts the Intention to use E-Wallet.

2.5 Intention to Use E-wallet (IT)

To investigate different aspects compared to previous studies, one of the research objectives was to explore how electronic word-of-mouth (eWOM) influences consumers' intentions to use online payment services through banks [54]. Discovered that acceptance factors significantly influence consumers' behavioral intentions regarding the use of mobile-based online payments [43]. The Technology Acceptance Model (TAM) was further extended to include factors such as perceived risk, emotional perception, compatibility, and, the interaction between individual and product-related factors. Regarding electronic word-of-mouth, it encompasses a broader scope where an individual acts as a spokesperson with access to more information and stories. They subsequently transmit and share the information they receive, significantly influencing consumers' intentions to use mobile wallets. Based on these findings, the following hypothesis is proposed.

H7: Electronic Word-of-Mouth positively impacts the Intention to use E-Wallet.

3 Methodology

3.1 Research Procedures

Research Process Consisting of Seven Steps, Described as Below. Research Design.

Step 1: Identify the Research Problem: Conduct a study on the impact of security factors, risk perception, satisfaction on mobile platforms, and satisfaction on mobile platforms influencing electronic word-of-mouth and consumer intentions to use electronic wallets.

Step 2: Database Research: Collect primary data by referring to relevant previous studies related to the author's intended use of electronic wallets. Subsequently, select and filter theories related to the research topic to build a research scale suitable for the research context. Then, construct a questionnaire.

Step 3: Build the Research Model: The author constructs a research model based on factors related to security, risk perception, satisfaction on mobile platforms, satisfaction on mobile platforms, electronic word-of-mouth, and consumer intentions to use electronic wallets.

Step 4: Refine the Measurement Scale: Qualitative research results will be conducted first, followed by adjustments, in-depth interviews, and refinement of concepts. Simultaneously, the construction of the formal measurement scale will be carried out to enhance its completeness and relevance to the research context.

Step 5: Formal Research–Quantitative Research: Quantitative research is the method extensively used, involving a survey of consumers in Ho Chi Minh City. The sample size for the survey, as set by the author, is 300 observation samples.

Step 6: Data Collection, Processing, and Analysis: The next step involves the preliminary examination and evaluation of these measurement scales using two commonly used assessment tools: Cronbach's Alpha coefficient and Exploratory Factor Analysis (EFA). These tools enable the author's team to eliminate predetermined variables not correlated with the model. This process helps consolidate them into a group of variables with significant factors that are more relevant to the research topic. Following the Preliminary Examination, the author will utilize the Structural Equation Modeling (SEM) framework to validate the model and hypotheses. This aims to confirm the model's structure and hypotheses, ensuring a comprehensive evaluation.

Step 7: Draw Conclusions and Propose Recommendations: The research team will leverage the results obtained above to conclude. Additionally, they will propose recommendations based on the findings.

3.2 Qualitative Data Collection Techniques:

To construct the measurement scale in the study, the author relied on relevant theoretical foundations. Subsequently, the author collected and synthesized measurement scales for variables within the research model. Following the author's research model, which includes variables in their study, a Likert scale design was employed to assess observational variables. The Likert scale measures the degree of agreement of respondents on a scale from 1 to 5 (ranging from completely disagree to completely agree): Completely Disagree, Disagree, Neutral, Agree, Completely Agree.

The author employed in-depth interview methods, and the process was conducted in Ho Chi Minh City.

Initially, the author conducted in-depth interviews, which involved a dialog between respondents and the author, with the conversation being repeated. In this phase, the author conducted interviews with seven different individuals. The majority of these individuals were in the age range of 18–20, consisting of students, and office workers who regularly use electronic wallets for various transactions such as purchasing goods or paying for services like watching movies or food delivery fees. Among the seven interviewees, one was the owner of a Beauty Garden cosmetics store, providing a diverse perspective.

Step 1: Once the measurement questions have been determined, the author will read the questions to the interview participants (hereafter referred to as respondents). While listening to the respondents' answers, the author will observe facial expressions and response delays. If a question is too complex, unclear, or irrelevant to the topic, the author will make notes and listen to the respondent's suggestions for improvement.

Step 2: After receiving feedback from the first respondent, the author will adjust suggestions related to questions that confused the first respondent.

Step 3: Subsequently, after adjusting suggestions from the first respondent, the author will use the modified set of questions to interview the second respondent. The process then returns to Step 1.

Step 4: If these respondents agree and find the set of questions clear, coherent, and relevant to the topic, the author will conclude the interview. The table below contains the questions recorded by the author during the interviews with respondents.

Step 5: The author refines the set of questions and prepares an online survey using Google Forms. Through this process, with the consensus of the author and experts, the research model and measurement scale have been tested, screened, and adjusted to fit the research topic. Due to differences in space and time in previous studies, the scale was not entirely suitable in Ho Chi Minh City. Therefore, the author continued to use qualitative methods to modify and improve the measurement tool.

The construction of the quantitative research survey questionnaire was based on the qualitative results.

3.3 *Quantitative Research*

Sample Determining

The sample size of this research model using the exploratory factor analysis (EFA) statistical analysis method requires a sufficiently large number of samples to ensure the reliability of the measurement scale. Researchers suggest that the sample size should follow a minimum variability ratio of 5:1 or higher [19]. This means that a measurement scale should have a minimum of 5 observations to ensure reliability.

The author's study consists of a total of 30 observed variables, using a 5-point Likert scale with 30 observed variables. Hence, the minimum sample size is determined using the following formula:

$$\text{Sample size} = \text{total number of observed variables x 5} = 30 \text{ x } 5 = 150$$

The minimum sample size is established as 150. However, to increase the confidence level, the research opted to survey an estimated sample size of 300 observations to ensure diverse samples and obtain the most robust results.

Research Instrument and Data Collection

This study collected and developed the initial questionnaire by constructing a robust theoretical framework. The questions were synthesized and data were collected using both secondary and primary data sources. Once the theoretical foundation and questionnaire were established, the questions were ensured to be reliable for the measurement scale and aligned with the research model. The questions were constructed on a Likert scale ranging from 1 to 5, corresponding to the values from "strongly disagree" to "strongly agree."

Data Analysis

The research aims to assess the reliability of the measurement scale in this study. Cronbach's Alpha coefficient is a statistical test used to measure the reliability of the measurement scale. The reliability of the measurement scales, as determined by Cronbach's Alpha coefficient, is all greater than 0.6, and the inter-item correlations are all greater than 0.3, indicating that the measurement scales meet the required reliability criteria [37, 41]. After testing the reliability using Cronbach's Alpha, exploratory factor analysis (EFA) is conducted to explore the data. When conducting EFA, attention should be given to the following criteria [40].

The research employs several criteria for evaluating the model fit:

- Kaiser-Mayer-Olkin (KMO) coefficient: $0.5 \leq \text{KMO} \leq 1$.

- Significance level of Bartlett: ≤ 0.05, indicating that the variables have relationships with each other.
- Eigenvalue < 1: factors with Eigenvalue less than 1 will be discarded.
- Total variance extracted (TVE) below 50%: factors will not be retained in the model; if TVE is above 50%, the factors will be retained [4].
- Factor loadings of observed variables > 0.3: the minimum condition to retain observed variables in the factor model [17].

To assess the appropriateness of the model, the research uses various indices in the model evaluation, such as:

- CMIN/df: ≤ 2 indicates a good fit; ≤ 5 indicates an acceptable fit.
- Comparative Fit Index (CFI): ≥ 0.8 indicates an acceptable fit; ≥ 0.9 indicates a good fit; ≥ 0.95 indicates a very good fit.
- Goodness of Fit Index (GFI): ≥ 0.9 indicates a good fit; ≥ 0.95 indicates a very good fit.
- Tucker-Lewis Index (TLI): ≥ 0.9 indicates a good fit; ≥ 0.95 indicates a very good fit.
- Root Mean Square Residual (RMR): ≤ 0.08 indicates a good fit; ≤ 0.03 indicates a very good fit.
- Root Mean Square Error of Approximation (RMSEA): ≤ 0.08 is considered good; ≤ 0.03 is considered very good.

Finally, the Structural Equation Model (SEM) is used to test relationships between observed and latent variables while providing information on the reliability and values of observed variables [14].

4 Result and Discussion

The study results must be clear and concise. Use an appendix or additional documentation if needed.

4.1 Result

After collecting and screening responses, a total of 344 valid questions were retained for further analysis. First, in terms of gender, the proportion of male respondents is 45.5% and the remaining 55.5% are female. For age criteria, the subjects focused on age groups: from 18 to 25 years old (accounting for 30.8%) and 26 to 35 years old (accounting for 44.5%). For the income criterion, it can be seen that the majority of the respondents have an income of 5–10 million VND, accounting for 36.3%. Followed by those with incomes below 5 million and 10 to 20 million are 28.2% and 30.2% respectively. The frequency of use collected from the respondents is quite uniform. The frequency of use is collected from the respondents. Respondents were quite similar. As for occupations, it is not surprising that students and office workers accounted for the highest percentage of occupations at 30.8% and 44.5%, respectively. Finally, the purpose of use, in general, the payment purpose does not have a high difference between users using e-wallets when paying for purchases (accounting for 37.2%), transferring money (32.3%), and the rest paying service charges.

4.2 EFA Analysis and Test of Reliability and Validity

This study utilized a total of 30 observed variables, out of which 10 were dependent variables and 20 were independent variables. The results of the study demonstrated that all observed variables achieved a satisfactory level of reliability and are presented in detail in Table 2.

The results showed that the Kaiser-Mayer-Olkin (KMO) measure was 0.900 ($0.5 \leq KMO \leq 1$), and the significance value in the Bartlett test was 0.000 (< 0.05), indicating that the selected observed variables were suitable for factor analysis using the exploratory factor analysis (EFA) method. Conducting the EFA, all factor loadings were greater than 0.3, the Eigenvalue was 1.638 (greater than 1), and the total variance extracted was 62.812% (greater than 50%). These results indicate that 60.035% of the data's variance was explained by 6 factors.

4.3 Adjusted Research Model After EFA

After conducting the Exploratory Factor Analysis (EFA), the Confirmatory Factor Analysis (CFA) was performed using AMOS 24 software. The obtained indices were as follows: CMIN/df = 1.230 (< 2), CFI = 0.985, TLI = 0.983, GFI = 0.916, TLI = 0.983, all greater than 0.9. The Root Mean Square Residual (RMR) was 0.046 (< 0.05), and the Root Mean Square Error of Approximation (RMSEA) was 0.026 (< 0.03). The Hoelter index values were 313 (at 0.05 level) and 328 (at 0.01 level), both higher than 200.

Furthermore, all observed variables were evaluated with standardized factor loadings (λi), which met the criterion of being greater than or equal to 0.5 (ranging from $\lambda i = 0.58$ to $\lambda i = 0.90$).

The results indicate that the measurement scale is completely suitable and fits well with the proposed model in this research (Table 3).

To evaluate the convergent validity and discriminant validity, we consider the indices AVE, CR, and MSV, as suggested [18, 20]. According to him if CR has a value greater than 0.7, it is considered to have good reliability. In the research model, all measurement scales have CR values greater than 0.7 [18]. Specifically, the maximum CR value is 0.911, and the minimum CR value is 0.87.

Table 1 KMO results, Bartlett's test, and Patter matrix

Symbol	Measure	Source	Factor
Electronic word-of-mouth 3 (EW3)	I review online customer ratings when making decisions about using electronic wallets	Lee [28]	0.856
Electronic word-of-mouth 5 (EW5)	I review online customer ratings when making decisions about using electronic wallets	Lee [28]	0.854
Electronic word-of-mouth 1 (EW1)	Whenever I need information about electronic wallets, my first thought is to search for online word-of-mouth reviews	Lee [28]	0.808
Electronic word-of-mouth 4 (EW4)	I believe that I have more accurate information about electronic wallets from the online feedback of other users	Lee [28]	0.786
Electronic word-of-mouth 2 (EW2)	I believe that I have more accurate information about electronic wallets from the online feedback of other users	Lee [28]	0.765
Mobile satisfaction 5 (MS5)	I believe that I have more accurate information about electronic wallets from the online feedback of other users	Lee [28]	0.902
Mobile satisfaction 4 (MS4)	I am satisfied with the company that provided this application service	Lee et al. [26]	0.836
Mobile satisfaction 1 (MS1)	I think that the functionality of the electronic wallet service meets my needs	Lee et al. [26]	0.788
Mobile satisfaction 3 (MS3)	I believe that the application service of the electronic wallet company has met my expectations	Lee et al. [26]	0.758
Mobile satisfaction 2 (MS2)	Based on all my experiences with this electronic wallet application service, I feel very satisfied	Lee et al. [26]	0.704
Perceived risk 1 (PR1)	The provider can verify the identity of users to ensure the safety of transactions	Senali et al. [44]	0.850

(continued)

Table 1 (continued)

Symbol	Measure	Source	Factor
Perceived risk 5 (PR5)	I feel secure when conducting transactions with electronic wallets	Senali et al. [44]	0.838
Perceived risk 4 (PR4)	I feel secure about transactions conducted through electronic wallets	Senali [44]	0.805
Perceived risk 3 (PR3)	The provider implements security measures to protect my payment transactions	Senali et al. [44]	0.739
Perceived risk 2 (PR2)	The provider can ensure the security of the electronic wallet	Senali et al. [44]	0.683
Security 4 (SE4)	I believe that the likelihood of losing money stored in a mobile wallet is low	Chawla and Joshi [7]	0.839
Security 5 (SE5)	I will confidently make payments through the mobile wallet	Chawla and Joshi [7]	0.815
Security 1 (SE1)	I believe that the technology used in mobile wallets is very secure	Chawla, and Joshi [7]	0.781
Security 3 (SE3)	I believe that this service is potentially safer than traditional payment methods such as credit cards and cash	Chawla and Joshi [7]	0.719
Security 2 (SE2)	I believe that transactions conducted through mobile wallets are safe	Chawla and Joshi [7]	0.712
Mobile trust 4 (MT4)	I trust that electronic wallets will uphold their commitments and promises	Chawla, and Joshi [7]	0.844
Mobile trust 5 (MT5)	I trust that in any situation or issue, the service provider will support me	Chawla, and Joshi [7]	0.814
Mobile trust 1 (MT1)	I trust transactions conducted through electronic wallets	Chawla and Joshi [7]	0.774
Mobile trust 3 (MT3)	I believe that electronic wallet service providers adhere to consumer protection laws	Chawla and Joshi [7]	0.750
Mobile trust 2 (MT2)	I trust that electronic wallet service providers will not disclose any of my personal information to third parties	Chawla and Joshi [7]	0.679

(continued)

Table 1 (continued)

Symbol	Measure	Source	Factor
Intention to use 5 (IT5)	I expect my use of the mobile wallet to increase in the future	Senal et al. [44]	0.888
Intention to use 3 (IT3)	I intend to use e-wallet services in the future	Senali et al. [44]	0.777
Intention to use 2 (IT2)	I intend to use e-wallet services when I purchase items	Senali, M. G et al. (2023)	0.771
Intention to use 4 (IT4)	I intend to recommend the use of e-wallets to friends	Senali et al. [44]	0.731
Intention to use 1 (IT1)	I plan to use e-wallet services in the future	Senali et al. [44]	0.605

Table 2 Comparison between criteria and CFA results

CMIN/df	<2	1.230
GIF	≥0.9	0.916
TLI	≥0.9	0.983
CFI	≥0.9	0.985
IFI	≥0.9	0.985
RMR	<0.05	0.046
RMSEA	≤0.8	0,026
Hoelter 0.05 và 0.01	>200	313 và 328

Table 3 Convergent and discriminant validity

	CR	AVE	MSV	MaxR
EW	0,911	0,673	0,258	0,919
MS	0,898	0,639	0,077	0,913
PR	0,890	0,618	0,183	0,893
SE	0,884	0,604	0,267	0,893
MT	0,882	0,601	0,078	0,892
IT	0,873	0,582	0,267	0,891

Next, we examine the convergent validity of the measurement scales through the Average Variance Extracted (AVE) index. A measurement scale achieves convergent validity if the AVE value is 0.5 or higher. According to the results in Table 4, the AVE values of all measurement scales are greater than 0.05. Specifically, the maximum AVE value is 0.67, and the minimum AVE value is 0.582. Therefore, the measurement scales of the research model demonstrate reliable convergence for the observed variables, such as EW, MS, SE, PR, MT, and IT.

Table 4 Construct a correlation matrix

EW	MS	PR	SE	MT	IT
0,820					
0,278***	0,799				
0,427***	0,150*	0,786			
0,385***	0,173**	0,377***	0,777		
0,280***	0,211***	0,157*	0,082	0,776	
0,508***	0,200**	0,305***	0,516***	0,160**	0,763

*, **, *** Construct and correlation matrix

To assess discriminant validity, the authors rely on the Maximum Shared Variance (MSV) index, where MSV should be smaller than both AVE and the value of AVE squared. This shows the distinction between variables EW, MS, SE, PR, MT, and IT. According to the results in Table 4, all MSV values are smaller than the AVE values. The minimum MSV value is 0.077, and the maximum MSV value is 0.267. Thus, the MSV values meet the requirement, ensuring discriminant validity among the variables. Overall, the results in Tables 4 and 5 confirm the discriminant validity of the research model.

Based on the results from Table 5, we can observe that all observed variables meet the criterion for Composite Reliability (CR) ($\geq$0.7), indicating good and accurate data with a reliability of 0.68. The average variance extracted (AVE) values of the observed variables are also determined and are greater than 0.5, indicating reliable convergent validity for variables such as EW, MS, SE, PR, MT, and IT. Moreover, all six observed variables have MSV values < AVE and the square root of AVE is greater than the correlation values between the variables, demonstrating reliable discriminant validity among the variables EW, MS, SE, PR, MT, and IT (Fig. 1).

The regression weights yielding the above results also support all the remaining relationships (P-value < 0.05). Therefore, they are statistically significant.

Table 5 Standardized regression weights: (group number 1—default model)

Hypothesis		Standardized regression coefficient	Value P	Result
H1	MS → EW	0.175	0.005	Accept
H2	MT → EW	0.199	0.004	Accept
H3	PR → EW	0.354	0.004	Accept
H4	PR → IT	0.026	0.714	Refute
H5	SE → EW	0.259	0.004	Accept
H6	SE → IT	0.378	0.004	Accept
H7	EW → IT	0.354	0.004	Accept

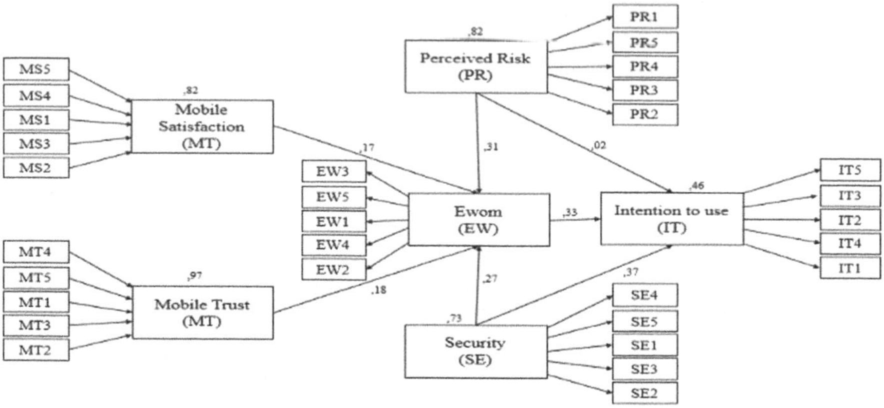

Fig. 1 Structural equation modeling (SEM)

5 Conclusions and Implications

5.1 Conclusion

Mobile Satisfaction has a positive impact on electronic word-of-mouth. As in the conceptual part that analyzed articles on satisfaction [10, 36, 38], it can be seen that satisfaction is one of the factors equally important factors for the intention to use the e-wallet. The research articles [2]; and [47] are different in the research context, but the results from the two studies show that satisfaction has a positive impact on Word of mouth and customer satisfaction will spread the word about that experience to other customers online. Similarly, research by the author group [16, 42] shows that customer satisfaction in online shopping will lead to positive word-of-mouth to others because of its convenience, ease of finding the product customers want, and ease of comparison. Price and quality of products from online shops. In technological contexts such as e-commerce [13, 49], and mobile commerce, trust is considered a key factor [15, 24, 32]. According to research, trust has a positive impact on electronic word-of-mouth in E-servicescape [53]. The studies also demonstrated that perceived risk has a positive impact on electronic word-of-mouth and that the level of perceived risk determines how consumers interpret and use information for word-of-mouth [6, 29]. Electronics increases with the consumer's feelings and level of trust before receiving information. In the context of shopping behavioral intention in the digital age, security, and privacy for electronic word-of-mouth are positively related to each other [22]. Previous studies said that high security can increase consumers' intention to use electronic payment systems on a platform [25]. Finally, previous research results also demonstrate that electronic word-of-mouth influences usage intention [52]. At the same time, the research [34] is also consistent with the author's research. This study investigates and identifies the factors influencing electronic word-of-mouth and the intention to use e-wallets among users in Ho Chi Minh City.

In this research, the authors examined two dependent variables: electronic word-of-mouth and Intention to use e-wallets, and four independent variables: Mobile Trust (M-Trust), Mobile Satisfaction (M-Satisfaction), Perceived Risk, and Security. The study collected 344 valid survey samples and determined that the identified factors were statistically significant. The results from Cronbach's Alpha coefficients were all greater than 0.8, indicating that the measurement scales used in the study are reliable. Subsequently, the authors conducted an Exploratory Factor analysis (EFA), and the results showed that the Kaiser-Mayer-Olkin (KMO) value was 0.900, and Sig. was 0.000, both of which are statistically significant. Moreover, all 344 observed variables from the six factors had factor loadings greater than 0.5, demonstrating the adequacy of the measurement scales. Finally, confirmatory factor analysis (CFA) was performed, and the various indices, such as CFI, TLI, GFI, RMR, CMIN/df, and Hoelter, met the standard criteria. Based on the findings, the authors proposed some managerial implications to enhance the intention to use e-wallets for online payment providers in Ho Chi Minh City.

5.2 Managerial Implications

This study emphasizes the importance of mobile trust and mobile satisfaction in promoting eWOM and the intention to use e-wallets. Therefore, e-commerce companies need to focus on building trust and user satisfaction to encourage positive eWOM and increase the intention to use e-wallets. Establishing trust and credibility, as indicated by the research results, can also help businesses build trust and credibility with their users.

The findings of this study can help businesses design user-friendly e-wallets that cater to the needs and preferences of Vietnamese consumers. The key is for managers to optimize the design of e-commerce websites on mobile applications. Additionally, mobile trust is a crucial factor in promoting e-wallet usage; thus, companies can concentrate on creating secure and highly secure e-wallets. This can be achieved by implementing measures to enhance security, reduce usage risks to protect user information, provide the best services to customers, and improve positive user experiences.

Businesses can leverage eWOM to boost the intention to use e-wallets. They can focus on encouraging positive eWOM, such as prompting users to leave reviews after experiencing their services, highlighting positive reviews on social media platforms, and addressing negative customer feedback to demonstrate their responsiveness and customer-centric approach. Furthermore, businesses need to maintain their competitive edge in the e-wallet market in Vietnam. By understanding the factors that drive e-wallet usage and user behavior, companies can design better e-wallets, establish trust and credibility, and capitalize on eWOM to promote adoption. This can help them stay ahead of their competitors and achieve success in the rapidly growing e-wallet market in Vietnam.

E-commerce companies should consider the cultural context in which their users operate. The study shows that mobile trust and mobile satisfaction significantly influence eWOM and the intention to use e-wallets, but these factors may vary depending on the cultural context. Therefore, e-commerce companies should take cultural differences into account when designing websites and mobile applications, as well as when developing their marketing strategies.

In conclusion, this scientific research on the impact of mobile trust and satisfaction on eWOM to the intention to use e-wallets in Vietnam has managerial implications for businesses. By understanding the factors that drive e-wallet usage among users, businesses can design better e-wallets, establish trust and credibility, and capitalize on eWOM to promote adoption. This can help businesses maintain their competitiveness in the rapidly growing e-wallet market in Vietnam and achieve long-term success.

5.3 Limitations and Future Research

The limitations are as follows. First, this research only focuses on the study conducted in Ho Chi Minh City; therefore, it cannot accurately assess the influencing factors and common characteristics in Vietnam as a whole. Secondly, the survey data obtained from respondents may not be representative of the broader population. The majority of respondents were students and office workers, who may not fully represent the diverse consumer groups using e-wallets in Vietnam.

Future research directions can be pursued as follows. First, further studies should expand geographically, for example, conducting research in other major cities such as Hanoi, Hai Phong, or Da Nang, to gain a more objective view of the six factors mentioned above. Second, in this study, the authors delved deeper into the factors of trust and satisfaction. The authors thoroughly investigated these two factors to measure the level of impact on consumers when they use mobile phones for cashless transactions through e-wallets. Future studies could consider further exploring the impact of risk or security factors (e.g., M-Risk and M-Security) when consumers increasingly adopt mobile devices for online payments. By addressing these limitations and exploring these future research directions, scholars can gain a more comprehensive understanding of the factors influencing e-wallet usage in Vietnam, and businesses can make more informed decisions and develop effective strategies to enhance user adoption and satisfaction.

References

1. Abu-Taieh, E.M., AlHadid, I., Abu-Tayeh, S., Masa'deh, R.E., Alkhawaldeh, R.S., Khwaldeh, S., Alrowwad, A.A.: Continued intention to use of M-Banking in Jordan by integrating UTAUT, TPB, TAM and service quality with ML. J. Open Innov.: Technol., Market, Complexity **8**(3), 120 (2022)
2. Alrwashdeh, M., Jahmani, A., Ibrahim, B., Aljuhmani, H.Y.: Data to model the effects of perceived telecommunication service quality and value on the degree of user satisfaction and e-WOM among telecommunications users in North Cyprus. Data Brief **28**, 104981 (2020)
3. Al-Zadjali, M., Al-Jabri, H., Al-Balushi, T.: Assessing customer satisfaction of m-banking in Oman using SERVQUAL model. In: 2015 6th IEEE International Conference on Software Engineering and Service Science (ICSESS) (2015)
4. Anderson, J.C., Gerbing, D.W.: Structural equation modeling in practice: a review and recommended two-step approach. Psychol. Bull. **103**(3), 411 (1988)
5. Babić Rosario, A., De Valck, K., Sotgiu, F.: Conceptualizing the electronic word-of-mouth process: what we know and need to know about eWOM creation, exposure, and evaluation. J. Acad. Mark. Sci. **48**, 422–448 (2020)
6. Chatterjee, P.: Online reviews: do consumers use them? (2001)
7. Chawla, D., Joshi, H.: Consumer attitude and intention to adopt mobile wallet in India—an empirical study. Int. J. Bank Market. **37**(7), 1590–1618 (2019)
8. Cheung, C.M., Lee, M.K., Rabjohn, N.: The impact of electronic word-of-mouth: the adoption of online opinions in online customer communities. Internet Res. **18**(3), 229–247 (2008)
9. Davis, F.D.: A technology acceptance model for empirically testing new end-user information systems: theory and results (Doctoral dissertation, Massachusetts Institute of Technology) (1985)
10. Dianat, I., Adeli, P., Jafarabadi, M.A., Karimi, M.A.: User-centered web design, usability, and user satisfaction: the case of online banking websites in Iran. Appl. Ergon. **81**, 102892 (2019)
11. Donthu, N., Kumar, S., Pandey, N., Pandey, N., Mishra, A.: Mapping the electronic word-of-mouth (eWOM) research: a systematic review and bibliometric analysis. J. Bus. Res. **135**, 758–773 (2021)
12. Fan, Y.W., Miao, Y.F.: Effect of electronic word-of-mouth on consumer purchase intention: the perspective of gender differences. Int. J. Electron. Bus. Manage. **10**(3), 175 (2012)
13. Gefen, D., Karahanna, E., Straub, D.W.: Trust and TAM in online shopping: an integrated model. MIS Q. 51–90
14. Gefen, D., Rigdon, E.E., Straub, D.: Editor's comments: an update and extension to SEM guidelines for administrative and social science research. MIS quarterly, iii-xiv (2003)
15. Guangming, Y., Yuzhong, M.: A research on the model of factors influencing consumer trust in mobile business. In: 2011 International Conference on E-Business and E-Government, pp. 1–5 (2011)
16. Giao, H., Vuong, B., Quan, T.: The influence of website quality on consumer's e-loyalty through the mediating role of e-trust and e-satisfaction: an evidence from online shopping in Vietnam. Uncertain Supply Chain Manage. **8**(2), 351–370 (2020)
17. Hair, J.F., Anderson, R.E., Babin, B.J., Black, W.C.: Multivariate data analysis: a global perspective, vol. 7 (2010)
18. Hair, J.F., Black, W.C., Babin, B.J., Anderson, R.E.: Multivariate Data Analysis, 7th edn. Pearson Education International, Upper Saddle River, New Jersey (2010)
19. Hair, J.F., Black, W.C., Babin, B.J., Anderson, R.E., Tatham, R.L.: Multivariate Data Analysis, 5th edn. Prentice Hall, Upper Saddle River, NJ (1998)
20. Hair, J.F., Jr., Sarstedt, M., Matthews, L.M., Ringle, C.M.: Identifying and treating unobserved heterogeneity with FIMIX-PLS: part I–method. Eur. Bus. Rev. **28**(1), 63–76 (2016)
21. Hennig-Thurau, T., Gwinner, K.P., Walsh, G., Gremler, D.D.: Electronic word-of-mouth via consumer-opinion platforms: what motivates consumers to articulate themselves on the Internet? J. Interact. Mark. **18**(1), 38–52 (2004)

22. Hermawan, D.: The effects of web quality, perceived benefits, security, and data privacy on behavioral intention and e-WOM of online travel agencies. Int. J. Data Netw. Sci. **6**(3), 1005–1012 (2022)
23. Jalilvand, M.R., Esfahani, S.S., Samiei, N.: Electronic word-of-mouth: challenges and opportunities. Procedia Comput. Sci. **3**, 42–46 (2011)
24. Kim, G., Shin, B., Lee, H.G.: Understanding dynamics between initial trust and usage intentions of mobile banking. Inf. Syst. J. **19**(3), 283–311 (2009)
25. LAI, P.C.: Design and Security impact on consumers' intention to use single platform E-payment. Interdisc. Inf. Sci. **22**(1), 111–122 (2016)
26. Lee, C.Y., Tsao, C.H., Chang, W.C.: The relationship between attitude toward using and customer satisfaction with mobile application services: an empirical study from the life insurance industry. J. Enterp. Inf. Manage. **28**(5), 680–697 (2015)
27. Lee, M.-C.: Factors influencing the adoption of Internet banking: an integration of TAM and TPB with perceived risk and perceived benefit. Electron. Commer. Res. Appl. **8**(3), 130–141 (2009)
28. Lee, Y.C.: Impacts of decision-making biases on eWOM retrust and riskreducing strategies. Comput. Hum. Behav. **40**, 101–110 (2014)
29. Liao, S.H., Hu, D.C., Chung, Y.C., Huang, A.P.: Risk and opportunity for online purchase intention—a moderated mediation model investigation. Telematics Inform. **62**, 101621 (2021)
30. Lin, A., Foster, J.: Electronic word-of-mouth (eWOM) and its influence on book purchasing decisions: a study of the Anobii Digital Bookshelf. In: Consumer Information Systems and Relationship Management: Design, Implementation, and Use, pp. 156–172. IGI Global (2013)
31. Liu, Y., Zhao, Y.: Compound attitudes, customer engagement and eWOM: an empirical study on WeChat
32. Liu, Z., Min, Q., Ji, S.: An empirical study on mobile banking adoption: the role of trust. In: 2009 Second International Symposium on Electronic Commerce and Security, vol. 2, pp. 7–13. IEEE (2015)
33. Malik, A.N.A., Annuar, S.N.S.: The effect of perceived usefulness, perceived ease of use, reward, and perceived risk toward e-wallet usage intention. In: Eurasian Business and Economics Perspectives: Proceedings of the 30th Eurasia Business and Economics Society Conference, pp. 115–130. Springer International Publishing (2021)
34. Mensah, I.K.: Perceived usefulness and ease of use of mobile government services: the moderating impact of electronic word of mouth (eWOM). Int. J. Technol. Diffusion (IJTD) **11**(1), 1–16 (2020)
35. Morgan, P.J., Trinh, L.Q.: Determinants and impacts of financial literacy in Cambodia and Vietnam. J. Risk Financial Manage. **12**(1), 19 (2019)
36. Muylle, S., Moenaert, R., Despontin, M.: The conceptualization and empirical validation of website user satisfaction. Inf. Manage. **41**(5), 543–560 (2004)
37. Nunnally, J.C., Bernstein, I.H.: Psychometric Theory. McGraw-Hill, New York (1994)
38. Oliver, R.L.: Satisfaction: A Behavioral Perspective on the Consumer. Irwin/McGraw-Hill, New York (1997)
39. Olivia, M., Marchyta, N.K.: The influence of perceived ease of use and perceived usefulness on E-wallet continuance intention: intervening role of customer satisfaction. Doctoral dissertation, Petra Christian University (2022)
40. Pallant, J.F., Bailey, C.M.: Assessment of the structure of the hospital anxiety and depression scale in musculoskeletal patients. Health Qual. Life Outcomes **3**, 1–9 (2005)
41. Peterson, R.A.: A meta-analysis of Cronbach's coefficient alpha. J. Consum. Res. **21**(2), 381–391 (1994)
42. Sanyal, S., Hisam, M.W., Baawain, A.M.S.: The impact of individual and technological factors on online customer satisfaction and repurchase intention: the moderating role of EWOM and personality. Int. J. Econ. Manage. Account. **29**(1), 23–44 (2021)
43. Senali, M.G., Iranmanesh, M., Ismail, F.N., Rahim, N.F.A., Khoshkam, M., Mirzaei, M.: Determinants of intention to use e-Wallet: personal innovativeness and propensity to trust as moderators. Int. J. Human–Comput. Interact. 1–13

44. Senali, M.G., Iranmanesh, M., Ismail, F.N., Rahim, N.F.A., Khoshkam, M., Mirzaei, M.: Determinants of intention to use e-Wallet: personal innovativeness and propensity to trust as moderators. Int. J. Human–Comput. Interact. **39**(12), 2361–2373 (2023)
45. Shaw, N.: The mediating influence of trust in the adoption of the mobile wallet. J. Retail. Consum. Serv. **21**(4), 449–459 (2014)
46. Shu, M., Scott, N.: Influence of social media on Chinese students' choice of an overseas study destination: an information adoption model perspective. J. Travel Tour. Mark. **31**(2), 286–302 (2014)
47. Sohaib, M., Hui, P., Akram, U., Majeed, A., Akram, Z., Bilal, M.: Understanding the justice fairness effects on eWOM communication in social media environment. Int. J. Enterprise Inf. Syst. (IJEIS) **15**(1), 69–84 (2019)
48. Subaramaniam, K., Kolandaisamy, R., Jalil, A.B., Kolandaisamy, I.: The impact of E-Wallets on the current generation. J. Adv. Res. Dyn. Control Syst **12**(1), 751–759 (2020)
49. Suh, B., Han, I.: Effect of trust on customer acceptance of Internet banking. Electron. Commer. Res. Appl. **1**(3–4), 247–263 (2002)
50. Sussman, S.W., Siegal, W.S.: Informational influence in organizations: an integrated approach to knowledge adoption. Inf. Syst. Res. **14**(1), 47–65 (2003)
51. Tang, Y.M., Chau, K.Y., Hong, L., Ip, Y.K., Yan, W.: Financial innovation in digital payment with WeChat towards electronic business success. J. Theor. Appl. Electron. Commer. Res. **16**(5), 1844–1861 (2021)
52. Tarigan, Z.J.H., Jonathi, M., Siagian, H., Basana, S.R.: The effect of e-WOM through intention to use technology and social media community for mobile payments during the COVID-19. Doctoral dissertation, Petra Christian University (2022)
53. Tran, G.A., Strutton, D.: Comparing email and SNS users: Investigating e-servicescape, customer reviews, trust, loyalty, and E-WOM. J. Retail. Consum. Serv. **53**, 101782 (2020)
54. Zalloum, L., Alghadeer, H., Nusairat, N.: The effect of using mobile banking services applications on electronic word of mouth: the mediating role of perceived trust. Int. Bus. Res. **12**(9), 62–80 (2019)
55. Zhou, T.: An empirical examination of initial trust in mobile payment. Wireless Pers. Commun. **77**, 1519–1531 (2014)
56. Zoghlami, A.T., Yahia, K.B., Berraies, S.: From mobile service quality evaluation to e-word-of-mouth: what makes the users of mobile banking applications speak about the bank?: the moderating role of brand reputation. Int. J. E-Serv. Mobile Appl. (IJESMA) **10**(2), 36–57 (2018)

Analyzing the Influence of Artificial Intelligence on Consumers' Online Purchase Intentions

Chi Thi Kim Nguyen, Y Thi Nhu Nguyen, and Anh Ngoc Tuan Bui

Abstract Artificial intelligence (AI) is rapidly advancing and has a significant impact on the online shopping market. The purpose of this study is to identify the factors that influence attitudes toward AI and online purchase intentions. The factors under investigation include perceived usefulness, perceived e-WOM, and perceived customization. The study uses qualitative and quantitative research methods. Through 366 data collected, we have information about people who used to shop online in Ho Chi Minh City. The results analyzed through PLS-SEM showed similarities with the previous findings. Previous studies have shown that perceived usefulness, perceived e-WOM, and perceived customization affect attitude toward AI and this study is no exception. Limitations include sample size, and future research could benefit from implementing probability sampling methods for increased generalizability. This research offers valuable insights for e-commerce businesses aiming to effectively utilize AI by focusing on developing functionalities that improve perceived usefulness and user experience.

Keywords Perceived e-WOM · Perceived customization · Attitude toward AI · Online purchase intention · TAM

1 Introduction

E-commerce sales are booming, with online shopping gradually replacing traditional brick-and-mortar retail in many sectors [1]. This shift in consumer behavior is driven in part by significant technological advancements, with Artificial Intelligence (AI) emerging as a pivotal force in this ongoing revolution [2]. AI has found widespread application in online retail environments [3], encompassing diverse platforms such as mass customization technology [4], virtual reality technology, and virtual personal assistants [2]. By enabling the collection and analysis of intricate data on consumer

C. T. K. Nguyen · Y. T. N. Nguyen · A. N. T. Bui (✉)
Ho Chi Minh City Open University, 35-37 Ho Hao Hon, Ho Chi Minh City 700000, Vietnam
e-mail: anh.bnt@ou.edu.vn

L. T. Tung et al. (eds.), *Disruptive Technology and Business Continuity*,
https://doi.org/10.1007/978-981-97-5452-6_5

preferences, behavior patterns, and online interactions, AI technology has revolutionized the way online businesses cater to their customers' evolving needs and desires.

AI is increasingly asserting its importance in automating enterprise processes, providing market statistics and consumer records quickly, and analyzing them accurately [5]. Therefore, AI is extensively applied in applications that include chatbots, virtual assistants, and product navigation systems to enhance consumers' shopping experiences both online and offline. These traits have been identified as the appropriate technique to stimulate demand and enhance users' shopping experience [5].

In the context of the continuous improvement of AI and the significance of the online purchasing market, research on the impact of AI on customer attitudes and behavior are essential [6]. This study aims to find out an essential issue of the present-day technological revolution: how AI impacts the way we shop and make decisions online. In particular, the studies focus on further investigating the impact of AI through potential factors that consist of usefulness, customization, and electronic word-of-mouth. These elements play a key function in consumers' purchasing decisions and determine whether they consider and accept AI technology in their shopping experience. This study's result helps managers understand the significance of AI in procurement and offers treasured data to create suitable techniques and solutions. This will guide businesses in successfully applying AI to enhance customer purchasing experiences, create value, and meet the increasingly diverse desires of the online purchasing market. Therefore, this research not only aims to provide references for the theoretical foundation in the field of customer shopping behavior but also aims to provide useful implications for businesses about applying AI to their business model.

2 Literature Review and Hypotheses Development

2.1 Artificial Intelligence in Online Shopping

Artificial intelligence (AI) is increasingly being widely applied in the marketing field, offering numerous benefits to both businesses and consumers. AI has emerged as a transformative tool for revenue growth in businesses. AI serves a variety of purposes, including predicting future trends, evaluating and comparing different marketing channels, and tailoring promotional communications [7]. AI can automate various business processes, provide insights based on historical data, and generate market and consumer insights through algorithmic programs [5].

If properly supervised and guided, AI can perform specific marketing tasks more effectively than humans. For example, consumer service chatbots use AI technology, which can assist or even replace human workers [8]. AI assistance can enhance efficiency, improve performance, and yield numerous benefits. For example, a consumer unsure about which skincare product to buy from an online store can benefit from AI-powered skin assessment tools that recommend suitable products, enhancing the customer experience. AI can personalize customers' shopping experiences, offering them products and services tailored to their specific needs and preferences. This can significantly boost conversion rates and foster customer loyalty.

2.2 Online Purchase Intention

Ajzen and Fishbein defined shopping intention as a consumer's objective intention toward a product [9]. Purchase intention is a conscious plan or intention to make an effort to purchase a product [6]. Online purchase intention specifically refers to whether consumers are willing and intending to purchase a certain product through online channels. Shoppers are more likely to make purchases from online stores that provide sufficient information about product/service categories, effective search functions, website trustworthiness, competitive prices, secure online payment systems, and product simulators [10]. It is proposed that a combination of internet users' personality traits and their perceptions of technology can influence users' online shopping intentions, thereby providing insights into their purchasing behavior [6].

2.3 Technology Acceptance Model (TAM)

Originally proposed by Davis in 1986, the Technology Acceptance Model (TAM) serves as a prominent framework for understanding and explaining the factors influencing individual technology adoption behavior [11]. TAM primarily aims to assess how external factors impact users' decisions to accept new technologies. It has been widely applied in research related to information technology [12]. Furthermore, researchers have leveraged TAM across various contexts to investigate the variations in consumers' intentions to adopt technology across different industries.

The TAM posits a causal relationship between usefulness and attitude with usage intention and behavior [3]. However, in recent times, technology has been increasingly developed and applied in many areas of our social life. Therefore, TAM has been considered to be expanded in many contexts by identifying and adding new variables. Therefore, in addition to perceived enjoyment, compatibility, and attitude forward technology [13], e-WOM [12], customization [14] was added to expand the original TAM. In this study, perceived usefulness, perceived e-WOM, perceived customization, attitude toward AI were considered and proposed in the model to examine the relationship between variables with consumers' online purchase intention.

2.4 Perceived Usefulness

Perceived usefulness is "the degree to which a person believes that using a particular system will enhance his or her job performance" [11]. Perceived usefulness in TAM has been found to have a significant impact on attitudes toward technology use [11]. Kelly and Palaniappan [15] demonstrated a significant influence of perceived usefulness on user attitudes, which subsequently impacted the continuous adoption of mobile money services within the Ghanaian context. According to Hajli [16], perceived usefulness is an important construct in the e-commerce context and there is a positive relationship between the perceived usefulness of a website and a user's purchase intention to buy. In this study, perceived usefulness is the benefits and conveniences that the online environment brings to customers such as saving money and time. From here, understanding the role of usefulness in attitude toward AI and online purchase intention has created the following two hypotheses.

H1: Perceived usefulness affects attitudes toward AI.
H2: Perceived usefulness affects online purchase intention.

2.5 Perceived e-WOM

Perceived electronic word-of-mouth (e-WOM) as informal communication between customers about a specific product or service using network technologies delivered on a large scale, instantly, and anonymously [17]. Regarding the context of the Internet and online channels, e-WOM communication refers to any positive or negative statements made by potential, actual, and former customers about an organization or its products via the Internet. When users are satisfied with the functions and services that online platforms provide based on technological applications, they are more likely to share positive feedback. This positive feedback can influence the attitudes of others toward AI technology and online platforms [18]. E-WOM is more influential than traditional word-of-mouth. A substantial body of literature has shown that e-WOM has a positive impact on consumer attitudes and behavior. For example, Li and Hitt [12] found that e-WOM influences consumer attitudes toward products in both online and offline shopping within the retail and fashion industry context. Additionally, the study Chetioui, Butt and Lebdaoui [17] also demonstrated that e-WOM has a significant impact on purchase intention regardless of the type of virtual community. The study found that e-WOM is a positive effect related to purchase intention. Based on the arguments presented above, the following hypothesis is proposed:

H3: Perceived e-WOM affects attitudes toward AI.
H4: Perceived e-WOM affects online purchase intention.

2.6 *Perceived Customization*

Perceived customization is a crucial factor in the success of e-commerce. Customization is the ability of retailers to provide customers with a transaction environment, products, and services tailored to each individual [19]. Perceived customization is the extent to which an organization meets customers' diverse needs, and it is a crucial factor influencing consumer behavior in online shopping [20], e-commerce [21]. AI technology in online shopping provides customized experiences for customers, influencing a positive attitude [21]. Studies have shown that online customization can positively influence consumer purchase intention [19]. From here, the following hypothesis is proposed:

H5: Perceived customization affects attitudes toward AI.
H6: Perceived customization affects online purchase intention.

2.7 *Attitude Toward AI*

Consumer attitudes and purchase intentions are well-established concepts in marketing research. Ajzen and Fishbein define them as an individual's predisposition toward performing a specific behavior [9]. Prior studies have consistently shown a positive relationship between consumer attitudes and purchase intentions [6, 13, 21, 22]. In this context, our study focuses on attitudes toward AI, specifically the reception and reaction to AI tools such as chatbots and virtual assistants. Building on existing research [4, 13], we hypothesize that a positive attitude toward AI will positively impact online purchase intention. Therefore, we propose the following hypothesis:

H7: Attitude toward AI affects Online purchase intention.

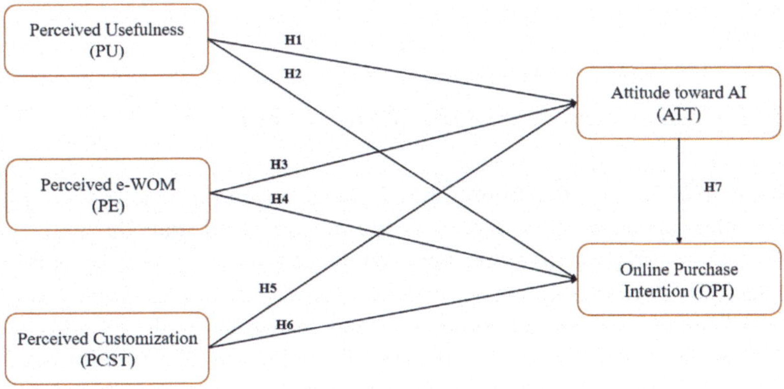

Fig. 1 Conceptual research model

3 Research Methods

The research was carried out in two phases. The preliminary stage is conducted using qualitative methods. The study utilizes references from highly reputable sources to identify factors of AI that influence attitudes toward AI and online purchase intentions. In addition, thanks to the synthesis of previous research, the authors have been able to build a model to study the impact of AI on online purchase intention. The formal phase is conducted using quantitative methods.

In particular, the questionnaire uses a 5-point Likert scale, following the convention where 1 represents "completely disagree" and 5 represents "completely agree." The measurement scales are inherited from previous studies. Liang, Lee and Workman [23] scale was used to measure components of the Technology Acceptance Model (TAM), including perceived usefulness (PU, 6 items), attitude toward AI (ATT, 3 items), and online purchase intention (OPI, 3 items). In addition, the scale of perceived e-WOM (PE, 3 items) was adapted from the study by Chetioui, Butt and Lebdaoui [17]). The scale of perceived customization (PCST, 4 items) was adapted from the study by Pillai, Sivathanu and Dwivedi [24]. To ensure the validity and clarity of the research instrument, the original scales were refined through in-depth interviews. Two experienced e-commerce researchers from a university in Ho Chi Minh City will collaborate on this project. Their expertise will be invaluable in confirming the scale's validity and refining the questionnaire's wording for optimal clarity. This meticulous approach will guarantee a well-prepared questionnaire for the subsequent survey.

Research data was collected through an online survey method using Google Forms. The survey participants were individuals who had previously shopped online. The data collection period will last from June 2023 to August 2023. Out of a total of 379 questionnaires received, only 366 were valid for analysis. SPSS 20.0 and Smart PLS 4.0.8.7 software were used during the implementation process.

4 Results

4.1 The Information About the Study Sample

Descriptive statistical results from Table 1 show that in the research sample, the female gender accounts for a higher proportion (52.5%) than the male gender (47.5%). The majority of them are between 18 and 24 years old, accounting for 41.8%, and 25–35 years old, accounting for 30.3%. The sample collected mainly consisted of officers (27%) and students (24%). In particular, the monthly income level accounting for the highest rate is above 20 million at 27.9%, followed by the income level of 10–20 million at 25.1%, and the lowest rate is under 5 million at 23%.

Table 1 Descriptive statistics of the sample

Demographic	N = 366	Percent (%)
Gender		
Female	192	52.5
Male	174	47.5
Age		
Under 18 years old	37	10.1
18–24 years old	153	41.8
25–35 years old	111	30.3
Above 35 years old	65	17.8
Occupation		
Student	88	24
Officer	99	27
Worker	41	11.2
Housewife	32	8.7
Teacher	47	12.8
Freelancer	35	9.6
Others	24	6.6
Income (VND)		
Under 5 million	84	23
5–9 million	88	24
10–20 million	92	25.1
Above 20 million	102	27.9

4.2 The Measurement Model

In this study, the validity of the model's scales has been theoretically tested as we primarily utilized scales from previous studies. The data was analyzed using the two-step modeling approach for SEM: Confirmatory Factor Analysis (CFA) was conducted to check the validity of the data [25]. The reliability was tested using two indicators: Cronbach's Alpha (CA) and Composite Reliability (CR). CA to be considered good when the CA index is greater than 0.7. Similar to [25], it is suggested that for satisfactory reliability, the Composite Reliability (CR) indexes should be greater than 0.7. The results of Table 2 show that the CR indexes range from 0.892 to 0.924, while the CA indexes range from 0.831 to 0.876. Thus, both indicators are good, and these scales are suitable for further analysis.

Assessing convergence in the research model is important to describe the convergence of hypotheses measuring the model's constructs [26]. Convergent validity was assessed based on the average variance extracted (AVE) and outer loadings. Hair et al. [25] proposed that variables in the model should be considered explained when AVE is greater than 50% and outer loadings are required to be greater than 0.7 to be

Table 2 The reliability

	Number of variables	Composite reliability (CR)	Cronbach's alpha
PU	6	0.908	0.878
PE	3	0.891	0.817
PCST	4	0.910	0.868
ATT	3	0.898	0.829
OPI	3	0.922	0.874

deemed satisfactory. The VIF was used to evaluate multicollinearity. If VIF is less than 5, the model does not exhibit multicollinearity [25]. The results (Table 3) show that the indices AVE, outer loadings, and VIF all satisfy the specified conditions. This proves that the model has convergence and does not violate multicollinearity.

As suggested by Fornell and Larcker [26], the discriminant validity of the scale is tested by comparing the AVE of each research variable in the model with the squared correlations with the remaining research variables. According to the results from Table 3, the square root test results of AVE are larger in magnitude than the correlations with other research variables. Therefore, the model's measurement scales all adapt to the requirements.

The coefficient of determination (R^2) and path coefficient (β) are used to evaluate the level of influence between the research variables proposed in the model [25]. R^2 explains the degree of bias in potential endogenous variables is explained, and the values are evaluated as strong (0.67), moderate (0.33), and weak (0.19) [25]. From

Table 3 The convergent validity and multicollinearity

Variables	Number of variables	Outer loadings	AVE	VIF	R^2
PU	6	[0,728–0,835]	0,622	(1,650–2,224)	
PE	3	[0,848–0,862]	0,732	(1,692–1,928)	
PCST	4	[0,838–0,858]	0,717	(2,075–2,392)	
ATT	3	[0,853–0,880]	0,745	(1,834–2,060)	0,604
OPI	3	[0,878–0,912]	0,798	(2,251–2,704)	0,646

Table 4 The discrimination

Variables	ATT	OPI	PCST	PE	PU
ATT	0.863				
OPI	0.717	0.893			
PCST	0.455	0.462	0.847		
PE	0.682	0.655	0.397	0.855	
PU	0.714	0.740	0.402	0.664	0.788

Table 5 The results of the research hypotheses

Hypotheses	Relationship	Path coefficient	STDVE	T values	P values	Result
H1	PU -> ATT	0.429	0.043	10.061	0.000	Accept
H2	PU -> OPI	0.388	0.052	7.491	0.000	Accept
H3	PE -> ATT	0.338	0.044	7.758	0.000	Accept
H4	PE -> OPI	0.163	0.045	3.625	0.000	Accept
H5	PCST -> ATT	0.148	0.037	4.048	0.000	Accept
H6	PCST -> OPI	0.115	0.035	3.260	0.001	Accept
H7	ATT-> OPI	0.277	0.049	5.710	0.000	Accept

the results presented in Table 3, all the values are greater than 0.10. Path coefficients can be utilized to assess the influence of study variables.

4.3 The Structural Model

A bootstrapping technique with 5000 samples was employed to measure the hypothesized relationship.

The results from Table 5 indicate that hypotheses H1, H2, H3, H4, H5, H6, and H7 are all accepted. Regarding the impact relationship on ATT, PU has the highest impact (β = 0.429), followed by PE (β = 0.338), and the lowest is PCST (β = 0.148). Meanwhile, the relationship between variables on online purchase intention shows that PU has the strongest impact (β = 0.388), followed by attitude toward AI (β = 0.277), and the lowest impact is from PCST (β = 0.115).

4.4 Discussion

The analysis revealed that perceived usefulness (PU) has the strongest positive impact on attitude toward AI (ATT) (β = 0.429), followed by perceived e-WOM (PE) (β = 0.338) and perceived customization (PCST) (β = 0.148). This finding aligns with Liang, Lee and Workman [23] who reported a similar effect of PU on ATT (β = 0.445). These results support the idea that AI can enhance consumer expectations and satisfaction by offering functionalities that address their needs [3, 22]. Notably, the mediating role of attitude toward AI is confirmed, with a positive influence on online purchase intention (β = 0.277). Results are similar to previous research, suggesting that a positive attitude formed through perceived usefulness translates into a higher likelihood of online purchase [23].

This study highlights the significant role of perceived e-WOM (PE) in shaping consumer attitudes toward AI. Positive electronic word-of-mouth about AI functionalities, shared by other users, can influence a user's perception of the usefulness and benefits of AI in online shopping. This aligns with research by sook Lee and An [18], Liang, Lee and Workman [23], who emphasize the influence of e-WOM on consumer behavior. These findings contribute to a deeper understanding of how various factors, including social influence, interact with perceived usefulness to ultimately influence online purchase intention [23, 24].

5 Conclusion

This study investigated the factors influencing consumer attitudes toward AI and their online purchase intention in the context of e-commerce. The analysis confirms the relationships between perceived usefulness (PU), perceived customization (PCST), perceived e-WOM (PE), and attitude toward AI (ATT), all of which positively influence online purchase intention (OPI), consistent with TAM theory. The findings further reveal that perceived usefulness (PU) has the strongest positive impact on both attitudes toward AI and online purchase intention. This aligns with existing research suggesting that AI's ability to enhance user experience and satisfaction is a key driver of positive attitudes and purchase behavior. Additionally, the study demonstrates the mediating role of attitude toward AI, highlighting the importance of fostering positive perceptions to increase online purchase intention.

This finding highlights the role of positive electronic word-of-mouth (e-WOM) in shaping consumer attitudes. When users encounter positive experiences shared by others, it reinforces their perception of AI's usefulness and benefits in online shopping. These findings offer valuable insights for e-commerce businesses looking to effectively leverage AI. By focusing on developing AI functionalities that enhance perceived usefulness and ensure user-friendliness, businesses can cultivate positive consumer attitudes and ultimately drive online purchase intention.

This research paves the way for further exploration of the relationship between AI and consumer behavior in e-commerce. Future studies could investigate the impact of specific AI applications, such as chatbots or virtual assistants, on various consumer segments. Additionally, research could explore the role of ethical considerations and user trust in shaping attitudes toward AI in online shopping environments.

References

1. Yeo, S.F., Tan, C.L., Kumar, A., Tan, K.H., Wong, J.K.: Investigating the impact of AI-powered technologies on Instagrammers' purchase decisions in digitalization era—a study of the fashion and apparel industry. Technol. Forecast. Soc. Change. **177**, 121551 (2022)
2. Makridakis, S.: The forthcoming Artificial Intelligence (AI) revolution: its impact on society and firms. Futures **90**, 46–60 (2017)
3. Kim, H.-Y., Lee, J.Y., Mun, J.M., Johnson, K.K.: Consumer adoption of smart in-store technology: assessing the predictive value of attitude versus beliefs in the technology acceptance model. Int. J. Fashion Design, Technol. Educ. **10**(1), 26–36 (2017)
4. Lee, H.-H., Chang, E.: Consumer attitudes toward online mass customization: an application of extended technology acceptance model. J. Comput.-Mediat. Commun. **16**(2), 171–200 (2011)
5. Davenport, T., Guha, A., Grewal, D., Bressgott, T.: How artificial intelligence will change the future of marketing. J. Acad. Mark. Sci. **48**, 24–42 (2020)
6. Nazir, S., Khadim, S., Asadullah, M.A., Syed, N.: Exploring the influence of artificial intelligence technology on consumer repurchase intention: the mediation and moderation approach. Technol. Soc. **72**, 102190 (2023)
7. Kulkov, I.: The role of artificial intelligence in business transformation: a case of pharmaceutical companies. Technol. Soc. **66**, 101629 (2021)
8. Sheehan, B., Jin, H.S., Gottlieb, U.: Customer service chatbots: anthropomorphism and adoption. J. Bus. Res. **115**, 14–24 (2020)
9. Ajzen, I., Fishbein, M., Lohmann, S., Albarracín, D.: 'The influence of attitudes on behavior', The Handbook of Attitudes, vol. 1: Basic principles, pp. 197–255 (2018)
10. Peña-García, N., Gil-Saura, I., Rodríguez-Orejuela, A., Siqueira-Junior, J.R.: Purchase intention and purchase behavior online: a cross-cultural approach. Heliyon **6**(6) (2020)
11. Davis, F.D.: Perceived usefulness, perceived ease of use, and user acceptance of information technology. MIS Q. 319–340 (1989)
12. Li, X., Hitt, L.M.: Self-selection and information role of online product reviews. Inf. Syst. Res. **19**(4), 456–474 (2008)
13. De Cicco, R., Iacobucci, S., Aquino, A., Romana Alparone, F., Palumbo, R.: 'Understanding users' acceptance of chatbots: an extended TAM approach', in Editor (Ed.)^(Eds.): 'Book Understanding users' acceptance of chatbots: an extended TAM approach', pp. 3–22. Springer (2021)
14. Luo, Y., Yang, L., Ye, Q., Liao, Q.: Effects of customization and personalization affordances on perceived value and continuance intention of smartwatch use. Technol. Forecast. Soc. Chang. **194**, 122752 (2023)
15. Kelly, A.E., Palaniappan, S.: Using a technology acceptance model to determine factors influencing continued usage of mobile money service transactions in Ghana. J. Innov. Entrepreneurship **12**(1), 34 (2023)
16. Hajli, M.N.: A study of the impact of social media on consumers. Int. J. Mark. Res. **56**(3), 387–404 (2014)
17. Chetioui, Y., Butt, I., Lebdaoui, H.: Facebook advertising, eWOM and consumer purchase intention—evidence from a collectivistic emerging market. J. Glob. Mark. **34**(3), 220–237 (2021)
18. Sook Lee, M., An, H.: A study of antecedents influencing eWOM for online lecture website: personal interactivity as moderator. Online Inf. Rev. **42**(7), 1048–1064 (2018)
19. Kim, H.Y., Lee, Y.: The effect of online customization on consumers' happiness and purchase intention and the mediating roles of autonomy, competence, and pride of authorship. Int. J. Human-Comput. Interact. **36**(5), 403–413 (2020)
20. Cho, H., Fiorito, S.S.: Acceptance of online customization for apparel shopping. Int. J. Retail Distrib. Manage. **37**(5), 389–407 (2009)
21. Kalinic, Z., Marinkovic, V.: Determinants of users' intention to adopt m-commerce: an empirical analysis. IseB **14**, 367–387 (2016)

22. Wu, L.-H., Wu, L.-C., Chang, S.-C.: Exploring consumers' intention to accept smartwatch. Comput. Hum. Behav. **64**, 383–392 (2016)
23. Liang, Y., Lee, S.-H., Workman, J.E.: Implementation of artificial intelligence in fashion: are consumers ready? Cloth. Text. Res. J. **38**(1), 3–18 (2020)
24. Pillai, R., Sivathanu, B., Dwivedi, Y.K.: Shopping intention at AI-powered automated retail stores (AIPARS). J. Retail. Consum. Serv. **57**, 102207 (2020)
25. Hair, J.F., Risher, J.J., Sarstedt, M., Ringle, C.M.: When to use and how to report the results of PLS-SEM. Eur. Bus. Rev. **31**(1), 2–24 (2019)
26. Fornell, C., Larcker, D.F.: Evaluating structural equation models with unobservable variables and measurement error. J. Mark. Res. **18**(1), 39–50 (1981)

How Interactivity Has Effects on Satisfaction and Vising Intention: Non-immersive Virtual Reality Technology

Dinh Tien Minh, Nguyen Thi My Xuyen, Thai Hong Son, and Nguyen Thi Lien

Abstract Virtual reality (VR) technology creates a virtual environment that feels authentic through the use of software and auxiliary technological equipment. Expanding upon this unique feature, we carried out supplementary studies to examine the possible impacts of interactive, non-immersive settings on virtual reality (VR) users. The study examines whether the unique features of VR affect perceived values in non-immersive environments and whether this component promotes satisfaction and actual travel intentions by combining model TAM and model SOR. Following the examination of 316 Gen Z survey respondents. The results noted that the typical interactive features of VR technology affect the perceived values of virtual reality technology (VR) in a non-immersive environment. Simultaneously, the data reveal that satisfaction when experiencing virtual tourism considerably influences reality intention.

Keywords Virtual reality (VR) · Non-immersive · Stimulus–organism-response (SOR) · Technology acceptance model (TAM) · Behavioral intention · Tourist

1 Introduction

In the last months of 2020, due to the severe impact of the COVID-19 pandemic, the entire global tourism system has undergone significant changes, shifting from open tourism [1] to more restricted tourism and most countries have implemented travel bans. The challenging circumstances of restricted and distanced activities during the pandemic Many businesses have effectively utilized this trend, creating opportunities and increasing economic value. In particular, the tourism industry has successfully transformed with virtual tourism. Virtual tourism is a product derived from real and virtual service models, providing diverse experiences and entertainment for

D. T. Minh · N. T. M. Xuyen (✉) · T. H. Son · N. T. Lien
University of Economics Ho Chi Minh, Ho Chi Minh City, Vietnam
e-mail: xuyennguyen.211109056@st.ueh.edu.vn

L. T. Tung et al. (eds.), *Disruptive Technology and Business Continuity*,
https://doi.org/10.1007/978-981-97-5452-6_6

customers [2]. By posting local travel information on social media platforms or using Google Maps to provide 3D images of art and cultural landmarks, tourism developers can offer tourists a rich experience of different locality areas with convenient observation points. At the Vietbuild 2020 exhibition in Ho Chi Minh City, some companies introduced virtual reality products for the tourism industry, such as virtual reality tours of famous landmarks and 3D interactive experiences to learn about the tourism products [3]. As online business platforms expand, so does the demand for online advertising space and a variety of advertising formats. According to Statista, the VR market in Vietnam is predicted to increase at an annual rate of 11.36% between 2024 and 2028 [4]. The developers in Vietnam continue to strive to bring virtual reality technology closer to customers by B2C strategy.

Previous studies have been conducted in different countries to assess the overall impact of virtual reality technology on the actual travel intentions of potential customers. The study supports the integration of hedonic factors (i.e., flow experience) into the TAM to enhance its predictive ability to understand consumers' behavioral intentions toward new technology [5]. The explores user experiences in terms of hedonic and utilitarian satisfaction, information content, and ease of use and examines their impact on consumer perception [6]. In addition, other studies also mentioned empirical evidence to confirm the effectiveness of VR in shaping consumer attitudes and behaviors based on the SOR framework [7]. The findings are used to build a theoretical foundation for investigating the interactive features of non-role-playing virtual reality in tourism and their impact on user responses and intentions to participate in actual tourism. The study's goal will be to look into how interactivity affects potential customers' experience of value, including perception and emotion. Additionally, the study will investigate the correlation between the perceived value of non-role-playing virtual reality and customer satisfaction, as well as their intention to engage in actual tourism. The study adopts the SOR framework and the perceived value factors from the TAM model. Thus, the proposed model will ensure a comprehensive study that includes the application of interactive features in non-role-playing VR to enhance the user experience and provide feedback through customer satisfaction. With secondary data, the study has developed the proposed model and corresponding hypotheses. The use of qualitative and quantitative analysis methods is appropriate for confirming the proposed hypotheses. The subjects of this study are individuals with travel preferences who are living and working in Ho Chi Minh City.

2 Literature Review

2.1 Virtual Reality Tourism (VRT)

Virtual reality (VR) is the use of computer-generated 3D environments, known as virtual environments (VE), in which users can navigate and interact with one or more of their senses [2]. Therefore, VR provides an interactive computer-simulated environment where users feel present [8]. Furthermore, VR has two types of experiential environments: immersive and non-immersive. With the non-immersive factor, users can utilize VR technology through personal electronic devices or laptops without the need for dedicated headsets. Applying VR technology in the tourism industry creates a new tourism model known as virtual tourism or virtual reality tourism (VRT). VRT is defined as virtual experiences that take place in a virtual environment through computer-mediated means [9]. VR allows users to immerse themselves in various levels of virtual environments through the hardware and/or software used, such as from screens to hidden headphones [10]. As a result, users can easily control navigation, and virtual tours can stimulate better emotions than static images [11] and create positive advertising attitudes [12]. From a humanistic perspective, VR tourism also supports providing opportunities for disabled tourists to travel without leaving their homes, allowing users to experience virtual tours [13].

2.2 Interactivity

From a theoretical perspective, interaction refers to the two-way communication between machines and users with timely reactive controls in the virtual world [14]. Individuals evaluate the level of interaction of websites based on their perception of two-way communication, control level, user activity, sense of place, and time sensitivity [14]. Interaction is one of the important criteria for evaluating the overall "authentic experience" that must include humans, products, and the physical environment in which tourists interact, creating their own optimal experience [15]. The key to stimulating interaction in non-immersive virtual space is to create a perfect "virtual" experiential environment where customers can rotate and zoom on a 2D display screen, having a similar impact to physical contact with "reality". Based on the research by [7], enhancing interactive features in VR travel experiences may be related to immersion. Therefore, it can be said that non-immersive virtual reality tourism is considered a perfect replica of real tourism as both provide customers with interaction and realistic experiences at each tourist destination.

2.3 Research Model and Hypothesis

The synthesis of secondary data reveals that there have been numerous previous studies integrating factors from the TAM model and the SOR theory to demonstrate the correlation between independent and dependent variables. Integration of TAM elements with the SOR framework is thought to be relevant for this study issue. By confirmed the level of interaction capability in the virtual reality environment directly affecting perceived value and post-usage attitudes [6]. Another study applied an extended technology acceptance model with flow theory to examine the positive impact on attitude and behavioral intention toward real-life experience after virtual web surfing [5]. User satisfaction, as an evaluative attitude after engaging in the experience, affects behavioral intention [5, 6, 16]. By grouping the independent variables in the SOR framework, researchers can acquire a deeper understanding of visitors' behavioral patterns regarding technology experiences. In summary, based on the theoretical foundations and previous research models, the author proposes the following model for this study (Fig. 1).

Interaction is considered as the most crucial part of the supplementary design aspect aimed at creating a conducive environment for consumers to fully explore the virtual world [17]. Due to the given ideas, several theories are proposed. Hypothesis 1: The ability to interact with VR has a positive influence on perceived value.

That collectivity enables users to direct as well as innovate the virtual world more effectively [2]. The interactive features of VR updated information, and user-friendliness can affect their perception of the convenience of using the online environment [18]. From this reasoning, the following hypothesis is derived. Hypothesis 2: The ability to interact with VR has a helpful impact on perception value.

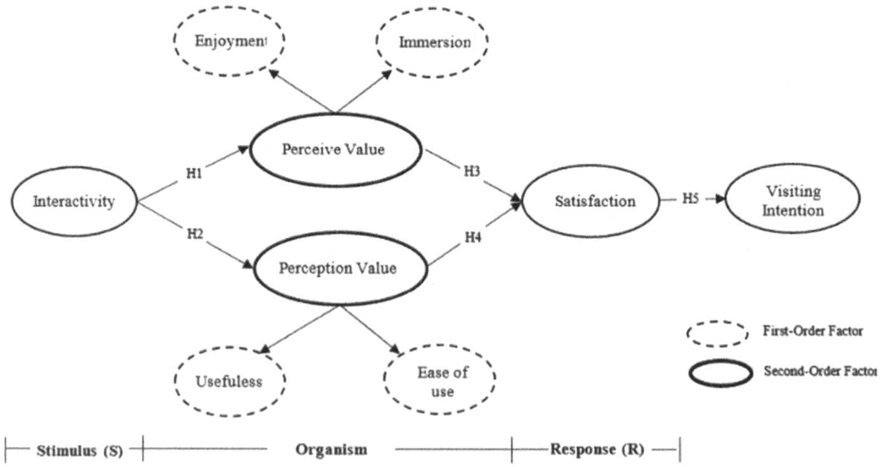

Fig. 1 Research model

User experience is used to explain users' feedback on their attitudes and behavioral intentions in VR [16, 19]. Psychological value guides to a remarkable level of flow experience and fulfillment [16]. Through the mentioned argument, the following hypothesis is being came up with. Hypothesis 3: Perceived value positively influences user satisfaction with VR.

Perceived usefulness and comfort of use are primary factors of the TAM to predict the approval of a technology and the attitude of the user [20, 21]. Vishwakarma's research used useful factors in cognition to investigate the objective of tourists to accept VR [21]. Li's research used perceived comfort of use to classify people's view and approval of automation [22]. From the said reasoning, the final hypothesis is derived from Hypothesis 4: Perception value positively influences user satisfaction with VR.

The VR connection not only positively but also straightforwardly affects contentment and habitual intention in virtual environment experiences [23]. Thus, VR experiences demonstrate that satisfaction is a key motivator for tourists' behavioral intentions. Hypothesis 5: Satisfaction positively influences the intention to visit.

3 Method

Based on the theoretical foundation of existing studies, the author inherits and constructs a research scale with observed variables from previous studies. Specifically, the interaction scale is inherited [24]. The value experience scales are inherited [21, 25]. In addition, a 5-point Likert scale is used to collect data in this study. Preston argued that scales with 5, 7, or 10 response categories are relatively easy to use and allow respondents to express their emotions reasonably [26]. Therefore, the authors agree to combine a 5-point Likert scale with the corresponding observed variables when constructing the survey questionnaire.

Currently, in other developed countries, virtual reality (VR) technology has been successfully applied in various fields such as education, healthcare, film, tourism, and retail, etc. However, in Vietnam, VR technology is still in its early stages, so the focus is on researching the application of VR in marketing and advertising domestic tourism destinations. The target audience for this study will be young people aged 18–38. Previous studies have shown that younger people are more likely to be interested in VR technology [7]. In fact, it is easy to see that young people tend to adopt new technologies quickly, resulting in better experiences. Therefore, the study participants will be young individuals who have traveled in the past year and reside in Ho Chi Minh City.

The convenience sampling method will save time and support quick sampling. Determining an appropriate sample size for the research model is important and challenging. According to Hair, a concept scale should have at least 5 observed variables, meaning the ratio of observed variables to measurement variables should be 5:1 [27]. For this research model, there are 26 observed variables and 7 scale variables, so the minimum sample size for analysis is 26 * 5 = 130 observed variables. An online survey will be conducted using a questionnaire to conveniently collect data and distributed widely to respondents through social media channels. Respondents will be introduced to the virtual reality tourism website in Ho Chi Minh City, map3d.visithcmc.vn, or other VR tourist destinations. Then they were asked to answer a small question about any detail included in the virtual tour to verify their participation or not. After that, respondents will be asked to complete the survey questionnaire immediately and send it back to the author. In total, 374 online surveys were sent out via Google Forms through social networking sites, and 331 responses were received from participants. The author will check and eliminate any duplicate or incomplete data that is not suitable for analysis. The result will consist of 310 valid survey responses for further analysis.

The quantitative research section will be conducted in four stages: constructing the official survey questionnaire, determining the research sample size, distributing the questionnaire to the research participants, and checking and encoding the data using SPSS version 20 software. With a total of 310 collected samples, SMART PLS 4 software will be used to evaluate criteria such as the internal consistency of the scale, the scale model, and the structural model.

4 Results

4.1 Measurement Model

Cronbach's Alpha is a measure of the internal consistency among observed variables in a scale, with coefficient values ranging from 0.6 to below 0.9 [28]. The correlation coefficient between each variable and the total score, known as the Corrected Item-Total Correlation, should have a value of ≥ 0.3 [28]. The results of testing the Cronbach's Alpha coefficient for the measured variables in the scale indicate that the α coefficient meets the standard of being greater than 0.6, and the correlation coefficient meets the standard of being greater than 0.3. The square root of the Average Variance Extracted (AVE) values is higher than the correlation coefficients of other factors in the same column, as all factors have distinct values (Table 1).

The KMO (Kaiser–Meyer–Olkin) value of 0.718 and Sig value of 0, as presented in Table 2, demonstrate that the observed variables in the measurement scale are correlated with each other. The eigenvalue is greater than 1, the factor loading is greater than 0.5, and the total variance explained is above 70%. Therefore, all variables in the measurement scale should be retained in their original form.

Table 1 Result of Cronbach's alpha reliability coefficient

Factor	Cronbach's alpha	CR	AVE
Interactivity	0.850	0.899	0.689
Perceived enjoyment	0.924	0.946	0.824
Perceived immersion	0.835	0.889	0.67
Perceived useful	0.858	0.914	0.779
Perceived ease of use	0.876	0.916	0.732
Satisfaction	0.729	0.831	0.552
Behavioral intention	0.764	0.865	0.681

Table 2 KMO and Bartlett's test

Kaiser–Meyer–Olkin measure of sampling adequacy		0.718
Bartlett's test of sphericity	Approx. chi-square	2465.300
	df	231
	Sig	0.000

4.2 Structural Model

Using the operations in the PLS-SEM tool to evaluate the relationships between structures, it was observed that all path coefficients were positive. In terms of assessing the impact relationships, after conducting a Bootstrapping analysis with a sample size of 1000, the results showed that all P-values were equal to 0. The level of variation in the endogenous variable Satisfaction (SA) explained by the exogenous variables was relatively high, with an adjusted R2 coefficient of 60%. Thus, the independent variables accounted for 60% of the variance in the dependent variable. The f2 coefficient is used to evaluate the effectiveness of the impact of each independent variable on the dependent variable. According to Cohen's recommended f2 values, the results indicated that the variables Perceived Value and Perceived Quality had a large impact on SA, and SA also had a large impact on Behavioral Intention (BI) [29]. Furthermore, when testing the estimated coefficients (β) of the independent variables on the dependent variable, it was found that each independent variable had a varying level of impact, ranging from strong to weak. Therefore, based on the standardized coefficients (β), the levels of influence on Satisfaction were as follows: Perceived Value ($\beta = 0.44$), Perceived Quality ($\beta = 0.5$), and Visiting Intention ($\beta = 0.53$). Thus, the overall synthesized results support all the hypotheses put forward (Fig. 2).

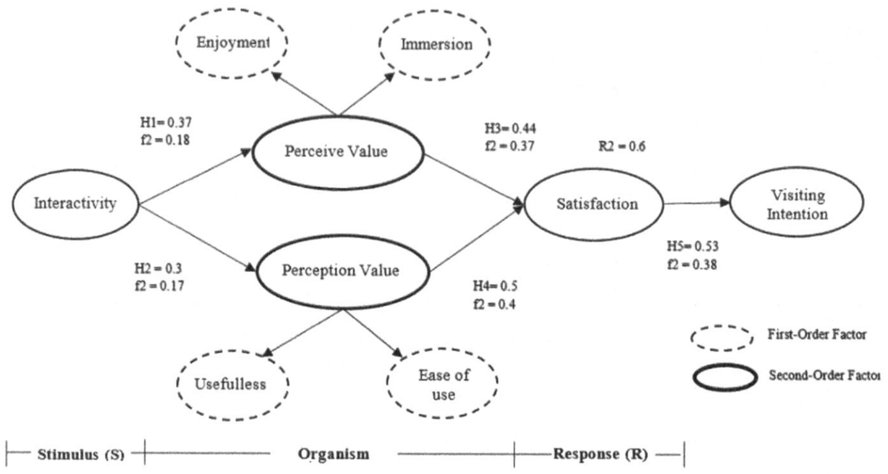

Fig. 2 Structural model

5 Discussion and Implication

5.1 Theoretical Implications

This study is a synthesis of various concepts aimed at evaluating in detail the user trends in VR technology for the future scenario of the tourism industry. Furthermore, VR is seen as a groundbreaking improvement in the diverse ways of marketing tourism. Based on the conclusions of previous scholarly articles, the authors propose a study on the relevance of tourists' reaction mechanisms to VR stimulation. Secondly, the study examines the relevance of VR technology to experiential satisfaction and visitation intention through the use of perceived value in the TAM model and perceived value. Connecting the theoretical frameworks in the proposed model has shown that the emotional factor of VR users strongly influences the realism of VR. Finally, the research results determined that the integration of factors in the model significantly contributes to customer satisfaction. The results have demonstrated that users' perception of emotional attitude and VR functionality in tourism is an important condition in shaping the consumer habits of participants. In other words, psychological factors have a significant impact on the final decision. Therefore, this study contributes additional literature on the user behavior trends of VR in the future.

5.2 Managerial Implications

The development of VR devices has brought convenience and ease of use for various purposes in recent years. This presents great potential for the widespread use of

VR tourism in the development and preservation of tourism in Vietnam. Previous research by Williams and Hobson suggests that scaling or creating travel experiences [30] through VR will have a significant impact on the tourism industry and can provide interactive experiences or rich data for potential travelers seeking destination information [31].

The results recorded in Chap. 4 show that the interactive features in virtual reality tourism are still limited when experienced in a non-immersive environment. Therefore, the goal of creators or destination marketers should pay attention to both content and visuals. Additionally, videos should be designed to contain useful information such as history, geographical location, etc., to provide tourists with an overview when participating in virtual travel and preparing for real travel plans. Interaction has an impact on the perceived value and emotional value of potential customers. Therefore, based on the recorded results, the research aims to provide additional information to help tourism managers have an overview of the relationship between interaction, emotional value, perceived value, satisfaction, and stimulating actual travel behavior of customers. Therefore, providing beautiful images in a non-immersive virtual environment will stimulate interest and attract customers to fully immerse themselves in the virtual travel experience. Thus, with the above results, the benefits of emotional value will attract potential tourists to visit destinations as demonstrated in VR.

Comparing the relationship between interaction and emotional value during VR travel experiences, it is stronger than the relationship between interaction and perceived value. Developers can use research results to propose development goals for programs that allow customers to increase navigation in the virtual environment, thereby highlighting images, space, and sound to make VR tourism more interesting, enjoyable, engaging, and impressive. As previous research has shown, interest, surprise, and enjoyment are the prerequisites for creating memorable experiences for each traveler [32]. Recently, some studies have also focused on designing services to enhance the customer experience [21]. Furthermore, destination marketers should use VR tourism content as a marketing and promotional tool for potential customers by combining emotional and cognitive aspects. Destination marketing strategies can be established by designing VR programs with creative content including images, sound, or instructional information.

Therefore, in a developing economy like Vietnam, VR tourism is a comprehensive solution for current environmental economic programs. This will attract a large number of tourists to Vietnam and contribute to the local economic development.

6 Conclusion

In general, content developers should rely on the unique interactive features in VR to create a more stimulating and immersive experience for users. The user-friendly nature of VR in tourism will motivate users to regularly use the technology and enhance their sense of immersion. In addition to these factors, there are other complementary elements that increase satisfaction in the experience. By promoting satisfaction in the experience, there is an opportunity to increase users' intention to experience it in reality.

However, this study has some limitations that serve as potential focal points for future research. Firstly, different users may have different concerns about VR technology. Secondly, the inconsistent factors of the flow due to different emotional states play a role in the purpose of the study. Next, the statistical analysis relies on data collected from a random sample of participants who completed an online survey. Consequently, it's important to recognize that the findings of this study may have limitations when it comes to applying them more broadly. Additionally, it's worth noting that a majority of the participants in this study were young people, which is consistent with previous research suggesting a greater interest in VR technology among this age group [7]. Previous findings have also found that younger individuals tend to be more skilled in using digital technology [33]. While it's acknowledged that the age distribution of participants could be seen as a limitation, it's reassuring to know that similar concerns have been addressed in previous research through careful participant selection [33]. Lastly, future studies could benefit from incorporating qualitative research methods to gain deeper insights into how user behavior influences their willingness to participate in programs. This is related to theoretical questions to know more about VR technology and VR applications in tourism. Or research on the potential use to enhance useful awareness of VR in tourism, thereby improving communication effectiveness and attracting more customers without being restricted by anthropological characteristics.

Funding This research is funded by the University of Economics Ho Chi Minh Vietnam City.

References

1. Dodds, R., Butler, R.: The phenomena of over tourism: a review. Int. J. Tour. Cities **5**(4), 519–528 (2019)
2. Griffin, T., Guttentag, D., Lee, S.H. (Mark), Giberson, J., Dimanche, F.: Is VR always better for destination marketing? Comparing different media and styles. J. Vacation Market. **29**(1), 135676672210782 (2022)
3. Vietbuild 2020 International Exhibition in Ho Chi Minh City. https://vietbuildexhibition.com.vn/en/news/vietbuild-2020-international-exhibition-in-ho-chi-minh-city/. Last accessed 20 Nov 2023
4. AR & VR—Vietnam. https://www.statista.com/outlook/amo/ar-vr/vietnam. Last accessed 20 Nov 2023
5. Huang, Y.-C.: Integrated concepts of the UTAUT and TPB in virtual reality behavioral intention. J. Retail. Consum. Serv. **70**, 103127 (2023)
6. Qin, H., Osatuyi, B., Xu, L.: How mobile augmented reality applications affect continuous use and purchase intentions: a cognition-affect-conation perspective. J. Retail. Consum. Serv. **63**, 102680 (2021)
7. Tussyadiah, I.P., Wang, D., Jung, T.H., Tom Dieck, M.C.: Virtual reality, presence, and attitude change: empirical evidence from tourism. Tour. Manage. **66**, 140–154 (2018)

8. Diemer, J., Alpers, G.W., Peperkorn, H.M., Shiban, Y., Mühlberger, A.: The impact of perception and presence on emotional reactions: a review of research in virtual reality. Front. Psychol. **6** (2015)
9. Cho, Y.-H., Wang, Y., Fesenmaier, D.R.: Searching for experiences. J. Travel Tour. Mark. **12**(4), 1–17 (2002)
10. Debbabi, S., Daassi, M., Baile, S.: Effect of online 3D advertising on consumer responses: the mediating role of telepresence. J. Market. Manage. **26**(9–10), 967–992 (2010)
11. Burigat, S., Chittaro, L.: Passive and active navigation of virtual environments versus traditional printed evacuation maps: a comparative evaluation in the aviation domain. Int. J. Human-Comput. Stud. **87**, 92–105 (2016)
12. Feng, Y.: Facilitator or inhibitor? The use of 360-degree videos for immersive brand storytelling. J. Interact. Advertising **18**(1), 28–42 (2018)
13. Standen, P.J., Brown, D.J.: Virtual reality in the rehabilitation of people with intellectual disabilities: review. Cyber Psychol. Behav. **8**(3), 272–282 (2005)
14. McMillan, S.J., Hwang, J.-S.: Measures of perceived interactivity: an exploration of the role of direction of communication, user control, and time in shaping perceptions of interactivity. J. Advertising **31**(3), 29–42 (2002)
15. Mossberg, L.: A marketing approach to the tourist experience. Scandinavian J. Hospital. Tourism **7**(1), 59–74 (2007)
16. Kim, K.-H., Park, D.-B.: Relationships among perceived value, satisfaction, and loyalty: community-based ecotourism in Korea. J. Travel Tour. Market. **34**(2), 171–191 (2016)
17. Bae, S., Jung, T.H., Moorhouse, N., Suh, M., Kwon, O.: The influence of mixed reality on satisfaction and brand loyalty in cultural heritage attractions: a brand equity perspective. Sustainability **12**(7), 2956 (2020)
18. Yung, R., Khoo-Lattimore, C., Prayag, G., Surovaya, E.: Around the world in less than a day: virtual reality, destination image and perceived destination choice risk in family tourism. Tour. Recreation Res. pp. 1–16 (2020)
19. Kim, D., Ko, Y.J.: The impact of virtual reality (VR) technology on sport spectators' flow experience and satisfaction. Comput. Hum. Behav. **93**, 346–356 (2019)
20. Huang, Y.C., Backman, K.F., Backman, S.J., Chang, L.L.: Exploring the implications of virtual reality technology in tourism marketing: an integrated research framework. Int. J. Tour. Res. **18**(2), 116–128 (2016)
21. Vishwakarma, P., Mukherjee, S., Datta, B.: Travelers' intention to adopt virtual reality: a consumer value perspective. J. Destin. Mark. Manage. **17**, 100456 (2020)
22. Li, X., Du, J., Long, H.: Dynamic analysis of international green behavior from the perspective of the mapping knowledge domain. Environ. Sci. Pollut. Res. **26**(6), 6087–6098 (2019)
23. Wu, H.-C., Ai, C.-H., Cheng, C.-C.: Virtual reality experiences, attachment and experiential outcomes in tourism. Tour. Rev. **75**(3), 481–495 (2019)
24. Yim, M.Y.-C., Chu, S.-C., Saucer, P.: Is augmented reality technology an effective tool for E-commerce? An interactivity and vividness perspective. J. Interact. Mark. **39**(1), 89–103 (2017)
25. Rahimizhian, S., Ozturen, A., Ilkan, M.: Emerging real of 360-degree technology to promote tourism destination. Technol. Soc. **63**, 101411 (2020)
26. Preston, C., Colman, A.: Optimal number of response categories in rating scales: reliability, validity, discriminating power, and respondent preferences. Acta Psychological **104**(1), 1–15 (2000)
27. Hair, J.F.: Multivariate Data Analysis, 7th edn. Pearson, New York (2010)
28. Nunnally, J.C., Bernstein, I.H.: The assessment of reliability. Psychom. Theory **3**, 248–292 (1994)
29. Cohen, J.: Statistical Power Analysis For the Behavioral Sciences, 2nd edn. Lawrence Erlbaum Associates, Hillsdale, N.J. (1988)
30. Williams, P., Hobson, P.: Virtual reality and tourism: fact or fantasy? Tour. Manage. **16**(6), 423–427 (1995)

31. Guttentag, D.: Virtual reality: Applications and implications for tourism. Tour. Manage. **31**(5), 637–651 (2010)
32. Oliver, R.: Satisfaction: a Behavioral Perspective on the Consumer, 1st edn. M. E. Sharpe, New York (1997)
33. Baek, E., Choo, H., Wei, X., Yoon, S.-Y.: Understanding the virtual tours of retail stores: how can store band experience promote visit intentions? Int. J. Retail Distrib. Manage. **48**(7), 649–666 (2020)

Factors Influencing the Intention and Behavior to Use E-Wallets of Customers in Ho Chi Minh City

Nguyen Khanh Ngan and Le Dinh Nghi

Abstract This paper examines the factors affecting customers' intention and behavior in using E-Wallets in Ho Chi Minh City (HCMC). The study employed a combination of qualitative and quantitative methodologies. The PLS-SEM model demonstrates that intention and behavior are influenced by perceived usefulness, perceived ease of use, attitude toward using mobile payment services, subjective norm, and individual mobility using data from 300 individuals who had first-hand experience with e-wallets. This research proposes meaningful implications for financial managers and marketers, stepping up factors that increase customers' intention to use E-Wallets in HCMC.

Keywords Behavior · e-wallets · Intention · Ho Chi Minh City

1 Introduction

Many nations have seen remarkable technical growth in recent years. These developments benefit several sectors: financial, education, and health. Within the financial sector, businesses aim to offer their clients faster and more effective payment services [20]. An e-wallet, an electronic account on a mobile phone or laptop that can store and transfer money and replace a traditional wallet [15], aids users in managing payment details, and allows them to view transaction history [8], is an essential component of the mobile payment system.

In Vietnam, E-Wallets have been developed for a long time, but since 2014, they have become widely known thanks to the appearance of many different E-Wallets such as MoMo, ZaloPay, Payoo, True Money, and VNPay. Several companies have focused on expanding payments for essential public services and collecting loans for banks and consumer finance companies. In the future, they will accelerate finance development, deploy agency systems throughout the state, and execute paid services, collection, and money transfers to people in the suburban area. E-Wallets

N. K. Ngan · L. D. Nghi (✉)
Saigon University, 273 An Duong Vuong, Ward 3, District 5, Ho Chi Minh City, Vietnam
e-mail: nghiledinh@sgu.edu.vn

L. T. Tung et al. (eds.), *Disruptive Technology and Business Continuity*,
https://doi.org/10.1007/978-981-97-5452-6_7

also integrate functions to help users maximize "idle money" in wallets for investment and accumulation. From the perspective of a strategic partner, using an e-wallet channel to conduct marketing campaigns will dominate the market share of youth who are sensitive to technology and enjoy internet marketing. Therefore, continuing to study the factors influencing the intention and behavior to use e-wallets is needed to help corporation managers have more information for their decision-making.

2 Theoretical Basis

2.1 *Literature Review*

After user verification, an e-wallet, or virtual wallet, can store credit card information on a computer or mobile device for online purchases and payments at physical retail POS terminals [34]. It is an electronic tool that may be used with a computer or a smartphone to conduct online transactions [25].

One of the most important and fundamental theories of human behavior, the Theory of Reasoned Action (TRA), is derived from social psychology. According to TRA, a person's intention, affected by attitude toward the behavior and subjective norm, determines their behavior [14]. The Theory of Planned Behavior (TPB) is an extension of the TRA. Behavioral intent is a crucial element of TPB's model. It is shaped by an individual's subjective assessment of the risks and benefits of a behavior, as well as their attitude towards the likelihood that the behavior will produce the desired result [22]. Based on these theories, along with the TAM model [11], some literature investigates the customer attitude and behavior to use e-wallets [4, 21, 29, 32]. These studies hint at potential factors driving consumer acceptance of mobile payment solutions, such as Perceived Usefulness (PU), Perceived Ease of Use (PEU), Subjective Norm (SN), Intention to Use (IU), Behavior to Use (BU), based on background theories TAM, TRA, and TPB. However, Individual Mobility (IM) is a factor that is scarcely examined in the context of HCMC. So, there is a need to have formal research on this factor as a feature that is inherent in mobile payments and has a role in increasing the intention of using mobile payments. This perfectly accords with a research context and is a prerequisite for building a model to evaluate the intention to use E-Wallets.

2.2 *Hypotheses and Conceptual Model*

PU and IU. The degree to which a person believes utilizing a specific information technology would increase productivity is known as PU [11]. A primary cause of the sluggish adoption of mobile applications in general and mobile payments in particular may be the inability to clearly explain the advantages to prospective users

[32]. Venkatesh and Davis [35] have examined the TAM model and indicated that PU positively affects the end-users behavioral intention. Prior studies have also shown that PU is the axiom of consumers' intention to use technology [4, 24]. Therefore, the following hypothesis is formed:

H1: PU of e-wallets will positively influence intention to use E-Wallets.

PEU and IU. The degree to which a person believes utilizing a system will be effortless is known as PEU [12], which is the prerequisite for consumers to use payment services. This is particularly true for mobile payment services, which must offer advantages in terms of usability in order to compete with more established payment methods [32]. The PEU of mobile payment services is influenced by various factors, such as the presence of intuitive icons and function buttons, a minimal number of stages in the payment process, a graphic display, and assistance features [26]. Therefore, if consumers see how easy it is to use technology, they will be interested in using it instead of learning how to use it. Therefore, the following hypothesis is formed:

H2: PEU of e-wallets will positively influence intention to use E-Wallets.

SN and IU. A person's belief that most people who matter to him believe he should or should not engage in the conduct is known as his SN [14]. Initially, SN was launched to explore the impact of social pressure on individual behavior [1]. Shaw and Kesharwani [33] stated that, with the development of the Internet, when choosing a new payment method, consumers would like to find out about it with someone who has previously experienced it. Venkatesh and Davis [35] also indicated that SN significantly manipulates the acceptance of technology of users, while Riemenschneider et al. [31] discovered that SN affects adoption decisions. Celuch et al. [9] observed that SN positively impacts using intention the Internet to manage purchasing and information. Therefore, the following hypothesis is formed:

H3: SN of e-wallets will positively influence intention to use E-Wallets.

Attitude Toward Using (ATU) Mobile Payment Services and IU. According to the TAM model, a person's attitude toward using technology is the primary antecedent of their intention to use it [11]. Kadir et al. [18] demonstrated that users' attitudes toward using E-Wallets are more positive when they have a positive experience. Several previous studies indicated a positive nexus between IU and ATU [21, 29, 32]. Therefore, the following hypothesis is formed:

H4: Attitude toward using mobile payment services of e-wallets will positively influence intention to use E-Wallets.

Individual Mobility (IM) and IU. In addition to conventional payment methods, mobile services can be used anytime, almost anywhere [10], and fulfill users' requests by solving everyday issues [30]. Although there is a general trend in our society toward increased mobility, individual mobility varies significantly [32]. According to Schierz et al. [32], highly mobile individuals will have a more positive attitude toward mobile payment services and a higher intention to use them. Arvidsson [5] asserts that the critical influence in the IM to adopt a new product or service is

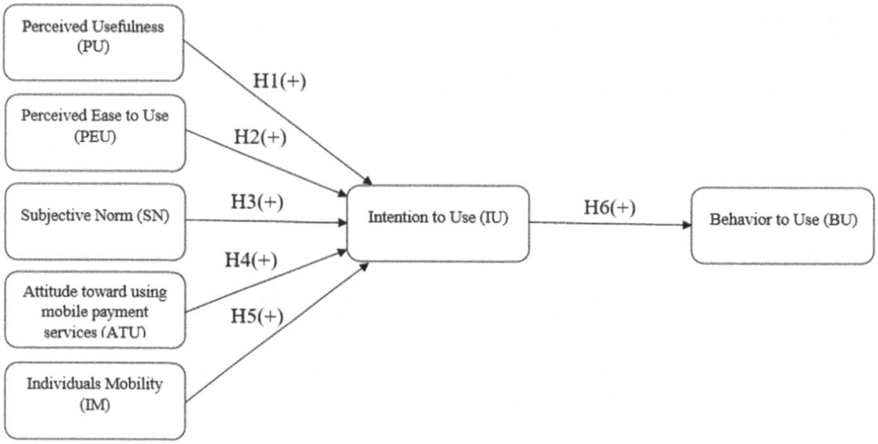

Fig. 1 Proposed research model

independent of time and location in use. Thus, mobile services are a perfect match for a mobile lifestyle, and IM is a significant factor in Vietnamese consumers' decision to use mobile payment services to pay for goods and services [23]. Therefore, the following hypothesis is formed:

H5: IM of e-wallets will positively influence the intention to use E-Wallets.

IU and BU. A person's behavioral intention is the subjective probability that they hope to achieve within a given time frame [2], whereas an individual's intention is the course of action they hope to accomplish [36]. Using the TRA and TAM model, many studies evident the relationship between IU and BU [6, 13]. Therefore, the following hypothesis is formed:

H6: IU e-wallet will have a positive influence on BU E-Wallets.

Our six hypotheses imply the proposed research model presented in Fig. 1.

3 Methodology

Both qualitative and quantitative research methods are used in this study. The qualitative approach was performed through in-depth interviews with experts to complete and adjust the scale. After that, the PLS-SEM model was applied for quantitative analysis procedures.

The measurement scales used to evaluate the research model with seven constructs were modified from earlier research [27, 32]. The measurement questions were developed based on a 5-point Likert scale, ranging from 1 ('strongly disagree') to 5 ('strongly agree').

The researcher employed convenience sampling, a non-probability sampling technique, including those using E-Wallets in HCMC. The primary data were collected throughout June 2023 by conducting a standardized online questionnaire in the form of Google form, which was subjected to comprehensive testing before implementation. A total of 306 questionnaires were collected from HCMC in Vietnam, but only 300 were taken into consideration for data analysis. To test the measurement and structural model, we used SmartPLS software version 4.0.

4 Result and Discussion

4.1 Result

Measurement Model. We conducted analyses separately for the factor loading and calculated Cronbach's Alpha (CA), Composite Reliabilities (CR), and Average Variances Extracted (AVE) to measure the validity and reliability. All items are reliable, with CA ranging from 0.707 to 0.874, and CR also show internal consistency with a value greater than 0.6 [16]. AVE and Outer Loading (OL) to measure convergent validity extracted surpass values of 0.5 [16]. Furthermore, the squared correlation of each construct with all other factors is less than the AVE for this construct. To sum up, the measuring model showed sufficient reliability, convergent validity, and discriminant validity (Table 1 and 2).

Common Method Bias (CMB). The authors employed Harman's one-factor and VIF test to check for CMB in the data. The results show that in Harman's one factor, the first unadjusted factor accounted for 34.223% (< 50%) [28], and the VIF value is less than 3 [16], indicating no single, general factor was extracted in the analysis.

Structural model. SRMR values vary from 0 to 1. Well-fitting models yield values less than 0.05 [7]; however, values up to 0.08 are considered reasonable [17]. Specifically, in this study, the value is 0.067, showing the model has a good fit.

Adjusted R-square Test. This analyses how the exogenous latent variables explain the endogenous variable. A higher value indicates a stronger dependency between the variables [16]. The outcomes reveal that R-square adjusted values reach as much as 0.237 with BU and 0.687 with IU.

Testing the hypothesis. It can be seen in Table 3, all of the hypotheses H1, H2, H3, H4, H5, and H6 are supported. More specifically, PU ($\beta = 0.070$; $p = 0.041$), PEU ($\beta = 0.115$; $p = 0.0154$), SN ($\beta = 0.108$; $p = 0.005$), ATU ($\beta = 0.649$; $p = 0.000$), IM ($\beta = 0.092$; $p = 0.010$) have positive influence on IU. Moreover, IU ($\beta = 0.489$; $p = 0.000$) also positively influences BU.

The mediating relationship. Table 4 tests the mediating specific indirect effects of IU with independent variables. This study has five indirect relationships at a 5% level. PU, PEU, ATU, SN, and IM influence BU, which is mediated by IU, which can be seen from the sample mean and the p-values. These values mean that the indirect relationships between PU, PEU, ATU, SN, IM, and BU have a positive

Table 1 Construct validity and reliability test

Measure	Mean	Kurtosis	Skewness	OL	CA	CR	AVE
Perceived usefulness (PU)							
PU1	3.540	−0.320	−0.674	0.906	0.874	0.922	0.798
PU2	3.447	−0.730	−0.332	0.890			
PU3	3.400	−0.533	−0.464	0.884			
Perceived ease of use (PEU)							
PEU1	3.747	−0.080	−0.393	0.872	0.849	0.908	0.768
PEU2	3.760	−0.265	−0.398	0.863			
PEU3	3.733	0.108	−0.522	0.894			
Subjective norms (SN)							
SN1	3.103	−0.744	−0.108	0.834	0.765	0.864	0.680
SN2	3.067	−0.359	−0.134	0.799			
SN3	3.067	−0.678	0.143	0.840			
Attitude towards using mobile payment services (ATU)							
ATU1	3.903	1.530	−0.963	0.833	0.778	0.855	0.597
ATU2	3.767	−0.218	−0.374	0.762			
ATU3	3.857	0.148	−0.535	0.750			
ATU4	3.890	0.796	−0.721	0.741			
Individual mobility (IM)							
IM1	3.237	−0.692	−0.226	0.734	0.787	0.862	0.611
IM2	3.067	−0.652	0.102	0.732			
IM3	3.367	−0.984	0.090	0.823			
IM3	3.440	−0.649	−0.322	0.831			
Intention to use (IU)							
IU1	3.903	1.530	−0.963	0.796	0.707	0.835	0.629
IU2	3.797	−0.150	−0.337	0.813			
IU3	3.843	0.498	−0.663	0.769			
Behavior to use (BU)							
BU1	3.603	−0.167	−0.576	0.872	0.822	0.894	0.738
BU2	3.713	−0.228	−0.522	0.834			
BU3	3.587	−0.286	−0.320	0.870			

and significant impact and are mediated successfully by IU. Thus, IU successfully mediates the relationship between PU, PEU, ATU, SN, IM, and BU.

Table 5 indicates that SN, PEU, PU, ATU, and IM have a total indirect effect on BU, as seen from the sample mean and p-values. These values mean that the connections between SN, PEU, PU, ATU, IM, and BU have a positive influence and that factors can be an additional incentive for customers to be keen on using E-Wallets instead of traditional transactions.

Table 2 Discriminant validity test

	SN	BU	PEU	PU	ATU	IM	IU
SN	**0.824**						
BU	0.399	**0.859**					
PEU	0.507	0.612	**0.876**				
PU	0.224	0.312	0.353	**0.893**			
ATU	0.355	0.462	0.52	0.303	**0.772**		
IM	0.289	0.365	0.421	0.186	0.328	**0.782**	
IU	0.439	0.489	0.571	0.348	0.798	0.398	**0.793**

Table 3 Hypothesis summary

Path	Hypotheses	β	T statistics	P values	Decision
PU → IU	H1	0.070	2.043	0.041	Supported
PEU → IU	H2	0.115	2.433	0.015	Supported
SN → IU	H3	0.108	2.838	0.005	Supported
ATU → IU	H4	0.649	17.997	0.000	Supported
IM → IU	H5	0.092	2.566	0.010	Supported
IU → BU	H6	0.489	7.922	0.000	Supported

Table 4 Specific indirect effects

Path	Original sample	Sample mean	Standard deviation	T statistics	P values
SN → IU → BU	0.053	0.053	0.020	2.640	0.008
PEU → IU → BU	0.056	0.056	0.026	2.193	0.028
IM → IU → BU	0.045	0.046	0.019	2.363	0.018
PU → IU → BU	0.034	0.034	0.017	2.001	0.045
ATU → IU → BU	0.317	0.317	0.040	7.982	0.000

Table 5 Total indirect effect test

Path	Original sample	Sample mean	Standard deviation	T statistics	P values
SN → BU	0.053	0.053	0.020	2.640	0.008
PEU → BU	0.056	0.056	0.026	2.193	0.028
PU → BU	0.034	0.034	0.017	2.001	0.045
ATU → BU	0.317	0.317	0.040	7.982	0.000
IM → BU	0.045	0.046	0.019	2.363	0.018

4.2 Discussion

The study uses the TRA, TPB, and TAM as ground theories to explain consumer behavior that is able and willing to accept a new technology based on PU and PEU. In addition, TRA has demonstrated the importance of attitude toward behavior and intention to use E-Wallets for transaction settlements. Consumers have positive perceptions toward PEU and SN as factors to be considered when deciding to use E-Wallets. Therefore, online marketing also needs to pay attention to consumer attitudes, and the vital things are PEU and SN when paying transactions.

Users utilize e-wallets because they are efficient in various transactions, which explains the relationship between PU and IU. They are a provoking factor for users to prefer using e-wallets over traditional payment. Because of this, the intention to use it increases with increasing perception of usefulness. According to the results, users are more likely to use E-wallets when their PEU is higher because their platforms are now designed with an intuitive interface and easy to use for all user objects. Consumers have no difficulty using it, so it is more convenient and highly recommended for using E-Wallets. These results are comparable to findings by several authors worldwide, such as [19, 20].

The better their ATU to use E-Wallets, the higher the consumer's IU them, similar to [3, 11, 32]. Evaluating anything with a certain amount of favoritism or disfavor is known as attitude; a more positive user attitude can increase acceptance and approval of utilizing e-wallets for payments. This is true in HCMC, Vietnam's largest economic hub, where new technologies are invaded and shared or commented on in forums. It helps users have more interesting views or attitudes about technology products and services. Thus, they accept using of new products.

IM is a new facet that impacts IU and is a crucial driver of mobile transaction acceptance. By way of a possible explanation for what was found, Schierz et al. [32] point out that because perceived compatibility was not included in the original TAM, researchers frequently overlook it. People must discover mobile payment services consistent with their current behavioral patterns before considering adopting them. As society becomes more mobile, mobile payment services are expected to become more critical.

Furthermore, the study discovered a significant correlation between IU and BU, indicating that IU determines BU. Therefore, users will use E-wallets if they intend to use them, which is affected by PU, PEU, SN, ATU, and IM.

5 Conclusions and Implications

The study proposes a model to investigate the behavior of using e-wallets in HCMC. Data analyzed with 300 respondents and the research results show that PU, PEU, SN, and ATU significantly affect IU, and IU significantly affects BU. The seven factors summarized in the study can serve as a guideline for increasing market penetration of mobile payment services in today's context.

Those who take the survey pay much attention to PU and PEU before agreeing to use technology. So, marketing directors and marketers leverage social media to implement advertising campaigns that stress E-Wallets' advantages and spread information across all platforms from those that have used services. It can be done via social networking sites or websites for notification of applications about the news.

The factor SN—a key driver of consumer acceptance—can imply that reference groups (parents, friends, teammates, etc.) play an essential role in spreading mobile payments. They will introduce and promote the e-wallet services when they realize they are good and valuable. Therefore, firms need to identify early adopters, then focus on preferential policies for them and proactively step up communications to stimulate their usage of paying to become "Reference" in the future.

To gain a competitive advantage, the quality of technology is a crucial element. When applying modern technology, customers should not have to go through many steps in the process; they should only enter their basic information like name, phone number, and touch ID with NFC. Customers' ATU will improve and accept to make mobile payments only when certain expectations have been met.

IM is another crucial driver of the consumer's acceptance of mobile payment services. The company cannot derive it; they only help managers by offering recommendations. Hence, the firm can focus on customer segmentation, who have a strong demand to pay for the service in every circumstance. It can help managers in the segmentation and prioritization of potential customers.

In summary, this study contributes to the diversity of research models in identifying, conceptualizing, and operationalizing relevant acceptance drivers of mobile payment systems. Our study was restricted to HCMC, so it would be more accurate by expanding a range of respondents, adding essential factors to improve attitudes toward using mobile payment services and analyzing the results in other cities to get more comprehensive information. Moreover, future research can compare e-wallets with competing methods such as credit cards, Visa, and MasterCard.

References

1. Ajzen, I.: From intentions to actions: a theory of planned behavior. In: Action Control, pp. 11–39. Springer Berlin Heidelberg (1985). https://doi.org/10.1007/978-3-642-69746-3_2
2. Ajzen, I.: Attitude structure and behavior. In Attitude structure and function, pp. 241–274. Lawrence Erlbaum Associates, Inc. (1989)
3. Ajzen, I.: The theory of planned behavior. Organ. Behav. Hum. Decis. Process. **50**(2), 179–211 (1991). https://doi.org/10.1080/10410236.2018.1493416
4. Alavi, S., Ahuja, V.: An empirical segmentation of users of mobile banking apps. J. Internet Commerce **15**(4), 390–407 (2016). https://doi.org/10.1080/15332861.2016.1252653
5. Arvidsson, N.: Consumer attitudes on mobile payment services—results from a proof of concept test. Int. J. Bank Market. **32**(2), 150–170 (2014). https://doi.org/10.1108/IJBM-05-2013-0048

6. Barry, M., Jan, M.T.: Factors influencing the use of m-commerce: an extended technology acceptance model perspective. Int. J. Econ., Manage. Account. **26**(1), 157–183 (2018)
7. Byrne, B.M.: Structural Equation Modeling With Lisrel, Prelis, and Simplis. Psychology Press (2013).https://doi.org/10.4324/9780203774762
8. Caldwell, T.: Locking down the e-wallet. Comput. Fraud Security **2012**(4), 5–8 (2012). https://doi.org/10.1016/S1361-3723(12)70028-3
9. Celuch, K., Walz, A., Saxby, C., Ehlen, C.: Understanding SME intention to use the internet for managing supplier information. New England J. Entrepreneurship **14**(1), 9–21 (2011). https://doi.org/10.1108/NEJE-14-01-2011-B001
10. Dahlberg, T., Mallat, N., Ondrus, J., Zmijewska, A.: Past, present and future of mobile payments research: a literature review. Electron. Commer. Res. Appl. **7**(2), 165–181 (2008). https://doi.org/10.1016/j.elerap.2007.02.001
11. Davis, F.D., Bagozzi, R.P., Warshaw, P.R.: User Acceptance of computer technology: a comparison of two theoretical models. Manage. Sci. **35**(8), 982–1003 (1989). https://doi.org/10.1287/mnsc.35.8.982
12. Davis, F.D., Venkatesh, V.: Toward preprototype user acceptance testing of new information systems: implications for software project management. IEEE Trans. Eng. Manage. **51**(1), 31–46 (2004). https://doi.org/10.1109/TEM.2003.822468
13. Faqih, K.M.S., Jaradat, M.-I.R.M.: Assessing the moderating effect of gender differences and individualism-collectivism at individual-level on the adoption of mobile commerce technology: TAM3 perspective. J. Retail. Consum. Serv. **22**, 37–52 (2015). https://doi.org/10.1016/j.jretconser.2014.09.006
14. Fishbein, M., Ajzen, I.: Belief, Attitude, Intention and Behaviour: An Introduction to Theory and Research. Addison-Wesley, Reading, MA (1975)
15. Gorczynski, P., Faulkner, G.: Exercise therapy for schizophrenia. Cochrane Database of Systematic Reviews (5) (2010). https://doi.org/10.1002/14651858.CD004412.pub2
16. Hair, J., Black, W., Babin, B., Anderson, R.: Multivariate Data Analysis: A Global Perspective (2010)
17. Hu, L., Bentler, P.M.: Cutoff criteria for fit indexes in covariance structure analysis: conventional criteria versus new alternatives. Struct. Equ. Modeling **6**(1), 1–55 (1999). https://doi.org/10.1080/10705519909540118
18. Kadir, H.A., Ismail, R., Wok, S., Manan, K.A.: The mediating effect of attitude on E-wallet usage among users In Malaysia. J. Commun. Educ. **2**(1), 58–77 (2022)
19. Karim, M.W., Haque, A., Ulfy, M.A., Hossain, M.A., Anis, M.Z.: Factors influencing the use of E-wallet as a payment method among Malaysian young adults. J. Int. Bus. Manage. **3**(2), 1–11 (2020). https://doi.org/10.37227/jibm-2020-2-21
20. Koo, F., Cuandra, F.: Analysis of factors affecting international E-wallet use. Jurnal Bisnis Dan Akuntansi, 24(2), 337–352 (2022). https://doi.org/10.34208/jba.v24i2.1603
21. Kustono, A.S., Nanggala, A.Y.A., Mas'ud, I.: Determinants of the use of E-wallet for transaction payment among college students. J. Econ., Bus., Accountancy Ventura **23**(1) (2020). https://doi.org/10.14414/jebav.v23i1.2245
22. LaMorte, W.W.: The theory of planned behavior. Boston University School of Public Health (2019)
23. Liu, G.-S., Tai, P.T.: A study of factors affecting the intention to use mobile payment services in Vietnam. Econ. World **4**(6), 249–273 (2016)
24. Lu, J., Wei, J., Yu, C., Liu, C.: How do post-usage factors and espoused cultural values impact mobile payment continuation? Behav. Inf. Technol. **36**(2), 140–164 (2017). https://doi.org/10.1080/0144929X.2016.1208773
25. Pachpande, B.R., Kamble, A.A.: Study of E-wallet awareness and its usage in Mumbai. J. Commerce Manage. Thought **9**(1), 33–45 (2018). https://doi.org/10.5958/0976-478X.2018.00004.6
26. Pagani, M., Schipani, D.: Motivations and barriers to the adoption of 3G mobile multimedia services: an end user perspective in the Italian market. In: End-User Computing: Concepts, Methodologies, Tools, and Applications, pp. 2329–2340. IGI Global (2008)

27. Phan, T.N., Ho, T.V., Le-Hoang, P.V.: Factors affecting the behavioral intention and behavior of using E–wallets of youth in Vietnam. The J. Asian Finance, Econ. Bus., **7**(10), 295–302 (2020). https://doi.org/10.13106/jafeb.2020.vol7.n10.295
28. Podsakoff, P.M., MacKenzie, S.B., Lee, J.-Y., Podsakoff, N.P.: Common method biases in behavioral research: a critical review of the literature and recommended remedies. J. Appl. Psychol. **88**(5), 879–903 (2003). https://doi.org/10.1037/0021-9010.88.5.879
29. Pradipta, I.A., Tresia, M.: Analysis of factors affecting the acceptance or use of e-wallet in Jakarta. J. Econ. Bus. Lett. **1**(4), 27–32 (2021). https://doi.org/10.55942/jebl.v1i4.129
30. Rao, S., Troshani, I.: A conceptual framework and propositions for the acceptance of mobile services. J. Theor. Appl. Electron. Commer. Res. **2**(2), 61–73 (2007). https://doi.org/10.3390/jtaer2020014
31. Riemenschneider, C.K., Harrison, D.A., Mykytyn, P.P.: Understanding it adoption decisions in small business: integrating current theories. Inf. Manage. **40**(4), 269–285 (2003). https://doi.org/10.1016/S0378-7206(02)00010-1
32. Schierz, P.G., Schilke, O., Wirtz, B.W.: Understanding consumer acceptance of mobile payment services: an empirical analysis. Electron. Commer. Res. Appl. **9**(3), 209–216 (2010). https://doi.org/10.1016/j.elerap.2009.07.005
33. Shaw, B., Kesharwani, A.: Moderating effect of smartphone addiction on mobile wallet payment adoption. J. Internet Commerce **18**(3), 291–309 (2019). https://doi.org/10.1080/15332861.2019.1620045
34. Tolety, R.K.: E-wallets their cause rise and relevance. Int. J. Res. IT Manage. (IJRIM) **8**(7), 1–8 (2018)
35. Venkatesh, V., Davis, F.D.: A theoretical extension of the technology acceptance model: four longitudinal field studies. Manage. Sci. **46**(2), 186–204 (2000). https://doi.org/10.1287/mnsc.46.2.186.11926
36. Zhao, W., Othman, M.N.: Predicting and explaining complaint intention and behaviour of Malaysian consumers: an application of the planned behaviour theory. In: International Marketing, vol. 21, pp. 229–252. Emerald Group Publishing Limited (2011)

Virtual Reality as a Tool for Destination Marketing of Sustainable Tourism During the COVID-19 Pandemic

Sinh Duc Hoang, Diep T. N. Nguyen, and Minh Pham

Abstract This study examines the utilization of virtual reality (VR) as a tool for promoting sustainable tourism amid the challenges posed by the COVID-19 pandemic. We distributed a questionnaire to a group of 249 students who were exposed to a video presentation showcasing low-impact tourism in Vietnam. The study outcomes reveal that the enjoyment derived from the VR experience amplifies the inclination of potential travellers to embark on trips. Contrary to our initial assumptions, this heightened enjoyment is not linked to the extent of immersion facilitated by VR technology. Surprisingly, we find that the degree of immersion, known as telepresence, has a positive influence on the intentions of practising social distancing. This, in turn, leads to a decrease in the desire to travel. Our findings suggest that during the pandemic, VR may be seen as a substitute for actual travel, rather than a motivator for it. This trend is particularly noticeable in a pandemic context, where the decision to maintain social distancing is driven by evaluations of potential threats and coping strategies. Although we expect these factors to weaken in a post-COVID era, the beneficial impact of telepresence provided by VR on social distancing intentions will continue to shape travellers' intentions even after the pandemic has subsided.

Keywords COVID-19 · Protection motivation theory · Sustainable tourism · TAM · Virtual reality

S. D. Hoang
School of Business, International University, Ho Chi Minh City, Vietnam

Vietnam National University, Ho Chi Minh City, Vietnam

S. D. Hoang
e-mail: hdsinh@hcmiu.edu.vn

D. T. N. Nguyen (✉) · M. Pham
Ho Chi Minh City Open University, 35-37 Ho Hao Hon, Co Giang Ward, District 1, Ho Chi Minh City, Vietnam
e-mail: diep.ngtn@ou.edu.vn

M. Pham
e-mail: minh.p@ou.edu.vn

L. T. Tung et al. (eds.), *Disruptive Technology and Business Continuity*,
https://doi.org/10.1007/978-981-97-5452-6_8

1 Introduction

In mid-December 2019, a new and extremely infectious coronavirus (COVID-19) arose and swept the whole planet away. The epidemic evolved into a pandemic, posing enormous problems to the tourist industry. There are growing concerns about a "new normal" [1]. WTTC invented the word to allude to the required routine that begins after lockdowns expire and limitations are relaxed. New norms and practices, such as increased cleanliness, contactless payment, and safe distance, will be part of the new normal [1]. Touchless travel and integrated digital identification solutions are gaining popularity [2]. The World Travel and Tourism Council (WTTC) is in the process of formulating a strategic vision for the future of the Travel and Tourism sector that takes into account the altered landscape we now face. WTTC has pinpointed sustainable development, innovation, as well as security and safety as pivotal concerns for the industry [1]. Our perspective aligns with this vision as we see a clear connection between the utilization of virtual reality (VR) in the realm of tourism and these critical issues. We firmly believe that integrating VR into the operational framework of tourism enterprises has the potential to both alleviate the repercussions of the COVID-19 pandemic and catalyse the industry's transformation into a more resilient and robust entity. These strategies are not only adept at helping industry players navigate the current crisis but also at laying the foundation for a healthier and safer tourism ecosystem in the foreseeable future.

Advancements in technology are reshaping how products and services are marketed to consumers. For decades, conventional media like television and radio dominated the advertising landscape. However, the rise of the internet has elevated the significance of digital channels, including online and mobile advertising [3]. Until recently, virtual reality (VR) was dismissed as a passing trend, akin to 3D glasses. Yet, the expanding array of applications across various sectors such as gaming, film, training, simulation, medicine, and the emergence of metaverse concepts indicates its enduring appeal. This trend presents a lucrative opportunity for marketers to harness VR as an advertising platform [4, 5]. In 2021, the global VR market was valued at nearly $28 billion, with projections forecasting its growth to exceed $252 billion by 2028, marking an impressive annual growth rate of over 35% [6].

VR's defining feature, setting it apart from traditional media, is the complete immersion it offers, resulting in heightened sensory engagement, referred to as telepresence [7]. This characteristic makes VR an ideal marketing tool for industries that sell experiences, such as hospitality and tourism [8]. Indeed, there is evidence supporting the notion that implementing VR in the hotel industry can stimulate impulsive consumer behaviour and enhance intentions to visit [9].

Existing research has reached a consensus regarding the impact of destination image on tourists' travel intentions, and this impact can be amplified through the application of VR technologies and their telepresence effects [9–12]. Nonetheless, the utilization of VR introduces a paradoxical dimension, as virtual tours of destinations have the potential to supplant the inclination of tourists to embark on actual journeys [13, 14]. However, there remains an unaddressed question in recent studies: why does the influence of VR stimulate tourist intentions in some scenarios while diverting tourists from visiting the destination in others? This is a gap that this study tries to fill. We hypothesise that VR could be viewed as a substitute for real travel by tourists with high levels of environmental involvement. By opting for VR tours instead of real tours, they try to preserve the environment from human impact. We apply this moderating effect to the extended version of the Technology Acceptance Model (TAM) and argue that telepresence provided by this technology triggers an increase in perceived enjoyment when the viewer is exposed to a VR video of a nature-based destination. Still, the impact of the enjoyment on actual travel intentions will be moderated by the level of environmental involvement of the viewer.

One additional factor that could potentially hinder the effectiveness of VR-based marketing in driving real travel to the promoted destination pertains to the promotion of social distancing practices. We posit that the presence of VR, with its immersive qualities, has the potential to further reinforce the adoption of social distancing measures. Social distancing was a universal measure enforced during the recent COVID-19 pandemic [15]. While some practised social distancing voluntarily appraising the threat and their own abilities to cope, others had to follow mandatory social distancing measures such as limits on public gatherings [16]. Even though social distancing has negatively affected tourism [17], we expect that the social distancing habits developed by people will be preserved in the post-pandemic period and will affect actual travel. Drawing from prior research into immersive experiences like computer gaming [18, 19] and the implications of social networks and smartphones on health and psychology [20], we anticipate that heightened telepresence offered by VR will stimulate individuals' inclinations to seek solitude and distance themselves from real-world interactions. Essentially, this voluntary social isolation, driven by greater telepresence, is expected to endure even in the post-pandemic era and exert an adverse influence on travel intentions.

It is unclear how the ongoing pandemic or environmental concerns may impact the effect of VR on decision-making behaviour [21]. As technological development continues to influence the tourism industry, it will become particularly relevant for businesses to understand and adjust to individual consumer preferences [22]. Therefore, it is important to explore how individual-level concerns about the environment and social distancing practices could influence the use of VR as a destination marketing tool for sustainable tourism.

2 Literature Review and Hypothesis Development

2.1 Telepresence and Perceived Enjoyment

Telepresence, which refers to the sense of being present in a virtual environment, is a key factor in determining the enjoyment experienced by tourists in virtual reality (VR) technology [23]. The perceived enjoyment of using VR technology to experience tourism destinations is an important aspect of measuring VR enjoyment [23]. Studies have shown that telepresence mediates the relationship between interactivity, vividness, and perceived enjoyment in VR shopping experiences [22]. Additionally, a good telepresence experience in a blended reality setting has been found to significantly enhance customers' perceived enjoyment [24].

Furthermore, the use of VR technology in tourism has been explored using the stimulus-organism-response (SOR) theory, which considers factors such as authentic experience, cognitive and affective responses, attachment, and visit intention [22]. Immersion and presence in VR tours have been found to indirectly impact tourists' choices and enhance their enjoyment of the experience [4]. The perception of VR technology also plays a role in tourist engagement, with positive perceptions leading to greater engagement [7].

In the context of destination marketing, Ying et al. [25] claim that VR commercials with higher telepresence have been found to elicit stronger intentions to (re)visit, with cognition and affection mediating this effect. Additionally, factors such as telepresence and control have been found to enhance consumer flow and increase intentions to adopt and utilize VR technology in a consumer setting [26]. Based on this, the following hypothesis is formulated:

H1: Telepresence from VR technology stimulates greater perceived enjoyment in tourists.

2.2 VR and Travel Intentions

Extensive study has been conducted on the correlation between emotions and consumer behaviour, as evidenced by studies conducted by Li et al. [27]. Therefore, it can be inferred that the enhanced perception of satisfaction resulting from the utilization of virtual reality (VR) technology among tourists will positively influence their plans to travel and their inclination to personally visit the advertised place [26, 28]. Numerous scholarly investigations have elucidated this phenomenon by positing that the utilization of virtual reality (VR) engenders good feelings, hence contributing to the development of a more favourable destination image [5, 10, 21]. Previous studies have examined the relationship between telepresence, perceived enjoyment, and travel intention using the Stimulus-Organism-Response (SOR) framework. Within this framework, telepresence is considered a stimulus that influences the psychological state of the individual, leading to perceived enjoyment. This perceived enjoyment then prompts a response in the form of a desire to physically visit the destination. This relationship has been explored in research conducted by Loureiro et al. [29]. Drawing from the discourse at hand, the subsequent hypothesis is posited:

Hypothesis 2: The favourable impact of virtual reality (VR) on visitors' travel intentions is mediated by their perceived enjoyment.

According to Hammady et al. [30] and Sancho-Esper [31], behavioural aims may be hindered if the virtual reality (VR) technology proves to be difficult to utilize or if the user deems it to lack utility. However, based on Technology Acceptance Model (TAM), the rate at which consumers adopt and accept new technologies, such as virtual reality (VR), is influenced by their perception of the technology's usefulness and simplicity of use [32]. The level of user-friendliness is correlated with the degree of proficiency needed to operate the novel technology with ease. Nevertheless, the concept of perceived ease of use is a subjective construct that is contingent upon various socio-demographic factors, including but not limited to the user's age, gender, level of education, occupation, and prior familiarity with the technology [20]. If it takes a large amount of time or expertise to learn how to use the new technology, users will be reluctant to adopt it and will not enjoy the process [33], which will lead to lower behavioural intentions. This series of arguments aids in the formulation of the subsequent hypothesis:

Hypothesis 3: The perception of virtual reality (VR) being easy to use has a beneficial impact on the perception of enjoyment and intentions to engage in travel.

The perceived utility of virtual reality (VR) technology is a significant determinant of individuals' satisfaction with and inclination to engage in this technology [34]. The concept of perceived usefulness refers to the utilitarian benefit that individuals derive from their utilization of technology, as described by Wei and Li [35]. The presence of technology that is deemed valuable and capable of fulfilling the user's needs has been found to positively influence perceived enjoyment and travel intentions [36–38]. Based on the preceding discourse, the ensuing proposition can be formulated as follows:

Hypothesis 4: The perceived usefulness of virtual reality (VR) exhibits a statistically significant positive impact on both perceived enjoyment and travel intentions.

2.3 COVID-19 Pandemic and Travel Intentions

Besides the mentioned technological barriers that marketers could experience when applying VR for promoting destinations, there are huge structural breaks in the tourism industry caused by the COVID-19 pandemic. When the pandemic started to spread, most countries introduced social distancing measures. The latter implied limitations on public gatherings and the minimum distance between people in public places [2, 15]. This practically meant restrictions on travel, dining in, movie theatres, and similar public activities [14, 16]. Not surprisingly, the tourism industry was among the worst hit by the pandemic [17].

Interestingly, social distancing is not only a regulatory response but also a volunteer measure that people, who have encountered with COVID-19 or are afraid of catching the disease, will impose on themselves [17]. Evidence shows that people continue to take precautionary measures such as social distancing even in the post-pandemic period when most travel bans have been lifted [27]. This long-term change in people's behaviour will have implications for travel intentions even in the post-pandemic period. Hence, the further hypothesis this article proposes is as follows:

H5: People practising social distancing will have lower travel intentions.

Protection Motivation Theory (PMT) helps predict which tourists are more likely to practice social distancing and, thus, have weaker travel intentions despite the VR technology's stimuli. PMT highlight the role of threat-appraisal and coping-appraisal elements in understanding health-linked intentions [39]. Threat appraisal assesses risk based on perceived severity and perceived susceptibility [40]. Perceived severity represents the perceived degree of harm to an individual linked to the event, while perceived susceptibility describes the perceived probability of the event happening [41]. In the context of the COVID-19 pandemic, perceived severity enhances as there is news of virus mutations and more lethal disease cases [42]. Upon hearing such news, people will respond by increasing social distancing and taking more precautionary measures. Perceived susceptibility increases during the pandemic when the number of people affected by the virus grows exponentially [43]. Conversely, when the number of new daily reported cases declines, perceived susceptibility declines and people may adopt more relaxed social distancing measures [44]. This discussion prompts the following hypothesis:

H6: Threat appraisal, comprised of perceived and perceived susceptibility, produces a positive effect on social distancing.

According to Rogers [40], coping appraisal involves response efficacy and self-efficacy. Response efficacy is the perception of the effectiveness of recommended risk prevention practices, while self-efficacy describes the perceived ability to adopt and exhibit such practices [45]. Tourists hold individual beliefs on the degree to which social distancing and similar policies effectively fight the threat. Thus, the more they believe in the efficacy of the measure, the more they will practice social distancing [46]. People also individually assess their ability to comply with the social distancing recommendations, and if they have a high enough level of self-efficacy, they will be more likely to adhere to social distancing [47]. Previous studies documented the positive role of both response efficacy and self-efficacy in stimulating protection behaviour concerning threats from human papillomavirus [48], natural disasters [49] and sexually transmitted diseases [50]. Based on this, the article expects these two coping appraisal types will also positively influence social distancing measures. Hence, the next hypothesis is as follows:

H7: Coping appraisal, comprised of response efficacy and self-efficacy, produces a positive effect on social distancing.

Applied to tourism and destination marketing, the PMT implies that the threat- and coping-appraisal processes would translate into risk-preventative behaviours, namely: social distancing, leading to travel avoidance or a shift from traditional tourism to ecotourism where social distancing is easier to preserve [16, 17]. As such, the influence of more effective marketing, such as VR tours, may be partially offset by health and safety concerns reflected in social distancing practices.

2.4 Moderating Role of Environmental Involvement

Another stream of research argues that people practising social distancing will prefer VR tours to actual visits for health-related reasons and environmental involvement [33]. Indeed, environmental involvement can be defined as the attitudes and actions of people towards preserving and protecting the natural environment [51]. If human visits to tourism locations are believed to cause harm to the natural environment, the people with higher environmental involvement will choose to visit the destinations in the VR world only and abstain from the actual travel. Conversely, Kim and Hall [52] argue that tourists with stronger hedonistic values and lower degree of environmental involvement will be prompted to visit the destination in real life after having enjoyed the VR experience. These arguments lead to the following hypothesis:

H8: At higher levels of environmental involvement, the relationship between perceived enjoyment and travel intentions will be weaker.

2.5 Telepresence and Social Distancing

While telepresence is expected to enhance perceived enjoyment among VR users, which many researchers believe should trigger tourist intentions [26, 28], they overlook one of the potential negative influences of telepresence. Previous studies document that technologies that offer a high level of telepresence and immersion of users facilitate the development of greater addiction and abuse of the use of the technology, which would have negative effects on social interaction and social activities in the real world [53]. For example, computer games can stimulate human cognitive functions [19] and contribute to psychological addiction [18]. The excessive use of social network sites similarly changes people's values, attitudes and behaviour [54]. On the one hand, the telepresence provided by VR can result in higher perceived enjoyment. On the other hand, this telepresence will contribute to developing a psychological addiction to this state, prompting users to spend more time in the virtual world rather than the real world, effectively making them social distance. Therefore, the ultimate hypothesis of this investigation is presented as follows:

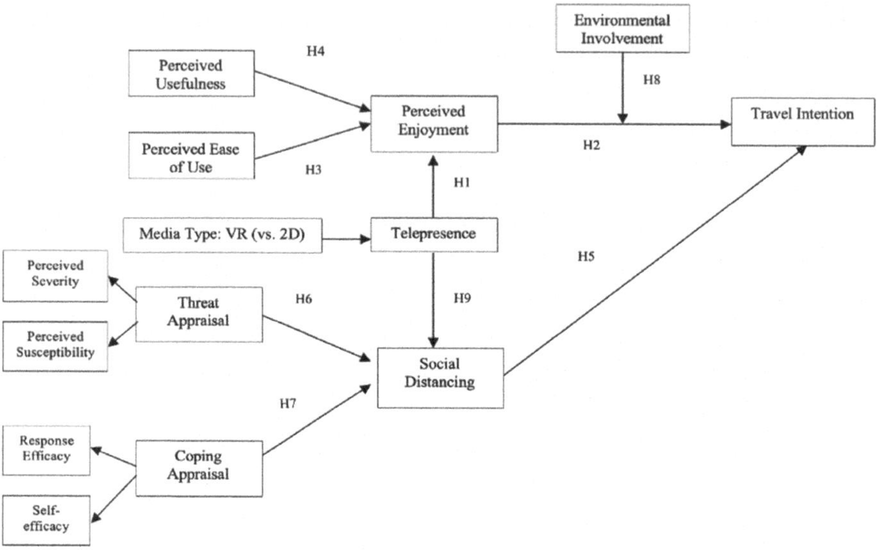

Fig.1 The conceptual model

H9: Telepresence from VR produces a positive effect on social distancing practices.

Based on the theories and existing literature mentioned above, the proposed hypotheses are summarised in conceptual model below (Fig. 1).

3 Research Methodology and Findings

The study employs structural equation modelling (SEM) to test the research hypotheses. A total of 260 individuals participated in the study, with 130 people randomized to the 2D treatment and another 130 participants assigned to the VR condition. A total of 249 respondents were included in the study, with 122 individuals seeing the film on a PC screen and 127 individuals watching the video on a virtual reality (VR) headset.

3.1 Measurement Model

Convergent validity was assessed by the utilization of many markers, including Cronbach's alpha, omega, and average variance explained (AVE). The findings are succinctly presented in Table 1. All constructs in the study exhibit alpha values that

Table 1 Convergent validity

Construct	Cronbach's alpha	Omega	AVE
TP	0.789	0.791	0.558
PU	0.912	0.912	0.675
PEU	0.835	0.836	0.560
PE	0.876	0.876	0.586
EI	0.831	0.832	0.554
TID	0.840	0.839	0.636
TIA	0.845	0.845	0.646
PSE	0.887	0.887	0.663
PSU	0.881	0.882	0.651
RE	0.869	0.870	0.690
SE	0.848	0.848	0.651
SD	0.904	0.905	0.543

surpass the established threshold of 0.70. Comparable findings are achieved for the omega measure. The average variance extracted (AVE) demonstrates a minimum value of 0.50 across all hidden variables. Nevertheless, there are other constructs that surpass the established barrier, such as telepresence, perceived ease of use, environmental participation, and social separation. However, the aforementioned data indicate that the constructs fulfil the criteria of reliability and convergent validity. Put simply, the objects that align with each concept have a tendency to be interconnected, hence bolstering the notion that they gauge some underlying latent factor.

Table 2 displays the outcomes obtained from the implementation of the HTMT ratio criterion for assessing discriminant validity. According to the criterion, it is necessary for the HTMT ratio between two constructions to be below 0.90. The latent variable pairings that displayed strong correlations also coincide with the highest ratios, often ranging from 0.6 to 0.7. As such, discriminant validity is determined among every combination of included constructs.

Finally, possible multicollinearity issues are investigated by considering the Variance Inflation Factors (VIFs) for variables that directly or indirectly explain travel intention (Table 3). None of the VIFs exceed the cut-off value of 3.3 [55], which suggests that the model is free of multicollinearity and common method bias. The largest VIF of 2.68 is estimated for the Social Distancing construct, which indicates a relatively high degree of collinearity with other covariates. This may be due to the Social Distancing construct being indirectly explained by four latent variables: Perceived Severity, Perceived Susceptibility, Self-Efficacy, and Response Efficacy.

In conclusion, the measuring approach utilized in the current investigation demonstrates evidence of validity. Variables that are related share similarities in their underlying constructions, whereas unique constructs can be easily distinguished from one another. Once construct validity has been proven, it is suitable to estimate the structural model of intentions to travel using the latent variables that have been created.

Table 2 Discriminant validity (heterotrait–monotrait ratio)

Construct	TP	PU	PEU	PE	EI	TID	TIA	PSE	PSU	RE	SE	SD
TP	1.000											
PU	0.392	1.000										
PEU	0.066	0.071	1.000									
PE	0.291	0.297	0.225	1.000								
EI	0.387	0.069	0.068	0.082	1.000							
TID	0.071	0.055	0.033	0.411	0.160	1.000						
TIA	0.145	0.070	0.060	0.419	0.503	0.584	1.000					
PSE	0.157	0.061	0.128	0.076	0.070	0.060	0.044	1.000				
PSU	0.189	0.083	0.100	0.073	0.131	0.157	0.061	0.698	1.000			
RE	0.040	0.054	0.069	0.068	0.073	0.069	0.055	0.255	0.253	1,000		
SE	0.090	0.087	0.070	0.066	0.055	0.099	0.119	0.260	0.239	0.633	1.000	
SD	0.166	0.082	0.052	0.121	0.080	0.599	0.178	0.323	0.212	0.320	0.316	1.000

Table 3 Multicollinearity test

Construct	VIF
TP	1.642
PU	1.379
PEU	1.115
PE	1.772
EI	1.851
PSE	2.161
PSU	2.290
RE	1.787
SE	1.778
SD	2.683

3.2 Structural Model

Table 4 summarizes the direction of effects and route coefficients, while the assessment of the goodness of fit of the final model in relation to other models was previously supplied.

The structural model exhibits significant coefficients for seven out of nine variables, indicating support for seven original hypotheses whereas two hypotheses are not supported by the findings. Specifically, the findings do not provide evidence for the influence of environmental participation in the relationship between perceived satisfaction and travel intentions. Consistent with anticipated outcomes, the influence of perceived satisfaction on travel intentions is found to be positive, regardless of individuals' level of environmental engagement.

Table 4 Structural model: goodness-of-fit

Effects	Coefficient	Std. error	z	p-value
PE—TI	0.468***	0.080	5.879	0.000
PE*EI -> TI	0.001	0.075	0.009	0.993
SD—TI	−0.478***	0.073	−6.568	0.000
PU —» PE	0.143**	0.062	2.315	0.021
PEU—PE	0.185***	0.065	2.829	0.005
TP—PE	−0.008	0.082	−0.100	0.920
TP SD	0.207**	0.083	2.496	0.013
TA-»SD	0.170**	0.068	2.501	0.012
CA-» SD	0.270***	0.067	4.027	0.000

Notes: * $p < 0.10$; ** $p < 0.05$; *** $p < 0.01$

Another hypothesis that lacked validation was the influence of telepresence on the perception of enjoyment. The findings fail to demonstrate this effect's statistical significance, showing that these two constructs are relatively independent. However, we do have support of the hypothesis that telepresence produces a positive effect on social distancing, and social distancing negatively affects travel intentions. These results have strong implications for the tourism industry in the post-pandemic period. During the pandemic, the two constructs for coping appraisal and threat appraisal based on the Protection Motivation Theory hold; however, the effect can be expected to diminish when the pandemic ends.

In contrast, the significant positive effect of telepresence on social distancing will persist as telepresence is independent of threat appraisal and coping appraisal. The absence of a significant enhancement in enjoyment through telepresence suggests that VR serves more as an alternative to actual travel than as an efficient tool for endorsing genuine nature-centric locations. Consequently, tourism enterprises might consider developing comprehensive VR journeys to offer as replacements for tangible trips, rather than generating brief marketing content for VR platforms.

4 Contributions

4.1 Theoretical Contribution

The key purpose of this study was to assess the use of VR as a tool for destination marketing of sustainable tourism during the COVID-19 pandemic. Numerous past research efforts have highlighted that telepresence is a distinguishing characteristic of VR compared to other 2D technologies. This feature has the potential to enhance the marketing efficiency of the VR platform when promoting eco-friendly travel destinations [30]. This study has extended the previous findings by reporting alternative channels through which telepresence can affect tourist behaviour and their ultimate travel intentions. In particular, this research provides support for a theoretical argument that telepresence can positively contribute to social distancing practices, which the recent pandemic has also reinforced. However, in contrast to the short-term effects of threat appraisal and coping appraisal on social distancing, as predicted by PMT [41], this study argues that telepresence will have lasting effects on voluntary social distancing as people will prefer the flow state of being in VR to actual visits to destinations. Therefore, our research adds to the existing knowledge of by illustrating that in addition to telepresence's beneficial impact on image creation [11], enjoyment [38] and ultimate travel behaviour [26, 28], VR-induced telepresence also contributes to social distancing, which reduces the travel behaviour.

This article also has practical implications. Instead of shooting short promotional VR videos of tourist destinations to advertise actual travel, tourism businesses should rather focus on producing full-scale virtual tours that can be sold as standalone products to customers. This strategy will be a winner not only during the period of the pandemic when people are restricted from travelling but also in the post-pandemic time, as telepresence can allow people to experience nearly the same emotions as during the actual trip but at lower cost and lower effort.

Contrary to several studies suggesting that VR-enhanced telepresence can amplify enjoyment due to heightened image clarity [24] and interactivity [37], this study documents that telepresence is independent of perceived enjoyment. On the one hand, the discrepancy between the findings can be explained by the lack of agreement among researchers on the best way to describe perceived enjoyment, with some arguing that it should reflect the enjoyment of the VR experience [34, 36] and others asserting that it should indicate anticipated enjoyment from a future or potential visit to the shown destination [11]. The lack of a significant link between telepresence and perceived enjoyment reported in this study can be explained by the argument that in VR, people can experience similar emotions as in the real world as similar senses are engaged. Thus, the level of enjoyment will depend on what they view in VR, and these emotions can vary even though the state of telepresence remains the same. By clarifying these exciting findings, the study is helpful in contributing to the existing literature on destination marketing and sustainable tourism.

4.2 Practical Contribution

The insights garnered have multiple implications for tourist destinations. Firstly, the data suggests that tourist spots can benefit from offering VR-enhanced excursions, potentially offsetting some revenue losses incurred due to the COVID-19 crisis. It's also apparent that destinations planning to operate amidst the pandemic (prior to the roll-out of an effective treatment or vaccine) can expect diminished footfall, a reasonable expectation considering the mandatory social distancing measures. Therefore, these spots are encouraged to develop and promote VR-enhanced tours as a strategy to boost visitations during these challenging times.

Virtual reality, when utilized optimally, can serve as a potent instrument for tourism marketing. Past studies, including those by Leung et al. [9], Wu and Lai [10], Skard et al. [11], and Zheng e al. [12], highlight its efficacy in bolstering intentions to visit. Our counsel revolves around enriching VR offerings. For instance, industry professionals could look to heighten the anticipated pleasure of viewers by integrating more engaging interactive VR elements into promotional videos, devising immersive VR scenarios that augment the overall experience, or crafting VR simulations of traditional events and festivities. Incorporating VR tools and 360-degree visualizations into official websites and mobile apps can furnish potential visitors with pertinent and captivating details.

Lastly, the value proposition of VR-enhanced tours isn't limited to the pandemic era. Post-pandemic, such virtual visits remain beneficial for those desiring a preliminary glimpse of a destination, those keen on experiencing destinations from their homes, individuals constrained by factors like finances from touring exotic places, or those hindered by physical challenges, as noted by Lin et al. [21]. Offering VR tours can thereby cater to a broader audience base, ensuring a more sustainable footprint. These virtual excursions also offer the advantage of accommodating countless visitors simultaneously, sidestepping issues like prolonged wait times or ticketing fraud that physical tours might encounter.

5 Limitations and Further Studies

This research has certain limitations that can be addressed in subsequent studies. Firstly, our participants were mainly students from higher education institutions, which might restrict the broader applicability of our findings. Factors such as age, academic background, and job status can significantly sway travel inclinations and habits. This raises questions about the universality of our conclusions in different settings. Additionally, our primary data-gathering tool was a survey. Given that it captures anticipated travel actions based on personal declarations and not on actual purchasing behaviours, real-world decisions might vary from those indicated. This highlights the typical disparity between expressed preferences and actual behavioural outcomes. Moreover, there is a limitation of the sample size associated with the difficulties of surveying many people during the COVID-19 pandemic when restrictions on social gatherings were enforced. The conclusions of this study are made based on the analysis of 249 responses. Previous studies often disagree on the best criteria for choosing the minimum sample size, with some arguing that the minimum sample size should be determined as a rule of thumb with the consideration of 5–10 responses per estimated parameter [56], while others arguing that more precise criteria such as power tests should be used [57, 58]. This study used the lower bound test of Westland [59], targeting the anticipated effect size of 0.3, desired power of 0.8 and a conventional significance level of 0.05 with nine latent variables and 49 observed variables. This test resulted in the lower bound for the minimum sample size to be 184 observations. This number of observations should be sufficient to detect effects. The final sample resulted in 249 observations, which exceeds this lower bound; however, alternative tests and rules of thumb can demonstrate different outcomes for the minimum sample size. Lastly, the current model doesn't offer a quantifiable willingness-to-pay metric that would be beneficial for policymakers. Future studies could tackle these shortcomings by exploring a more diverse demographic sample and employing actual behaviour analysis to determine how utilizing VR in destination promotion might influence the readiness to pay for sustainable tourism.

References

1. World Travel & Tourism Council—WTTC: https://wttc.org/, Corona virus brief April 14, 2020. Last accessed 30 July 2022
2. Schiopu, A.F., Hornoiu, R.I., Padurean, M.A., Nica, A.M.: Virus tinged? Exploring the facets of virtual reality use in tourism as a result of the COVID-19 pandemic. Telematics Inform. **60**, 101575 (2021)
3. Maseeh, H.I., Jebarajakirthy, C., Pentecost, R., Ashaduzzaman, M., Arli, D., Weaven, S.: A meta-analytic review of mobile advertising research. J. Bus. Res. **136**, 33–51 (2021)
4. Colombo, V., Aliverti, A., Sacco, M.: Virtual reality for COPD rehabilitation: a technological perspective. Pulmonology **28**(2), 119–133 (2022)
5. Lee, M., Lee, S.A., Jeong, M., Oh, H.: Quality of virtual reality and its impacts on behavioral intention. Int. J. Hosp. Manage. **90**, 102595 (2020)
6. Statista, Augmented reality (AR), virtual reality (VR), and mixed reality (MR) market size worldwide in 2021 and 2028 (2022): https://www.statista.com/statistics/591181/global-augmented-virtual-reality-market-size/. Last accessed 04 Nov 2022
7. Xi, N., Hamari, J.: Shopping in virtual reality: a literature review and future agenda. J. Bus. Res. **134**, 37–58 (2021)
8. Perry Hobson, J.S., Williams, A.P.: Virtual reality: a new horizon for the tourism industry. J. Vacat. Mark. **1**(2), 124–135 (1995)
9. Leung, X.Y., Lyu, J., Bai, B.: A fad or the future? Examining the effectiveness of virtual reality advertising in the hotel industry. Int. J. Hosp. Manage. **88**, 102391 (2020)
10. Wu, X., Lai, I.K.W.: Identifying the response factors in the formation of a sense of presence and a destination image from a 360-degree virtual tour. J. Destin. Mark. Manage. **21**, 100640 (2021)
11. Skard, S., Knudsen, E.S., Sjåstad, H., Thorbjørnsen, H.: How virtual reality influences travel intentions: the role of mental imagery and happiness forecasting. Tour. Manage. **87**, 104360 (2021)
12. Zheng, C., Chen, Z., Zhang, Y., Guo, Y.: Does vivid imagination deter visitation? The role of mental imagery processing in virtual tourism on tourists' behavior. J. Travel Res. **61**(7), 1528–1541 (2022)
13. Chang, H.H.: Virtual reality, YouTube, or social media? Assessing promotional effects on tourism destination. J. Vacat. Mark. **28**(2), 211–227 (2022)
14. Medai, N., Wu, L.: A study of determinants that affect the intention to participate in online tours and the role of constraints under COVID-19 pandemic. Curr. Issue Tour. **26**(7), 1132–1146 (2023)
15. Rather, R.A.: Demystifying the effects of perceived risk and fear on customer engagement, co-creation and revisit intention during COVID-19: a protection motivation theory approach. J. Destin. Mark. Manage. **20**, 100564 (2021)
16. Wen, H., Liu-Lastres, B.: Consumers' dining behaviors during the COVID-19 pandemic: an application of the protection motivation theory and the safety signal framework. J. Hosp. Tour. Manage. **51**, 187–195 (2022)

17. Nazneen, S., Xu, H., Din, N.U., Karim, R.: Perceived COVID-19 impacts and travel avoidance: application of protection motivation theory. Tour. Rev. **77**(2), 471–483 (2021)
18. Inoue, K., Fujita, Y., Takeshita, H., Hashioka, S., Kamura, M.: The use of video games, smartphones, and PCs/tablet PCs based on a survey of students' lifestyles: necessary actions. Public Health **205**, 43–44 (2022)
19. Reynaldo, C., Christian, R., Hosea, H., Gunawan, A.A.: Using video games to improve capabilities in decision making and cognitive skill: a literature review. Procedia Comput. Sci. **179**, 211–222 (2021)
20. Zhang, M., Shu, L., Luo, X., Yuan, M., Zheng, X.: Virtual reality technology in construction safety training: extended technology acceptance model. Autom. Constr. **135**, 104113 (2022)
21. Lin, L.P.L., Huang, S.C.L., Ho, Y.C.: Could virtual reality effectively market slow travel in a heritage destination? Tour. Manage. **78**, 104027 (2020)
22. Kim, J.H., Kim, M., Park, M., Yoo, J.: How interactivity and vividness influence consumer virtual reality shopping experience: the mediating role of telepresence. J. Res. Interact. Mark. **15**(3), 502–525 (2021)
23. Tussyadiah, I.P., Wang, D., Jung, T. H., Tom Dieck, M.C.: Virtual reality, presence, and attitude change: empirical evidence from tourism. Tour. Manage. **66**, 140–154 (2018)
24. Wu, J., Song, S., Whang, C.H.: Personalizing 3D virtual fashion stores: exploring modularity with a typology of atmospherics based on user input. Inf. Manage. **58**(4), 103461 (2021)
25. Ying, T., Tang, J., Ye, S., Tan, X., Wei, W.: Virtual reality in destination marketing: telepresence, social presence, and tourists' visit intentions. J. Travel Res. **61**(8), 1738–1756 (2022)
26. Wu, D.Y., Lin, J.H.T., Bowman, N.D.: Watching VR advertising together: How 3D animated agents influence audience responses and enjoyment to VR advertising. Comput. Hum. Behav. **133**, 107255 (2022)
27. Li, Y., Kim, H.J., Do, B., Choi, J.: The effect of emotion in thumbnails and titles of video clips on pre-roll advertising effectiveness. J. Bus. Res. **151**, 232–243 (2022)
28. Han, S.L., An, M., Han, J.J., Lee, J.: Telepresence, time distortion, and consumer traits of virtual reality shopping. J. Bus. Res. **118**, 311–320 (2020)
29. Loureiro, S.M.C., Guerreiro, J., Japutra, A.: How escapism leads to behavioral intention in a virtual reality store with background music? J. Bus. Res. **134**, 288–300 (2021)
30. Hammady, R., Ma, M., Strathearn, C.: Ambient information visualisation and visitors' technology acceptance of mixed reality in museums. J. Comput. Cultural Heritage (JOCCH) **13**(2), 1–22 (2020)
31. Sancho-Esper, F., Ostrovskaya, L., Rodriguez-Sanchez, C., Campayo-Sanchez, F.: Virtual reality in retirement communities: technology acceptance and tourist destination recommendation. J. Vacat. Mark. **29**(2), 275–290 (2023)
32. Israel, K., Zerres, C., Tscheulin, D.K.: Presenting hotels in virtual reality: does it influence the booking intention? J. Hosp. Tour. Technol. **10**(3), 443–463 (2019)
33. Schiopu, A.F., Hornoiu, R.I., Padurean, A.M., Nica, A.M.: Constrained and virtually traveling? Exploring the effect of travel constraints on intention to use virtual reality in tourism. Technol. Soc. **71**, 102091 (2022)
34. Zhang, X., Guo, X., Wu, Y., Lai, K.H., Vogel, D.: Exploring the inhibitors of online health service use intention: a status quo bias perspective. Inf. Manage. **54**(8), 987–997 (2017)
35. Wei, N., Li, Z.: Telepresence and interactivity in mobile learning system: its relation with open innovation. J. Open Innov.: Technol., Market, Complexity **7**(1), 78 (2021)
36. Trunfio, M., Jung, T., Campana, S.: Mixed reality experiences in museums: exploring the impact of functional elements of the devices on visitors' immersive experiences and post-experience behaviours. Inf. Manage. **59**(8), 103698 (2022)
37. Cowan, K., Ketron, S.: A dual model of product involvement for effective virtual reality: the roles of imagination, co-creation, telepresence, and interactivity. J. Bus. Res. **100**, 483–492 (2019)
38. Holdack, E., Lurie-Stoyanov, K., Fromme, H.F.: The role of perceived enjoyment and perceived informativeness in assessing the acceptance of AR wearables. J. Retail. Consum. Serv. **65**, 102259 (2022)

39. Seow, A.N., Choong, C.K., Chen, I.C., Choong, Y.O.: Can protection motivation theory explain the perception of international tourists' on medical tourism? J. Hosp. Tour. Insights **5**(2), 394–412 (2022)
40. Rogers, R.W.: A protection motivation theory of fear appeals and attitude change1. J. Psychol. **91**(1), 93–114 (1975)
41. Seow, A.N., Choong, Y.O., Choong, C.K., Moorthy, K.: Health tourism: behavioural intention and protection motivation theory. Tour. Rev. **77**(2), 376–393 (2022)
42. Fragkaki, I., Maciejewski, D.F., Weijman, E.L., Feltes, J., Cima, M.: Human responses to Covid-19: the role of optimism bias, perceived severity, and anxiety. Personality Individ. Differ. **176**, 110781 (2021)
43. Raza, S.A., Zhang, X., Oluyomi, A., Adepoju, O.E., King, B., Amos, C.I., Badr, H.: Predictors of COVID-19 perceived susceptibility: insights from population-based self-reported survey during lockdown in the United States. J. Infect. Public Health **15**(5), 508–514 (2022)
44. Wong, R., Grullon, J.R., Lovier, M.A.: COVID-19 risk factors and predictors for handwashing, masking, and social distancing among a national prospective cohort of US older adults. Public Health **211**, 164–170 (2022)
45. Ruan, W., Kang, S., Song, H.: Applying protection motivation theory to understand international tourists' behavioural intentions under the threat of air pollution: a case of Beijing, China. Curr. Issues Tour. **23**(16), 2027–2041 (2020)
46. Chang, T.S.: Social distancing in retail: Influence of perceived retail crowding and self-efficacy on employees' perceived risks. J. Retail. Consum. Serv. **62**, 102613 (2021)
47. Kim, Y.R., Liu, A.: Social distancing, trust and post-COVID-19 recovery. Tour. Manage. **88**, 104416 (2022)
48. Myhre, A., Xiong, T., Vogel, R.I., Teoh, D.: Associations between risk-perception, self-efficacy and vaccine response-efficacy and parent/guardian decision-making regarding adolescent HPV vaccination. Papillomavirus Res. **10**, 100204 (2020)
49. Gumasing, M.J.J., Prasetyo, Y.T., Ong, A.K.S., Nadlifatin, R.: Determination of factors affecting the response efficacy of Filipinos under Typhoon Conson 2021 (Jolina): an extended protection motivation theory approach. Int. J. Disaster Risk Reduction **70**, 102759 (2022)
50. Jin, S.S., Kai, B.U., Chen, F.F., Xu, H.F., Yi, L.I., Zhao, D.H., Fang, X.U., Li, J.Y., Han, M.J., Ning, W.A.N.G., Lu, W.A.N.G.: Correlates of condom-use self-efficacy on the EPPM-based integrated model among Chinese college students. Biomed. Environ. Sci. **30**(2), 97–105 (2017)
51. Sánchez, M.R., Palos-Sanchez, P.R., Velicia-Martin, F.: Eco-friendly performance as a determining factor of the adoption of virtual reality applications in national parks. Sci. Total Environ. **798**, 148990 (2021)
52. Kim, M.J., Hall, C.M.: Can sustainable restaurant practices enhance customer loyalty? The roles of value theory and environmental concerns. J. Hosp. Tour. Manage. **43**, 127–138 (2020)
53. Stavropoulos, V., Alexandraki, K., Motti-Stefanidi, F.: Flow and telepresence contributing to Internet abuse: differences according to gender and age. Comput. Hum. Behav. **29**(5), 1941–1948 (2013)
54. Stănculescu, E., Griffiths, M.D.: Social media addiction profiles and their antecedents using latent profile analysis: the contribution of social anxiety, gender, and age. Telematics Inform. **74**, 101879 (2022)
55. Kock, N.: Common method bias in PLS-SEM: a full collinearity assessment approach. Int. J. e-Collaboration (ijec) **11**(4), 1–10 (2015)
56. Nicolaou, A.I., Masoner, M.M.: Sample size requirements in structural equation models under standard conditions. Int. J. Account. Inf. Syst. **14**(4), 256–274 (2013)
57. MacCallum, R.C., Browne, M.W., Sugawara, H.M.: Power analysis and determination of sample size for covariance structure modeling. Psychol. Methods **1**(2), 130 (1996)
58. Saris, W.E., Satorra, A.: Power evaluations in structural equation models. In: Bollen, K.A., Long, J.S. (eds.) Testing Structural Equation Models. Sage, Newbury Park, CA (1993)
59. Westland, J.C.: Lower bounds on sample size in structural equation modeling. Electron. Commer. Res. Appl. **9**(6), 476–487 (2010)

Intention to Accept Smart Contracts Based on Blockchain Technology in Vietnamese Businesses

Thi Hong Nhung Vo, The Huu Chau, and Quan Tri Dang

Abstract Blockchain technology's recent rapid growth has caused a significant impact on several industries such as logistics, banking, and construction. Since its introduction in 1994 through up to the present, smart contracts based on decentralized ledger data have assisted businesses in resolving several unresolved issues between parties engaged in cooperative activities. Therefore, this study aims to identify the variables influencing firms' intentions to use smart contracts in Vietnam. It has been confirmed from the research that considerable influence on Vietnamese enterprises' intention to accept smart contracts use is demonstrated through three out of nine hypotheses, i.e. Government support (GOV), Trading Partner Pressure (TPP), and Relative advantage (ADV), whose levels of impact decrease, respectively. The study's limitation lies in its focus on some specific places in spite of the country's large territory and the number of respondents to the survey. It is suggested that future research should take these two factors into consideration for more significant findings.

Keywords Smart contracts · Blockchain · TOE framework · Use intention

1 Introduction

Research on the Function of Corporate Governance in Corporate Social and Environmental Responsibility claims that Disclosure, a crucial component of corporate governance [1–3]. Currently, according to PRNewswire, E-commerce and technology activities are forecasted to grow at a real CAGR in the period 2020–2025 of 5.1% [4]. In short, this will not only help Vietnamese businesses, and readers

T. H. N. Vo · Q. T. Dang
Faculty of Business Administration, HCMC University of Foreign Languages–Information Technology, Ho Chi Minh, Vietnam

T. H. Chau (✉)
HCMC University of Foreign Languages—Information Technology, Ho Chi Minh City, Vietnam
e-mail: huuct@huflit.edu.vn

Department of Business Adminstration, National Chengchi University, Taipei, Taiwan

L. T. Tung et al. (eds.), *Disruptive Technology and Business Continuity*,
https://doi.org/10.1007/978-981-97-5452-6_9

raise awareness when applying smart contracts but also have the most complete preparation when implementing the application.

2 Literature Review

2.1 *Smart Contract Based on Blockchain Technology*

Smart contracts were first proposed in the 1990s, as an automated transaction method for executing contract terms [5]. A smart contract can automatically execute the terms of a legal contract without human intervention [6]. Specifically, SC is seen as a hash-encrypted container of information. Indeed, in today's trusted payments environment, the adoption of SC is said to be still at the forefront of business processes [6, 7].

2.2 *Technology-Organization-Environment Framework (TOE)*

As technology advances, more and more studies and models explore behavioral intention using new technology. Several theories have been developed to test this new application such as the Technology Acceptance Model (TAM) [8], Technology-Organization- Environment Theory (TOE), Unified Theory of Technology Adoption and Use (UTAUT) [9], Theory of Planned Behavior (TPB) [10]. This study will further complete the factors affecting the intention to accept Smart contracts in enterprises in Vietnam.

3 Conceptual Model and Hypothesis Formulation

According to the TOE model, the study proposes a model based on hypothetical perceptions of the levels when an enterprise decides to adopt smart contract implementation, this model includes three decisive factors: technological, organizational, and environmental contexts. The related structures will be presented in this research model.

3.1 Technological Characteristics—Related Factors and Smart Contract Adoption Intentions

According to the Diffusion of Innovation Theory (DOI), there are five primary criteria that determine whether technological innovation succeeds or fails: Relative Advantage, Compatibility, Complexity, Trialability, and Observability [11]. Relative advantage is defined by Rogers as the degree to which a new innovation is thought to be superior than the concept, scheme, or item it replaces [11].

Hypothesis 1 (H1). Relative advantage is positively associated with SC adoption intention.

The degree to which an invention is consistent with the values, experiences, and requirements of potential adopters is known as compatibility [11]. Compatibility with corporate beliefs is also a factor to consider.

Hypothesis 2 (H2). Compatibility is positively associated with SC adoption intention.

The third factor influencing technological innovation is complexity. According to Technological Diffusion, complexity is an innovation that is difficult to understand or use [11]. Indeed, uncertainty and technological complexity can hinder their adoption [6].

Hypothesis 3 (H3). Complexity is positively associated with SC adoption intention.

Observability, also known as the fourth element influencing technological innovation, is understood as the degree to which innovation yields measurable outcomes [11]. The following theory is put out in light of the observations made above:

Hypothesis 4 (H4). Observability is positively associated with SC adoption intention.

3.2 Organizational Characteristics—Related Factors and Smart Contract Adoption Intentions

According to research on factors affecting an organization's readiness for change, including Top Management Support and Organizational Readiness [12, 13], Top Management Support is considered the most important factor leading to the success of innovation [14]. Therefore, the study proposes the following hypothesis:

Hypothesis 5 (H5). Top Management Support is positively associated with SC adoption intention.

The second factor is organizational readiness. This is defined as the availability of necessary resources within the business [15]. Therefore, the study proposes the hypothesis:

Hypothesis 6 (H6). Organizational Readiness is positively associated with SC adoption intention.

3.3 Environmental Characteristics—Related Factors and Smart Contract Adoption Intentions

According to research on environmental factors affecting the intention to adopt new technology [16], these factors include Competitive Pressure, Government Support, and Trading Partner Pressure. Suggested comments are as follows:

Hypothesis 7 (H7). Competitive Pressure is positively associated with SC adoption intention.

The second factor is government support. This is demonstrated through guidance and support from the government such as technical training, knowledge enhancement seminars, and innovation funding [17]. As a result, this study suggests the following:

Hypothesis 8 (H8). Government Support is positively associated with SC adoption intention.

The third factor affecting the intention to adopt innovation is trading partner pressure. Several studies have emphasized the importance of business partners in putting innovation into practice [12, 18]. Therefore, the conjecture hypothesis is formed:

Hypothesis 9 (H9). Trading Partner Pressure is positively associated with SC adoption intention.

4 Research Methodology

4.1 Sample and Procedure

In this study, the target sample is determined based on people working in enterprises using traditional contracts in Vietnam. In addition, G*Power 3.1 software was additionally used to calculate the required sample size [19]. The results show that for the study determining the minimum sample with an effect size $f2 = 0.15$, probability of error $\alpha = 0.05$ and power level (1-β error probability) $= 0.8$ and the number of predictors $= 9$, so the size of the recommended minimum sample is 111.

4.2 Instrument Development

The survey is based on a linear range questionnaire and is divided into two parts. The first part describes the demographics of the study population. The second part is structural measurement questions on the linear range. The questionnaire is built on a 7-point Likert scale because it tended to produce better data distributions. Therefore, using a 7-point Likert scale from (1) Strongly Disagree to (7) Strongly Agree was appropriate in this study.

4.3 Pre-test and Pilot Test

The questionnaire is designed based on the theoretical framework of Technology—Organization and Environment Environment, as well as reviewing relevant documents that have been done before. Excluding the demographic section, the survey with a total of 29 questions was used. First, survey questions were conducted by the operator and two instructors. They assisted practitioners to enhance relevance to the research context. Through the testing process, potential problems in data processing would be eliminated by reality. Second, the study runs a test sample of a survey panel with 316 samples on a 7-level Likert scale. And a panel experiment was once again conducted, based on subjects not included in the survey sample. Through the second test, the experimenter will be asked about the problem they encountered while performing the test. And finally, the survey was adjusted to better match the actual survey (see Table 1).

4.4 Common Method Bias

The questionnaire used to collect data is based on a validated scale and has been used in previous studies. The results show that a single factor explains only 32.451% of the variance of the data and is less than 50% of the threshold recommended by Podsakoff and Organ (1986). This indicates no serious problems for the CMB. The data are regarded as genuine and reliable to perform regression analysis based on the aforementioned tests.

Table 1 Construct, measurement

Construct	Measurement items	Sources
Part 1: technology characteristics		
	Relative advantage (three items)	
ADV1	A smart contract reduces transaction costs and makes business more efficient	[9]
ADV2	A smart contract enhances trust among contract stakeholders	
ADV3	A smart contract reduces the execution time of the contract process	
	Compatibility (three items)	
CPT1	A smart contract is compatible with existing contract management systems and administrative procedures in the enterprise	[9, 14]
CPT2	A smart contract fits our corporate culture	
CPT3	A smart contract in line with enterprise business practices	
	Complexity (three items)	
CPX1	A smart contract is easy to understand	[13]
CPX2	A smart contract is easy to use and manage documents	
CPX3	A smart contract is easily integrated with existing contracts in the enterprise through a programming language	
	Observability (three items)	
OSB1	The positive effects of using smart contracts are easily observed	[13]
OSB2	We observe many other organizations using smart contracts	
OSB3	I have a good understanding of the positive impact of smart contracts	
Part 2: organization characteristics		

(continued)

Table 1 (continued)

Construct	Measurement items	Sources
	Top management support (two items)	
TMS2	Top management communicates its support to employees about the benefits smart contracts can bring	[13]
TMS3	Senior leadership has set goals and provided enough resources for employees to adopt smart contracts	
	Organizational readiness (three items)	
ORG1	My organization has the necessary resources such as IT systems, a team of technicians with a lot of experience to apply smart contracts	[19]
ORG2	Current technologies in my enterprise are suitable for smart contract adoption	
ORG3	The IT staff in my business have the skills and experience to support the adoption of smart contracts	
Part 3. environment characteristics		
	Competitive pressure (three items)	
COP1	Using smart contracts will give my organization a competitive edge over competitors	[14]
COP2	My organization will be at a competitive disadvantage if a smart contract is not passed	
COP3	Using smart contract will allow to generate more profit for my organization	
	Government support (three items)	
GOV1	The government provides seminars and courses on smart contracts for businesses	[19]

(continued)

Table 1 (continued)

Construct	Measurement items	Sources
GOV2	The government has conducted seminars to solicit opinions on improving the legal framework on the economy and improving the efficiency of law enforcement	
GOV3	Government agencies are helping businesses market their products and services	
	Trading partner pressure (two items)	
TPP2	My organization's partners require the adoption of smart contracts in their operations	[14, 19]
TPP3	My organization is under pressure from business partners to adopt smart contracts	
Part 4: smart contract adoption intention		
USI1	My organization intends to use smart contract in digital transformation	[17]
USI2	My organization intends to actively introduce smart contracts to others	
USI3	We plan to use smart contract in the future	

5 Data Analysis and Result

5.1 Assessing the Outer Measurement Model

This study evaluated the reliability of the study through standardized Composite Reliability (CR) and Cronbach's Alpha (CA), and this validity was validated through assembly and discriminant validity. According to previous studies, CR, and CA values $\geq$0.7 are considered reliable and consistent . In Table 4, CR is greater than the threshold value of 0.7, demonstrating the measurement model's high dependability. The lowest AVE value is 0.616, which is also greater than the minimum 0.5.

Table 2 Model's fitness

	Saturated model	Estimated model
SRMR	0.039	0.039
d_ULS	0.656	0.656
d_G	0.319	0.319
Chi-square	568.454	568.454
NFI	0.889	0.889

5.2 *Inspecting the Model Fit and the Inner Structural Model*

The study uses the Standardized Root Mean Square Residual (SRMR) and Normed Fit Index (NFI) to evaluate the fit of both the model through saturated models and the estimated. These indicators are evaluated for approximate fit with a certain threshold of NFI > 0.90 and SRMR < 0.08. Normed Fit Index (NFI) value is considered as one of the normalized fit indexes, according to Table 2, the NFI value is 0.889 < 0.90 compared to the recommended level. This shows that the fit of the model in the study is satisfied (Tables 3, 4 and 5).

Table 4 shows 3 out of 9 supported hypotheses. When the T-statistic > 1.96 at the 95% confidence level (α=0.05), the relationship is significant in the study. Therefore, H1 is accepted to support; and H2, H3, H4 are not supported. In addition, regarding the Organizational context,neither Top Management Support (t= 1.111, ρ > 0.05) nor Organizational Readiness (t= 1.145, ρ > 0.05) does not support the intent to use smart contracts. On the other hand, Table 2 shows that the Root Mean Square Error (RMSE) is consistent with those in the linear model criteria.

Table 6 shows three out of nine supported hypotheses. When the T-statistic >1.96 at the 95% confidence level ($\alpha = 0.05$), the relationship is significant in the study. Therefore, H1 is accepted to support; and H2, H3, H4 are not supported. In addition, regarding the Organizational context, neither Top Management Support ($t = 1.111$, $\rho > 0.05$) nor Organizational Readiness ($t = 1.145$, $\rho > 0.05$) does not support the intent to use smart contracts. On the other hand, Table 7 shows that the Root Mean Square Error (RMSE) is consistent with those in the linear model criteria.

Table 3 Collinearity statistics (VIF)

	ADV1	**ADV2**	**ADV3**	**COP1**	**COP2**	**COP3**	**CPT1**	**CPT2**
VIF	1.512	1.954	1.734	1.853	1.878	1.643	1.565	1.705
	CPT3	**CPX1**	**CPX2**	**CPX3**	**GOV1**	**GOV2**	**GOV3**	**ORG1**
VIF	1.582	1.462	1.802	1.493	1.432	1.564	1.434	1.420
	ORG2	**ORG3**	**OSB1**	**OSB2**	**OSB3**	**TMS2**	**TMS3**	**TPP1**
VIF	1.597	1.440	1.461	1.812	1.488	1.347	1.347	1.371
	TPP2	**TPP3**	**USI1**	**USI2**	**USI3**			
VIF	1.552	1.267	1.557	1.529	1.484			

Table 4 Loading, composite reliability, Cronbach's alpha, and average variance extracted

Latent constructs	Items	Loadings	Cronbach's alpha (CA)	Composite reliability	Average variance extracted (AVE)
ADV	ADV1	0.822	0.790	0.870	0.692
	ADV2	0.795			
	ADV3	0.876			
CPT	CPT1	0.846	0.777	0.863	0.679
	CPT2	0.754			
	CPT3	0.867			
CPX	CPX1	0.833	0.753	0.851	0.657
	CPX2	0.778			
	CPX3	0.819			
OSB	OSB1	0.761	0.753	0.858	0.669
	OSB2	0.901			
	OSB3	0.784			
TMS	TMS2	0.828	0.721	0.858	0.751
	TMS3	0.904			
ORG	ORG1	0.831	0.738	0.851	0.656
	ORG2	0.789			
	ORG3	0.808			
COP	COP1	0.860	0.811	0.886	0.722
	COP2	0.827			
	COP3	0.861			
GOV	GOV1	0.868	0.739	0.842	0.640
	GOV2	0.729			
	GOV3	0.798			
TPP	TPP1	0.800	0.708	0.828	0.616
	TPP2	0.814			
	TPP3	0.738			
USI	USI1	0.832	0.757	0.860	0.672
	USI2	0.818			
	USI3	0.809			

Table 5 Discriminant validity—cross-loadings

	ADV	COP	CPT	CPX	GOV	ORG	OSB	TMS	TPP	USI
ADV1	**0.822**	0.461	0.497	0.513	0.415	0.448	0.428	0.466	0.412	0.494
ADV2	**0.795**	0.593	0.559	0.578	0.517	0.504	0.523	0.502	0.526	0.478
ADV3	**0.876**	0.567	0.565	0.524	0.479	0.443	0.492	0.478	0.460	0.526
COP1	0.567	**0.860**	0.550	0.570	0.445	0.569	0.534	0.573	0.480	0.509
COP2	0.488	**0.827**	0.549	0.525	0.459	0.541	0.515	0.589	0.447	0.489
COP3	0.545	**0.861**	0.603	0.559	0.593	0.547	0.564	0.538	0.505	0.510
CPT1	0.560	0.554	**0.846**	0.554	0.416	0.476	0.499	0.475	0.460	0.490
CPT2	0.522	0.606	**0.754**	0.535	0.457	0.499	0.481	0.485	0.453	0.437
CPT3	0.521	0.552	**0.867**	0.640	0.481	0.459	0.509	0.489	0.476	0.502
CPX1	0.570	0.522	0.620	**0.833**	0.477	0.472	0.539	0.449	0.444	0.502
CPX2	0.488	0.532	0.513	**0.778**	0.416	0.478	0.493	0.436	0.425	0.469
CPX3	0.467	0.541	0.549	**0.819**	0.468	0.419	0.499	0.442	0.448	0.494
GOV1	0.436	0.479	0.474	0.454	**0.868**	0.494	0.445	0.474	0.519	0.536
GOV2	0.414	0.476	0.411	0.434	**0.729**	0.416	0.418	0.492	0.441	0.450
GOV3	0.481	0.500	0.409	0.488	**0.798**	0.427	0.446	0.444	0.521	0.492
ORG1	0.421	0.520	0.426	0.427	0.445	**0.789**	0.477	0.490	0.480	0.442
ORG2	0.419	0.535	0.435	0.482	0.468	**0.808**	0.491	0.488	0.448	0.453
ORG3	0.469	0.526	0.498	0.441	0.446	**0.831**	0.444	0.532	0.447	0.466
OSB1	0.452	0.477	0.495	0.496	0.395	0.437	**0.761**	0.450	0.453	0.442
OSB2	0.479	0.525	0.512	0.547	0.451	0.482	**0.901**	0.458	0.450	0.523
OSB3	0.457	0.568	0.463	0.508	0.484	0.509	**0.784**	0.477	0.446	0.455
TMS2	0.494	0.566	0.479	0.503	0.472	0.532	0.485	**0.828**	0.500	0.468
TMS3	0.495	0.583	0.518	0.450	0.515	0.552	0.487	**0.904**	0.515	0.511
TPP1	0.418	0.443	0.429	0.421	0.521	0.440	0.514	0.435	**0.800**	0.484
TPP2	0.422	0.507	0.463	0.501	0.505	0.520	0.443	0.512	**0.814**	0.493
TPP3	0.427	0.383	0.415	0.356	0.425	0.377	0.312	0.435	**0.738**	0.447
USI1	0.508	0.468	0.480	0.491	0.541	0.446	0.482	0.512	0.508	**0.832**
USI2	0.481	0.471	0.425	0.469	0.532	0.490	0.456	0.447	0.476	**0.818**
USI3	0.488	0.518	0.520	0.523	0.443	0.444	0.489	0.430	0.505	**0.809**

Table 6 Results of the hypothesized direct effects of the variables in the structural model

Hypothesis	PLS Path	Original sample (O)	Sample mean (M)	Standard deviation (STDEV)	T statistics (|O/STDEV|)	P values	2.5%	97.5%	Remarks
H1	ADV -> USI*	0.152	0.151	0.066	2.302	0.022	0.026	0.276	Supported
H2	CPT -> USI^{NS}	0.049	0.046	0.068	0.728	0.467	−0.086	0.176	Unsupported
H3	CPX -> USI^{NS}	0.120	0.117	0.070	1.705	0.088	−0.022	0.259	Unsupported
H4	OSB -> USI^{NS}	0.108	0.106	0.059	1.832	0.067	−0.010	0.225	Unsupported
H5	TMS -> USI^{NS}	0.060	0.055	0.054	1.111	0.267	−0.050	0.161	Unsupported
H6	ORG -> USI^{NS}	0.067	0.071	0.058	1.145	0.253	−0.040	0.186	Unsupported
H7	COP -> USI^{NS}	0.025	0.032	0.068	0.368	0.713	−0.105	0.163	Unsupported
H8	GOV -> USI**	0.192	0.197	0.054	3.558	0.000	0.102	0.308	Supported
H9	TPP -> USI**	0.167	0.171	0.057	2.930	0.003	0.055	0.280	Supported

Note (s) ADV: Relative advantage; CPT: Compatibility; CPX: Complexity; OSB: Observability; COP: Competitive Pressure; GOV: Government support; TPP: Trading Partner Pressure; TMS: Top Management Support; ORG: Organizational Readiness, USI: Smart Contract Adoption Intention

* Significant at the 95% confidence level, $p < 0.05$

** Significant at the 99% confidence level, $p < 0.01$

^{NS} Not supported

Table 7 Effect size f-square and importance-performance map analysis

Predictor construct	USI	Total effect	Performance
ADV	0.024	0.152	71.959
COP	0.000	0.025	74.267
CPT	0.002	0.049	73.225
CPX	0.013	0.120	76.773
GOV	0.040	0.192	66.593
ORG	0.005	0.067	75.668
OSB	0.012	0.108	72.991
TMS	0.004	0.060	77.085
TPP	0.031	0.167	75.119

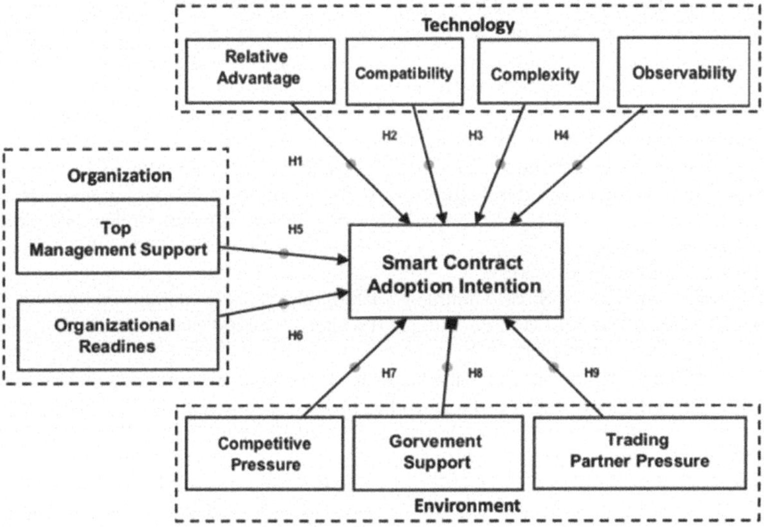

Fig. 1 Presents the research model with the hypothesis development

6 Conclusion

The findings indicate that three out of nine hypotheses significantly impact the intention to accept SC use in enterprises in Vietnam, namely ADV, GOV, and TPP. The results show that Government Support has the strongest impact on behavioral intention, followed by Trading Partner Pressure, and Relative Advantage.

7 Limitations and Future Direction

Firstly, although the study was conducted in enterprises in Vietnam, however, given the large geographical size, the study may limit the results to different locations. Based on data collected from only 341 individuals working in enterprises in Vietnam, the study should choose a larger sample size over a longer period to improve the generalizability of the findings.

References

1. Dicks, D.L.: Executive compensation and the role for corporate governance regulation. Rev. Financ. Stud. **25**(6), 1971–2004 (2012). https://doi.org/10.1093/RFS/HHS055
2. Diamastuti, E., Muafi, M., Fitri, A., Faizaty, N.E.: The role of corporate governance in the corporate social and environmental responsibility disclosure. The J. Asian Finance, Econ. Bus. **8**(1), 187–198 (2021). https://doi.org/10.13106/JAFEB.2021.VOL8.NO1.187
3. Alsalim, M., Amin, H., Youssef, A.: The role of corporate governance in achieving accounting information quality (field study in the Mishraq sulfur state co.)," Studies and scientific researches. economics edition, no. 27 (2018). https://doi.org/10.29358/SCECO.V0I0.399
4. PRNewswire: "Digital Logistics Market worth $46.5 billion by 2025 - Exclusive Report by MarketsandMarkets™," Sep. 2022 https://www.prnewswire.com/news-releases/digital-logistics-market-worth-46-5-billion-by-2025--exclusive-report-by-marketsandmarkets-301129979.html. Last accessed 06 May 2023
5. Nick Szabo: "The Idea of Smart Contracts," 1990. https://www.fon.hum.uva.nl/rob/Courses/InformationInSpeech/CDROM/Literature/LOTwinterschool2006/szabo.best.vwh.net/idea.html. Last accessed 11 May 2023
6. Badi, S., Ochieng, E., Nasaj, M., Papadaki, M.: Technological, organisational and environmental determinants of smart contracts adoption: UK construction sector viewpoint. Constr. Manage. Econ. **39**(1), 36–54 (2021). https://doi.org/10.1080/01446193.2020.1819549
7. Taherdoost, H.: Smart contracts in blockchain technology: a critical review. Information (Switzerland) **14**(2). MDPI (2023). https://doi.org/10.3390/info14020117
8. Davis: *Technology Acceptance Model*. 1989. https://www.igi-global.com/chapter/davis-technology-acceptance-model-tam-1989/127133. Last accessed 12 May 2023
9. Venkatesh, V., Morris, M.G., Davis, G.B., Davis, F.D.: User acceptance of information technology: toward a unified view. MIS Q. **27**(3), 425–478 (2003). https://doi.org/10.2307/30036540
10. Ajzen: The theory of planned behavior. Organ. Behav. Hum. Decis. Process **50**(2), 179–211 (1991). https://doi.org/10.1016/0749-5978(91)90020-T
11. Rogers: Diffusion of Innovation Theory. 1962. https://sphweb.bumc.bu.edu/otlt/mph-modules/sb/behavioralchangetheories/behavioralchangetheories4.html. Last accessed 15 May 2023
12. Sila: Factors affecting the adoption of B2B e-commerce technologies. Electron. Commerce Res. **13**(2), 199–236 (2013). https://doi.org/10.1007/S10660-013-9110-7/METRICS
13. Weiner, B.J.: A theory of organizational readiness for change. Implement. Sci. **4**(1) (2009). https://doi.org/10.1186/1748-5908-4-67
14. Young, R., Jordan, E.: Top management support: mantra or necessity? Int. J. Project Manage. **26**(7), 713–725 (2008). https://doi.org/10.1016/J.IJPROMAN.2008.06.001
15. Ramdani, B., Chevers, D., Williams, D.A.: SMEs' adoption of enterprise applications: a technology-organisation-environment model. J. Small Bus. Enterp. Dev. **20**(4), 735–753 (2013). https://doi.org/10.1108/JSBED-12-2011-0035

16. Lee, J.: Environmental factors of acceptance organization affecting intention to accept BIM. Int. J. Manage. **11**(04), 188–200 (2020). haattp://waaww.iaeme.com/IJM/index.asp188, haattp://waaww.iaeme.com/ijm/issues.asp?JType=IJM&VType=11&IType=4JournalImpactFactor
17. Nguyen, T.H., Le, X.C., Vu, T.H.L.: An extended technology-organization-environment (TOE) framework for online retailing utilization in digital transformation: empirical evidence from Vietnam. J. Open Innov.: Technol., Market, Complexity **8**(4) (2022). https://doi.org/10.3390/joitmc8040200
18. Bany Mohammad, A., Al-Okaily, M., Al-Majali, M., Masa'deh, R.: Business intelligence and analytics (BIA) usage in the banking industry sector: an application of the TOE framework. J. Open Innov.: Technol., Market, Complexity **8**(4) (2022). https://doi.org/10.3390/joitmc8040189
19. Erdfelder, E., FAul, F., Buchner, A., Lang, A.G.: Statistical power analyses using G*Power 3.1: tests for correlation and regression analyses. Behav. Res. Methods **41**(4), 1149–1160 (2009). https://doi.org/10.3758/BRM.41.4.1149/METRICS

Do the Uses of Technology Increase Firm Performance? Evidence from the WBES Dataset

Thuy An Chung and Quynh Trang Phan

Abstract This study investigates the effect of technology use on firm performance in an international setting. Using the World Bank Enterprise Surveys (WBES) dataset in 10 European countries, the results show that technology helps firms enhance their performance. Particularly, the use of technology licenses from foreign companies, the adoption of technology for managing suppliers, and the diversification of sales channels by online and telephone sales help firms increase their size in terms of sales and labour scales. This study proposes some policy implications. Policymakers should promote and incentivize the adoption of technology. The government should implement several technology transfer programs that connect local firms with foreign technology providers. The government can foster international collaboration and partnerships in technology and innovation. Further, managers should pay attention to technology as it helps to enhance firms' supply management and to promote sales through several channels such as online or telephone sales.

Keywords Firm size · Online sales channel · Supplier-managed technology · Technology license

1 Introduction

It is widely accepted that technology is a key driver of economic growth [1–3]. At the firm level, the use of technology brings a lot of benefits for business activities, such as customer relationship management [4], for salespersons to improve their outcome performance [5, 6]. Overall, technology is very important for firms since it helps firms enhance competitive advantage [7, 8] and improve firm performance [9, 10].

Firm performance is a central issue in business and finance research since it relates to several perspectives of a firm, such as CEO compensation [11, 12]; corporate social responsibility [13]; internalization [14]; firm innovation [15]; corporate governance

T. A. Chung (✉) · Q. T. Phan
Faculty of Finance—Banking, Ho Chi Minh City Open University, 35–37 Ho Hao Hon, District 1, Ho Chi Minh, Vietnam
e-mail: an.ct@ou.edu.vn

L. T. Tung et al. (eds.), *Disruptive Technology and Business Continuity*,
https://doi.org/10.1007/978-981-97-5452-6_10

[16]. Therefore, several studies aim to seek determinants of firm performance [17–19] or investigate the relationship between specific firm characteristics and firm performance such as competitive advantage and firm performance [20]; corporate governance and firm performance [21]; firm-wide integration and firm performance [22] and so on. However, previous studies show mixed findings between information technology investments and firm performance [23, 24].

Understanding the relationship between the uses of technology and firm performance is important to help firms maintain their leading with competitors, identify opportunities in business to reduce cost and increase sales, diversify their sales channels to reach their target customers, allow firms to deliver products and services efficiently, and manage their supplier chain efficiently. In this study, we obtained the cross-sectional dataset from the World Bank Enterprise Survey (WBES) to examine how the uses of technology impact firm performance. In particular, we consider the impact of three ways of technological usage: adoption of technology license from foreign firms (TECH), application of technology in managing and communicating with suppliers (TECH_MNG), and application of technology in product sales (TECH_SELL). The analysis controls for the potential impact of firm-specific characteristics and country-specific variables. Using the 2020–2021 WBES dataset of 10 countries, we found that the use of technology helps firms improve their performance.

The rest of this paper is structured as follows. Section 2 briefs a literature review of country-level governance quality, foreign ownership, and firm investment. Section 3 describes the model and data used in this study. Section 4 reports the results and robustness checks. Section 5 concludes.

2 Theoretical Framework and Literature Reviews

Many studies have focused on several facets of technology and its effect on firm performance [9, 10, 25–27]. Technology is defined as "it (technology) is the application of scientific knowledge to a particular technical field: materials or computer technology" [28]. In this study, we narrow down three dimensions of technology: external technology license, application of technology in supplier management, and application of technology in sales.

2.1 External Technology License and Firm Performance

The use of external technology helps firms enhance their competitive advantage [8, 29] and firm performance [30, 31] since firms can accumulate technological knowledge [32] and empower technological capability [33]. Ref. [34] reported that corporate-sponsored new ventures utilised external technology sources more intensively than independent ventures using the dataset of 112 ventures. Similarly, based on a sample of corporations in Europe [35], Japan and the United States [35] to examine the relationship between acquisition of technology and firm performance. This study showed that external acquisition of technology is essential to sales growth.

Regarding the indirect effect of obtaining external technology, SubbaNarasimha et al. [36] found that firms would improve their performance at the given level of technological knowledge unitisation using a sample of 29 U.S. pharmaceutical firms. Ref. [37] used a sample of 133 Brazilian firms to test the relationship between technological capability and firm performance. By grouping firms into seven industries, they found a significant relationship between technological capability and firm performance.

However, some studies have found that firms gain few benefits by acquiring external technology. For example, ref. [38] used the 188 domestic and foreign U.S. firms dataset to evaluate the relationship between external technology acquisition and firm performance. The findings indicated that external technology acquisition had a negative impact on performance. Ref. [31] used the dataset of 341 Taiwanese firms over the period 1998–2002 to investigate the role of external technology acquisition in firm performance. Using the least square dummy variable method, they found no evidence of the significant effect of inward technology license on firm performance. The impact of technology licenses on firm performance is still under debate, but we expect that the acquisition of external technology licenses could help the firm expand its sales and scales by shortening its research and development timeline, reducing capital expenditures, and increasing efficiency and innovation.

Hypothesis 1: Technology licenses from foreign firms have a positive effect on firm performance.

2.2 The Use of Technology in Supplier Management and Firm Performance

The use of technology in managing the supplier chain can impact firm performance since it brings many benefits to firms through supplier selection, monitoring practices [39], communications between seller and buyer [40], and cost reduction management [41]. Information technology in the supply chain helps firms collect and utilise information about their stores, customers, and suppliers, influencing firm performance [42].

Ref. [43] investigated how supply chain management links to firm performance using survey data of 20 senior managers. They found that supply chain management practices influence the relationship between knowledge management and firm performance. Ref. [39] indicated that advanced selection and monitoring practices tend to increase profitability and supplier performance in Canada, Germany, Japan, and the United States. They employed a set of tests, such as cluster analysis, general linear model (GLM) method, and ANOVA F-test.

Investment in information technology can create value when technology is integrated across the supply chain process [44]. Ref. [45] developed a new conceptualisation of supply chain capabilities: information exchange, coordination, activity integration and supply chain responsiveness. Using the interviews of 1949 managers, results indicated that supply chain capabilities can transform IT-related resources into higher value for a firm. Ref. [46] used survey data from UK firms to investigate the link between Internet-enabled supply chains and firm performance. Using the confirmatory factor analyses, he found that upstream and downstream supply chain integration improves performance. In addition, ref. [47] also showed that better information sharing among business partners helps firms reduce transaction costs and improve performance in electronic commerce.

Based on the many benefits of technology implemented in supply chain management, we expect that using technology in managing suppliers helps firms reduce costs, mitigate risks in supplier selection, better information flow between buyer and seller, and improve performance.

Hypothesis 2: Using technology in supplier management helps firms enhance performance.

2.3 The Use of Technology in Sales and Firm Performance

Using technology in sales activity can help firms enhance productivity in many ways. The application of technology can reduce sales costs and maintain customer relationships to maximise revenue. Indeed, several studies have shown that sales technologies are employed to increase the productivity of a firm and to establish long-term relationships between businesses and consumers [48, 49] since salespeople can spend less time to target prospective customers [23, 50].

The utilisation of technology in sales is progressively transformed from traditional sales channels to modern sales channels, such as online sales through websites and telephone. For example, ref. [51] suggested that firms should focus on website design to improve their sales using a sample of 465 internet users in Spain. Ref. [52] employed an explanatory study to explain why technology is important in direct sales. They argued that technology can serve as a tool to lower expenses, enhance efficiency, and facilitate supply chain activities. Moreover, firms could improve their competitive advantages by using technology to enhance the communication between firm-to-sales representatives, salesperson-to-consumer, and firm-to-consumer. Ref. [48] developed a theoretical framework to conclude that Email is used to alert customers about new products, promotions, coupons, and store openings. Ref. [53] indicated that a salesperson's technology orientation positively influences their internal role performance. Ref. [54] tested the impact of a retailer's online channel use on its financial and operating performance. Their results showed that sales, net operating income, total assets, and inventory turnover are better using a sample of over a hundred publicly traded U.S. retailers from 1996 to 2008.

Digital technologies have several potential impacts on business activities, such as improving the marketing of products and services, establishing new distribution channels, reducing the expenses of delivering information to customers, and shortening the delivery time [55]. Ref. [56] used the dataset of 272 Taiwanese firms to show that digital technology usage positively affects firm performance. Ref. [10] obtained a sample of 93 production centres in 10 countries to evaluate the different facets of business digitalisation on organisational performance. The results of the structural equation modelling showed that business digitisation can substantially increase the development of value activities. Ref. [57] used data from 465 IT firms to explore the relationship between using technological innovation and firm performance. Using the Generalized Method of Moment (GMM) approach, the results confirmed that technological innovation is essential for firm performance.

Based on the literature reviews, we expect that technology improves firm performance by adding a tool to sell products to traditional sales channels through online or telephone sales, improve communication between buyers and sellers to maximise revenue, and efficiently approach the potential client to increase sales. Therefore, our hypothesis is following:

Hypothesis 3: The use of technology in sales helps firms improve performance.

3 Data and Model Description

3.1 *Sample and Data*

We collected the data from the World Bank Enterprise Survey (WBES) and the World Bank Development Indicators (WBDI). The WBES data provide detailed information about firm performance and firm-specific characteristics through survey data. Although the WBES dataset is cross-sectional data, the WBES dataset has been commonly used in corporate finance [58–64]. We then excluded all missing observations. The final sample consists of 8,722 firm-level observations in 10 European countries: Austria, Belgium, Denmark, Finland, France, Germany, Ireland, Luxembourg, the Netherlands, and Sweden for the 2020–2021 period. Table 1 shows the list of countries and firms in the dataset.

3.2 *Model Description*

To test our hypotheses, we employ pooled Ordinary Least Squares (OLS) regression with robust standard error to examine the impact of technology on firm performance. We employ the following model specifications:

$$PER_{i,j} = \beta_0 + \beta_1 TECH_{i,j} + \beta_{2-5}(Firm\_Control)_{i,j} + \beta_{6-9}(Country\_Control)_j + \varepsilon_i$$

Table 1 Countries and observations

Countries	Observations
Austria	569
Belgium	550
Denmark	863
Finland	701
France	1,286
Germany	2,826
Ireland	571
Luxembourg	152
Netherlands	777
Sweden	477
Total	**8,772**

The dependent variable in this study is firm performance (PER), which is proxied by total sales (PER_SALE) and labour (PER_LABOUR) last year. PER_SALE is measured by the natural logarithm of total sales last year. In robustness tests, we measure firm performance as the natural logarithm of total permanent full-time workers (PER_LABOUR).

The firm-level independent variable of interest is a technology the firm employs in business activities. The technology variable is proxied by technology license (TECH) that is obtained from foreign-owned firms, technology that is applied to manage suppliers (TECH_MNG) and technology that is used to sell products via online channel or phone channel (TECH_SELL). The other firm-level controlled variables are firm ownership, firm age, firm debt and firm export. Firm age (AGE) is the natural logarithm of years. Firm debt (DEBT) is measured by the ratio of debt obtained from suppliers, banks, and non-bank sources for working capital. The country-level controlled variables are GDP growth rate (GDP), inflation (INF), and unemployment rate (UNE). εi is the characteristic error. Table 2 presents details on the computation of the firm-level variables.

4 Results and Discussions

4.1 Descriptive Statistics

Table 3 reports the basic descriptive statistics for the variables used in this study. The mean value of performance, which is proxied by total sales, is 15.43. This value is lower than in some developing countries, such as Chile (26.64) and Brazil (27.31) [65]. Next, the average value of DEBT is 24.39, showing that nearly 24.39% of working capital is financed by debt. Next, the mean values of INF, UNE, and GDP

Table 2 Variable description

Variables	Measurement	Data source
PER_SALE	Natural logarithm of total sales	WBES
PER_LABOR	Natural logarithm of total permanent full-time workers	WBES
TECH	Get 0 if technology license is obtained from foreign-owned firms; otherwise, get 1	WBES
TECH_MNG	Get 0 if a firm does not use technology to manage their suppliers Get 1 if a firm manages its suppliers by manual search Get 2 if a firm manages its suppliers with an updated database Get 2 if a firm manages its suppliers by a Relation Management software Get 2 if a firm manages its suppliers by E-procurement with electronic orders Get 5 if a firm manages its suppliers in other ways	WBES
TECH_SELL	Percentage of sales if a firm sells products via online channel or phone channel	WBES
FO	Get 0 if a firm does not have foreign ownership; otherwise, get 1	WBES
FAM	Percentage of firms owned by the same family	WBES
DEBT	Percentage of working capital financed by debt	WBES
AGE	Natural logarithm of years	WBES

are 0.98, 5.28, and −1.31, respectively. Appendix A presents the mean value of the main variables by country.

Table 3 Descriptive statistics

Variable	Observations	Mean	Standard deviation	Min	Max
PER_SALE	8,772	15.43	1.89	9.21	25.26
TECH	8,772	0.17	0.37	0.00	1.00
TECH_MNG	8,772	2.37	1.26	0.00	5.00
TECH_SELL	8,772	47.21	44.22	0.00	100.00
DEBT	8,772	24.39	33.07	0.00	100.00
FO	8,772	0.12	0.32	0.00	1.00
FAM	8,772	69.95	40.64	0.00	100.00
AGE	8,772	3.23	0.88	0.00	5.39
INF	8,772	0.98	0.87	-0.33	3.06
UNE	8,772	5.28	1.65	3.14	8.41
GDP	8,772	-1.31	3.96	-7.78	6.18

Table 4 Correlation matrix

	PER_ SALE	TECH	TECH_ MNG	TECH_ SELL	DEBT	FO	FAM	AGE	INF	UNE	GDP
PER_ SALE	1.00										
TECH	0.12	1.00									
TECH_ MNG	0.18	0.03	1.00								
TECH_ SELL	0.04	0.02	−0.01	1.00							
DEBT	0.10	0.01	0.01	-0.03	1.00						
FO	0.29	0.10	0.06	0.01	−0.02	1.00					
FAM	−0.22	−0.09	−0.06	−0.04	0.001	−0.26	1.00				
AGE	0.26	−0.01	0.04	0.01	−0.02	0.01	0.08	1.00			
INF	−0.01	0.04	−0.01	−0.08	0.04	0.04	−0.02	−0.02	1.00		
UNE	0.12	−0.01	−0.02	−0.07	−0.01	0.04	−0.02	0.03	−0.24	1.00	
GDP	0.10	0.07	0.03	−0.04	0.07	0.05	0.01	−0.02	0.51	−0.29	1.00

4.2 Correlation Analysis

Table 4 presents the correlations among firm performance and the independent variables. The PER_SALE is positively correlated with TECH, TECH_MNG, and TECH_SELL. The figures imply that when firms use technology, their performance in terms of sales increases. For firm-level control variables, only FAM is negatively related to PER_SALE, while DEBT, FO, FAM, and AGE are positively related to PER_SALE. Overall, the signs of the correlation coefficients between PER_SALE and controlled variables are consistent with the literature. Further, none of the VIF reached the accepted threshold of 10. This implies that this study may not have a problem of multicollinearity.

4.3 Regression Analysis

We present and discuss our findings in this section. To test hypotheses 1–3, we apply the OLS estimator with robust standard errors to control for heteroscedasticity issues. As can be seen in Table 5, the R-squares of the models are approximately 0.22–0.24, indicating that the models explain 22–24% of the change in firm performance. Columns (1), (2), and (3) in Table 5 show the positive signs that the coefficients of TECH, TECH_MNG, and TECH_SELL are statistically significant at 1% level. The results provide strong support for the research hypotheses. The findings reflect that technology improves firm performance in terms of sales, although technology is examined in three different aspects: external technology license, technology that

Table 5 The effect of technology on firm performance in terms of sale

Independent variables	(1)	(2)	(3)
TECH	0.4180*** (8.41)		
TECH_MNG		0.2170*** (15.27)	
TECH_SELL			0.0020*** (4.90)
DEBT	0.0062*** (11.36)	0.0062*** (11.37)	0.0630*** (11.51)
FO	1.3040*** (20.97)	1.302*** (21.11)	1.3420*** (21.51)
FAM	−0.0082*** (−17.45)	−0.0081*** (−17.28)	−0.0083*** (−17.76)
AGE	0.5810*** (27.21)	0.567*** (26.90)	0.579*** (27.00)
INF	−0.1720*** (−7.35)	−0.1600*** (−6.88)	−0.1620*** (−6.87)
UNE	0.1440*** (12.67)	0.1480*** (13.15)	0.1500*** (13.09)
GDP	0.0762*** (13.90)	0.0763*** (14.13)	0.0794*** (14.52)
Cons	13.26*** (134.10)	12.82*** (122.77)	13.21*** (128.17)
Number of observations	**8,772**	**8,772**	**8,772**
R-squared	**0.2275**	**0.2414**	**0.2228**
Prob > F	**0.0000**	**0.0000**	**0.0000**

is applied to manage suppliers, and technology that is used to sell products. The findings are consistent with Tsai's [31] finding that technological capability increases firm performance regarding productivity growth. Firm-level control variables are statistically positive and significant, except FAM. The coefficients of these control variables are generally consistent with previous findings in the literature.

4.4 Robustness Checks

In this section, we discuss our robustness checks, showing how our findings vary according to alternative measures, alternative sub-sample used, and alternative methods.

Alternative Measure of the Dependent Variable

We replace PER_SALE with PER_LABOR in the model to test the hypotheses. The coefficients of TECH, TECH_MNG, and TECH_SELL shown in columns (1), (2), and (3) in Table 6 are significantly positive. Overall, the findings in Tables 5 and 6 are very similar, except for country-level control variables such as UNE and GDP, which are found insignificant.

Endogeneity Tests

Previous studies have identified the potential endogeneity between technology and firm performance. We employ the two-stage least squares (2SLS), which can help eliminate possible biased results using instrumental variables [58, 66]. Table 7 shows the coefficients of TECH and TECH_MNG that are significant and positive with PER_SALE and PER_LABOR at the 1% and 5% levels. Overall, the findings in Tables 5 and 7 are very similar.

Table 6 The effect of technology on firm performance in terms of labour

Independent variables	(1)	(2)	(3)
TECH	0.3180*** (9.29)		
TECH_MNG		0.1100*** (11.40)	
TECH_SELL			0.0010*** (3.47)
DEBT	0.0035*** (9.62)	0.0035*** (9.58)	0.0035*** (9.76)
FO	0.7370*** (17.23)	0.7460*** (17.50)	0.7670*** (17.86)
FAM	−0.0057*** (−17.79)	−0.0058*** (−17.82)	−0.0059*** (−18.10)
AGE	0.3730*** (25.78)	0.3670*** (25.37)	0.373*** (25.56)
INF	−0.131*** (−8.40)	−0.1240*** (−7.98)	−0.1260*** (−8.01)
UNE	0.0034 (0.44)	0.0057 (0.75)	0.0065 (0.85)
GDP	0.0000 (0.00)	0.0007 (0.20)	0.0022 (0.66)
Cons	2.114*** (30.61)	1.9130*** (26.58)	2.1150*** (29.32)
Number of observations	**8,772**	**8,772**	**8,772**
R-squared	**0.1852**	**0.1884**	**0.1771**
Prob > F	**0.0000**	**0.0000**	**0.0000**

Table 7 The effect of technology on firm performance—2SLS

Independent variables	PER_SALE	PER_LABOR	PER_SALE	PER_LABOR
TECH	5.0840** (2.76)	4.1894** (2.98)		
TECH_MNG			1.6601*** (5.93)	0.5469*** (3.66)
DEBT	0.0059*** (7.35)	0.0032*** (5.28)	0.0057*** (7.10)	0.0033*** (8.13)
FO	0.8579*** (4.29)	0.3670* (2.40)	1.0236*** (10.23)	0.6618*** (12.29)
FAM	−0.0050*** (−3.42)	−0.0031** (−2.79)	−0.0054*** (−6.38)	−0.0050*** (−11.22)
AGE	0.5780*** (19.38)	0.3713*** (16.47)	0.4765*** (13.38)	0.3392*** (18.28)
INF	−0.1781*** (−5.21)	−0.1360*** (−5.25)	−0.0843* (−2.19)	−0.1016*** (−5.29)
UNE	0.1369*** (8.45)	−0.0022 (−0.18)	0.1726*** (9.96)	0.0132 (1.51)
GDP	0.0468** (3.25)	−0.0244* (−2.24)	0.0591*** (6.89)	−0.0045 (−1.07)
lCons	12.2935*** (30.31)	1.3157*** (4.24)	9.3171*** (13.49)	0.8536* (2.32)
Number of observations	**8,772**	**8,772**	**8,772**	**8,772**

Sub-Samples

We divide the sample into two groups based on the use of technology license (TECH). TECH is one or zero, indicating that firms use or do not use external technology, respectively. Overall, the coefficients of firm-level control variables in both tech and non-tech groups with two different measures of firm performance in Table 8 are significant.

5 Conclusions

This study addresses the equivocal findings in the literature regarding the relationship between the use of technology and firm performance. We use the WBES database comprising 8,772 firm-level observations in 10 European countries from 2020 to 2021. This study contributes to work on how technology improves firm performance. The findings show that three different aspects of technology (including external technology license (TECH), technology that is used to manage the supply chain (TECH_MNG), and technology that is used to drive sales channels (TECH_SELL) are significant and positive with firm performance. The findings reflect that technology is an

Table 8 The effect of technology on firm performance—TECH classification

Independent variables	TECH = 0	TECH = 1	TECH = 0	TECH = 1
	PER_SALE	PER_SALE	PER_LABOR	PER_LABOR
DEBT	0.0065*** (10.88)	0.0052*** (3.73)	0.0037*** (9.492)	0.0024** (2.65)
FO	1.3144*** (18.24)	1.2956*** (10.62)	0.7499*** (15.29)	0.7226*** (8.27)
FAM	−0.0083*** (−16.15)	−0.0073*** (−6.58)	−0.0058*** (−16.75)	−0.0051*** (−6.34)
AGE	0.5289*** (23.06)	0.8241*** (14.81)	0.3330*** (21.52)	0.5605*** (14.74)
INF	−0.1957*** (−7.74)	−0.0447 (−0.75)	−0.1448*** (−8.71)	−0.0551 (−1.33)
UNE	0.1535*** (12.70)	0.0958** (2.98)	0.0137 (1.68)	−0.0513* (−2.33)
GDP	0.0757*** (12.54)	0.0839*** (6.37)	−0.0015 (−0.41)	0.0118 (1.36)
Cons	13.3958*** (128.09)	12.9875*** (46.12)	2.2013*** (30.36)	2.0354*** (9.95)
Number of observations	**7,246**	**1,526**	**7,246**	**1,526**
R-squared	**0.208**	**0.261**	**0.167**	**0.215**

important factor of firm performance as technology enhances firm performance in terms of sales and labour scales.

These results propose some policy implications. Policymakers should promote and incentivize the adoption of technology. The government should implement several technology transfer programs that connect local firms with foreign technology providers. The government can also foster international collaboration and partnerships in technology and innovation.

Firm managers use technology from foreign firms to improve products and save internal expenditures on research and development. Firms should focus on techniques that enhance their supply management and promote sales through several channels. Specifically, firms should first encourage innovative sales channels, such as online or telephone sales, instead of traditional sales channels, such as offline stores. Second, firms should manage the supplier chain effectively, such as by implementing software to track performance metrics and maintaining good communications.

The limitation of this study is related to the sample. This study only focuses on European-developed countries. Future studies could examine the impact of technology on firm performance using data from developing countries, which are very different from developed countries, such as regulations, demand for using technology, funds for investing in technology, technology approaches, and so on.

Appendix A: Summary means the value of variables by country.

	PER_SALE	TECH	TECH_MNG	TECH_SELL	DEBT	FO	FAM	AGE	INF	UNE	GDP
Australia	14.59	0.22	1.96	44.76	22.77	0.11	67.56	3.09	1.40	5.25	−5.46
Belgium	15.16	0.18	2.28	29.18	29.83	0.16	76.61	3.25	1.44	5.37	2.23
Denmark	17.69	0.22	2.53	50.26	36.65	0.21	64.82	3.45	0.67	5.18	0.58
Finland	15.29	0.25	2.38	53.16	27.75	0.15	58.67	3.12	0.78	7.04	0.08
France	15.06	0.08	2.36	37.95	21.59	0.09	74.94	3.27	0.57	8.06	−6.37
Germany	14.94	0.14	2.40	57.81	19.22	0.06	71.25	3.21	0.67	3.77	−2.42
Ireland	14.57	0.19	2.37	35.19	23.73	0.06	84.08	3.07	0.65	5.10	5.61
Luxembourg	15.21	0.25	2.26	37.70	17.44	0.49	54.52	2.97	1.72	5.60	2.24
Netherlands	15.20	0.19	2.51	36.24	33.12	0.14	68.64	3.18	2.51	3.42	1.42
Sweden	18.15	0.23	2.31	54.07	19.93	0.17	59.90	3.45	1.33	7.34	0.52

References

1. Justman, M., Teubal, M.: A structuralist perspective on the role of technology in economic growth and development. World Dev. **19**(9), 1167–1183 (1991)
2. Rosenberg, N.: Capital goos, technology, and economic growth. Oxf. Econ. Pap. **15**(3), 217–227 (1963)
3. Yousefi, A.: The impact of information and communication technology on economic growth: evidence from developed and developing countries. Econ. Innov. New Technol. **20**(6), 581–596 (2011)
4. Jayachandran, S., Sharma, S., Kaufman, P., Raman, P.: The role of relational information processes and technology use in customer relationship management. J. Mark. **69**(4), 177–192 (2005)
5. Robinson, L., Marshall, G.W., Stamps, M.B.: Sales force use of technology: antecedents to technology acceptance. J. Bus. Res. **58**(12), 1623–1631 (2005)
6. Román, S., Rodríguez, R.: The influence of sales force technology use on outcome performance. J. Bus. Indus. Market. **30**(6), 771–783 (2015)
7. Fagerberg, J.: Technology and competitiveness. Oxf. Rev. Econ. Policy **12**(3), 39–51 (1996)
8. Porter, M.E.: Technology and competitive advantage. J. Bus. Strateg. **5**(3), 60–78 (1985)
9. Li, M., Richard, Y.L.: Information technology and firm performance: linking with environmental, strategic and managerial contexts. Inf. Manage. **35**(1), 43–51 (1999)
10. Martínez-Caro, E., Cegarra-Navarro, J.G., Alfonso-Ruiz, F.J.: Digital technologies and firm performance: the role of digital organisational culture. Technol. Forecast. Soc. Change. **154**, 119962 (2020)
11. Chukwuma, N.J., Famba, T., Sun, H., Mensah, I.A., Kurauone, O., Li, L., Chituku-Dzimiro, G.: The effect of firm performance on CEO compensation: the moderation role of SOE reform. SN Bus. Econ. **1**(11), 158 (2021)

12. Rath, C., Deo, M.: The effect of firm performance on executive compensation in socially responsible firms: the Indian evidence. Int. J. Indian Culture Bus. Manage. **29**(2), 200–220 (2023)
13. Li, Q., Luo, W., Wang, Y., Wu, L.: Firm performance, corporate ownership, and corporate social responsibility disclosure in China. Bus. Ethics: A Eur. Rev. **22**(2), 159–173 (2013)
14. Jung, J.C., Bansal, P.: How firm performance affects internationalization. Manage. Int. Rev. **49**(6), 709–732 (2009)
15. Audretsch, D.B.: Firm profitability, growth, and innovation. Rev. Ind. Organ. **10**(5), 579–588 (1995)
16. Sethi, P., Sahu, T.N., Maity, S.: Firm performance, vertical agency crisis and corporate governance of Indian listed companies. Asian J. Econ. Banking **7**(1), 86–98 (2022)
17. Burger, A., Damijan, J.P., Kostevc, Č, Rojec, M.: Determinants of firm performance and growth during economic recession: the case of Central and Eastern European countries. Econ. Syst. **41**(4), 569–590 (2017)
18. Hansen, G.S., Wernerfelt, B.: Determinants of firm performance: the relative importance of economic and organizational factors. Strateg. Manage. J. **10**(5), 399–411 (1989)
19. Selvam, M., Gayathri, J., Vasanth, V., Lingaraja, K., Marxiaoli, S.: Determinants of firm performance: a subjective model. Int. J. Soc. Sci. Stud. **4**, 90 (2016)
20. Ma, H.: Competitive advantage and firm performance. Competitiveness Rev.: An Int. Bus. J. **10**(2), 15–32 (2000)
21. Bhagat, S., Bolton, B.: Corporate governance and firm performance. J. Corp. Finan. **14**(3), 257–273 (2008)
22. Chen, H., Mattioda, D.D., Daugherty, P.J.: Firm-wide integration and firm performance. The Int. J. Logistics Manage. **18**(1), 5–21 (2007)
23. Johnson, D.S., Bharadwaj, S.: Digitization of selling activity and sales force performance: an empirical investigation. J. Acad. Mark. Sci. **33**(1), 3–18 (2005)
24. Ambekar, S.S., Deshmukh, U., Hudnurkar, M.: Impact of purchasing practices, supplier relationships and use of information technology on firm performance. Int. J. Innov. Sci. **13**, 118–130 (2020)
25. Collins, J.D., Worthington, W.J., Reyes, P.M., Romero, M.: Knowledge management, supply chain technologies, and firm performance. Manage. Res. Rev. **33**(10), 947–960 (2010)
26. Kim, H.J.: Information technology and firm performance: the role of supply chain integration. Oper. Manage. Res. **10**(1), 1–9 (2017)
27. Liang, T., You, J., Liu, C.: A resource-based perspective on information technology and firm performance: a meta analysis. Ind. Manage. Data Syst. **110**(8), 1138–1158 (2010)
28. Salomon, J.: What is technology? The issue of its origins and definitions. Hist. Technol. **1**, 113–156 (1984)
29. Chatterji, D.: Accessing external sources of technology. Res. Technol. Manage. **39**(2), 48–56 (1996)
30. Bapuji, H., Loree, D., Crossan, M.: Connecting external knowledge usage and firm performance: an empirical analysis. J. Eng. Tech. Manage. **28**(4), 215–231 (2011)
31. Tsai, K.-H.: The impact of technological capability on firm performance in Taiwan's electronics industry. J. High Technol. Manage. Res. **15**(2), 183–195 (2004)
32. Cohen, W.M., Levinthal, D.A.: Innovation and learning: the two faces of R & D. Econ. J. **99**(397), 569–596 (1989)
33. Jonash, R.S.: Strategic technology leveraging: making outsourcing work for you. Res. Technol. Manage. **39**(2), 19–25 (1996)
34. Zahra, S.A.: Technology strategy and new venture performance: a study of corporate-sponsored and independent biotechnology ventures. J. Bus. Ventur. **11**(4), 289–321 (1996)
35. Granstrand, O., Bohlin, E., Oskarsson, C., Sjöberg, N.: External technology acquisition in large multi-technology corporations. R&D Manage. **22**(2), 111–134 (1992)
36. SubbaNarasimha, P.N., Ahmad, S., Mallya, S.N.: Technological knowledge and firm performance of pharmaceutical firms. J. Intellec. Capital **4**, 20–33 (2003)

37. Reichert, F.M., Zawislak, P.A.: Technological capability and firm performance. J. Technol. Manage. Innov. **9**(4), 20–35 (2014)
38. Jones, G.K., Lanctot, A., Teegen, H.J.: Determinants and performance impacts of external technology acquisition. J. Bus. Ventur. **16**(3), 255–283 (2001)
39. Ittner, C.D., Larcker, D.F., Nagar, V., Rajan, M.V.: Supplier selection, monitoring practices, and firm performance. J. Account. Public Policy **18**(3), 253–281 (1999)
40. Sanders, N.R.: The benefits of using E-business technology: the supplier perspective. J. Bus Logistics **28**, 177–207 (2007)
41. Shank, J.K., Govindarajan, V.: Strategic cost management: the new tool for competitive advantage. Simon and Schuster (1993)
42. Tippins, M.J., Sohi, R.S.: IT competency and firm performance: is organizational learning a missing link? Strateg. Manage. J. **24**(8), 745–761 (2003)
43. Peng Wong, W., Yew Wong, K.: Supply chain management, knowledge management capability, and their linkages towards firm performance. Bus. Process. Manage. J. **17**(6), 940–964 (2011)
44. Powell, T.C., Dent-Micallef, A.: Information technology as competitive advantage: the role of human, business, and technology resources. Strateg. Manage. J. **18**(5), 375–405 (1997)
45. Wu, F., Yeniyurt, S., Kim, D., Cavusgil, S.T.: The impact of information technology on supply chain capabilities and firm performance: a resource-based view. Ind. Mark. Manage. **35**(4), 493–504 (2006)
46. Frohlich, M.T.: E-Integration in the supply chain: barriers and performance*. Decis. Sci. **33**(4), 537–556 (2002)
47. Lin, F., Huang, S., Lin, S.: Effects of information sharing on supply chain performance in electronic commerce. IEEE Trans. Eng. Manage. **49**(3), 258–268 (2002)
48. Ailawadi, K.L., Beauchamp, J.P., Donthu, N., Gauri, D.K., Shankar, V.: Communication and promotion decisions in retailing: a review and directions for future research. J. Retail. **85**(1), 42–55 (2009)
49. Enrique Bigné, J., Aldás, J., Andreu, L.: B2B services: IT adoption in travel agency supply chains. J. Serv. Mark. **22**(6), 454–464 (2008)
50. Rapp, A., Agnihotri, R., Forbes, L.P.: The sales force technology–performance chain: the role of adaptive selling and effort. J. Personal Selling Sales Manage. **28**(4), 335–350 (2008)
51. Bigné, E., Ruiz, C., Blas, S.: The impact of internet user shopping patterns and demographics on consumer mobile buying behaviour. J. Electron. Commerce Res. 6 (2005)
52. Ferrell, L., Gonzalez-Padron, T.L., Ferrell, O.C.: An assessment of the use of technology in the direct selling industry. J. Personal Selling Sales Manage. **30**(2), 157–165 (2010)
53. Hunter, G.K., Perreault, W.D.: Sales technology orientation, information effectiveness, and sales performance. J. Personal Selling Sales Manage. **26**(2), 95–113 (2006)
54. Xia, Y., Zhang, G.P.: The impact of the online channel on retailers' performances: an empirical evaluation. Decis. Sci. **41**(3), 517–546 (2010)
55. Gunasekaran, A., Marri, H.B., McGaughey, R.E., Nebhwani, M.D.: E-commerce and its impact on operations management. Int. J. Prod. Econ. **75**(1), 185–197 (2002)
56. Tsou, H.-T., Chen, J.-S.: How does digital technology usage benefit firm performance? Digital transformation strategy and organisational innovation as mediators. Technol. Anal. Strategic Manage. **35**(9), 1114–1127 (2023)
57. Lin, W.L., Yip, N., Ho, J.A., Sambasivan, M.: The adoption of technological innovations in a B2B context and its impact on firm performance: an ethical leadership perspective. Ind. Mark. Manage. **89**, 61–71 (2020)
58. Allison, L., Liu, Y., Murtinu, S., Wei, Z.: Gender and firm performance around the world: the roles of finance, technology and labor. J. Bus. Res. **154**, 113322 (2023)
59. Chavis, L.W., Klapper, L.F., Love, I.: The impact of the business environment on young firm financing. The World Bank Econ. Rev. **25**(3), 486–507 (2011)
60. Lashitew, A.A.: The effect of political connections on credit access: does the level of financial development matter? Kyklos **67**(2), 227–254 (2014)
61. Liu, Y., Xu, J.: Residual state ownership, foreign ownership and firms' financing patterns. Emerg. Mark. Rev. **51**, 100868 (2022)

62. O'Toole, C.M., Tarp, F.: Corruption and the efficiency of capital investment in developing countries. J. Int. Dev. **26**(5), 567–597 (2014)
63. Presbitero, A.F., Rabellotti, R., Piras, C.: Barking up the wrong tree? measuring gender gaps in firm's access to finance. The J. Dev. Stud. **50**(10), 1430–1444 (2014)
64. Xu, J., Liu, Y., Abdoh, H.: Foreign ownership and productivity. Int. Rev. Econ. Financ. **80**, 624–642 (2022)
65. Martins, H.C., Schiehll, E., Terra, P.R.S.: Country-level governance quality, ownership concentration, and debt maturity: a comparative study of Brazil and Chile. Corp. Gov. Int. Rev. **25**, 236–254 (2017)
66. Bhagat, S., Bolton, B.: Corporate governance and firm performance. J. Corp. Finance **14**, 257–273 (2008)

Impact of Work-Life Balance on Employee Work Performance: The Mediating Role of Employee Creativity

Nguyen Minh Ha, Nguyen Thanh Phuong Thuy, and Ngo Thanh Trung

Abstract Modern people have many personal and professional obligations. Work-life balance has become a key factor that attracts more people. This study investigates the relationships between work-life balance, employee creativity, and work performance. Five main aspects of work-life balance are explored, including work overload, work stress, flexible work arrangements, family responsibilities, and organizational support. 419 accounting and auditing personnel in Vietnam are surveyed to obtain research data. Qualitative research methods were used to better understand the relationships and improve the pre-designed questionnaire. The Structural Equation Modeling (SEM) method is used to estimate the relationships between concepts. Three dimensions of work-life balance, including work overload, work stress, and family responsibilities, have harmful impacts on work performance, according to the findings. On the other hand, increasing flexible work arrangements and organizational support promote work performance. In addition, employee creativity acts as a mediating variable, enhancing the positive effect of organizational support on work performance. The findings provide important empirical evidence for management recommendations to improve employee work performance by reducing the negative effects of work overload, work stress, and family responsibilities while increasing the positive effects of flexible work arrangements, organizational support, and employee creativity.

N. M. Ha
Ho Chi Minh City Open University, Ho Chi Minh City, Vietnam

N. M. Ha · N. T. Trung (✉)
Finance, Economic and Management Research Group (FEMRG), Ho Chi Minh City Open University, Ho Chi Minh City, Vietnam
e-mail: trung.nt@ou.edu.vn

N. M. Ha
Research Centre in Business, Economics and Resources (CBER), Ho Chi Minh City Open University, Ho Chi Minh City, Vietnam

N. T. P. Thuy
The Graduate School, Ho Chi Minh City Open University, Ho Chi Minh City, Vietnam

N. T. Trung
Faculty of Finance and Banking, Ho Chi Minh City Open University, Ho Chi Minh City, Vietnam

L. T. Tung et al. (eds.), *Disruptive Technology and Business Continuity*,
https://doi.org/10.1007/978-981-97-5452-6_11

Keywords Work-life balance · Employee creativity · Work performance

1 Introduction

Employees are a critical component of any organization, and their participation is a core value of organizational health [1]. Employers can develop a work environment improvement plan based on employee performance reviews to increase employee motivation, behavior, and productivity. Managers want their corporations to be stronger and more competitive due to the skills and talents of their human resources, and no organization will tolerate the loss of high-performing personnel to competitors [2]. However, in this new era, people's and organizations' needs are constantly changing and improving, requiring employees to constantly strive to meet the needs of both work and life [3]. As a result, they no longer have time to spend with family and friends, or to enjoy and feel the interesting things in life because the imbalance between work and life occurs frequently, causing many negative consequences for both individuals and organizations [4].

Ref. [5] conducted a comprehensive review of previous empirical research on work-family concepts in Asia. They discover the relationship between work-life balance (WLB) and work performance (WP). Numerous studies have been conducted to determine the factors affecting the WP from the pressure to balance work and life, including those by [1, 4, 6–8]. The common theme among the studies is that the components of WLB are frequently focused on the family aspect and are frequently conducted on subjects who must allocate time and money to both work and family.

Similarly, employee creativity (EC) and WP are closely related [9]. EC is the most essential asset, contributing significantly to the success or failure of a business [10]. Workplace innovation and creativity are becoming more essential factors of company performance, success, and long-term survival [11]. Ref. [12, 13] agreed that EC has both individual and organizational benefits; specifically, it helps employees acquire new knowledge, thereby increasing the company's chances of survival and success. In reality, there is a significant difference in business performance between companies that use a great deal of innovation at work and those that rely solely on imposition and traditional methods.

Yet, differences in cultures, values, social structures, and human resource management (HRM) practices may have a distinct impact on the work-life experiences of Asian employees than those of Western employees [5]. On more specific and smaller scales, such as the level of a country or an industry, these factors can also contribute to variations in work-life experiences. Vietnam is a developing economy in Asia. There are approximately 900,000 enterprises operating in various fields in Vietnam today. A large number of accountants and auditors are employed by businesses. Due to the nature of their profession, they are always under a great deal of pressure in terms of time, knowledge, qualifications, exact data requirements, and especially the harsh rejection of their profession. Their work-life experiences are negative, and they lack balance between their work and personal lives.

Consequently, research on the influence of WLB and EC on WP is required. This study examines the relationship between WLB, creativity, and WP among accountants and auditors in Vietnam, as well as the mediating role of EC in the relationship between WLB and WP. Based on the obtained research results, suggestions are made to support administrators in developing management solutions that will help their employees in completing their work with the greatest efficiency.

2 Literature Review

2.1 *Work-Life Balance*

WLB is frequently defined as simultaneously fulfilling the demands of work and life. It is the relationship between work and non-work aspects of a person's life [14], the evaluation of an individual's ability to effectively balance multiple roles [9], or the degree to which an individual participates in an organization and feels satisfied completing work and family responsibilities [15]. It occurs when the employer and employee make working arrangements that take into account the nature of the organization's operations and the employee's personal life needs [1]. Ref. [4] argued that WLB is associated with the ability to perform well at work and to minimize conflict between the roles of an employee and a person's daily life. In conclusion, research on the topic of WLB combines work and family factors [2]. Numerous studies have described work as the setting of formal duties performed by employees to achieve an organization's goal, whereas life is characterized as a succession of activities unconnected to work. Consequently, the work-life imbalance is out of control in each of the above roles. Using the approach of research of [4], this study also examines WLB from five distinct perspectives: (1) work overload (WO), (2) work stress (WS), (3) flexible work arrangements (FWA), (4) organizational support (OS), and (5) family responsibilities (FR).

2.2 *Employee Creativity*

EC in the context of the workplace is the result of novel concepts and enhanced assignments in the form of products or work procedures [11]. According to [8], a new product, idea, or process must meet two criteria: (1) originality and novelty and (2) utility and relevance to the organization. EC is one of the affirmative behaviors that encourages employees to participate in more organizational activities and to contribute more to the organization's success [16]. Thus, it should be viewed as the creation of unique things that are either completely or relatively separate from what has come before and may be applied to one or more aspects of the business to increase the organization's advantages or worth. EC can also be viewed as a source of a company's competitive advantage [8].

2.3 Work Performance

WP is correlated with an employee's capacity to perceive specified objectives, meet expectations, and accomplish organizational objectives or tasks [17]. Ref. [18] defined WP as the collection of expected work-related activities. WP focuses on the employee's behavior while executing the job in order to contribute to the attainment of the established goals of the assigned jobs [19]. Individuals' spirit and psychology are also associated with employee performance [6]. WP is the effort that individuals exert to attain organizational objectives and is not always regarded as the end result [20].

2.4 Theories Related to the Research Topic

The work-family border theory, proposed by [21], refers to a person's balance between work and family. According to this theory, everyone has a role to play in a specific aspect of life, and these aspects can be separated by physical, temporal, or psychological borders. In order to achieve a balance between work and life, employees must create a clear line between the roles that must complete the organization's work and assigned duties and the roles that must meet responsibilities with family, social interactions, and life activities. When any of these roles is violated excessively, the employee loses control of his or her behavior and is unable to generate new ideas or perform well.

The componential model of individual creativity, proposed by [22], suggests that creativity consists of three primary components: expertise, talent; creativity skills; and task motivation. The first component is characterized as the memorization of practical information, technical expertise, and specialized talent in a particular sector. The second component is regarded as a creative skill to be able to approach obstacles with adaptable and innovative thought. Meanwhile, work motivation is a concept comprised of two different components: extrinsic motivation and intrinsic motivation. This theory is used to explain employees' creativity in the workplace.

2.5 Research Hypotheses

The relationship between WLB and WP. WO refers to the excessive workload of employees who must complete it in a short or lengthy period while under time constraints, resulting in poor WP. WO was discovered in [4]'s research of Ethiopian office workers employed by the United Nations. Frequently, they are required to work long, nonstop hours, and as their burden increases, their job efficiency drops. In his study, ref. [8] obtained comparable results. The WO leaves employees with absolutely little time to examine upcoming tasks extensively and thoroughly. As a result, they lack the enthusiasm and positive emotions necessary to generate new, more efficient methods of completing their work. In other words, an excessive task that must be finished in a short period of time causes an employee's time and mental resources to be depleted to accomplish the work with the best possible result. Even if this condition persists for an extended period of time, it will deplete them psychologically and physically, making them more prone to errors and failures at work. Therefore, WO reduces employee effectiveness, which is consistent with both theory and practice. Consequently, this research proposes the following hypothesis:

Hypothesis H1: WO has a negative impact on WP.

WS is the capacity to tolerate work-related stressors such as job burnout and performance anxiety [23, 24]. In prior research, numerous researchers have identified stress in the workplace as a negative factor that has several detrimental effects on the working environment, the stability of the organization's personnel structure, and WP. WS is frequently related to an increase in absenteeism, workplace violence, staff turnover, bad morale, or lower productivity as a result of burnout, poor performance, etc. [25]. Ref. [6] also demonstrated that work-related stress impairs employees' ability to generate beneficial work-related solutions. WS is also seen as a circumstance that threatens, requires, or challenges an organization's output or service delivery growth [9]. WP will alter if the issue of work balance is scrutinized, particularly in terms of enhancing paid work flexibility and improving working environment, according to research by [20]. The study therefore proposes the following research hypothesis:

Hypothesis H2: WS has a negative impact on performance.

Additionally, FWA significantly impacts employees' attitudes toward their jobs and other aspects of their lives [26]. Work arrangement is the process of determining the tasks that must be accomplished and then allocating the proper amount of time to complete them, demonstrating the duties and abilities of each employee [4]. Work arrangement and management abilities enable each individual to rapidly handle difficulties and achieve desired outcomes [6]. Besides, other resources, such as health, money, etc., are also utilized more efficiently in their task. As a result, individuals can perform the specified tasks more efficiently. These individuals, according to [1], have a good WLB, greater job satisfaction, less stress, and less criticism. Therefore, the following hypothesis is proposed:

Hypothesis H3: FWA has a positive impact on WP.

In addition to having roles and responsibilities within his organization, an individual also has roles and responsibilities within his family. FR are considered as the division of roles and responsibilities in a certain area of life, which might be separated by physical, temporal, or psychological boundaries [21]. Incompatibilities between work and family role expectations are a common source of conflict [27]. Ref. [21] discusses this in his family-work boundary theory. In a limited amount of time, the more responsibilities an individual must simultaneously fulfill at work and at home, the greater the likelihood that he or she will be unable to meet all of the requirements for each role. In reality, with 24 hours in a day, each employee spends at least 10 hours at work (including short breaks), and with 6–8 hours to re-energize for the upcoming working day, there is not enough time to care for other family members or engage in other family-related social activities. Thus, it is difficult for them to perform their roles at work and at home. Employees must be under pressure from their own families, especially married women attempting to fulfill mother and wife responsibilities, which severely restricts their ability to contribute to the organization's success [15]. Consequently, the study offers the following hypothesis:

Hypothesis H4: FR has a positive impact on WP.

Ref. [4] argues that OSs, such as expanding welfare and health insurance programs and creating a more comfortable work environment, will assist in reducing employee stress and burnout. OS is also defined as managers' and superiors' interest in areas of work and life, whether directly or indirectly, to promote employee happiness when participating in the organization's operations [28]. Employees frequently view managers as organizational representatives and correlate management activities with organizational behaviors [29]. Trust, empathy, support, encouragement, and the provision of opportunities for employees to expand their potential are the values brought by the manager, which are also perceived by employees as the organization's support for their work. The stronger the organization's support, the more favorable feelings they must increase their work output. Therefore, the following hypothesis is proposed by the study:

Hypothesis H5: OS has a positive impact on WP.

The relationship between WLB and EC. In this study, the only aspect of WLB examined in relation to EC is OS. It, according to [29], comprises emotional support, facility support, role model support, and creative support. All of these have a positive impact on enhancing employees' expertise, creativity, and motivation. Support for models and facilities can help the development of employees' skills and work experience. The support of working facilities or the offer of fresh opportunities to try innovative approaches also inspires employees' creativity. The emotional support of the management encourages employees to learn new knowledge and work abilities. In addition, this support boosts the confidence and optimism of employees over the new ways and methods of work they develop. The creative motivation and work motivation of the employees were also enhanced. Work motivation is one of three key aspects that directly or indirectly affect employees' emotions for them to be creative at work, alongside expertise and creative skills [30]. The support of the company or the support of the boss inspires individuals to be more enthusiastic about their work, interested in discovering new and better ways of doing things, and willing to accomplish new achievements. Research of [11, 13, 16] finds a positive relationship between OS and EC. Therefore, the hypothesis could be expressed as follows:

Hypothesis H6: OS has a positive impact on EC.

The relationship between EC and WP. Creativity is dependent on the expertise required to make appropriate decisions and develop stimuli such as information, relationships, motivation, etc. This can generate alternative solutions and boost organizational performance in a sustainable manner [8]. Intrinsic motivation stimulates the creativity of employee, considerably enhancing their performance at work [6]. Workplace activities and efforts, innovative products, and the quality of products and services all demonstrate the abilities of the employees. Work creativity will influence the quantity of work done and will be measured by productivity, customer happiness, profit growth, or shareholder value [8]. So, the hypothesis can be stated as follows:

Hypothesis H7: EC has a positive impact on WP.

3 Methods

3.1 Measurements

Previous research employed a variety of scales to measure WLB, but ref. [5] assert that a well-validated WLB scale is lacking and must be developed. The original scales are based on previous research by [4, 8]. Following that, the study uses qualitative research methodologies to complete these scales. One-on-one interviews were conducted with two management researchers and three auditing business managers. Group interviews were done with five staff members with at least two years of expertise in the field of accounting and auditing. Experts were polled on the importance of each observed variable on the scale, as well as revisions and additions to new observed variables. The opinions of specialists about the interview approach, questionnaire format, and ease of interpreting the questionnaire were also recorded and considered. As a result, the official scale and questionnaire were developed. The official questionnaire contained 42 statements concerning WLB, EC, and WP. The responses of the interviewees were recorded using a 5-point Likert scale. Personal information regarding respondents (gender, age, work experience, marital status, and so on) was also included.

3.2 Data

Vietnamese employees in the fields of accounting and auditing are the respondents. Face-to-face and online surveys with a pre-designed questionnaire were used to collect data. Convenience sampling method was used. The question "Do you perform accounting or auditing work?" was inserted at the top of the questionnaire to ensure the correct respondents. Incomplete response sheets or answer sheets with only one option were also eliminated. The study circulated 450 questionnaires and received 419 valid replies (about 93.11%) for the subsequent quantitative analytic procedures. The majority of respondents (about 62%) is female. Because the accounting and auditing profession involves great thoroughness and attention to detail, more women than men are employed in the field. Therefore, the gender features of the survey sample are appropriate for the Vietnam context. Regarding age, 40% of survey respondents are between the ages of 31 and 45, 31% are between the ages of 22 and 30, and the remainder are over the age of 45. About working experience, 47% of survey respondents have 1 to 4 years, 31% have 5 or more years, and the rest have less than one year. Regarding family-related features, 64% of respondents are married; 57% have one or two children; 83% do not live with their in-laws' family members; and 63% do not financially support their spouse's family.

4 Results

The research conducted scale reliability analysis and exploratory factor analysis (EFA). The overall Cronbach's Alpha values of the scales are all greater than 0.70, and the total correlation coefficient of each observed variable is greater than 0.30, therefore it can be stated that all the scales are reliable. An exploratory factor analysis (EFA) is conducted using the Principal Axis Factoring extraction method and Promax rotation. The obtained analytical results are as follows: KMO index = 0.9455 > 0.5, Barlett's test with Sig. = 0.000 < 0.05, total variance extracted = 56.267%, and seven factors are retrieved. Since no observable variables are deleted and the composition of the factors did not change, the initial seven factors were kept.

The next stage of the quantitative analysis performed in the research is confirmatory factor analysis (CFA). The measurement model consists of seven latent constructs: FR, WS, WO, WP, OS, EC, and FWA. This measurement model is determined to be appropriate for the gathered data when the CMIN/df index = 1.135, the GFI value = 0.909, the CFI value = 0.987, and the RMSEA value = 0.018. In addition, the acquired CR, AVE, and MSV values all met the standards established by [31], hence this measurement model is reliable, discriminative, and convergent.

The structural equation modeling (SEM) technique is used to determine the connection between concepts. Based on the study's findings, the structural model is assessed as appropriate. The results in Table 1 show that all correlations between concepts are statistically significant at the 5% level of significance.

The study will continue to conduct Bootstrap tests to assess the reliability of the model's estimates. This test employed 1000 replicate samples. All C.R values (–1.96 < C.R. < 1.96) are within the acceptable range. So, the model's estimates are reliable (Fig. 1).

Table 1 The results of regression weights

Path	Regression weights			
	Estimate	S.E.	C.R.	P
OS → EC	0.446	0.058	7.673	0.000***
FR → WP	–0.125	0.048	–2.625	0.009**
OS → WP	0.151	0.056	2.673	0.008**
FWA → WP	0.155	0.047	3.332	0.000***
WS → WP	–0.135	0.048	–2.83	0.005**
WO → WP	–0.129	0.046	–2.791	0.005**
EC → WP	0.253	0.061	4.161	0.000***

5 Results

WO, WS, and FR have a statistically significant negative impact on the employee's WP at the 5% significance level. As a result, the proposed study hypotheses H_1, H_2, and H_4 are supported. The findings on the negative impact of WO and WS on WP are consistent with previous studies by [1, 4, 9]. Accounting and auditing employees are frequently overloaded due to the enormous and careful task, which requires absolute correctness and completion of work on time. This leaves the employee with little time to consider the job in general, resulting in a lack of motivation to come up with innovative ways to manage work efficiently [8]. Employees in the accounting and auditing fields are constantly under pressure from factors such as time, knowledge, qualifications, etc. Not only that, but the huge workload comes with a lot of pressure, pushing staff to work most of the day. As a result, employees no longer have enough time to accomplish important tasks as family members. When employees are required to complete work in the business as well as satisfy family commitments, their WP suffers dramatically due to a lack of time and energy. This result is consistent with the work and family boundary theory of [21], which addresses the issue of crossing boundaries across areas of life, particularly work and family, and causes people to lose control of their behavior, reason, and emotions. When either of these roles is violated excessively, employees lose control of their behavior and are unable to think clearly enough to generate new ideas or perform well.

WP is positively impacted by three factors: FWA, OS, and EC. FWA and EC have a statistically significant impact at the 1% significance level, whereas OS has a statistically significant impact at the 5% significance level. Hypotheses H_3, H_5, and H_7 are thus all supported. The findings of a positive relationship between FWA, OS, and employee WP are consistent with previous research [4, 6, 8, 9]. An organization in any business field is always operated according to a specific process to maintain consistency and efficiency. Accounting and auditing professionals are no exception. With the nature of work requiring speed, meticulousness, and high correctness, a suitable arrangement of the sequence of dealing with the assigned job tasks or the private work of the family helps them solve the issue more quickly. In other words,

WP is enhanced. The positive relationship found in this study between EC and WP is similar to the results in prior studies such as [6, 8]. Creativity in the workplace enables employees to find better ways to operate in order to complete tasks more efficiently.

According to the findings of this study, OS has a statistically significant positive effect on EC at the 1% significance level. This impact has a relatively large magnitude, 0.446. Previous research by [4, 6, 8, 9, 11, 13, 16] support the above view. Employees will have more confidence and excitement to be more creative to find the ideal way to operate at peak performance if they are encouraged and inspired to be creative in the process of doing work and their creativity is respected and appreciated by the organization and manager. The manager's dedicated assistance, training programs, financial support from the organization, or just giving employees the opportunity to try new things in the organization will create the most suitable conditions for employees to encourage their own creativity in the workplace.

Aside from the direct influence, OS has an indirect impact on WP via the mediating role of EC. In this scenario, the magnitude of indirect influence is $0.446*0.253 = 0.113$, and the indirect effect is positive. That is, as the OS increased, so did the EC, and the growth in this EC boosted their WP. With EC as the mediator variable, the aggregate impact of OS on WP is: $0.151 + 0.113 = 0.264$. Thus, when compared to its direct impact, EC as a mediator variable has boosted the influence of OS on WP.

6 Conclusions and Recommendations

Many studies have been undertaken to discover the factors influencing employee WP, ranging from stress to WLB. However, there have not been many studies proving the impact of EC on WP, particularly for employees working in the fields of accounting and auditing, where the profession is constantly under pressure and has high standards. WO, WS, FWA, OS, FR, EC, and WP are all factors in the suggested research model. EC is a mediator variable impacting accountants' and auditors' employee performance in Vietnam.

Adjustments are required to reduce negative factors that affect WP, such as WS and WO. Employees in accounting and auditing, in particular, frequently work extra due to a heavy workload, especially when it comes time to inventory and report monthly, quarterly, and annually to shareholders and tax offices, resulting in mistakes in the reported data. However, when managers are required to guide and provide flexible workloads for their employees, the effects will be more beneficial. This is similar to [8]'s argument that important jobs are prioritized to be completed earlier, providing a sense of ease when there is more time to do tasks that need less time. They take less time and are less important. Reference [6] concur that job management abilities are crucial for individuals to efficiently address issues and achieve desired outcomes. Besides, the importance of creativity in accounting and auditing, as well as other fields in general, must constantly be appropriately cared for through OS. Managers should consider the following suggested activities: periodic health care, professional

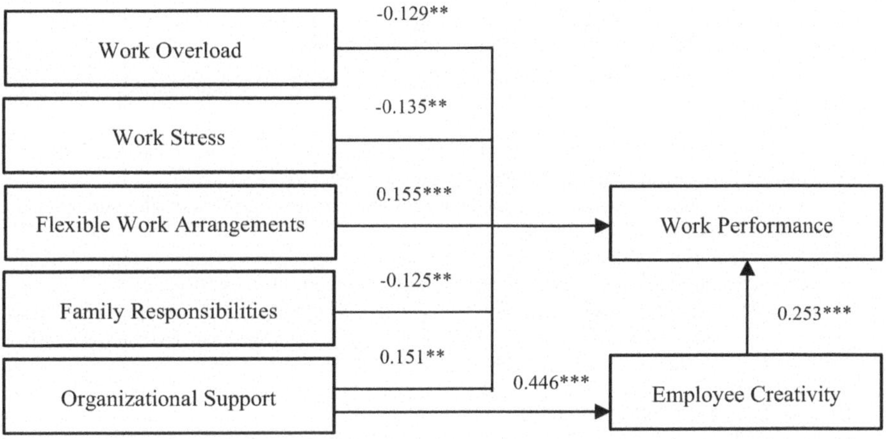

Fig. 1 The results of structural model

training, and retraining, motivating, encouraging, and listening to employees' aspirations, as well as reducing negative influences by adjusting and arranging the appropriate workload, allowing employees to actively choose a working location, and reporting the progress of processing records remotely without entering the company so that employees do not feel overloaded at work. As a result, EC is increased, and WP is improved.

Limitations and Future Research

This study examines the relationship between WLB, EC, and WP using a non-probability sampling technique. Therefore, they lack representativeness and cannot be generalized to the population. This is the study's first limitation. The study will be of greater value if it is conducted using stratified probability sampling. Moreover, the study examines the effects of WLB and EC on WP. There are many other factors that affect an employee's WP and creativity, including fair compensation, reasonable working time allocation, flexible working location, professional knowledge, colleague cooperation, and so on. Therefore, further studies that add the above factors to the existing research model are necessary.

References

1. Haider, S., Jabeen, S., Ahmad, J.: Moderated mediation between work life balance and employee job performance: The role of psychological wellbeing and satisfaction with coworkers. J. Work Organ. Psychol. **34**(1), 29–37 (2018)
2. Dousin, O., Collins, N., Kler, B.K.: Work-life balance, employee job performance and satisfaction among doctors and nurses in Malaysia. Int. J. Hum. Resour. Stud. **9**(4), 306–319 (2019)

3. Rusu, R.: Work-family balance: Theoretical and empirical perspectives. International Conference Knowledge-Based Organization **24**(2), 383–387 (2018)
4. Teklu, B.: The effect of work-life balance on employee performance: the case of UNDP Ethiopia. St. Mary's University, (2020). [Online]. Available http://hdl.handle.net/123456789/5608
5. Le, H., Newman, A., Menzies, J., Zheng, C., Fermelis, J.: Work–life balance in Asia: A systematic review. Hum. Resour. Manag. Rev. **30**(4), 100766 (2020)
6. Bodla, M.A., Naeem, B.: Creativity as mediator for intrinsic motivation and sales performance. Creat. Res. J. **26**(4), 468–473 (2014)
7. Johari, J., Tan, F.Y., Zulkarnain, Z.I.T.: Autonomy, workload, work-life balance and job performance among teachers. Int. J. Educ. Manag. **32**(1), 107–120 (2018)
8. Ximenes, M., Supartha, W.G., Manuati Dewi, I.G.A., Sintaasih, D.K.: Entrepreneurial leadership moderating high performance work system and employee creativity on employee performance. Cogent Bus. & Manag., **6**(1), 1697512 (2019)
9. Adnan Bataineh, K.: Impact of work-life balance, happiness at work, on employee performance. Int. Bus. Res., **12**(2), 99–112 (2019)
10. Henker, N., Sonnentag, S., Unger, D.: Transformational leadership and employee creativity: The mediating role of promotion focus and creative process engagement. J. Bus. Psychol. **30**, 235–247 (2015)
11. Anderson, N., Potočnik, K., Zhou, J.: Innovation and creativity in organizations: A state-of-the-science review, prospective commentary, and guiding framework. J. Manag. **40**(5), 1297–1333 (2014)
12. Ahmad, N., Ullah, Z., AlDhaen, E., Han, H., Scholz, M.: A CSR perspective to foster employee creativity in the banking sector: The role of work engagement and psychological safety. J. Retail. Consum. Serv. **67**, 102968 (2022)
13. Ibrahim, H.I., Isa, A., Shahbudin, A.S.M.: Organizational support and creativity: The role of developmental experiences as a moderator. Procedia Econ. Financ. **35**, 509–514 (2016)
14. Kelliher, C., Richardson, J., Boiarintseva, G.: All of work? All of life? Reconceptualising work-life balance for the 21st century. Hum. Resour. Manag. J. **29**(2), 97–112 (2019)
15. Nguyên, N.T.: Mối quan hệ giữa căng thẳng trong công việc và hiệu suất công việc, động lực làm việc. Tạp chí khoa học Yersin—Chuyên đề Quản lý Kinh tế **5**(8/2019), 36–48 (2019)
16. Fu, Q., et al.: Enhancing employee creativity in the banking sector: a transformational leadership framework. Sustainability **14**(8), 4643 (2022)
17. Miao, R., Cao, Y.: High-performance work system, work well-being, and employee creativity: Cross-level moderating role of transformational leadership. Int. J. Environ. Res. Public Health **16**(9), 1640 (2019)
18. Griffin, R.W., Phillips, J.M., Gully, S.M.: Organizational behavior: Managing people and organizations. Cengage Learning, (2016)
19. Saithong-in, S., Ussahawanitchakit, P.: Psychological capital and job performance: An empirical research of certified public accountants (CPAs) in Thailand. Bus. Manag. Rev. **7**(5), 499 (2016)
20. Gong, Y., Huang, J.-C., Farh, J.-L.: Employee learning orientation, transformational leadership, and employee creativity: The mediating role of employee creative self-efficacy. Acad. Manag. J. **52**(4), 765–778 (2009)
21. Clark, S.C.: Work/family border theory: A new theory of work/family balance. Human Relations **53**(6), 747–770 (2000)
22. Amabile, T.M.: Creativity and innovation in organizations. Harvard Business School Boston, (1996)
23. Allen, T.D., Shockley, K.M., Poteat, L.: Protégé anxiety attachment and feedback in mentoring relationships. J. Vocat. Behav. **77**(1), 73–80 (2010)
24. Firth, L., Mellor, D.J., Moore, K.A., Loquet, C.: How can managers reduce employee intention to quit? J. Manag. Psychol. **19**(2), 170–187 (2004)
25. Allen, T.D., Herst, D.E., Bruck, C.S., Sutton, M.: Consequences associated with work-to-family conflict: a review and agenda for future research. J. Occup. Health Psychol. **5**(2), 278 (2000)

26. Hayman, J.R.: Flexible work arrangements: Exploring the linkages between perceived usability of flexible work schedules and work/life balance. Community Work Fam. **12**(3), 327–338 (2009)
27. Netemeyer, R.G., Boles, J.S., McMurrian, R.: Development and validation of work–family conflict and family–work conflict scales. J. Appl. Psychol. **81**(4), 400 (1996)
28. Muñoz-Pascual, L., Galende, J., Curado, C.: Contributions to sustainability in SMEs: Human resources, sustainable product innovation performance and the mediating role of employee creativity. Sustainability **13**(4), 2008 (2021)
29. Hammer, L.B., Kossek, E.E., Yragui, N.L., Bodner, T.E., Hanson, G.C.: Development and validation of a multidimensional measure of family supportive supervisor behaviors (FSSB). J. Manag. **35**(4), 837–856 (2009)
30. Amabile, T.M.: Motivating creativity in organizations: On doing what you love and loving what you do. Calif. Manage. Rev. **40**(1), 39–58 (1997)
31. Hair, J.F., Black, W.C., Babin, B.J., Anderson, R.E., Tatham, R.L.: Multivariate data analysis, vol. 6. (2006)

Impact of the Authentic Leadership on Employee's Creativity: The Intermediate Role of Well-Being, Person-Job Fit, Person-Organization Fit

Anh Thuy Trinh, Tram Thi Bich Nguyen, and Nuong Thi Xuan Nguyen

Abstract Authentic leadership stands as a crucial determinant of individual creativity within organizational contexts, as evidenced by extensive scholarly research [1–4]. This study aims to construct and validate a comprehensive model elucidating the relationship between authentic leadership and individual creativity, considering intervening variables such as well-being, person-job fit, and person-organization fit [5–9], particularly within the service industry domain. Employing a mixed-method approach, qualitative techniques refine the research model and measurement instruments, followed by quantitative analysis involving 628 respondents. Findings underscore the mediating role of well-being, person-job fit, and person-organization fit in this relationship, with well-being notably influencing individual creativity within organizational contexts. Implications suggest that authentic leaders, by prioritizing meaningful relationships with employees, can foster beliefs, competencies, and efforts conducive to enhanced individual creativity, thereby augmenting organizational efficacy and quality of life. In conclusion, this study underscores the imperative for leaders to cultivate positive attributes and behaviors to effectively nurture creativity and innovation within organizations.

Keywords Authentic leadership · Employee well-being · Employee creativity · Well-being · Person-job fit · Person-organization fit

A. T. Trinh (✉)
University of Economics Ho Chi Minh City, Ho Chi Minh City, Vietnam
e-mail: thuyanh@ueh.edu.vn

T. T. B. Nguyen
Ho Chi Minh City Open University, Ho Chi Minh City, Vietnam

N. T. X. Nguyen
Vietnam Happy Human Resources Co, Ltd, Ho Chi Minh City, Vietnam

L. T. Tung et al. (eds.), *Disruptive Technology and Business Continuity*,
https://doi.org/10.1007/978-981-97-5452-6_12

1 Introduction

Numerous preceding studies have delved into the correlation between leadership and employee creativity, with a primary focus on leader-member exchange and self-leadership behaviors, notably transformational leadership [10, 11]. Despite the extensive exploration of these areas, scant attention has been paid to authentic leadership, although theoretical discourse posits its potential to stimulate creativity [3, 12–14]. Authentic leadership, distinguished by its cultivation of positive, supportive, fair, and transparent interactions, is posited to engender favorable employee emotions, thus offering compelling grounds to consider its association with individual creativity.

Early empirical research has indeed established a linkage between authentic leadership and individual creativity; however, the mechanisms underpinning this relationship remain inadequately explicated. Authentic leadership is deemed pivotal in fostering individual creativity, as underscored by extant literature [1, 3]. Moreover, individual creativity is purportedly influenced by the alignment between individuals and their jobs, as well as the compatibility between individuals and their organizations [5, 6].

Furthermore, there exists a discernible nexus between authentic leadership and employee well-being, reinforcing the significance of authentic leadership in organizational settings [8, 9].

Shifting our focus to the contemporary landscape of the labor market, a report detailing the labor market situation in 2022 reveals a resurgence in activity, with positive indications stemming from enterprise production activities. Nonetheless, the advent of the COVID-19 pandemic has precipitated transformative trends within the job market, affecting the employment preferences of workers.

Significantly, nearly 80% of full-time employees express an intent to transition to new employment opportunities, indicative of a paradigm shift away from conventional inclinations towards job stability. This trend persists even amidst the post-pandemic economic recovery, with workers displaying a pronounced inclination towards professional development and growth. Statistical insights gleaned from surveys underscore the prevalence of job-seeking behavior across various employment ranks, thereby accentuating the competitive dynamics of the labor market.

Survey respondents have articulated five key criteria driving their job-seeking endeavors, comprising salary, compensation, conducive work environment, career advancement prospects, and the organizational brand strength. Against this backdrop, the pivotal role of authentic leadership in fostering employee happiness, engagement, and productivity comes to the fore, with true leaders poised to enhance organizational competitiveness through volunteerism, creativity stimulation, and spontaneous goal achievement.

Consequently, the imperative to scrutinize the impact of authentic leadership on employee creativity, mediated by employee well-being, people-work compatibility, and people-organization compatibility, becomes increasingly salient in the current milieu. This study endeavors to contribute a novel theoretical framework, contextualized within the tourism industry, to illuminate the intricate interplay between authentic leadership and employee creativity.

2 Literature Review

2.1 *Authentic Leadership*

According to [12], authentic leadership is characterized by behaviors that foster positive psychological outcomes, such as creating an ethical environment, enhancing self-awareness, and promoting ethical attitudes. These traits lead to a more balanced approach to processing information, increased transparency, and stronger relationships with followers, ultimately contributing to their positive self-development. Research has identified four key aspects of authentic leadership: (1) Self-awareness—a deep understanding of one's strengths, weaknesses, and the multifaceted nature of the self, along with an awareness of the impact on and perceptions of others, continuously refined through feedback [12, 15]. (2) Transparency in relationships—demonstrated by openly sharing information, thoughts, and genuine emotions in interactions while avoiding inappropriate emotional expressions [13, 15]. (3) An intrinsic moral perspective—where leaders consistently uphold and adhere to principles, standards, and core moral values as a matter of personal choice [14]. (4) Balanced processing—the objective analysis of all relevant information before making decisions, promoting fairness in decision-making [8, 9, 12, 16, 17]. In this study, the authors define authentic leadership based on these four dimensions.

2.2 *Employee Well-Being*

Employee well-being is defined as the happiness or positive emotional state derived from evaluating one's job or work experience [18]. Earlier studies have highlighted affect, anxiety, and frustration as key psychological indicators of happiness, while physiological indicators include blood pressure and heart condition [19]. Scholars have approached understanding employee well-being through two lenses: positive and negative. The negative approach focuses on studying burnout and occupational stress, while the positive approach pertains to a state of happiness comprising two dimensions: pleasure and arousal [8, 19]. Consequently, emotional happiness has been termed general happiness [17]. Well-being has been utilized in several studies to measure overall happiness [18, 20, 21].

2.3 Person-Job Fit

In the literature on occupational compatibility and characteristics, John Holland's Person-Environmental fit theory has been extensively utilized. This compatibility is defined as person-job fit [17, 22]. Person-job fit is conceptualized as the degree to which an individual's knowledge, skills, abilities, and values meet the requirements of a particular job or job duties [5, 17, 22, 23].

2.4 Person-Organization Fit

Person-organization fit studies originate from Moley's [17] definition of human behavior as a function of the individual and the individual's environment. In the organizational context, person-organization fit is a process that influences employees' attitudes and behaviors towards work. In a broader sense, it pertains to the compatibility between individuals' personal values, beliefs, norms, and expectations with those of the organization [5]. People-organizational fit is defined as the alignment between personal and organizational values, such as creativity and focus on teamwork [7, 24]. People-organization fit entails the overall harmony between individuals and the values of the organization they work for, including the alignment between leaders and the organization's purpose, and the balance of satisfaction between the organization's overall structure and its employees' needs [20, 21].

2.5 Employee Creativity

Employee creativity, a crucial aspect of human capital, involves the generation of novel and valuable ideas. Creativity is the creation of valuable and useful new products, services, ideas, procedures, or processes by individuals within a complex social system [25]. Defined as the manifestation of novel and useful ideas, creativity is a social process comprising three main components: expertise, creative thinking skills, and motivation [26]. According to [7], creativity is akin to a "combination game," where the mind juggles various ideas until they collide in novel ways. Environmental factors such as creativity, autonomy, resources, pressure, and organizational obstacles influence creativity [11]. Innovation suffers as creativity declines and workplace obstacles increase [10]. Unstructured, stress-free time to generate and develop new ideas can foster creativity [2]. Intrinsic motivation enhances creativity [25].

2.6 Leader-Member Exchange Theory (LMX)

Numerous studies have explored authentic leadership's role in fostering positive relationships between leaders and members, thereby improving attitudes and enhancing employee creativity [10, 25]. However, scant attention has been paid to the mediating effects of employee well-being, person-job fit, and person-organization fit on the relationship between authentic leadership and employee creativity [6]. In this study, the authors propose to investigate the impact of authentic leadership on employee creativity and the mediating role of employee well-being, person-job fit, and person-organization fit within the framework of the LMX.

2.7 Theory of Planned Behavior (TPB)

The TPB predicts an individual's intention to engage in specific behavior at a particular time and place. It posits that individual behavior is governed by behavioral plans, which are influenced by the individual's attitude towards the behavior, subjective norms, and perceived behavioral control [27]. The strength of TPB lies in its inclusion of the "perceived control behavior" factor, enabling individuals to exert control over their behavior rather than being solely driven by emotions. By synthesizing elements from authentic leadership styles that impact employees' creative consciousness, TPB aims to promote employees' creative intentions.

3 Hypothesis Development

The link between authentic leadership and person-job fit can be elucidated by leaders' capacity to comprehend employee needs. Early leadership research by [13] suggested that authentic leaders elevate employees' needs from lower level (including physiological and safety) to higher level (including self-esteem and self-actualization) according to Maslow's hierarchy of needs. Specifically, authentic leaders are expected to employ inspirational methods to influence employees' attitudes towards their work [15] and enhance job significance [12], while also connecting work to a broader purpose [14]. By consistently offering support to employees, authentic leadership fosters experiential learning opportunities [23], bolstering employees' confidence in their abilities as they receive positive feedback on their efforts and performance [28]. Consequently, it is plausible to posit that authentic leaders increase the likelihood of person-job fit for employees [17, 22]. Based on these arguments, we hypothesize that:

H1: *Authentic leadership is positively related to person-job fit.*

Person-job fit can be associated with employee well-being for several reasons. Firstly, a positive perception of the match between person and job enables employees to experience greater job satisfaction. Ref. [5] noted that perceiving task alignment fosters greater work enjoyment. Additionally, ref. [5] and [9] have demonstrated that a suitable match between employees' skills and job demands enhances job satisfaction. Secondly, when employees perceive a close alignment between their abilities and job requirements, they experience reduced stress, burnout, and anxiety [7], thus mitigating the negative impact of burnout on employee well-being [17], as evidenced in [8].

Lastly, ref. [3] suggested that employees' personal resources contribute to happiness by fostering personal growth and goal attainment. Person-job fit enables employees to perform their roles effectively [23] because individuals possessing the requisite skills for the job can execute their tasks proficiently [17], thereby enhancing their efficacy. Therefore, we propose the following hypothesis:

H2: *Person-job fit is positively related to employee well-being.*

Researchers contend that authentic leaders cultivate a sense of collective pride among organizational members by articulating visionary and attainable goals while emphasizing shared values [13]. Consequently, these members perceive organizational values as relevant not only to the leader's vision but also aligned with their own values, fostering a sense of worth within the organization [14]. Moreover, authentic leaders are adept at fostering a high degree of alignment with person-organization fit, as they effectively communicate these values to others, thereby establishing people-organization compatibility [20]. From a theoretical standpoint, both social identity theory and organizational identity offer insights into how leaders can foster a strong sense of person-organization fit [28]. Authentic leaders also assist members in tackling problems and finding creative solutions to organizational challenges, thereby fostering robust person-organizational linkages conducive to organizational success. Therefore, the authors hypothesize:

H3: *Authentic leadership is positively related to person-organization fit.*

Ref. [21] proposed the concept of fit between individuals and organizations (P-O fit), emphasizing the importance of considering selection and socialization processes when studying and predicting employee behavior. Ref. [24] demonstrated that person-organization fit reflects cultural alignment based on shared values between individuals and organizations. When employees perceive alignment between their preferences and those of the organization or their colleagues, they perceive the organizational environment more positively. Ref. [16] found that when employees' psychological needs are met, they experience motivation and happiness. When employees' values align with those of the organization, they exhibit positive work performance and attitudes [13, 21, 29]. Therefore, the authors posit:

H4: *Person-organization fit is positively related to employee well-being.*

Happiness can be defined as the balance between positive and negative emotions in one's life [3]. Employee well-being is crucial in organizations as it directly impacts employees' positive and negative emotions at work. Employees experiencing more positive emotions than negative ones are happier, more enthusiastic, and more confident [17], fostering commitment to organizational goals and values, increased effort, and a sense of organizational belonging. Therefore, employee well-being is positively associated with desirable organizational behaviors and attitudes, such as organizational commitment, citizenship behavior, and performance [8, 29].

Previous research has demonstrated that employee well-being is influenced by both the physical and psychological work environment [8]. Leadership style is a significant psychological factor in the work environment affecting employee well-being [19]. Leader support acts as a work resource that influences employee well-being through the quality of the leader-employee relationship [18]. Authentic leadership enhances employee well-being for three reasons. Firstly, authentic leaders foster trust among employees, thereby improving well-being by reducing risk, vulnerability, and potential stress [6]. Secondly, the supportive behavior of authentic leaders contributes to job satisfaction, an indicator of happiness, by helping employees achieve their job goals and fostering intrinsic job satisfaction [29]. Thirdly, the openness and accessibility of authentic leaders can reduce job stress and enhance employee well-being [19]. Consequently, the hypothesis is proposed as follows:

H5: *Authentic leadership is positively related to employee well-being.*

Given that creativity involves the generation of novel and valuable ideas, it can be argued that employee well-being at work influences creativity [25]. Positive emotions stimulate the formation of novel ideas and creativity [18]. Positive emotions at work increase the inclination to explore new ideas, seek out information, and develop one's potential, thereby promoting individual creativity [18]. Employees with high levels of happiness are more resilient physically and mentally, which enhances their creativity [17]. Regular experiences of positive emotions enable employees to thrive in challenging situations, stimulating their creativity [18]. Positive mood states facilitate more fluid and original creativity [26], as individuals with a positive mindset tend to have richer associations within existing knowledge structures, making them more flexible and creative. According to [30], the interaction between positive and negative affect influences employee creativity, with happier individuals demonstrating greater creativity [2]. Based on this evidence, the following hypothesis is proposed:

H6: *Employee well-being positively influences employee creativity.*

4 Research Methodology

In order to ensure the validity and reliability of the data, this study employed an online questionnaire as the instrument for data collection. The questionnaire offers ease of use and facilitates the analysis of data, particularly in quantitative research where data is numerical in nature. The constructs measured in this research study were selected and adapted from previous studies, namely authentic leadership, employee well-being, employee creativity, well-being, person-job fit, and person-organization fit, as presented in Table 1. The Likert scale technique was utilized for the research, with respondents indicating their agreement level on a scale ranging from 1 (strongly disagree) to 5 (strongly agree).

Table 1 Measurement indicators

Construct	Measurement indicators	Adapted source
Authentic leadership	My leadership seeks feedback to improve interactions with others My leader describes exactly how others view his/her abilities My leader shows that he/she clearly understands his/her strengths and weaknesses My leader is well aware of his/her impact on others My leader made it clear what he/she meant My leader acknowledges his/her mistakes as they happen My leadership openly shares information with others My leaders clearly communicate their ideas and thoughts to others My leadership is always asking for challenging ideas My leadership carefully listens to alternative points of view before drawing conclusions My leadership objectively analyzes relevant data before making a decision My leadership encourages others to voice opposing views My leader demonstrates consistency between his/her beliefs and actions My leaders always have faith when making decisions My leader resists pressure to force him/her to do things that are different from his/her beliefs My leader is guided in his/her actions by internal ethical standards	[7, 12, 13, 15, 19]
Person-job fit	My skills and abilities match my job My job requirements perfectly match my likes and dislikes There is a good fit between my work and me	[5, 22, 23, 32]
Creativity employee	You realize the opportunity when solving a new job Are you looking for new ideas/new ways to solve problems? You come up with a novel but doable idea You show originality in work	[7, 10, 11, 25]
Well-being	For the past 6 months, I've been feeling motivated In the past 6 months, I have felt a lot of energy In the past 6 months, I feel energetic For the past 6 months, I've been feeling energetic For the past 6 months, I have felt very happy In the past 6 months, I feel happy	[8, 16, 18, 33]
Person-organization fit	My personal values align well with my organization The values of the organization I work for align with my personal values The organization I work for has a value of honesty that aligns with my personal values The values of the organization I work for have values of fairness that align with my personal values	[5–7]

The authors conducted a survey and obtained responses from 631 individuals, out of which 628 questionnaires were deemed valid. Hence, the study was carried out with a sample size of 628 survey participants. The data analysis involved the utilization of SPSS 25.0 software for testing demographic variables, and Smart PLS 3.3.9 software for evaluating measurement models and structural models, as recommended by [31]. All survey respondents were aged 18 years or older and were located in Ho Chi Minh City.

Following the complete collection of data from the survey sample, the authors proceeded to analyze the data using SPSS and Smart PLS software. Various statistical tests were employed to draw conclusions, including descriptive statistics, evaluation of scale reliability using Cronbach's Alpha coefficient, exploratory factor analysis (EFA), and confirmatory factor analysis (CFA) to assess the scale of the research model for ensuring appropriate reliability. Subsequently, after conducting CFA analysis and checking reliability, discriminant validity, and convergence, structural equation modeling (SEM) was utilized to examine the hypotheses and confirm the relationships between variables.

Lastly, the authors employed bootstrap testing to assess the difference between the normalized estimate in the SEM model and the mean normalized estimate of the bootstrap. A negligible bias in this comparison indicates good reliability of the initial estimates in the SEM model.

5 Results and Discussion

The factors of employee well-being, person-job fit, and person-organization fit all serve as mediators in the relationship between authentic leadership and employee creativity. In this study, the impact level of person-job fit and person-organization fit factors is not particularly high. Firstly, the influence of authentic leadership on person-organization fit demonstrates a relatively high level of impact (beta = 0.870), consistent with prior research by [5, 17]. However, the impact of person-organization fit on employee well-being is at a moderate level (beta = 0.124), deviating slightly from findings in [17]. Conversely, the influence level of the relationship between person-job fit and employee well-being is also not high (beta = 0.124) (Fig. 1).

With the surveyed sample in this study, authentic leadership exhibits a notable impact on other factors, with beta coefficients of 0.918, 0.695, and 0.870 corresponding to the relationships between authentic leadership and person-job fit, authentic leadership and employee well-being, and authentic leadership and person-organization fit, respectively. This suggests that employee well-being is significantly bolstered by the role of authentic leadership, while person-job fit and person-organization fit make relatively minor contributions to employee well-being.

Lastly, the degree of influence of employee well-being on employee creativity is notably high (beta = 0.902). This implies that when employees experience higher levels of happiness, their creativity is significantly enhanced.

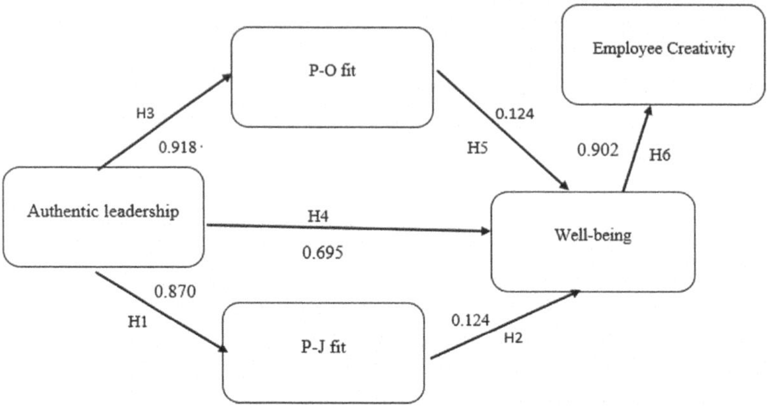

Fig. 1 Research framework

Table 2 Result

Hypothesis	Beta	P-value	Final conclusion
H1	0.807	0.000	Accept
H2	0.124	0.000	Accept
H3	0.918	0.000	Accept
H4	0.695	0.006	Accept
H5	0.124	0.000	Accept
H6	0.902	0.000	Accept

The results presented in Table 2 indicate that all hypotheses are accepted, as evidenced by the P values being less than 0.05. Specifically, authentic leadership demonstrates a positive impact on person-job fit (H1) and a robust relationship is observed between employee well-being and employee creativity (H6). Additionally, hypotheses (H2) and (H4) reveal that person-job fit and person-organization fit also positively affect employee well-being, albeit with relatively minor impacts. Similarly, hypotheses (H3) and (H5) highlight strong relationships between authentic leadership and person-organization fit, as well as between authentic leadership and employee well-being. These findings are further supported by the bootstrapping method [31].

6 Concluding Remarks

While the study makes significant theoretical and practical contributions, it is important to acknowledge its limitations. First, the research data used to measure and evaluate the scale and test the model were gathered from a restricted geographical area. Consequently, the findings may not be fully representative. Future research endeavors could expand to include a broader geographic scope, encompassing various provinces and cities, to provide a more comprehensive understanding.

Second, this study investigates the working age demographic without imposing limitations based on specific occupations. Future research avenues could explore more focused research directions within specific industries or fields, offering deeper insights into the dynamics at play.

Third, the survey sample is limited to individuals who have some form of association with the authors. This may introduce bias into the findings. Including a more diverse range of participants from various backgrounds would enhance the robustness and generalizability of the study outcomes.

Fourth, the scales used to assess authentic leadership, people-work compatibility, people-organization compatibility, employee well-being, and employee creativity are adapted from foreign sources. As such, there is a need to develop and validate measurement tools that are culturally tailored to the Vietnamese context to ensure the accuracy and relevance of the findings.

Last but not least, while this study focuses on authentic leadership, there exists a multitude of leadership styles that could impact employee creativity. Future research endeavors could delve into these alternative leadership styles to provide a more nuanced understanding of their influence on employee creativity and organizational outcomes.

Addressing these limitations and embracing future research directions will contribute to advancing knowledge in the field of leadership and its implications for employee creativity within the Vietnamese context.

References

1. Zhou, J., George, J.M.: Awakening employee creativity: The role of leader emotional intelligence. Leadersh. Q. **14**(4–5), 545–568 (2003)
2. Hirst, G., Van Dick, R., Van Knippenberg, D.: A social identity perspective on leadership and employee creativity. J. Organ. Behav. **30**(7), 963–982 (2009)
3. Semedo, A.S.D., Coelho, A.F.M., Ribeiro, N.M.P.: Authentic leadership and creativity: the mediating role of happiness. Int. J. Organ. Anal. **25**(3), 395–412 (2017)
4. Liu, X., Zhu, Z., Liu, Z., Fu, C.: The influence of leader empowerment behaviour on employee creativity. Manag. Decis. **58**, 2681–2703 (2020)
5. Afsar, B., Badir, Y., Khan, M.M.: Person–job fit, person–organization fit and innovative work behavior: The mediating role of innovation trust. J. High Technol. Managem. Res. **26**(2), 105–116 (2015)
6. Seong, J.Y., Choi, J.N.: Is person–organization fit beneficial for employee creativity? moderating roles of leader–member and team–member exchange quality. Hum. Perform. **32**(3–4), 129–144 (2019)
7. Liu, S., Chu, F., Guo, M., Liu, Y.: Authentic leadership, person-organization fit and collectivistic orientation: a moderated-mediated model of workplace safety. Leadersh. Org. Dev. J. **42**(8), 1295–1310 (2021)
8. Nelson, K., Boudrias, J.S., Brunet, L., Morin, D., De Civita, M., Savoie, A., Alderson, M.: Authentic leadership and psychological well-being at work of nurses: The mediating role of work climate at the individual level of analysis. Burn. Res. **1**(2), 90–101 (2014)

9. Rahimnia, F., Sharifirad, M.S.: Authentic leadership and employee well-being: The mediating role of attachment insecurity. J. Bus. Ethics **132**(2), 363–377 (2015)
10. Gumusluoglu, L., Ilsev, A.: Transformational leadership, creativity, and organizational innovation. J. Bus. Res. **62**(4), 461–473 (2009)
11. Gong, Y., Huang, J.C., Farh, J.L.: Employee learning orientation, transformational leadership, and employee creativity: The mediating role of employee creative self-efficacy. Acad. Manag. J. **52**(4), 765–778 (2009)
12. Goffee, R., Jones, G.: Authentic leadership. Lead.Ship Excel., **26**(7), 17 (2009)
13. Luthans, F., Avolio, B.J.: Authentic leadership development. Posit. Organ. Sch., **241**, 258 (2003)
14. Novicevic, M.M., Harvey, M.G., Ronald, M., Brown-Radford, J.A.: Authentic leadership: A historical perspective. J. Lead.Ship & Organ. Stud. **13**(1), 64–76 (2006)
15. Avolio, B.J., Griffith, J., Wernsing, T.S., Walumbwa, F.O.: What is authentic leadership development? p. 39, (2010)
16. Mansor, N.A., Wai, C.M., Mohamed, A., Shah, I.M.: The relationship between management style and employees' well-being: a case of non-managerial staffs. Procedia Soc. Behav. Sci. **40**, 521–529 (2012)
17. Choi, S.B., Tran, T.B.H., Kang, S.W.: Inclusive leadership and employee well-being: The mediating role of person-job fit. J. Happiness Stud. **18**(6), 1877–1901 (2017)
18. Wright, T.A., Cropanzano, R., Bonett, D.G.: The moderating role of employee positive well being on the relation between job satisfaction and job performance. J. Occup. Health Psychol. **12**(2), 93 (2007)
19. Ozkan, S., Ceylan, A.: Collective efficacy as a mediator of the relationship between authentic leadership and well-being at work. Int. Bus. Res. **9**(6), 17–30 (2016)
20. Piasentin, K.A., Chapman, D.S.: Subjective person–organization fit: Bridging the gap between conceptualization and measurement. J. Vocat. Behav. **69**(2), 202–221 (2006)
21. Morley, M.J.: Person-organization fit. J. Manag. Psychol., **22**(2), 109–117 (2007)
22. Bui, H.T., Zeng, Y., Higgs, M.: The role of person-job fit in the relationship between transformational leadership and job engagement. J. Manag. Psychol. **32**(5), 373–386 (2017)
23. Sekiguchi, T.: Person-organization fit and person-job fit in employee selection: A review of the literature. Osaka keidai ronshu **54**(6), 179–196 (2004)
24. Memon, M.A., Salleh, R., Baharom, M.N.R., Harun, H.: Person-organization fit and turnover intention: The mediating role of employee engagement. Glob. Bus. Manag. Res. **6**(3), 205 (2014)
25. Hennessey, B.A., Amabile, T.M.: Creativity. Annu. Rev. Psychol. **61**, 569–598 (2010)
26. Amabile, T.M., Barsade, S.G., Mueller, J.S., Staw, B.M.: Affect and creativity at work. Adm. Sci. Q. **50**(3), 367–403 (2005)
27. Ajzen, I.: The theory of planned behaviour. Organ. Behav. Hum. Decis. Process. **50**, 179–211 (1991)
28. Verquer, M.L., Beehr, T.A., Wagner, S.H.: A meta-analysis of relations between person–organization fit and work attitudes. J. Vocat. Behav. **63**(3), 473–489 (2003)
29. Mortier, A.: Acting upon the true self: the role of authentic leadership in enhancing followers' well-being at work. Doctoral dissertation, Ghent University, (2017)
30. Chen, M.H., Kaufmann, G.: Employee creativity and R&D: A critical review. Creat. Innov. Manag. **17**(1), 71–76 (2008)
31. Hair, J.F., Hult, T.M., Ringle, C., Sarstdt, M.: A Primer on Partial Least Squares Structural Equation Modeling (PLS-SEM), 3rd edn. Sage Publishing, (2022)
32. Westerman, J.W., Cyr, L.A.: An integrative analysis of person–organization fit theories. Int. J. Sel. Assess. **12**(3), 252–261 (2004)
33. Wu, T.J., Gao, J.Y., Wang, L.Y., Yuan, K.S.: Exploring links between polychronicity and job performance from the person–environment fit perspective—The mediating role of well-being. Int. J. Environ. Res. Public Health **17**(10), 3711 (2020)

Knowledge Sharing for Enhanced Job Engagement of Public Servants in Ho Chi Minh City

Le Quang Thang and Mai Ngoc Khuong

Abstract In public organizations, engaged employees are motivated by a sense of purpose and a commitment to serving the public interest. When knowledge is freely exchanged among public servants, a culture of collaboration emerges, leading to several positive outcomes that contribute to enhanced job engagement, pivotal for sustaining organizational operations. Additionally, within the changing landscape emphasizing sustainability, a knowledge-intensive environment enables public organizations to adapt to technological advancements and develop sustainable policies. Consequently, this study aims to identify the factors impacting knowledge sharing and job engagement among public servants in Ho Chi Minh City at all levels of government. The study employed quantitative research methods with a sample of 300 respondents. The results revealed that centralization, integration, support, social interaction, reciprocity, and trust affect knowledge sharing, while formalization, centralization, integration, social interaction, and reciprocity affect job engagement. Notably, knowledge sharing was found to promote public servants' job engagement. Despite lacking longitudinal data, the study provides valuable insights for public managers to encourage knowledge sharing in the workplace, thereby increasing public servants' commitment to the organization's success and sustainability.

Keywords Knowledge sharing · Job engagement · Public servants

1 Introduction

The government of Ho Chi Minh City, Vietnam, is under increasing pressure to enhance public services amidst rising demands from the public [30]. Consequently, understanding crucial areas such as knowledge sharing and job engagement within public organizations has become paramount. Job engagement is particularly vital for public servants navigating these changes and striving to contribute effectively to

L. Q. Thang (✉) · M. N. Khuong
School of Business, International University, Vietnam National University Ho Chi Minh City, Ho Chi Minh City, Vietnam
e-mail: BABAIU20132@student.hcmiu.edu.vn

L. T. Tung et al. (eds.), *Disruptive Technology and Business Continuity*,
https://doi.org/10.1007/978-981-97-5452-6_13

organizational goals [33]. Recognizing the determinants of employee engagement is crucial, especially in the era of globalization, where efficiency and collaboration are imperative [24]. Additionally, Ahmad and Karim [1] highlight the critical role of knowledge sharing in dynamic organizational environments, where staying current is vital for sustained operation. However, there is limited literature on job engagement and knowledge sharing within the Vietnamese public sector. Therefore, this study aims to explore the impact of knowledge sharing on job engagement and propose theoretically tested approaches to enhance organizational sustainability and meet evolving citizen demands.

To explore the intricate relationship between knowledge sharing and job engagement, our study focuses on 300 public servants working for People's Committees in Ho Chi Minh City. These public servants carry out administrative and public service functions on behalf of the government. Understanding the relationship between knowledge sharing and job engagement is crucial for enhancing organizational sustainability, particularly within the People's Committees of Ho Chi Minh City, chosen for their pivotal roles in policy formulation, operational oversight, and resource allocation [30].

2 Theoretical Basis

2.1 Knowledge Sharing

Knowledge sharing is a vital practice that cultivates relationships, fosters innovation, and generates valuable organizational resources [21, 34]. It entails the sharing of thoughts and insights among members and departments, leading to the creation of novel concepts and expanding the organization's knowledge [1]. According to this research, knowledge sharing is a cultural phenomenon that involves interpersonal relationships and the sharing of information, experiences, and abilities amongst people working for an organization [17, 32]. It involves making one's knowledge accessible to others, facilitating the mutual exchange of both implicit and explicit knowledge [28]. During this process, new insights are generated, and current information is clarified [23].

Knowledge management and sharing within public organizations have garnered attention in recent years, often drawing comparisons with the private sector [4, 20]. As noted by Muqadas et al. [21], sharing knowledge in public organizations can be challenging due to perceptions that it is linked to power dynamics and career advancement opportunities. Moreover, according to Henttonen et al. [12], there exists a fundamental disparity in knowledge-sharing approaches between public institutions and private enterprises, with bureaucratic nature often hindering the free flow of knowledge. However, Chawla and Joshi [4] mentioned that the public sector holds inherent advantages in knowledge sharing, such as being less concerned about guarding trade secrets and proprietary information compared to the private sector. Additionally, the public sector can provide a motivating environment for knowledge sharing, as public servants often derive motivation from a strong commitment to serving the community and society at large.

2.2 *Job Engagement*

Job engagement, initially defined by Kahn [13], is a pivotal aspect of organizational psychology that entails the simultaneous application of one's values and self-expression to tasks, fostering a strong connection with work and colleagues. It encompasses a holistic commitment of personal energy across physical, cognitive, and emotional domains [27]. Cognitive energy represents an individual's self, while engagement is linked to job demands, work resources, and performance, constituting the psychological state of employees at work [24]. Bakker et al. [2] delineate job engagement through three key facets: vitality, dedication, and absorption. Vitality denotes feeling mentally rejuvenated at work. Dedication signifies a profound connection to one's work characterized by eagerness, motivation, confidence, and readiness to tackle significant challenges. Absorption entails complete immersion in one's work, where time appears to fly and detachment becomes challenging. Job engagement is distinct from and bolstered by personality traits, reflecting an individual's current state of mind rather than a fixed personality characteristic [14, 19]. In this study, engagement is characterized by enthusiasm and deep involvement in the workplace, fostering a fulfilling state of mind related to work [26].

2.3 *Previous Studies*

Research on knowledge sharing in organizational contexts has identified trust, social interaction, community considerations, normative considerations, and self-interest as key drivers of knowledge sharing, while reciprocity has shown no substantial impact [18, 31]. Yasir et al. [35] highlighted that integration enhances knowledge sharing and emphasized the importance of improving employee attitudes towards knowledge sharing, allowing new tasks, and providing feedback for organizational operations. Conversely, the study found that formalization and centralization negatively affect knowledge sharing.

Moreover, job engagement is crucial for enhancing job performance and employee well-being, leading organizations to prioritize human capital management for sustainable success [24, 3]. Research has examined a range of factors that influence job engagement in diverse work environments [24, 9, 8]. They revealed that distributive justice and organizational support emerged as the main predictors of job engagement, with interpersonal and procedural distributive judgments and information predicting workplace engagement. Despite the pivotal roles knowledge sharing and job engagement play in fostering organizational sustainability, research on the relationship between these two factors in the public sector is still lacking [33]. Therefore, the purpose of this research is to address this gap by investigating the influencing factors of knowledge sharing and job engagement and exploring their interrelationships within the public sector context.

2.4 Proposing Research Model

Numerous factors impacting knowledge sharing and work engagement have been found in prior studies. However, specific factors relevant to public organizations in Ho Chi Minh City include (1) Formalization; (2) Centralization; (3) Integration; (4) Support; (5) Social Interaction; (6) Reciprocity; and (7) Trust. These factors collectively illuminate the intricate relationship between knowledge sharing and engagement among public servants. Therefore, we propose the following hypothesis:

H1: Factors including formalization (H1a), centralization (H1b), integration (H1c), support (H1d), social interaction (H1e), reciprocity (H1f), and trust (H1g) are correlated with public servants' knowledge sharing.

H2: Factors including formalization (H1a), centralization (H1b), integration (H1c), support (H1d), social interaction (H1e), reciprocity (H1f), and trust (H1g) are correlated with public servants' knowledge sharing.

H3: Knowledge sharing in public organizations in Ho Chi Minh City has a positive influence on public servants' job engagement.

3 Methodology

3.1 Measurement of Variables

The study's measurement instruments were adapted from previous empirical studies to ensure contextual relevance to the knowledge-sharing environment within public organizations. Specifically, formalization, or the level of organizational written guidelines and regulations, comprises five items adapted from Kim and Lee [15]. Six items were adapted from Liao et al. [16] to measure the concentration of decision-making authority, or centralization. Reflecting the organization's ability to coordinate between various functions or integration, a five-item scale adapted from Liao et al. [16] was used. The extent to which public servants feel supported in their work was measured using five items adapted from Yang et al. [34]. Social interaction, or the social dynamics and relationships among public servants, was measured by four items adapted from Chiu et al. [6]. Reciprocity, assessing whether public servants reciprocate favors, assistance, or cooperation with their colleagues, was measured by three items adapted from Chen and Hung [5]. Trust, representing the level of interpersonal and organizational trustworthiness, was assessed using five items derived from Chiu et al. [6]. Knowledge sharing was measured by four items adapted from Lin and Lee [17]. Finally, job engagement was measured by nine items in the UWES-9 scale adapted from Schaufeli et al. [26].

The questionnaire comprises two sections. The first section gathers personal information from survey participants, while the second section delves into various concepts within the research model by posing questions related to each research concept. The survey employs a 5-point Likert scale, where 1 represents "Strongly disagree" and 5 indicates "Strongly agree," to assess participants' perceived levels.

3.2 Data Collection and Sampling

This study employed quantitative research methodologies targeting public servants working for People's Committees, comprising approximately 12,245 individuals across ward-level, district-level, and city-level positions in Ho Chi Minh City, Vietnam. These public servants play crucial roles in policymaking, operational management, and resource allocation [30]. To ensure a representative sample, a total of 334 questionnaires were disseminated between June 15, 2023, and August 17, 2023, among employees in public organizations, guided by the "10-times rule" for sample size estimation [10]. The data collection process utilized a combination of Google Forms and paper-based questionnaires distributed through direct engagement and email to accommodate the geographical dispersion of the target population in Ho Chi Minh City while minimizing response bias [7]. Convenience and snowball sampling techniques were utilized to maximize participation. Subsequently, after careful evaluation, 300 valid responses were considered for further analysis.

3.3 Data Analysis

To evaluate the hypotheses, 3,000 non-parametric bootstrapping repetitions are performed in the data processing process using SmartPLS 4.0. Partial Least Squares Structural Equation Modeling (PLS-SEM), known for its regression-oriented approach, is advantageous in reducing residual variance in endogenous variables compared to CB-SEM, offering greater flexibility, and accommodating varying sample sizes with fewer specification requirements [25]. It addresses the limitations of CB-SEM, including issues related to measurement level, sample size, distributional properties, and unobserved factors. For this study, examining relationships among formalization, centralization, integration, support, social interaction, reciprocity, trust towards knowledge sharing, and job engagement, PLS-SEM is deemed suitable due to its capacity to manage intricate models with numerous indices and latent variables, empowering researchers to identify key factors. The study utilizes a measurement model to establish validity and reliability, construct validity, including convergent and discriminant validity, and internal reliability. The structural model and hypotheses are evaluated through path coefficients (β) and significance level using the PLS path model's asymmetric bootstrapping procedure.

4 Results and Discussions

4.1 Results

The authors distributed questionnaires across city-level, district-level, and ward-level public organizations in Ho Chi Minh City, collecting 334 survey responses, of which 300 were deemed valid. Among the valid responses, city-level public servants constituted the largest group, comprising 37.3% of the total, followed by ward-level public servants at 35% and district-level public servants at 27.7%. This distribution provides insights into the representation of various professional positions among respondents. Additionally, an analysis of years of service reveals that public servants with 11–15 years of experience formed the largest group at 36.3%, followed by those with over 15 years at 28.7%, 5–10 years at 25.3%, and less than 5 years at 9.7%.

This study employs PLS-SEM via SmartPLS 4.0 software, with bootstrapping involving 3,000 repetitions, to examine two models: the measurement model, focusing on variable and latent construct relationships, and the structural model, analyzing relationships among latent constructs [11]. Evaluation of the measurement model primarily entails assessing validity and reliability, with standards such as average variance extracted (AVE) being greater than 0.5 and composite reliability (CR) being greater than 0.7, all met by nine variables. Additionally, outer loadings range from 0.729 to 0.922, all within the acceptable range of 0.70 or higher (Table 1).

The structural model's adequacy is evaluated based on convergence and distinct values. Hair et al. [11] recommend that both Cronbach's alpha (α) and CR should surpass 0.7 to ensure construct reliability and consistency. α values range from 0.718 to 0.902, meeting this criterion. Similarly, CR values range from 0.89 to 0.90, all exceeding the 0.70 threshold. AVE values, ranging from 0.63 to 0.78, meet the threshold of 0.50 or higher, ensuring convergent validity [10]. All HTMT values are below the recommended 0.90 threshold by Hair et al. [11], confirming the discriminant validity. The determination coefficient (R2) measures the extent to which independent variables explain dependent variables. An R2 value of 0.695 for job engagement indicates a high-moderate level of prediction accuracy, suggesting that eight variables explain 69.50% of job engagement, while an R2 value of 0.472 for knowledge sharing in public organizations reflects a low-moderate level of prediction accuracy, with seven variables accounting for 47.20% of knowledge sharing. Additionally, the level of prediction (Q2 value) is assessed, indicating a large level of prediction for job engagement and an average level for knowledge sharing.

Table 1 Assessment results of reflective measurement model

Scale		Outer loading	CR	A	AVE
Formalization (FOR)	FOR1	0.841			
	FOR2	0.774			
	FOR3	0.824	0.921	0.893	0.700
	FOR4	0.906			
	FOR5	0.832			
Centralization (CEN)	CEN2	0.892			
	CEN3	0.769	0.829	0.712	0.620
	CEN6	0.689			
Integration (INT)	INT1	0.811			
	INT2	0.801			
	INT3	0.889	0.924	0.900	0.670
	INT4	0.815			
	INT5	0.866			
Support (SUP)	SUP1	0.821			
	SUP2	0.848			
	SUP3	0.865	0.904	0.868	0.655
	SUP4	0.712			
	SUP5	0.793			
Social Interaction (SI)	SI1	0.810			
	SI2	0.881	0.897	0.845	0.686
	SI3	0.861			
	SI4	0.753			
Reciprocity (REC)	REC1	0.838			
	REC2	0.922	0.914	0.859	0.781
	REC3	0.889			
Trust (TRUS)	TRUS1	0.796			
	TRUS2	0.825			
	TRUS3	0.856	0.920	0.895	0.659
	TRUS4	0.855			
	TRUS5	0.816			
Knowledge Sharing (KS)	KS1	0.867			
	KS2	0.897	0.907	0.862	0.709
	KS3	0.827			
	KS4	0.773			
Job Engagement (JOEN)	JOEN1	0.752			
	JOEN2	0.829			
	JOEN3	0.835			

(continued)

Table 1 (continued)

Scale		Outer loading	CR	A	AVE
	JOEN4	0.778			
	JOEN5	0.790	0.935	0.921	0.644
	JOEN6	0.849			
	JOEN7	0.779			
	JOEN8	0.803			
	JOEN9	0.712			

Table 2 Hypothesis testing

Relationships		Path Coefficient	p-value	Results
H1a	FOR → KS	0.079	0.346	*Rejected*
H1b	CEN → KS	-0.197	0.003**	Accepted
H1c	INT → KS	0.170	0.034*	Accepted
H1d	SUP → KS	0.159	0.031*	Accepted
H1e	SI → KS	0.140	0.036*	Accepted
H1f	REC → KS	0.217	0.001***	Accepted
H1g	TRUS → KS	0.151	0.026*	Accepted
H2a	FOR → JOEN	0.267	0.000***	Accepted
H2b	CEN → JOEN	0.113	0.027*	Accepted
H2c	INT → JOEN	0.134	0.031*	Accepted
H2d	SUP → JOEN	-0.037	0.582	*Rejected*
H2e	SI → JOEN	0.101	0.049*	Accepted
H2f	REC → JOEN	0.184	0.001***	Accepted
H2g	TRUS → JOEN	0.040	0.465	*Rejected*
H3	KS → JOEN	0.249	0.000***	Accepted

Note Significance level where, $*p < 0.05$, $**p < 0.01$, $***p < 0.001$

Table 2 details the relationships between variables, showcasing the outcomes of hypothesis testing. Notably, H1a, H2d, and H2g were rejected based on the path coefficients and associated p-values. Apart from the association between centralization and knowledge sharing (H1b), which displayed a significant negative correlation, all other hypotheses showcased positive and significant correlations.

4.2 Results

The research findings revealed critical factors that affect job engagement and knowledge sharing. First, the study revealed that KS ($\beta = 0.249$, $p = 0.000$) has a significant influence on JOEN. This indicates that knowledge sharing among employees positively contributes to their level of job engagement, which aligns with Vila-Vázquez et al.'s [33] study. The statistical significance of this relationship emphasizes how crucial it is to promote knowledge sharing inside public institutions.

Second, the findings regarding FOR (β = 0.267, p = 0.000), CEN (β = 0.113, p = 0.027), INT (β = 0.134, p = 0.031), SI (β = 0.101, p = 0.049), and REC (β = 0.184, p = 0.001) align with previous research on organizational factors influencing JOEN. For instance, Rich et al. [24] and Lu et al. [19] have demonstrated the positive impact of formalization on job engagement, highlighting the importance of well-defined processes and objectives. Similarly, Deepa [8] has emphasized the role of centralization in promoting higher levels of engagement by providing clear decision-making structures. In addition, integration has been shown to positively influence job engagement by Caesens et al. [3], indicating that collaborative work structures contribute to enhanced engagement. Social interaction has been highlighted as a significant factor in boosting job engagement by Nguyen and Ha [22], underscoring the importance of social connections in the workplace. Reciprocity has also been identified as a critical factor contributing to job engagement in studies by Khuong and Yen [14], suggesting that maintaining close social relationships and exchanging knowledge with colleagues enhance engagement. On the other hand, the absence of statistically significant relationships between SUP, TRUS, and JOEN indicates that these factors may not significantly influence job engagement.

Third, the following effects on KS are in line with previous studies: INT (β = 0.170, p = 0.034), SUP (β = 0.159, p = 0.031), SI (β = 0.140, p = 0.036), REC (β = 0.217, p = 0.001), and TRUS (β = 0.151, p = 0.026). Park and Gabbard [23] have demonstrated the positive impact of cohesive work structures, such as integration, on knowledge sharing, indicating that fostering interpersonal support facilitates information dissemination. Similarly, Tohidinia and Mosakhani [32] have highlighted the significance of organizational support in promoting knowledge sharing, suggesting that a climate that prioritizes employee well-being fosters mutual respect and information sharing. The importance of social interaction in promoting knowledge sharing, as noted by Lin et al. [18] and Tohidinia and Mosakhani [32], underscores the role of strong social connections and active information exchange. Moreover, the favorable effect of reciprocity on knowledge sharing aligns with research by Suppiah and Sandhu [28] and Tangaraja et al. [29], suggesting that mutual assistance among employees facilitates knowledge sharing. The significant influence of trust on knowledge sharing within public organizations aligns with Lin et al. [18] and Titi Amayah [31], indicating that trust-based relationships encourage a culture of knowledge sharing among employees. However, the adverse effect of CEN (CEN, β = –0.197, p = 0.003) on KS is also consistent with research by Yasir et al. [35], suggesting that reliance on superiors' approval for decision-making may hinder the exchange of knowledge. Lastly, the non-significant effect of FOR on KS indicates that following standardized processes may not significantly impact knowledge exchange [35].

5 Conclusions and Implications

In conclusion, the findings reveal key factors that influence job engagement and knowledge sharing within public organizations in Ho Chi Minh City. Formalization was found to significantly impact job engagement, while centralization of decision power played a significant role in both job engagement and knowledge sharing, emphasizing the importance of effective governance in adapting to changing landscapes. Moreover, the integration environment emerged as a critical factor positively affecting both job engagement and knowledge sharing, highlighting the value of collaboration and adaptability across departments amidst evolving business environments. Additionally, organizational support fosters knowledge sharing, essential for sustainability management, while social interaction was found to positively influence both job engagement and knowledge sharing, emphasizing the value of close relationships that could promote resilience in dynamic settings. Furthermore, reciprocity played a significant role in both job engagement and knowledge sharing, underscoring the importance of mutual assistance among colleagues as a sustainable practice. While trust significantly influenced knowledge sharing, it had no significant effect on job engagement. Finally, the study underscores the significant impact of knowledge sharing itself on work engagement, delineating its crucial role in the sustainable management of employees' engagement within public organizations amidst an evolving landscape.

This research significantly contributes to understanding the dynamics of job engagement and knowledge sharing, emphasizing their interconnectedness and their role in enhancing sustainability management within public organizations. Therefore, a set of sustainable practices is suggested to improve job engagement and knowledge sharing within public organizations in Ho Chi Minh City. These practices include cultivating a culture of knowledge exchange, recognizing and rewarding contributions to knowledge sharing, organizing team-building activities, and investing in personnel development. By encouraging reciprocal knowledge sharing, these practices can foster a positive work environment. Additionally, organizing team-building activities and thematic meetings can strengthen collaboration. Lastly, investing in personnel development can empower employees with the skills they need to flourish in their positions and support the objectives of their organizations. By implementing these recommendations, public organizations in Ho Chi Minh City can create a sustainable environment by leveraging collective intelligence and fostering continuous learning.

Despite its valuable insights, this study has several limitations. The moderate explanatory power suggests unexplored factors, while the cross-sectional descriptive research method and non-probability sampling technique may limit the representativeness of the findings. The lack of comparative studies within public organizations in Vietnam also affects the depth of analysis. Future research should expand the current knowledge base by conducting similar studies in diverse geographic regions outside Ho Chi Minh City. Researchers should also explore additional factors influencing knowledge sharing and job engagement, such as organizational culture, leadership styles, and technology adoption. This will provide more nuanced insights into how these aspects contribute to the effectiveness of public sector organizations, enhancing the potential for evidence-based policy recommendations and practical interventions.

Acknowledgements This research is funded by the International University, VNU-HCMC under grant number SV2022-BA-07.

References

1. Ahmad, F., Karim, M.: Impacts of knowledge sharing: a review and directions for future research. J. Work. Learn. **31**(3), 207–230 (2019)
2. Bakker, A.B., Schaufeli, W.B., Leiter, M.P., Taris, T.W.: Work engagement: An emerging concept in occupational health psychology. Work Stress. **22**(3), 187–200 (2008)
3. Caesens, G., Stinglhamber, F., Luypaert, G.: The impact of work engagement and workaholism on well-being: The role of work-related social support. Career Dev. Int. **19**(7), 813–835 (2014)
4. Chawla, D., Joshi, H.: Knowledge management initiatives in Indian public and private sector organizations. J. Knowl. Manag. **14**(6), 811–827 (2010)
5. Chen, C.J., Hung, S.W.: To give or to receive? Factors influencing members' knowledge sharing and community promotion in professional virtual communities. Inf. & Manag. **47**(4), 226–236 (2010)
6. Chiu, C.M., Hsu, M.H., Wang, E.T.: Understanding knowledge sharing in virtual communities: An integration of social capital and social cognitive theories. Decis. Support Syst. **42**(3), 1872–1888 (2006)
7. de Bernardo, D.H., Curtis, A.: Using online and paper surveys: the effectiveness of mixed-mode methodology for populations over 50. Res. Aging **35**(2), 220–240 (2013)
8. Deepa, S.M.: The effects of organizational justice dimensions on facets of job engagement. Int. J. Organ. Theory & Behav. **23**(4), 315–336 (2020)
9. Ghosh, P., Rai, A., Sinha, A.: Organizational justice and employee engagement: Exploring the linkage in public sector banks in India. Pers. Rev. **43**(4), 628–652 (2014)
10. Hair, J.F., Ringle, C.M., Sarstedt, M.: PLS-SEM: Indeed a silver bullet. J. Mark. Theory Pract. **19**(2), 139–152 (2011)
11. Hair, J.F., Risher, J.J., Sarstedt, M., Ringle, C.M.: When to use and how to report the results of PLS-SEM. Eur. Bus. Rev. **31**(1), 2–24 (2019)
12. Henttonen, K., Kianto, A., Ritala, P.: Knowledge sharing and individual work performance: an empirical study of a public sector organisation. J. Knowl. Manag. **20**(4), 749–768 (2016)
13. Kahn, W.A.: Psychological conditions of personal engagement and disengagement at work. Acad. Manag. J. **33**(4), 692–724 (1990)
14. Khuong, M.N., Yen, N.H.: The effects of leadership styles and sociability trait emotional intelligence on employee engagement. A study in Binh Duong City, Vietnam. Int. J. Curr. Res. Acad. Rev. **2**(1), 121–136 (2014)
15. Kim, S., Lee, H.: The impact of organizational context and information technology on employee knowledge-sharing capabilities. Public Adm. Rev. **66**(3), 370–385 (2006)
16. Liao, C., Chuang, S.H., To, P.L.: How knowledge management mediates the relationship between environment and organizational structure. J. Bus. Res. **64**(7), 728–736 (2011)
17. Lin, H.F., Lee, G.G.: Perceptions of senior managers toward knowledge-sharing behaviour. Manag. Decis. **42**(1), 108–125 (2004)

18. Lin, M.J.J., Hung, S.W., Chen, C.J.: Fostering the determinants of knowledge sharing in professional virtual communities. Comput. Hum. Behav. **25**(4), 929–939 (2009)
19. Lu, L., Lu, A.C.C., Gursoy, D., Neale, N.R.: Work engagement, job satisfaction, and turnover intentions: A comparison between supervisors and line-level employees. Int. J. Contemp. Hosp. Manag. **28**(4), 737–761 (2016)
20. Massaro, M., Dumay, J., Garlatti, A.: Public sector knowledge management: a structured literature review. J. Knowl. Manag. **19**(3), 530–558 (2015)
21. Muqadas, F., Rehman, M., Aslam, U., Ur-Rahman, U.: Exploring the challenges, trends and issues for knowledge sharing: A study on employees in public sector universities. VINE J. Inf. Knowl. Manag. Syst. **47**(1), 2–15 (2017)
22. Nguyen, C.M.A., Ha, M.T.: The interplay between internal communication, employee engagement, job satisfaction, and employee loyalty in higher education institutions in Vietnam. Hum. Soc. Sci. Commun. **10**(1), 1–13 (2023)
23. Park, J., Gabbard, J.L.: Factors that affect scientists' knowledge sharing behavior in health and life sciences research communities: differences between explicit and implicit knowledge. Comput. Hum. Behav. **78**, 326–335 (2018)
24. Rich, B.L., Lepine, J.A., Crawford, E.R.: Job engagement: Antecedents and effects on job performance. Acad. Manag. J. **53**(3), 617–635 (2010)
25. Rigdon, E.E., Sarstedt, M., Ringle, C.M.: On comparing results from CB-SEM and PLS-SEM: Five perspectives and five recommendations. Mark.: ZFP–Journal Res. Manag. **39**(3), 4–16 (2017)
26. Schaufeli, W.B., Bakker, A.B., Salanova, M.: The measurement of work engagement with a short questionnaire: A cross-national study. Educ. Psychol. Measur. **66**(4), 701–716 (2006)
27. Seppälä, P., Mauno, S., Feldt, T., Hakanen, J., Kinnunen, U., Tolvanen, A., Schaufeli, W.: The construct validity of the Utrecht Work Engagement Scale: Multisample and longitudinal evidence. J. Happiness Stud. **10**, 459–481 (2009)
28. Suppiah, V., Singh Sandhu, M.: Organisational culture's influence on tacit knowledge-sharing behaviour. J. Knowl. Manag. **15**(3), 462–477 (2011)
29. Tangaraja, G., Mohd Rasdi, R., Abu Samah, B., Ismail, M.: Knowledge sharing is knowledge transfer: a misconception in the literature. J. Knowl. Manag. **20**(4), 653–670 (2016)
30. Thuy, N.T.T., Phinaitrup, B.A.: The effect of public service motivation on job performance of public servants in Vietnam: The role of mediation of job satisfaction and person-organization fit. Int. J. Public Adm. **46**(5), 326–343 (2023)
31. Titi Amayah, A.: Determinants of knowledge sharing in a public sector organization. J. Knowl. Manag. **17**(3), 454–471 (2013)
32. Tohidinia, Z., Mosakhani, M.: Knowledge sharing behaviour and its predictors. Ind. Manag. Data Syst. **110**(4), 611–631 (2010)
33. Vila-Vázquez, G., Castro-Casal, C., Álvarez-Pérez, D., del Río-Araújo, L.: Promoting the sustainability of organizations: Contribution of transformational leadership to job engagement. Sustainability **10**(11), 4109 (2018)
34. Yang, H., van Rijn, M.B., Sanders, K.: Perceived organizational support and knowledge sharing: employees' self-construal matters. Int. J. Hum. Resour. Manag. **31**(17), 2217–2237 (2020)
35. Yasir, M., Majid, A., Yasir, M.: Nexus of knowledge-management enablers, trust and knowledge-sharing in research universities. J. Appl. Res. High. Educ. **9**(3), 424–438 (2017)

Factors Affecting Meaningful Work and Employee Engagement in the Information Technology Industry: Evidence in Ho Chi Minh City

Nong Quy Ngoc An and Le Dinh Nghi

Abstract Employee engagement (EG) and meaningful work (MW) are key factors that influence crucial organizational outcomes like performance, well-being, and job satisfaction. However, little research has been done on the connection between them. This study shows what factors influence MW, which may partly demonstrate the nexus between MW and EG. Confirmatory factor analysis (CFA) and structural equation modeling (SEM) were used to analyze survey data from 470 employees of information technology (IT) enterprises in Ho Chi Minh City. The results show that job variety, supervisor support, and autonomy are positively and significantly associated with MW. These factors also have a significant and positive impact on EG.

Keywords Meaningful work · Employee engagement · Information technology

1 Introduction

The gap between people's expectations and experiences at work indicates their degree of job satisfaction. People are motivated when they feel satisfied with their jobs. In addition to being more productive, motivated workers also have more excellent mental health. Organizations and their employees both benefit from it. Increased EG is one of the most essential consequences of positive attitudes toward work and job satisfaction.

EG can be impacted by various factors, such as compensation, the degree of stress experienced at work, the opportunity for both professional and personal development, and the sense of the attractiveness of the work. Reduced burnout, absenteeism, and intention to leave can all be attributed to increased EG.

So, how can companies raise EG levels? Exploring the connection between MW, EG, and job satisfaction may create the key to the solution. EG ensures organizational

N. Q. N. An · L. D. Nghi (✉)
Saigon University, 273 An Duong Vuong, Ward 3, District 5, Ho Chi Minh City, Vietnam
e-mail: nghiledinh@sgu.edu.vn

L. T. Tung et al. (eds.), *Disruptive Technology and Business Continuity*,
https://doi.org/10.1007/978-981-97-5452-6_14

effectiveness [19]. Employees who are engaged with the company are often satisfied at work, have high commitment, stay with their company longer, and thereby reduce the number of people leaving their jobs and significantly save on recruitment costs. Therefore, companies must create conditions to promote EG.

Many IT companies in Vietnam, especially in Ho Chi Minh City, were formed and grown in recent years. The development of an IT company depends heavily on innovation and creativity, so having talented employees and keeping them working at peak performance is the key to success. Furthermore, the IT industry job market is becoming more competitive than ever as the wave of Industrial Revolution 4.0 penetrates deeply into Vietnam. The demand for high-quality engineers in new technology fields such as big data, artificial intelligence, machine learning, or blockchain is incredibly high. Meanwhile, supply remains at a minimum level. The shortage of engineers leads to fierce competition for human resources in recruiting and retaining talented employees of IT companies. Therefore, the article aims to identify and measure the drivers of employee engagement at IT companies in Ho Chi Minh City. Once they have a clear picture of the critical drivers of employee engagement, executives of IT companies will be able to identify plans, strategies, and activities to improve results. Their performance creates a competitive advantage and maintains rapid and sustainable growth.

2 Theoretical Basis

2.1 Meaningful Work

EG, as perceived by an individual, is significantly impacted by MW. The concept of MW in relation to EG has been the subject of increasing research [5]. Fairlie [9] found a significant connection between MW and EG. Since employees spend a large portion of their time at work, Holbeche and Springett [13] contend that people must understand the meaning or purpose of their work.

2.2 Employee Engagement (EG)

In recent decades, there has been a rise in interest in the concept of engagement. [8, 12, 26]. While consulting businesses initially brought this issue to the public's attention, scholars also showed interest in conducting studies to establish the constructs, antecedents, and effects. Using the definition of Schaufeli et al. [27], the study defines EG as a motivational construct, described as an upbeat, satisfying state of mind associated with work that is marked by vigor, dedication, and absorption. Here, vigor alludes to a person's high degree of mental toughness and vitality and their willingness to work hard and persevere through challenging times. Dedication is the feeling of excitement, challenge, importance, and pride that one experiences when working, while absorption is the state of being wholly absorbed and focusing intently, which results in contentment and makes it impossible to separate even after the allotted time.

2.3 Fundamental Theory and Hypothesis

Saks [25] claims that Social Exchange Theory (SET) provides a solid theoretical foundation for understanding EG. According to SET, a succession of contacts between parties that are mutually dependent on one another results in responsibilities. A cornerstone of SET is that provided both parties follow specific "rules," relationships can develop over time into mutual dependability, devotion, and trust [7].

Most of the literature and research on meaningful work is theoretically grounded on the Job Characteristics Theory (JCT) [22]. Rich jobs (skill diversity, task identity, task relevance, autonomy, feedback) are associated with better work-related outcomes (motivation, satisfaction, performance, and lower absenteeism and turnover), according to JCT. Thus, we propose the following hypothesis:

H1: Job variety has a positive impact on MW.

Good relationships between supervisor and employee have been proven to be essential for MW [6]. Perceived Supervisor Support is determined to impact employees' work, emotions (motivation, work spirit), and MW. Thus, we propose the following hypothesis:

H2: Supervisor support has a positive impact on MW.

According to Bakker and Demerouti [3], employee training and development positively impact MW. Employees who have a positive perception of training, advancement, and personal development opportunities will be able to overcome obstacles and reduce pressure at work [17]. Especially in technical professions, training and advancement issues are even more critical. Support from superiors has been the focus of much research [23]. Thus, we propose the following hypothesis:

H3: Development opportunities (training and development) have a positive impact on MW.

Autonomy to enhance decision-making and autonomy in the workplace can be implemented as a valuable protective measure. Furthermore, conducting developmental conversations with employees can ensure that they have the opportunity to improve their skills and can experience various challenges in their work [1]. They all said that dissatisfaction with the lack of empowerment at an organization always harms employees' MW. Autonomy is one of the core job characteristics of JCT [22], and it may affect MW. Thus, we propose the following hypothesis:

H4: Autonomy at work has a positive impact on MW.

When managers provide feedback, staff members may feel pressured to improve their jobs in response to the input, potentially affecting MW. Furthermore, when workers get assistance from their supervisors, they see this as a formal relationship established by the organizational structure, becoming a part of the meaning of their work. Leaders are always required to welcome feedback and acknowledge their contributions [15]. Feedback is also one of the core job characteristics of JCT [22], and it may affect MW. Thus, we propose the following hypothesis:

H5: Feedback has a positive impact on MW.

Kahn [16] suggested that psychological meaning stems from positions that deliver challenging work, require diverse mastery, and let employees feel they create valuable contributions. As a result, these workers will believe that they can benefit both their company and other people, and they will also believe that they are getting the help and resources they need to do their jobs well. Thus, we propose the following hypothesis:

H6: Job variety has a positive impact on EG.

Supervisor support positively influenced EG [24, 10]. Due to the high-tech nature of IT companies, employees tend to work very closely with superiors (specifically project team leaders). Many employees quit their jobs because they do not receive enough support from their superiors. Thus, we propose the following hypothesis:

H7: Supervisor support has a positive impact on the EG.

Development opportunities include training, development, and career. This is the motivation that has a positive impact on EG [24]. An interesting point here is that when employees see a path to advancement in their organization, this factor has the most decisive impact on employees speaking well about the company, staying with it, and striving for their work. Thus, we propose the following hypothesis:

H8: Development opportunities have a positive impact on EG.

Autonomy is a factor that positively impacts EG, and managers should let subordinates participate in the decision-making process and make decisions that affect their work [18]. Habraken [10] found that autonomy positively influences EG. Thus, we propose the following hypothesis:

H9: Autonomy has a positive impact on EG.

Workers who consistently receive performance attention and detailed feedback show more interest in and engage in their work [20]. Research indicates that it makes little difference if they receive positive feedback or constructive criticism. Above all, they are grateful that their employer thinks highly enough of them to ensure success. Thus, we propose the following hypothesis:

H10: Feedback has a positive impact on EG.

MW arises when employees are clear about their abilities, expectations, and the goals they are working toward, both for the company and society [28]. People feel work is more meaningful when individuals see their efforts working toward clearly outlined goals within the organization. From then on, MW happens when people see their role as essential and serving some real purpose. On that basis, it can also be

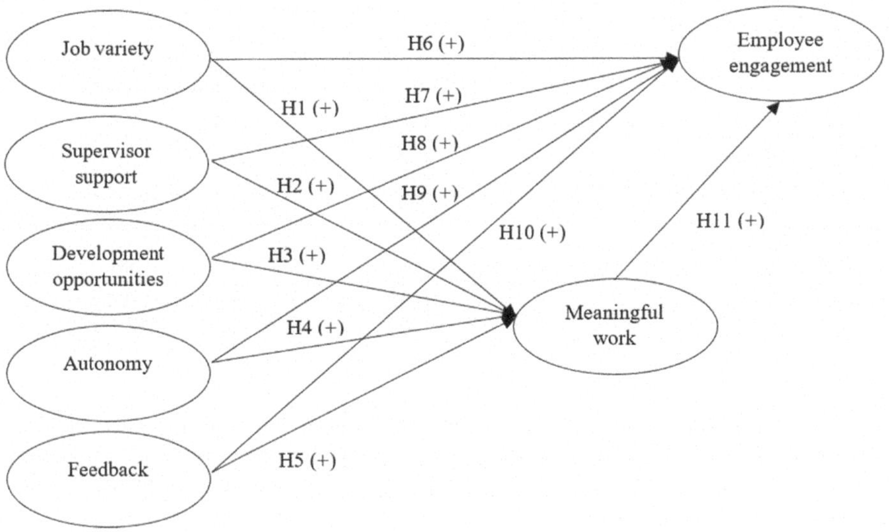

Fig. 1 Proposed research framework

affirmed that when employees work meaningfully, it will help them become more attached to their work and increase their engagement with the organization. Thus, we propose the following hypothesis:

H11: MW has a positive impact on EG.

Our hypotheses imply the conceptual research model in Fig. 1.

3 Methodology

The results were 470 valid questionnaires, of which the response rate from inspection staff was 41.3%, development staff was 39.8%, and other staff was 18.9%. Data analysis techniques are SPSS 21 and AMOS, including the following steps: Validity and reliability analysis (Exploratory Factor Analysis—EFA, Cronbach's Alpha), Confirmatory factor analysis (CFA), and hypothesis testing using Structural Equation Modeling (SEM).

First, we conducted qualitative interviews with two human resources of IT companies in Ho Chi Minh City to adjust the scale, thereby building a formal questionnaire. After completing the questionnaire, the next step will be collecting quantitative research data. The sample was selected by a non-probability method with a convenient sampling method. The survey was conducted directly and online. Boomsma and Hoogland [4] specify 400 as the best number of samples and suitable for the SEM model. Therefore, the number of final study samples used to include 470 samples is appropriate. The research sample has 77.4% male, female with 22.6%.

Table 1 Reliability test

Factor	No. of items	Cronbach's alpha	Corrected item-Total correlation range
Job variety (JV)	7	0.902	0.694–0.729
Supervisor support (SS)	4	0.901	0.759–0.789
Training & Development	4	0.869	0.673–0.764
Autonomy (AT)	5	0.862	0.666–0.693
Feedback (FB)	3	0.825	0.678–0.682
Meaningful work (MW)	5	0.878	0.686–0.780
Employee Engagement (EG)	6	0.880	–0.716

The age group that accounted for the most was under 25 years old, with 25.1%, followed by 25–34 years old, with 49.1%, 34–45 years old with 14.7%, and over 45 years old with 11.1%. The response rate from developers was 15.3%, testers was 14.3%, network security was 13.8%, web developer was 17.7%, software engineer was 14.7%, and other staff was 3%. Employees with college/university degrees accounted for the majority with 79.1%, at least having a postgraduate degree with 5.5%. Employees with income of 10–20 million VND the most with 40.9%, followed by 20–50 million VND and 50–80 million VND, accounting for 22.3% and 15.3%, respectively, income over 80 million VND with 8.3%. The data was entered into SPSS 20 and AMOS 24 software for analysis, performed Exploratory Factor Analysis (EFA), analyzed the reliability of Cronbach's Alpha for each group of factors, Confirmatory Factor Analysis (CFA), Structural Equation Modeling (SEM).

4 Result and Discussion

4.1 Cronbach's Alpha Reliability Test

Table 1 shows that the measured Cronbach's alpha values range from the lowest of 0.825 to the highest of 0.902. This result means all scales achieve Cronbach's Alpha reliability coefficient requirement and may be used in model analysis. The value of each criterion is also presented in this table.

4.2 Exploratory Factor Analysis

The analysis results show that the KMO coefficient is 0.968, which explains that the sample size is suitable for EFA, and Bartlett's coefficient has an observed significance level of $0.000 < 0.05$ (there is a correlation between variables). That confirms that the above analytical method is suitable (or satisfies the conditions for factor analysis). Thus, the KMO test results are satisfactory.

In EFA, the scales of each factor must achieve convergent value with eigenvalue > 1, 50% of the variance extracted, and factor loading $\geq$ 0.50 [2]. Furthermore, observed variables have Cronbach's alpha coefficient $\geq$ 0.6 and Item-Total Correlation coefficient > 0.3 to achieve reliability [21]. The study analyzed 34 observed variables of 7 factors of the model. The EFA results show all factors have loading factors (0.628 $\div$ 0.866) > 0.50, and variance is extracted (44.095% $\div$ 59.976%) > 50% and eigenvalue (1.040 $\div$ 15.389) > 1. Therefore, the scale has convergent validity.

4.3 Analyzing the Scale Validation Results with CFA

CFA is used to confirm the factors extracted in EFA. The results of the CFA analysis show that the values of the indexes (CMIN/df = 1.159, GFI = 0.934, TLI = 0.991, CFI = 0.992, RMSEA = 0.018) all meet acceptable thresholds [11]. Therefore, the fit indices of the proposed model are the overall fit of the model.

The Composite Reliability (CR) and Average Variance Extracted (AVE) metrics help assess validity and reliability. The CFA results indicate the CR value (0.825 $\div$ 0.902) is > 0.5, so all scales are reliable. The AVE value (0.550 $\div$ 0.695) is greater than > 0.5, and all scales have standardized regression weights (0.742 $\div$ 0.833) > 0.5 and are statistically significant ($p < 0.05$). Therefore, these scales have convergent validity. The scales also have discriminant validity because the square root of AVE is greater than the correlation between constructs. Therefore, the CFA measurement model meets the requirements of reliability and validity.

4.4 Hypothesis and Research Model Testing

This study uses SEM to test the hypothesis and examine the overall impact of MW on EG. The SEM results show that the model suits market data: CMIN/df = 1.159, TLI = 0.991, CFI = 0.992, and RMSEA = 0.018. Table 2 presents the results of testing the hypotheses. Hypotheses H1, H2, H4, H6, H7, H8, H9 and H11 were supported ($p < 0.05$), while H3, H5 and H10 was not supported ($p > 0.05$). The SEM results show that: (1) job variety positively correlated with MW ($p < 0.05$). Data support Hypothesis 1—individuals who possess a high level of MW when there is job variety. (2) Hypothesis 2 states a positive relationship between MW and supervisor support. Table 2 shows that MW positively correlated with supervisor support ($p < 0.05$). Data support Hypothesis 2. With supervisor support, individuals will accomplish high levels of MW. (3) Autonomy has a positive effect on MW; (4) Job variety has a positive effect on EG; (5) Supervisor Support has a positive effect on EG; (6)

Development opportunities have a positive effect on EG; (7) Autonomy has a positive effect on EG; (8) MW has a positive effect on EG (Fig. 2).

Table 2 SEM's results: Regression coefficients

			B	β	SE	p-value	Decision
MW	<—	JV	0.226	0.214	0.073	0.002	Supported
MW	<—	SS	0.246	0.267	0.062	0.00	Supported
MW	<—	TD	0.069	0.065	0.069	0.318	Not Supported
MW	<—	AT	0.306	0.259	0.080	0.00	Supported
MW	<—	FB	0.128	0.118	0.067	0.054	Not Supported
EG	<—	JV	0.166	0.163	0.071	0.020	Supported
EG	<—	SS	0.128	0.145	0.061	0.036	Supported
EG	<—	TD	0.208	0.201	0.067	0.002	Supported
EG	<—	AT	0.200	0.176	0.079	0.012	Supported
EG	<—	FB	0.068	0.066	0.064	0.286	Not Supported
EG	<—	MW	0.173	0.180	0.066	0.009	Supported

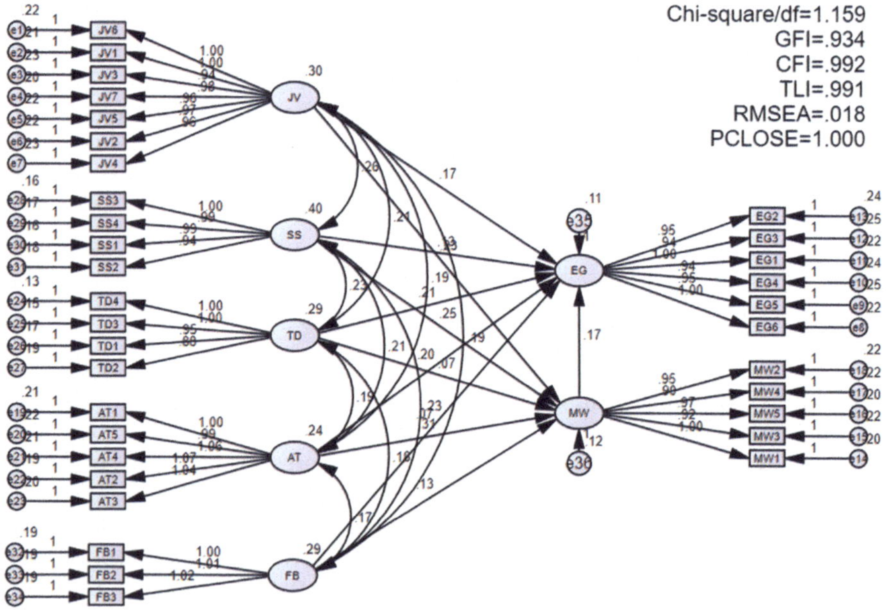

Fig. 2 Structural equation modeling (standardized estimates)

4.5 Discussion

The results of the SEM show that supervisor support (β = 0.267) is the strongest motivator for MW. Given the project-based nature of IT work, employees are often attached to their project team on the job, especially to the project team leader (direct superior). The project team leader also provides team members' feedback to higher management and guides them in daily tasks. Autonomy (β = 0.259) is the second motivating force behind MW. A high level of empowerment will allow employees to do whatever they want and push their creativity to the highest level. Job variety (β = 0.214) is the third motivator that affects MW. Development opportunities (β = 0.318) were not supported due to statistical significance greater than 0.05. This result contradicts the research results of authors Bakker & Demerouti [3], Kim [17]. It takes time to complete the training program framework and prepare personnel (trainers), documents, and assessment standards, leading to delays in accessing this knowledge for workers. Through online channels, employees can better serve their work without having to participate in training programs from the company,the characteristic of the IT industry is that to complete many tasks, workers need to work overtime to complete the job, so they neglect training and studying to improve their qualifications. That could be one of the reasons why the effect of this factor on MW in IT companies is insignificant at a 5% level. Besides that, feedback (β = 0.318) was also not supported.

Four factors (job variety, supervisor support, development opportunities, and autonomy) had a significant, direct positive relationship with EG with the following β, respectively: 0.163, 0.145, 0.201, 0.176. These results are evidence of JCT and are in line with other studies by Mani [18], Hoonakker et al. [14], and Saks [25]. Contrary to expectations, feedback (β = 0.66) does not impact EG at a 10% significance level. The predictable reason is that IT is a technical industry with personnel characterized by rationality. Therefore, emotional factors such as feedback have not significantly influenced their engagement.

5 Conclusions and Implications

More EG creates higher productivity, customer focus, and loyalty. In this study, the drivers of EG were of outstanding support, career opportunities, empowerment, and a creative work environment. From there, we propose management implications for IT companies. Firstly, businesses are interested in diversifying jobs and skills for workers. Working at IT businesses always requires improving professional knowledge and soft skills when working in groups and directly with customers, demonstrating professionalism. Companies should use techniques in the science of human resource management, including rotation and job enrichment so that workers are more satisfied with their jobs. Second, increase the level of support from superiors. Companies must consider strengthening the support of their management team (especially project team leaders) as a top priority in their human resource development strategy. This management team must have the necessary skills to support members and be open and friendly in communicating and understanding team members. Third, pay attention to employees' career development. Companies must not only pay their employees a fair salary and provide them with advancement opportunities but also train them in the necessary skills and provide a suitable working environment to enhance their competitive position. Fourth, empowerment must be practiced at work. In an IT project, the tasks of each development and testing employee are different, which means there is no strict procedure for a particular job, but it is entirely up to the person performing the task to perform it the best way. Therefore, companies need to empower employees to take control of their work. Finally, the company should define an open strategy for innovation and develop a plan for handling employee ideas. Providing innovative topics will help employees orient and develop appropriate knowledge and develop acceptable ideas that can be implemented into practice.

Overall, there are many factors that influence MW and EG. However, there is still little research on MW as a psychological mechanism that explains the impact on EG. Current research highlights the importance of MW, explaining in part how experiences of job resources lead to experiences of engagement. Since meaning is considered the strongest predictor of EG, future research should focus on how to create MW in the workplace.

References

1. Albrecht, S.L., Green, C.R., Marty, A.: Meaningful work, job resources, and employee engagement. Sustain. (Switz.), **13**(7), (2021)
2. Anderson, J.C., Gerbing, D.W.: Structural equation modeling in practice: A review and recommended two-step approach. Psychol. Bull. **103**(3), 411 (1988)
3. Bakker, A.B., Demerouti, E.: Job demands–resources theory: Taking stock and looking forward. J. Occup. Health Psychol. **22**(3), 273–285 (2017)
4. Boomsma, A., Hoogland, J.J.: The robustness of LISREL modeling revisited. Structural equation models: Present and future. A Festschr. Honor. Karl Jöreskog, **2**(3), 139–168 (2001)
5. Chalofsky, N., Krishna, V.: Meaningfulness, commitment, and engagement: The intersection of a deeper level of intrinsic motivation. Adv. Dev. Hum. Resour. **11**(2), 189–203 (2009)
6. Chen, Z., Zhang, X., Vogel, D.: Exploring the underlying processes between conflict and knowledge sharing: A work engagement perspective. J. Appl. Soc. Psychol. **41**, 1005–1033 (2011)
7. Cropanzano, R., Mitchell, M.S.: Social exchange theory: an interdisciplinary review. J. Manag. **31**(6), 874–900 (2005)
8. Demerouti, E., Bakker, A.B., Nachreiner, F., Schaufeli, W.B.: The job demands-resources model of burnout. J. Appl. Psychol. **86**(3), 499–512 (2001)
9. Fairlie, P.: Meaningful work, employee engagement, and other key employee outcomes: Implications for human resource development. Adv. Dev. Hum. Resour. **13**(4), 508–525 (2011)
10. Habraken, M.P.M.: Establishing employee engagement within a Dutch hotel. MBA thesis, University of Twente, Netherlands (2013)
11. Hair, J.F., Black, W.C., Babin, B.J., Anderson, R.E.: Multivariate data analysis. Pearson, (2014)
12. Hallberg, U.E., Schaufeli, W.B.: "Same same" but different? Can work engagement be discriminated from job involvement and organizational commitment? Eur. Psychol. **11**(2), 119–127 (2006)

13. Holbeche, L., Springett, N.: Roffey Park Institute Limited. In search of meaning at work. Roffey Park Institute, (2004)
14. Hoonakker, P., Carayon, P., Korunka, C.: Using the job-demands-resources model to predict turnover in the information technology workforce-general effects and gender differences. Horiz. Psychol. **22**, 51–65 (2013)
15. Humphrey, S.E., Nahrgang, J.D., Morgeson, F.P.: Integrating motivational, social, and contextual work design features: A meta-analytic summary and theoretical extension of the work design literature. J. Appl. Psychol. **92**(5), 1332–1356 (2007)
16. Kahn, W.A.: The essence of engagement: Lessons from the field. In: Handbook of employee engagement: Perspectives, issues, research and practice, pp. 20–30. Edward Elgar Publishing, (2010)
17. Kim, S.: Factors affecting state government information technology employee turnover intentions. Am. Rev. Public Adm. **35**(2), 137–156 (2005)
18. Mani, V.: Analysis of employee engagement and its predictors. Int. J. Hum. Resour. Stud. **1**(2), 15–26 (2011)
19. Mann, A., Harter, J.: The worldwide employee engagement crisis. Gallup Business Journal **7**(1), 1–5 (2016)
20. Menguc, B., Auh, S., Fisher, M., Haddad, A.: To be engaged or not to be engaged: The antecedents and consequences of service employee engagement. J. Bus. Res. **66**(11), 2163–2170 (2013)
21. Nunnally, J.C., Bernstein, I.H.: Psychometric Theory. McGraw-Hill, New York (1994)
22. Oldham, G. R., Hackman, J. R.: How job characteristics theory happened. In: Great minds in management: The process of theory development, pp. 151–170. Oxford University Press, (2007)
23. Podsakoff, P.M., MacKenzie, S.B., Bommer, W.H.: Transformational leader behaviors and substitutes for leadership as determinants of employee satisfaction, commitment, trust, and organizational citizenship behaviors. J. Manag. **22**(2), 259–298 (1996)
24. Robinson, D., Perryman, S., Hayday, S.: The drivers of employee engagement. Institute for Employment Studies, (2004)
25. Saks, A.M.: Antecedents and consequences of employee engagement. J. Manag. Psychol. **21**(7), 600–619 (2006)
26. Saks, A.M., Gruman, J.A.: Getting newcomers engaged: The role of socialization tactics. J. Manag. Psychol. **26**(5), 383–402 (2011)
27. Schaufeli, W.B., Martinez, I.M., Pinto, A.M., Salanova, M., Bakker, A.B.: Burnout and engagement in university students: A cross-national study. J. Cross Cult. Psychol. **33**(5), 464–481 (2002)
28. Steger, M.F., Dik, B.J.: Work as meaning: Individual and organizational benefits of engaging in meaningful work. In: Linley, P.A., Harrington, S., Garcea, N. (eds.) Oxford handbook of positive psychology and work, pp. 131–142. Oxford University Press (2010)

Linking Green Organizational Identity and Employee Pro-Environmental Behaviors: The Role of Green Shared Vision

Nguyen The Khai, Tran Quoc Cuong, Nguyen Ngoc Duy Phuong, and Do Thi Thanh Truc

Abstract This research sought to ecamine how Green Organizational Identity (GOI) influences the encouragement of Pro-Environmental Behaviors, specifically by assessing the influence of GOI on employees' green performance behaviors, with Green Shared Vision as a mediating factor. The research involved 696 employees from a hospital in Vietnam and employed a cross-sectional research design. The study utilized hierarchical regression analysis to test the proposed research model. The findings revealed that GOI significantly predicted Pro-Environmental Behaviors, and Green Shared Vision played a significant mediating role in this relationship. However, gender and environmental values were not found to moderate the association between GOI and Pro-Environmental Behaviors. These results underscore the crucial role of GOI in advancing environmental sustainability and highlight the pressing need to integrate sustainability principles into management systems to support the achievement of sustainable development goals.

Keywords Green human resource management · Green shared vision · Pro-environmental behaviors

1 Introduction

Sustainability is currently a prominent global concern. Businesses have recently recognized that the viability of their operations hinges on a consistent supply of natural resources. Depletion of these essential resources could disrupt not only

N. T. Khai · T. Q. Cuong
Ho Chi Minh City Open University, Vo Van Tan St, HCM 700000 Ho Chi Minh City, Vietnam

N. N. D. Phuong (✉)
International University, Vietnam National University Ho Chi Minh City, Quarter 6, Thu Duc, HCMC 700000, Vietnam
e-mail: nndphuong@hcmiu.edu.vn

D. T. T. Truc
Vietnam Aviation Academy, Nguyen Van Troi St, HCMC 700000, Vietnam

L. T. Tung et al. (eds.), *Disruptive Technology and Business Continuity*,
https://doi.org/10.1007/978-981-97-5452-6_15

ecological sustainability but also the financial sustainability of organizations [1]. Furthermore, corporate leaders have come to understand that a triple bottom line approach, which considers the social, environmental, and economic aspects of business simultaneously, is the key to gaining a competitive edge [2, 3]. Consequently, companies are undergoing a transformation by incorporating social and environmental considerations into their business models.

Hospitals with strategies to quickly adapt to the environment and climate change have adjusted product/process/method regulations to adapt to green practices and stakeholder demands. While most other units do not attach importance to pro-environmental behavior as a way to create long-term competitive advantage. Hospital administrators recognize that pro-environmental behavior requires a lot of costs and time [4]. Others believe that environmental protection behavior should be reserved for large organizations rather than small ones when they have many problems that need to be prioritized rather than changing all operations to green innovation.

Vietnam has been taken into consideration for empirical research as a case study. The destruction of the environment has had a substantial economic impact on Vietnam. Remarkably, relatively few hospitals have developed a road-map for execution and assessment of sustainable development goals and have particular procedures in place for doing so. The use of sustainable development is mentioned in the Ministry of Health's annual statistical yearbook of health activities, although there isn't much in-depth analysis on this topic. Coordinated procedures for creating a plan for carrying out and assessing sustainable development goals are lacking in hospitals. This study was conducted at hospitals in Vietnam, which has had strong development in health care services in recent times but is facing pollution problems from its activities. The objective of this study is to survey the perceptions of workers in hospitals about the effects of green organizational identification, sharing of green vision, and pro-environmental behavior. The findings from the study contribute significantly to helping hospitals have appropriate policies to encourage employees to be highly aware of environmental protection behaviors, contributing to the development of the healthcare industry towards sustainability. The following section outlines the theoretical foundation and proposed research hypotheses. It is followed by an explanation of the methodology, presentation of results, discussion, practical implications, identified limitations, and suggestions for future research.

2 Theoretical framework

2.1 Attitude-Behavior-Context Theory

Attitude-Behavior-Context theory (ABC) is based on the Lewinian idea that "behavior (B) is an interactive product of individual range of attitude variables (A) and contextual factors (C)" [5, 6]. This theory offers multiple benefits in this context. Primarily, the ABC theory is specifically designed for the realm of environmental studies, making it highly relevant for forecasting Pro-environmental behavior (PEB). Secondly, this theory has been refined through three decades of research [7] effectively capturing the dynamic characteristics of PEB. Additionally, it offers a versatile structure that supports ongoing refinement. Utilizing this adaptability, the thesis extends ABC theory by integrating subjectively perceived contextual elements and examining their interplay with PEB.

2.2 *Developing research models*

2.2.1 Green Organization Identity and Pro-Environmental Behavior

Pro-environmental behavior (PEB), often referred to as green behavior, sustainable behavior, or eco-friendly behavior, encompasses actions taken by individuals aimed at safeguarding the environment [8]. PEB encompasses conscientious involvement in activities aimed at safeguarding the environment, such as participating in recycling programs and reusing household items. PEB also includes actions taken to adapt to climate change effects, like purchasing eco-friendly products (organic products, energy saving products), limiting the use of plastic bags, save water or energy or change your mode of travel (walking, cycling, or public bus instead of riding a motorbike), actively contribute to environmental activities for the community [9].

From the standpoint of organizational identity theory, an individual's organizational identity and emotional foundation can shape organizational behavior and influence how employees pursue goals. Organizational identity emerges when the organization's identity aligns with the self-concept of its members. Green Organizational Identity (GOI) represents a collaboratively constructed identity focused on environmental management and an environmentally protective identity model [3, 10]. GOI describes a cognitive framework that legitimizes environmental management as an integral part of the organization's identity [11]. This collective cognitive structure can enhance members' value and sense of belonging within the organization so that members are motivated by the organization's unified identity and have a deeper understanding of the organization's environmental strategy, which ultimately contributes to both member and organizational performance [12]. When an employee demonstrates PEB in a company that promotes environmental friendliness in the workplace, the organizational identification between the employee and the company will be stronger than that of an employee who does not demonstrate PEB [13]. Based on this, the study suggests the following hypothesis.

H1: *Green organizational identity has a positive impact on employees' environmental protection behavior.*

2.2.2 Organization Identity and Green Share Vison

Academic researchers acknowledge the important role of sharing the green vision of organizations, in a green context. Specifically, sharing a green vision it can serve as a means to convey environmental policies and goals to the staff to achieve pro-environmental behaviors. Additionally, sharing an organization's green vision motivates employees to better identify with an environmentally beneficial organizational identity [14]. This expectation arises from the understanding that promoting a green vision aids GHRMP by examining and comprehending the protocols and regulations related to environmental matters. Therefore, sharing green vision can be recommended as a variable intervention between green human resource management and green organizational identity. This sharing will help the organization to foster a green organizational identity by offering employees opportunities to engage in environmental activities at work. Empirically, Dumont et al. [15] show that GHRM practices (including green training) are necessary to increase the effectiveness of environmentally friendly employee behavior, when their company cares more about creating a green environment at work.

Sharing a green vision provides a road-map for developing a common green vision among employees, so it is an important task of sharing a green vision to clarify and shape the common vision. Therefore, this factor is shown that the more organizations share green vision, the stronger green governance has an impact on green organizational identity. Therefore, the study proposed the sixth hypothesis as follows:

H2: *Green Organization identity has a positive impact on green share vision.*

2.2.3 Green Share Vision and Pro-environmental Behavior

Chen et al. [16] define Green share vision (GSV) as "a clear and shared strategic direction of shared environmental goals and aspirations that has been internalized by members of an organization". The authors further envisage that because it provides a collective strategic direction that can guide members' actions towards environmentalism, the GSV serves as a catalyst for GHRM to grow. Additionally, a shared vision provides a common' strategic direction' that can reveal converging goals. Similarly, Afsar and Umrani [17] argue that having a shared vision allows organizations to inspire desired behavior in their workforce, ensuring the achievement of long-term goals. But if organizations do not communicate their goals, "visions can become mere words, leading to disillusionment and distrust instead of inspiration and motivation".

ABC theory explains that a shared vision increases the satisfaction and joy inherent in activities by evoking positive emotions such as enthusiasm and optimism and giving organizational members direction on what to think about and what to change, allowing workers to tap into their cognitive resources (mindfulness), which they can use by 'questioning their assumptions' them, restrain problems, and think outside the box [18]. This is because a shared vision encourages employee self-determination and gives them the freedom to choose how to develop original and advanced ideas into actions that protect the environment [19]. When organizational managers have a flexible vision, achieving sustainability requirements is encouraged. This is important because HRM can create opportunities for employees to motivate themselves to accomplish organizational goals. Therefore, this factor is shown that the more organizations share green vision, the stronger green governance has an impact on green organizational identity. Therefore, the study proposed the sixth hypothesis as follows:

H3: *Sharing green vision has a positive impact on pro-environmental behaviors.*

2.2.4 Mediating Role of Green Share Vision

Rice et al. [20] point out that a shared vision can convey common understandings, visions, knowledge, and plans for the future ideals of members and that a common vision can provide overall strategic direction to facilitate and reveal converging goals. In addition, a shared vision uses the company's potential for success as the basis for far-sighted strategies. Similarly, Chang et al. [21] state that establishing a shared vision can be the basis for achieving a competitive advantage. A shared vision can help employees perceive their work through a broad and conscious context.

GSV can be used to motivate organizational members to increase their readiness to exceed expectations. In summary, a common vision can help senior members achieve many goals, such as establishing a common blueprint for future development, promulgating norms and values, promoting push to exceed performance expectations, and serving as a resource for developing future strategies. When developing future organizational policies, managers should build a green knowledge-sharing platform so that employees demonstrate more environmental protection behavior, thereby achieving the strategic goal of protection the organization's environment. Therefore, this study argues that sharing a green vision has a positive mediating role in the relationship between green organizational identity and employees' pro-environmental behavior, especially in the health sector. Therefore, the study proposes the following hypothesis:

H4: *Green share vision mediates the relationship between green organizational identification and pro-environmental behavior.*

Based on the hypotheses set forth, the research model is presented in Fig. 1.

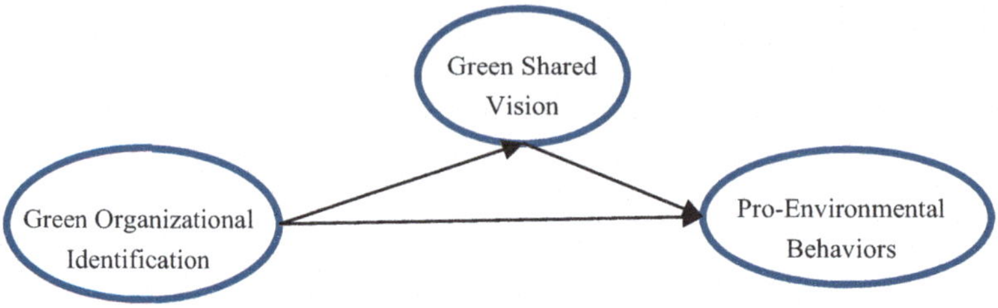

Fig. 1 Research model

3 Methodology

Prior to distributing the questionnaire, we sought the expertise of 10 academics to review it and chose five hospitals for preliminary testing. This process was instrumental in verifying the relevance of the items for healthcare professionals in Vietnamese hospitals and ensuring that our selected respondents possessed the necessary knowledge to complete the questionnaire. The feedback received was primarily centered on assessing GOI and PEB. First, 10 scholars suggested that the GOI scales should focus on the specific characteristics of hospitals in Vietnam and adjust the PEB scale to suit the daily work realities of medical staff. Second, the survey results at 5 hospitals suggest that this study should apply a 5-point Likert-type scale instead of a scale.

We received support from the Department of Health and hospital leaders in Ho Chi Minh City in approaching volunteer staff to participate in interviews to collect research data. We chose those 20 hospitals through a random selection process. We reached out to the medical personnel at these hospitals via email or phone, explained the study to them, and invited them to participate in the survey. This study uses 19 observed variables. Based on the 5:1 rule, the required sample size for this study is 95. However, to prevent errors during the interview and data entry process, the expected sample size is increased to 800 observations. According to expert opinions, all proposed observation variables are considered necessary for the research and the wording of some questions needs to be adjusted to make them smooth and understandable to respondents. Through synthesizing expert opinions, an official measurement scale for the study is proposed.

The GOI factor was measured using items developed by Chen [3] and Mittal and Dhar [22], with a total of 6 items. The GSV factor was measured using items developed by Chen et al. [16] with a total of 4 items. The PEB factor was measured using items developed by Mónus [23] with 9 items. A total of 800 employees agreed to participate in the survey after two reminders. We then sent questionnaires directly to these medical staff. After two reminders, 696 medical staff returned completed questionnaires. Of these returned questionnaires, 19 were excluded because respondents did not meet our criteria. Finally, we obtained 696 valid questionnaires.

4 Methodology

The official time period for the survey is going to be January 2023–April 2023. There were a total of 800 questionnaires distributed directly to the volunteer staff members who participated in the daily operations of the hospital. Once the answer sheets have been reviewed, the following criteria must be met for them to be considered valid: don't leave any unfilled space for observed variables; different respondents provide different levels of response on surveys; completely documented personal data, including gender, age, education, job position, and seniority at work. After eliminating invalid questionnaires, 696 valid questionnaires were collected, resulting in an effective recovery rate of 87.00%. Table 1 presents the sample descriptive statistics for the questionnaire.

4.1 Reliability and Validity

The internal consistency of the scales used in this study was assessed using Cronbach's α values, which were found to be greater than 0.7, indicating good reliability

Table 1 Sample characteristics (N = 696)

Characteristics	Classification	Counts	Frequency (%)
Gender	Female	438	62.93
	Male	258	37.07
Age	< 25	126	18.10
	26–35	350	50.29
	36–45	172	24.71
	46 and above	48	6.90
Position	Doctors	149	21.41
	Nurses	345	49.57
	Medical technicians	68	9.77
	Pharmacists	35	5.03
	Other staffs	99	14.22
Edu	High school	34	4.89
	Vocational school	145	20.83
	Bachelor degree	280	40.23
	Master or Ph.D.	237	34.05
Tenure (year)	< 1	39	5.60
	1–5	226	32.47
	6–10	259	37.21
	>10	172	24.71

Table 2 Reliability and validity

Variable	Item	Factor loading	AVE	Cronbach's α	CR
GOI	6	1	0.561	0.903	0.844
PEB	9	1	0.616	0.916	0.827
GSV	4	1	0.559	0.904	0.850

Table 3 Mean, standard deviation, and correlation

	Mean	Standard deviation	Correlation			
			1	2	3	4
1. GOI	3.568	.745	0.1	1		
2. GSV	3.597	.743	0.181**	0.144*	1	
3. PEB	3.564	.724	0.135*	0.173**	0.183**	1

Note * $p < 0.05$, ** $p < 0.01$

(see Table 2). Confirmatory factor analysis was conducted using AMOS software, and the results indicate good model fitting: $\chi 2/df = 1.947$ (< 3); RMSEA = 0.057 (< 0.080); CFI = 0.943 (> 0.900). The homogeneity, internal consistency, and reliability of each variable is supported by all CR values being greater than 0.8 and exceeding the 0.6 threshold. The convergent validity of the scale is demonstrated by AVE values exceeding 0.5 for each construct. Additionally, good discriminant validity is shown when the correlation coefficients between factors are lower than the AVE values.

Before proceeding with further analysis, the measures of sampling adequacy, including KMO and Bartlett's test, were evaluated. 0.947 is the KMO value for all factors, conforming to the Kaiser criterion for a "meritorious" evaluation. For this reason, the raw data were used to assess the model and measures' goodness.

4.2 Descriptive Statistics Analysis

Table 3 presents the mean, standard deviation, and correlation coefficients for each variable. The research findings indicate a significant correlation between each variable, which supports the hypotheses.

4.3 Hypothesis Testing

Green Shared Vision is expected to act as a mediator between Organizational Green Identity and Pro-Environmental Behaviors. Hierarchical regression analysis was the

Table 4 Regression results

	Dependent variables					
	PEB		GSV		PEB	
	Model 1	Model 2	Model 3	Model 4	Model 5	Model 6
Age	0.051	0.012	0.060	0.032	0.024	0.045
Education	0.028*	0.114*	0.036*	0.044*	0.018*	0.037*
GOI		0.512**		0.678*		0.487*
GSV					0.447*	0.319**
F	4.214*	49.178*	2.551	65.439*	77.084*	46.105**
R^2	0.061	0.421	0.0120	0.423	0.340	0.528
Adjusted R^2	0.050	0.451	0.009	0.527	0.346	0.523
ΔR2	0.051	0.452	0.008	0.500	0.302	0.041

Note * $p < 0.05$. ** $p < 0.01$

method we utilized to test this hypothesis. In this study, hypothesis testing was done using Baron and Kenny [24] technique.

As a first step, we investigated the impact of GOI on PEB.

We constructed Model 1 to assess the effects of the control variables (age and education) on PEB. Subsequently, Model 2 was developed to test Hypothesis 1 (H1). As indicated in Table 4, GOI demonstrated a significant and positive effect on PEB ($\beta = 0.512$, $p < 0.05$), thereby supporting H1.

Secondly, we analyzed the influence of GOI on GSV. Model 3 was designed to evaluate the effects of the control variables on GSV, and Model 4 was built upon Model 3 to test Hypothesis 2 (H2). According to Table 4, GOI significantly and positively affected GSV ($\beta = 0.678$, $p < 0.05$), confirming H2.

Lastly, we explored the effect of GSV on PEB. Using Model 1 as a foundation, Model 5 was created to verify Hypothesis 3 (H3). The results, shown in Table 4, revealed that GSV had a significant and positive impact on PEB ($\beta = 0.447$, $p < 0.05$), thus supporting H3.

5 Conclusion

The goal of the study is to establish a theoretical moderating mediation model by integrating variables such as GOI, GSV, and PEB into the model and examining the relationship between them to clarify the comprehensive picture in the context of the Vietnamese scene. According to the empirical results of this study, GOI has an immediate positive impact on both GSV and PEB. Additionally, the study results confirmed that there was a positive correlation between GOI and PEB in the study. Consistent with other works, our study shows that an increase in GOI also contributes to an increase in PEB. Furthermore, the results of this study are consistent with previous studies [25, 26] showing a positive effect of GOI on PEB.

The empirical findings of the study demonstrate that GSV has a significant mediating effect on both direct and indirect (mediation) relationships [27]. Interestingly, GSV levels appear to have a significant impact on PEB, as shown in the results. Furthermore, the study shows that GVS plays an intermediary role in the relationship between GHRM and PEB in Vietnam. Adding GSV to the model strengthened the association between PEB and GSV, contrary to the study's prediction. This study also supports the idea that GSV should be considered when analyzing PEB.

Our paper presents a critical assessment of the GOI construct and its correlations with various variables across different countries and regions. This forms a foundational basis for further exploration of GOI in diverse global settings. While our study possesses numerous strengths, it is important to acknowledge several limitations that open doors for future research.

Researchers in the future should take these limitations into consideration. Firstly, our sample was restricted to hospital employees in Vietnam, potentially restricting the applicability of our findings to other urban areas, industries, and nations with varying sociocultural and economic contexts. Thus, forthcoming investigations should aim to conduct research within their specific contexts to enhance the comprehensiveness and validity of their results, and to explore potential variations.

Secondly, all assessments were reliant on responses from either staff or management, which may introduce self-response bias. To mitigate this issue, future studies could collect data from multiple sources, including both employees and employers.

Thirdly, our study employed a cross-sectional design, limiting our capacity to make causal inferences. Consequently, future research endeavors could consider adopting a longitudinal research design to examine how relationships evolve over time. Additionally, integrating both qualitative and quantitative data could provide a more holistic understanding of the relationships under scrutiny.

References

1. Xu, Y., Zhao, F.: Impact of energy depletion, human development, and income distribution on natural resource sustainability. Resour. Policy **83**(2023), 103531 (2023)
2. Iqbal, Q., Ahmad, N.H., Halim, H.A.: How does sustainable leadership influence sustainable performance? empirical evidence from selected ASEAN countries. SAGE Open **10**(4), 1–16 (2020)
3. Chen, Y.: Green organizational identity: sources and consequence. Manag. Decis. **49**(3), 384–404 (2011)
4. Gürlek, M., Tuna, M.: Reinforcing competitive advantage through green organizational culture and green innovation. Serv. Ind. J. **38**(7–8), 467–491 (2018)
5. Stern, P.C.: New environmental theories: toward a coherent theory of environmentally significant behavior. J. Soc. Issues **56**(3), 407–424 (2000)
6. Stern, S.M, Porter, E., Furman, J.L.: The Determinants of national innovative capacity. Natl. Bur. Econ. Res., 7876 (2000)
7. Dietz, T.A., Fitzgerald, Shwom, R.: Environmental values. Annu. Rev. Environ. Resour. **30**(1), 335–372 (2005)

8. Yu, X.: Is environment "a city thing" in China? Rural–urban differences in environmental attitudes. J. Environ. Psychol. **8**, 39–48 (2014)
9. Lange, F., Dewitte, S.: Cognitive flexibility and pro-environmental behaviour: a multimethod approach. Eur. J. Pers. **33**(4), 488–505 (2019)
10. Dutton, J.E., Ashford, S.J.: Selling issues to top management. Acad. Manag. Rev. **18**(3), 397–428 (1993)
11. Soewarno, N., Tjahjadi, B., Fithrianti, F.: Green innovation strategy and green innovation: The roles of green organizational identity and environmental organizational legitimacy. Manag. Decis. **57**(11), 3061–3078 (2019)
12. Robertson, J.L., Carleton, E.: Uncovering how and when environmental leadership affects employees, voluntary pro-environmental behavior. J. Lead. & Organ. Stud. **25**(2), 197–210 (2018)
13. Gohoungodji, P., Bernadine, A.N. Latulippe, J.l, Adriana L.B.M.: What is stopping the automotive industry from going green? A systematic review of barriers to green innovation in the automotive industry. J. Clean. Prod. **277**(1), 123524 (2020)
14. Kim, W.G.S., McGinley, H.M., Choi, Agmapisarn, C.: Hotels' environmental leadership and employees' organizational citizenship behavior. Int. J. Hosp. Manag. **87**(1), 102375 (2020)
15. Dumont, J., Shen, J., Deng, X.: Effects of Green HRM practices on employee workplace green behavior: the role of psychological green climate and employee green values. Hum. Resour. Manag. **56**(4), 613–627 (2017)
16. Chen, Y.S., Chang, C.H., Yeh, S.L., Cheng, H.I.: Green shared vision and green creativity: the mediation roles of green mindfulness and green self-efficacy. Qual. & Quant.: Int. J. Methodol **49**(3), 1169–1184 (2015)
17. Afsar, B., Umrani, W.A.: Corporate social responsibility and pro-environmental behavior at workplace: The role of moral reflectiveness, coworker advocacy, and environmental commitment. Corp. Soc. Responsib. Environ. Manag. **27**(1), 109–125 (2020)
18. Eldor, L.: How collective engagement creates competitive advantage for organizations: a business-level model of shared vision, competitive intensity, and service performance. J. Manag. Stud. **57**(2), 177–209 (2020)
19. Ali, M.N.F., Shafique, I.: Green mindfulness and green creativity nexus in hospitality industry: examining the effects of green process engagement and CSR. Int. J. Contemp. Hosp. Manag. **33**(8), 2653–2675 (2021)
20. Rice, M.P., O'Connor, G., Peters, C.L.S., Morone, J.G.: Managing discontinuous innovation. Res.-Technol. Manag. **41**(3), 52–58 (1998)
21. Chang, T.W., Chen, F.F., Luan, H.D., Chen, Y.S.: Effect of green organizational identity, green shared vision, and organizational citizenship behavior for the environment on green product development performance. Sustainability **11**(3), 2–17 (2019)
22. Mittal, S., Dhar, R.L.: Effect of green transformational leadership on green creativity: A study of tourist hotels. Tour. Manag. **57**(C), 118–127 (2016)
23. Mónus, F.: Environmental perceptions and pro-environmental behaviour—comparing different measuring approaches. Environ. Educ. Res. **27**(1), 132–156 (2021)
24. Baron, R.M., Kenny, D.A.: The moderator–mediator variable distinction in social psychological research: Conceptual, strategic, and statistical considerations. J. Pers. Soc. Psychol. **51**(6), 1173–1182 (1986)
25. Dumont, J., Shen, J., Deng, X.: Effects of green HRM practices on employee workplace green behavior: The role of psychological green climate and employee green values: Effect of green HRM on employee workplace green behavior. Hum. Resour. Manag. **56**(4), 613–627 (2016)
26. Leroy, H., van Segers, J.D., den Hartog, D.: Managing people in organizations: Integrating the study of HRM and leadership. Hum. Resour. Manag. Rev. **28**(3), 249–257 (2018)
27. Younas et al., N.: Green shared vision: A bridge between responsible leadership and green behavior under individual green values. Heliyon **9**(11), e21511 (2023)

The Role of External Stimulation on the Relationship between Mental Imagery and Purchase Intentions: Case Study of Vietnamese Gen Z

Ha Nguyen Le Khanh and Linh Huynh Thi My

Abstract Online shopping is the current trend, and to accelerate their decision-making process, marketers must use a stimulating tool that can give customers an experience in all senses. Currently, product presentation videos can help marketers do that when videos provide a view of the product in images, text, sound, and lively interactions. However, brand familiarity makes the recall process in the consumer's mind faster and easier, and relevant information about the product is also displayed to strengthen trust. This study is supported by the SOR theory of the stimulus model, which considers the influence of external stimuli on mental imagery and purchase intention. The sample was collected from June to September 2023, resulting in 375 responses. The research subjects are Generation Z (born from 1997 to 2012). The data was analyzed using the PLS-SEM method with SmartPLS 4. The results revealed that processing fluency and product presentation videos have the most decisive impact on mental imagery. Besides, predicted happiness has a significantly strong effect on purchase intention. Additionally, happiness forecasting mediates the relationship between mental imagery and purchase intention.

Keywords Product presentation video · Processing fluency · Product knowledge · Brand familiarity · Mental imagery

1 Introduction

In a marketing environment, marketers often use external stimuli to influence consumers' minds so that they remember a product or brand. Among them, mental imagery is a popular experience for consumers to recall brands [1]. Nowadays, for imagery to be formed more clearly and specifically, to create mental imagery in customers' minds, more and more sellers use product presentation videos and

H. N. Le Khanh · L. H. T. My (✉)
Ho Chi Minh City Open University, 35-37 Ho Hao Hon, Co Giang Ward, District 1, Ho Chi Minh City, Vietnam
e-mail: 2054012080ha@ou.edu.vn

L. T. Tung et al. (eds.), *Disruptive Technology and Business Continuity*,
https://doi.org/10.1007/978-981-97-5452-6_16

graphic text beside traditional photo text to introduce products on the homepage of e-commerce platforms. Video not only provides dynamic visual information and auditory information [2] and [3] but is also more vivid than images and text. Flavián et al. [4] defined product presentation videos as audio-visual resources that help online consumers know about products. Among them, mental imagery is a popular experience for consumers to recall brands [1]. At the same time, other research also shows that product presentation videos provide a lot of product information to consumer perception, thus positively influencing attitude formation [5]. From what is shown in the product video, it helps customers enhance the imagery when thinking about it.

Besides, the brand's familiarity in customers' minds will help customers easily recognize and influence their memory more than unfamiliar brands [6]. On the other hand, previous research also did not find an interaction between brand familiarity and the frequency of advertising repetition in consumers' minds, but brand familiarity increases recall and recognition. Because of this, the brand is considered a stimulus that helps the brand's imagery return to the customer's mind when deciding to buy. Strong brands are associated with quality and other desired benefits, and therefore, they easily excite the minds of consumers [7].

Along with product presentation videos and brand familiarity, product knowledge is also seen as a factor stimulating consumer intention when product knowledge also provides customers with additional information in their minds. Location helps form imagery in consumers' minds and influences purchasing decisions [8]. Usually, customers will determine product value based on information. Product knowledge is formed through the customer's experience after using the product. Hauser and Lund [9] suggest that consumers with better knowledge about remanufactured products will better understand the quality considerations and features. Finally, with the support of processing fluency in the customer's mind, they can create vivid experiences and feelings when mental imagery exists, increasing purchase intention towards the product.

The article aims to assess the role of external stimulation in the relationship between mental imagery and purchase intentions. Except for the introduction, the structure of the article consists of four sections. The next section is a literature review underlying the study and the methodological considerations behind the data collection process, followed by the results of the study. We then discuss the results in the fourth section and then draw some concluding remarks in the last section of the paper.

2 Literature review

2.1 Purchase Intention

Intentions are the choices being considered for implementation, in which their steps are in the state of preparation for action after the intention stage will be the act. This stage is critical. The higher the implementation intention, the higher the likelihood of the action being taken. Because implementation intentions clarify the mechanisms that help reduce the "gap" between intentions and achieving behavioral goals. Intentions are realized in response to a specific situation that will result in a specific action [10]. Additionally, intention is a factor used to evaluate an individual's ability to perform an action. According to Ajzen [11], the intention is provisional and can attempt to motivate an individual to be willing to perform a particular behavior.

2.2 Stimulus, Organism, Response Theory (SOR)

The Stimulus, Organism, Response (SOR), also known as the stimulus model, was developed from the traditional stimulus-response theory of Woodworth [12] and then expanded through stimuli that affect the subject can and are responded to by actions. This theory is widely used in the study of stimuli. The SOR model supports the explanation of human behavioral responses when analyzing the subject's state, which can be cognitive, rational, or emotional, after being stimulated by the environment [13].

External stimuli: The model compiled by the author from related studies shows that the interaction relationship increases the ability to form images in the customer's imagination, ranging from brand familiarity, processing fluency, product knowledge, and product presentation videos to mental images [14–17]. At the same time, the mental image and predicted happiness in customer mind are also considered by related studies to affect each other and affect purchase intention [18, 19] and [20].

In this study, SOR is used as a background theory to support the model proposed for explaining purchase intention (R) after the subject predicted happiness and mental imagery (O) after being stimulated by external factors such as product presentation videos, brand familiarity, product knowledge, and processing fluency (S). In online shopping, purchase intention (R) will be higher if customers have more information about the product [21]. Having much information about the product helps customers easily visualize specific mental imagery of the product or service in their mind, and consumers can imagine situations and simulate consumer experiences used psychologically about predicted (O) they have never experienced and will happen in the future, which brings feelings of happiness to customers.

H1: Predicted happiness has a positive impact on purchase intention.

H2: Mental imagery has a positive impact on predicted happiness.

The subjects of the observed stimuli are mental imagery and predicted happiness. However, this study also found that there is always a link between mental imagery and predicted happiness. The spirit is formed by stimulating factors such as product presentation videos. The mental imagery of the subject becomes more precise than usual through the vividness of the product presentation video. Video visuals and audio can be designed to appeal to consumers' emotions, using music, images, and voice to evoke positive emotions and excitement about the product. Next, brand familiarity also contributes to creating mental imagery when consumers are directly or indirectly exposed to advertising through repeated exposure to the brand and the ability to recognize its brand in different situations and quickly receive advertising messages.

Furthermore, mental imagery is also formed from product knowledge about the product, such as uses, ingredients, and dosage. Mental imagery that is presented concretely or abstractly is also involved in processing fluency. Once information is processed, fluency can help customers form mental representations of products or related imagery [15]. It can be seen that how subjects visualize mental imagery is related to external stimuli. Based on that, we propose the following hypothesis:

H3: Video product presentation has a positive impact on mental imagery.

H4: Brand familiar has a positive impact on mental imagery.

H5: Product knowledge has a positive impact on mental imagery.

H6: Processing fluency has a positive impact on mental imagery.

3 Methodology

3.1 Measures

The model is based on the Stimulus, Organism, and Response theory. The Product Presentation Video, Processing Fluency and Mental Imagery scales were developed by [22]. The Brand familiarity scale was developed by [23] and [24] with six observed variables, Product knowledge was built based on the research of [25]. Predicted happiness scale is inherited from the research of Feizi et al. [26] with five observed variables. The Purchase Intention scale was built from the research of Wu et al. [27], including four observed variables.

The study subjects are Gen Z, born between 1997 and 2012. Data was collected by sending them to respondents via Google Forms. Because this is a research topic conducted by students, it is limited in terms of cost and time, so the group chose a non-probability sampling method, precisely the convenience sampling method.

The hypotheses were assessed by the PLS-SEM method with SmartPLS 4.0. PLS-SEM can identify very complex models with high confidence. Data are evaluated through the following steps: measurement model assessment and structural model assessment.

In the first step, the reliability test of the scale is determined through composite reliability (CR) and Cronbach's Alpha (CA). According to Hair Jr et al. [28], all contruct's CR must be over 0.7 and considered to meet the required reliability. Similarly, CA greater than 0.7 is reliable [29]. This index needs to be between 0.7 and 0.95 for the scale to be highly reliable. The average variance extracted (AVE) and the outer loading coefficient evaluate the convergent validity. Hair Jr et al. [28] suggest convergent validity is also achieved if AVE is more significant than 0.5 because the observed variables can explain more than 50% of the variance of the concept it represents [30].

Discriminant validity is assessed through a comparison matrix between each concept's inter-correlations with its AVE's square root. According to Henseler et al. [30], discriminant validity is achieved when the square root of the AVE of a concept is greater than the correlations between this concept and others.

The next step is structural model assessment, including evaluating the power of explanation through R2, predictive power with Q2 and the path coefficient test [28]. Typically, R2 is evaluated as strong, medium, and weak with values of 0.75, 0.50, and 0.25, respectively [29]. Evaluate the model's predictive power through the Q2 value.

3.2 Sample

Statistics show that most genZ people have a reasonably stable income from 5 to 10 million VND, accounting for 49.4%. In addition, statistics show that there are similarities between men and women (See Table 1).

Table 1 Sample characteristics

Variable	Category	Frequency	Percent (%)
Gender	Male	176	46.6
	Female	202	53.4
Income	Under 5 million	110	29.1
	Form 5 to 10 million	187	49.4
	From 10 to 20 million	48	12.7
	Over 20 million	33	8.8

4 Result

4.1 Measurement Model Assessment

In this stage, the data validity is assessed by verifying the scale's reliability and convergent and discriminant validity. Table 2 shows that the all scale has a value greater than 0.7. The measurement scales achieve the necessary reliability to continue with the following steps. Next, the study tests convergent validity. The results show that all AVE is more significant than 0.5 and outer loadings are above 0.7, also meeting the standards according to Gotz et al. [31].

Discriminant validity to evaluate whether the research concept it is explaining is distinct from other concepts included in the research model. According to Henseler et al. [30], concepts are distinct when the square root of the AVE of a concept (bold numbers in Table 3) is greater than the correlations between this concept and others (lowercase numbers in Table 3). The results show that the data satisfy the requirements. Therefore, the discriminant validity is guaranteed [32].

Table 2 Reliability and convergent validity

Variable	CA	CR	AVE	Outer loadings
Brand familiarity (BF)	0.758	0.845	0.578	0.706–0.796
Mental Imagery (MI)	0.909	0.926	0.610	0.748–0.818
Processing fluency (PF)	0.801	0.881	0.712	0.773–0.890
Predicted Happiness(PH)	0.834	0.883	0.601	0.740–0.810
Purchase intention (PI)	0.806	0.873	0.631	0.773–0.817
Product knowledge (PK)	0.821	0.881	0.650	0.767–0.828
Video product presentation (PPV)	0.855	0.896	0.633	0.785–0.827

Table 3 Discriminant validity

	BF	MI	PF	PH	PI	PK	PPV
BF	0.760						
MI	0.436	0.781					
PF	0.271	0.468	0.844				
PH	0.271	0.401	0.309	0.775			
PI	0.382	0.418	0.275	0.406	0.794		
PK	0.337	0.385	0.333	0.269	0.372	0.806	
PPV	0.428	0.475	0.356	0.365	0.449	0.393	0.796

Table 4 Bootstrapping analysis

Relationships	β	T-statistics	P-values	Results
BF –> MI	0.218	5.099	0.000	Accepted
MI –> PH	0.401	8.534	0.000	Accepted
PF –> MI	0.285	5.895	0.000	Accepted
PH –> PI	0.406	9.578	0.000	Accepted
PK –> MI	0.126	2.576	0.010	Accepted
PPV –> MI	0.230	4.261	0.000	Accepted

4.2 *Structural Model Assessment*

Table 4 shows that the path coefficients (β) are all positive. The bootstrapping technique demonstrates the statistical significance of the research hypotheses. The study uses bootstrapping confidence intervals (N = 5000) to test whether the reliability of the variable is significantly higher or lower than the recommended minimum threshold. In other words, bootstrapping is applied to test for direct effects. So, all P-values below 0.05 indicates that all hypothesis is accepted (see Table 4).

5 Discussion

Processing fluency has a positive effect on mental imagery. The results of the data analysis show that processing fluency positively impacts mental imagery ($\beta = 0.285$; $p = 0.000$). This result is consistent with the research of Huang and Ha [22]. This means that in reality, people with the ability to process information fluently will quickly create a brand image when reminded of the condition that the person must be able to fluently understand information, process, and have the ability to visualize the whole from simple to complex. The research results are also consistent with that of [19]. Processing fluency facilitates customers receiving and understanding information clearly and effectively, helping to form a positive mental image of the brand. When customers can process visual and semantic information easily, they can create positive mental imagery of the brand based on personal experience and a deep understanding of the product and service of the brand.

Brand familiarity directly impacts mental imagery ($\beta = 0.218, p = 0.000$). Consistent with the view of Gavilan and Avello [33], consumers are familiar with the brand from which many mental images are formed. When customers are continuously exposed to and interact with a brand, they often develop a sense of familiarity and connection with that brand. It can increase customer interest in the product, contributing to a positive mental image. Customers' mental image is higher when familiar and sympathetic to the brand. Yu et al. [14] stated that brand familiarity positively impacts mental imagery. Brand familiarity helps consumers easily recall the brand, activating stored information about that brand and forming mental imagery for an apparel brand in online shopping. Brand familiarity often creates an emotional bond with consumers through continuous experience and advertising, facilitating brand recall and stimulating brand-related stored information. This creates a positive mental imagery of the brand in the consumer's mind, which is critical in online shopping, where brand awareness and trust are decisive factors.

Besides, mental imagery positively affects the ability to predicted happiness. The analysis shows that this hypothesis is consistent with $\beta = 0.401$ and $p = 0.000$. It is similar to the findings of Skard et al. [34], showing that mental images created from virtual reality (VR) technology positively affect customer enjoyment and happiness. Usually, customers think about or daydream about the feeling the product can bring to satisfy their emotional needs. So, mental images help them make that thought concrete and more explicit, achieving a realistic feeling.

Predicted happiness positively affects purchase intent ($\beta = 0.406$; $p = 0.000$). This result is consistent with the discovery of authors in [34] that the correlation between mental images and predicting happiness increases purchase intentions. From the results of this study, when the increased mental image of other factors remained the same, the prediction of increased happiness resulted in an increase in intention to 0.163. Therefore, mental image affects consumer behavior by predicting happiness. Predicted happiness comes when customers feel satisfied when they imagine owning a product, which promotes consumer behavior that forms the intention to buy to be satisfied. Previous studies have also demonstrated that happiness and spending intentions are related. Customers will generally spend and plan to spend on products that make them feel happy to own them [35].

Furthermore, product knowledge positively impacts mental imagery ($\beta = 0.126$; $p = 0.010$). This result is consistent with research by Nielsen et al. [36], which suggests that consumers with much knowledge of a related product category are more likely to create vivid and attractive simulations that lead to mental images. Product knowledge helps customers better visualize the functions and uses of the product. Similar to the research of AI-Abbadi et al. [37]. product knowledge helps consumers better understand product features, advantages and differences. By collecting reviews from other consumers, they can build a comprehensive and accurate picture of the product, creating a positive mental image and increasing trust and confidence in their purchasing decisions.

Finally, product presentation videos positively impact mental imagery. Cheng et al. [17] state that product presentation videos improve consumers' mental image. Product presentation videos can create a strong positive impact in building a mental image. By combining images, sounds, and storytelling, this video helps create an enjoyable experience that contributes to building a mental image in the consumer's mind. From there, they feel like they are experiencing the product when watching the video. This is consistent with previous researchers of Orus et al. [38], who reported that product presentation videos were positively related to mental imagery. The formation of mental imagery depends on the vividness of the video. Vivid content helps stimulate consumers' imaginations about the product. In the online environment, vivid videos help consumers imagine what the product is like in reality, overcoming the lack of interaction with the product.

6 Conclusion

The study tested the influence of familiarity with the brand, processing fluency, product presentation video, and product knowledge on the relationship between mental image and purchase intention. The research was conducted based on an analysis of 375 samples using Smartpls 4.0. The data validity and other indicators of the scale all met the requirements.

The result shows that predicting happiness has the most decisive impact on purchase intention. It shows that when customers are psychologically stimulated by consumer product experiences about feelings they have never experienced and will happen in the future through mental images, it leads to a higher purchase intention. Next comes the impact mental imagery has on predicting happiness. Building specific mental images helps customers easily imagine specific usage situations. While analyzing four external stimulus factors that impact mental images, the processing fluency has the most substantial impact on mental image formation, followed by product presentation videos, familiar brands, and product knowledge (See Fig. 1).

The powerful indirect effect of mental imagery on purchase intention through happiness prediction is detected. Mental images are the customer's fantasies about the product in their mind and can create consumers' fantasies and expectations about the future state when using the product or service. When positive mental images and associations predicted happiness, they encourage and motivate consumers to form purchase intentions. Customers perceive that the product is the right choice to achieve their desired state of happiness, and this drives purchase intention and consumption actions.

In a time when online shopping is gradually becoming a trend like now, administrators need to clarify brand identity, simplify images, or use unique text to build strategies and implement consistently to be easily remembered in customers' minds. At the same time, you can encourage customer interaction by inviting them to comment and express EWOM or WOM for the brand/product to increase mental imagery and purchase intention.

The first limitation is that its population is Gen Z in Vietnam and uses convenience sampling. In addition, it can be seen that the study only surveyed general cases without focusing on each industry. If digging deeper, there may be differences between industries. Future research should be conducted in specific industries to understand how external stimuli influence mental imagery and purchase intention relationships.

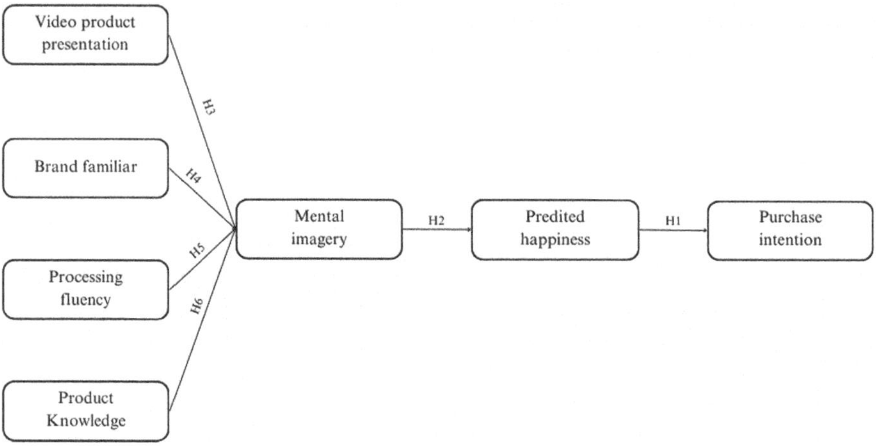

Fig. 1 Conceptual framework

References

1. Seurinck, R., de Lange, F.P., Achten, E., Vingerhoets, G.: Mental rotation meets the motion aftereffect: the role of hV5/MT+ in visual mental imagery. J. Cogn. Neurosci. **23**(6), 1395–1404 (2011)
2. Jiang, Z., Benbasat, I.: Research note—investigating the influence of the functional mechanisms of online product presentations. Inf. Syst. Res. **18**(4), 454–470 (2007)
3. Vonkeman, C., Verhagen, T., Van Dolen, W.: Role of local presence in online impulse buying. Inf. & Manag. **54**(8), 1038–1048 (2017)
4. Flavián, C., Gurrea, R., Orús, C.: The influence of online product presentation videos on persuasion and purchase channel preference: The role of imagery fluency and need for touch. Telemat. Inform. **34**(8), 1544–1556 (2017)
5. Park, D.H., Kim, S.: The effects of consumer knowledge on message processing of electronic word-of-mouth via online consumer reviews. Electron. Commer. Res. Appl. **7**(4), 399–410 (2008)
6. Martí-Parreño, J., Bermejo-Berros, J., Aldás-Manzano, J.: The effect of brand familiarity and repetition of product placement in video games. In: Global marketing conference, pp. 725–735 (2016)
7. San-Martín, S., Prodanova, J., Jiménez, N.: The impact of age in the generation of satisfaction and WOM in mobile shopping. J. Retail. Consum. Serv. **23**, 1–8 (2015)
8. Burton, S., Howlett, E., Tangari, A.H.: Food for thought: how will the nutrition labeling of quick service restaurant menu items influence consumers' product evaluations, purchase intentions, and choices? J. Retail. **85**(3), 258–273 (2009)
9. Hauser, W., Lund, R.T.: The remanufacturing industry: Anatomy of a giant. Department of Manufacturing Engineering Boston Universit, (2003)
10. Gollwitzer, P.M., Sheeran, P.: Implementation intentions and goal achievement: A meta-analysis of effects and processes. Adv. Exp. Soc. Psychol. **38**, 69–119 (2006)
11. Ajzen, I.: The theory of planned behavior. Organ. Behav. Hum. Decis. Process. **50**(2), 179–211 (1991)
12. Woodworth, R.S.: Psychology. New York: Henry Holt & Co. Department of Psychology University of Vermont Burlington Vermont 5405, (1929)
13. Shah, A.M., Yan, X., Shah, S.A.A., Ali, M.: Customers' perceived value and dining choice through mobile apps in Indonesia. Asia Pac. J. Mark. Logist. **33**(1), 1–28 (2020)

14. Yu, U.J., Cho, E., Johnson, K.K.C.: Effects of brand familiarity and brand loyalty on imagery elaboration in online apparel shopping. J. Glob. Fash. Mark. **8**(3), 193–206 (2017)
15. Chang, C.: Imagery fluency and narrative advertising effects. J. Advert. **42**(1), 54–68 (2013)
16. Visentin, M., Pizzi, G., Pichierri, M.: Fake news, real problems for brands: The impact of content truthfulness and source credibility on consumers' behavioral intentions toward the advertised brands. J. Interact. Mark. **45**(1), 99–112 (2019)
17. Cheng, Z., Shao, B., Zhang, Y.: Effect of product presentation videos on consumers' purchase intention: the role of perceived diagnosticity, mental imagery, and product rating. Front. Psychol. **13**, 812579 (2022)
18. Yoo, J., Kim, M.: The effects of online product presentation on consumer responses: A mental imagery perspective. J. Bus. Res. **67**(11), 2464–2472 (2014)
19. Maier, E., Dost, F.: Fluent contextual image backgrounds enhance mental imagery and evaluations of experience products. J. Retail. Consum. Serv. **45**, 207–220 (2018)
20. MacInnis, D.J., Patrick, V.M., Park, C.W.: Looking through the crystal ball: affective forecasting and misforecasting in consumer behavior. Rev. Mark. Res., 43–79 (2017)
21. De, P., Hu, Y., Rahman, M.S.: Product-oriented web technologies and product returns: An exploratory study. Inf. Syst. Res. **24**(4), 998–1010 (2013)
22. Huang, R., Ha, S.: The role of need for cognition in consumers' mental imagery: a study of retail brand's Instagram. Int. J. Retail. & Distrib. Manag. **49**(2), 242–262 (2021)
23. Doong, H.S., Wang, H.C., Foxall, G.R.: An investigation of consumers' webstore shopping: a view of click- and-mortar company. Int. J. Inf. Manag **31**(3), 210–216 (2011)
24. Ha, H.Y., Perks, H.: Effects of consumer perceptions of brand experience on the web: brand familiarity, satisfaction and brand trust. J. Consum. Behav **4**(6), 438–452 (2005)
25. Sun, Y., Wang, S.: Understanding consumers' intentions to purchase green products in the social media marketing context. Asia Pac. J. Mark. Logist. **32**(4), 860–878 (2020)
26. Feizi, S., Nasiri, M., Bahadori, H., Amiri, M.H., Mirhosseini, H.: The relationship between spiritual well- being and happiness among healthcare students: Application of the spiritual health questionnaire for the Iranian population. Heliyon **6**(11), (2020)
27. Wu, J., Wang, F., Liu, L., Shin, D.: Effect of online product presentation on the purchase intention of wearable devices: the role of mental imagery and individualism-collectivism. Front. Psychol. **11**, 6 (2020)
28. Hair Jr, J.F., Hult, G.T.M., Ringle, C.M., Sarstedt, M., Danks, N.P., Ray, S.: Partial least squares structural equation modeling (PLS-SEM) using R: A workbook. Springer Nature, 197 (2021)
29. Hair, J.F., Ringle, C.M., Sarstedt, M.: PLS-SEM: Indeed a silver bullet. J. Mark. Theory Pract., 139–152 (2011)
30. Henseler, J., Ringle, C.M., Sarstedt, M.: A new criterion for assessing discriminant validity in variance- based structural equation modeling. J. Acad. Mark. Sci. **43**, 115–135 (2015)
31. Gotz, O., Liehr-Gobbers, K., Krafft, M.: Evaluation of structural equation models using the partial least squares (PLS) approach. Handb. Part.L Least Sq.S: Concepts, Methods Appl. **1**(3), 691–711 (2010)
32. Hair, J.F., Jr., Sarstedt, M., Hopkins, L., Kuppelwieser, V.G.: Partial least squares structural equation modeling (PLSSEM): An emerging tool in business research. Eur. Bus. Rev. **26**(2), 106–121 (2014)
33. Gavilan, D., Avello, M.: Brand-evoked mental imagery: The role of brands in eliciting mental imagery. Sage Open, **10**(4), (2020)
34. Skard, S., Knudsen, E.S., Sjåstad, H., Thorbjørnsen, H.: How virtual reality influences travel intentions: The role of mental imagery and happiness forecasting. Tour. Manag. **87**, 104360 (2021)
35. Aknin, L.B., Wiwad, D., Hanniball, K.B.: Buying well-being: Spending behavior and happiness. Soc. Pers. Psychol. Compass, **12**(5), (2018)
36. Nielsen, J.H., Escalas, J.E., Hoeffler, S.: Mental simulation and category knowledge affect really new product evaluation through transportation. J. Exp. Psychol.: Appl. **24**(2), 145 (2018)

37. Al-Abbadi, L., Bader, D., Mohammad, A., Al-Quran, A., Aldaihani, F., Al-Hawary, S., Alathamneh, F.: The effect of online consumer reviews on purchasing intention through product mental image. Int. J. Data Netw. Sci. **6**(4), 1519–1530 (2022)
38. Orús, C., Gurrea, R., Flavián, C.: Facilitating imaginations through online product presentation videos effects on imagery fluency, product attitude and purchase intention. Electron. Commer. Res., **17**, 661–700 (2016)

How Does Knowledge Shape the Student's Entrepreneurial Intention? the S-O-R Theory Perspective

Tuyen Kim Thi Dinh, Trang Thuy Duong Mai, and Linh Thuy Thi Ly

Abstract While the effect of entrepreneurial knowledge on entrepreneurial intention has received plenty of attention, a microscopic study has been made on how this element affects the entrepreneurial intention of Vietnamese students. Therefore, this study was conducted to provide a better understanding of the impact of entrepreneurial knowledge, including knowledge from university and participation in the family business on entrepreneurial intention and the mediating role of entrepreneurial passion from the perspective of SOR theory. Questionnaires were sent to 605 university students in Vietnam and Vietnamese students at universities worldwide. The data were analyzed using partial least squares structural equation modeling (PLS-SEM) through SmartPLS 4 software. The investigation results show that an individual's entrepreneurial passion was greatly influenced by their entrepreneurial knowledge. Besides, entrepreneurial passion also has a favorable effect on entrepreneurial intention. Consequently, this study proposes that students' universities and families should pay attention to providing entrepreneurial knowledge and environment to optimize Vietnamese students' entrepreneurial passion, thereby motivating them to become entrepreneurs.

Keywords Entrepreneurial intention · Entrepreneurship education · Family business involvement · Entrepreneurial passion · S-O-R theory

1 Introduction

Entrepreneurs contribute significantly to economic progress in the twenty-first century through their entrepreneurship [1]. Researchers, governments, and politicians worldwide are becoming more interested in entrepreneurship due to its economic and social benefits [2]. Research on entrepreneurial intention is one of the critical fields of entrepreneurship. This is still relatively new knowledge regarding entrepreneurial intention and needs further research to understand the intention to

T. K. T. Dinh (✉) · T. T. D. Mai · L. T. T. Ly
Ho Chi Minh City Open University, Ho Chi Minh City 700000, Vietnam
e-mail: 2154110486tuyen@ou.edu.vn

L. T. Tung et al. (eds.), *Disruptive Technology and Business Continuity*,
https://doi.org/10.1007/978-981-97-5452-6_17

become an entrepreneur. The importance of considering entrepreneurial intention has been demonstrated in numerous earlier studies.

Identification, company formation, and other entrepreneurial activities are all related to entrepreneurial knowledge. Each individual's knowledge level will impact their intention to become an entrepreneur. However, one topic of entrepreneurship research that is frequently overlooked is how entrepreneurship knowledge affects entrepreneurial intention [3]. This research explores the connection between entrepreneurial knowledge and entrepreneurial intention to fill this neglected research gap. The article analyzes two aspects of entrepreneurial knowledge: entrepreneurship education and family business involvement. Entrepreneurship education can help students develop their entrepreneurial intention by stimulating their entrepreneurial thinking and providing them with a foundational knowledge of the field. Along with that, family business involvement also creates motivation for individuals to develop entrepreneurial intentions.

The foundational theory of the study is the theory of Mehrabian and Russell's [4] Stimulus, Organism, and Response (S–O-R). The research is carried out by analyzing the relationship between S–O-R factors: a stimulus (S) passing through the internal organism (O) of the human body will create an intention to respond (R). Hence, entrepreneurship educational programs can stimulate entrepreneurial activity by increasing entrepreneurial intention. Entrepreneurship education and family business involvement are treated as a stimulating factor (S). Entrepreneurial passion is the internal mechanism of the organism (O), as it is the combination of entrepreneurial activity and emotional awareness, so entrepreneurial passion is a unique emotional expression of the entrepreneur. Entrepreneurial intention is the outcome of the S and O process that causes the response (R).

The remaining portions of this research are divided into four main sections. The theoretical foundation is presented in the second section. Then, we integrate these theories into a proposed model of entrepreneurial intention. Part three presents the research method. The results of the study are discussed in section four. The final section summarizes the findings and presents the study's limitations.

2 Literature Review

2.1 Theory of SOR (Stimulus - Organism - Response)

Environmental psychology is the source of the SOR theoretical framework. It asserts that the environment contains stimulus (S) that can affect and change organisms (O). On the contrary, individuals exhibit approach or response (R) due to these internal states [5]. According to the stimulus-organism-response (SOR) model, environmental factors can affect people's behavior by forming unique psychological stimuli, particularly emotions and cognitions.

This model explains "stimulus" as an environmental factor that stimulates an internal [6]. Following the authors' research, family business involvement and entrepreneurship education serve as powerful stimuli that positively affect entrepreneurial passion. According to Souitaris et al. [7], entrepreneurial intentions are influenced by inspiration from entrepreneurship education. Therefore, educational entrepreneurship activities must foster and ignite a passion for the business world.

The term "organism" in the model refers to the intermediate states of the cognitive and emotional state of people that mediate the effect of a stimulus on a person's response [8]. To examine entrepreneurs' emotional and cognitive states for their entrepreneurial passion, this study uses entrepreneurs' beliefs about the stimulating effects of entrepreneurship education and family business involvement. Entrepreneurs who are passionate about their businesses are more likely to succeed. Because entrepreneurial passion inspires creativity and motivates innovation to take advantage of business opportunities, it is essential to entrepreneurship.

2.2 *Entrepreneurial Intention*

According to Fayolle and Lián [9], the intention is considered as an individual's involvement in an enterprise or the intention to start a business enterprise. Entrepreneurship activity results from entrepreneurial intention. By assisting a person in identifying business opportunities, creating a business plan, and carrying it out, the entrepreneurial intention serves as the foundation step toward entrepreneurship activities.

2.3 *Entrepreneurship Education and Family Business Involvement*

The goal of entrepreneurship education is to improve positive personal attitudes toward entrepreneurship and inspire them to be prepared to engage in entrepreneurial tasks. It is the primary source of knowledge and skills in business. The development of entrepreneurial knowledge and abilities is facilitated by entrepreneurship education.

The family businesses are defined in many different ways by researchers worldwide. Alcaraz [10] considers family involvement as a way to influence the business. People who have grown up in a family business and as employees of this business may have advantages or disadvantages. Thanks to their extensive exposure to the family business, they have the potential to contribute a special type of human capital in the form of specific tacit business knowledge. The founders' entrepreneurial spirit, the company's reputation, its management practices, and the trust and communication among family members are the types of resources that go into creating such an ethical combination family.

2.4 Entrepreneurial Passion

Entrepreneurial passion is a conscious, approachable, and positive emotion toward entrepreneurship. Through entrepreneurship education, one can foster or develop their entrepreneurial passion. Individuals will increase their support for entrepreneurship and relatively define themselves as entrepreneurs by gaining knowledge and skills through entrepreneurship education and completing practical activities related to creative entrepreneurship [11]. Entrepreneurial passion motivates wise decisions and contributes to high efficiency when embarking on business.

Hypothesis H1. Entrepreneurship education has a positive impact on entrepreneurial passion.

Hypothesis H2. Family business involvement has a positive impact on entrepreneurial passion.

Hypothesis H3. Entrepreneurial passion has a positive impact on entrepreneurial intention (Fig. 1).

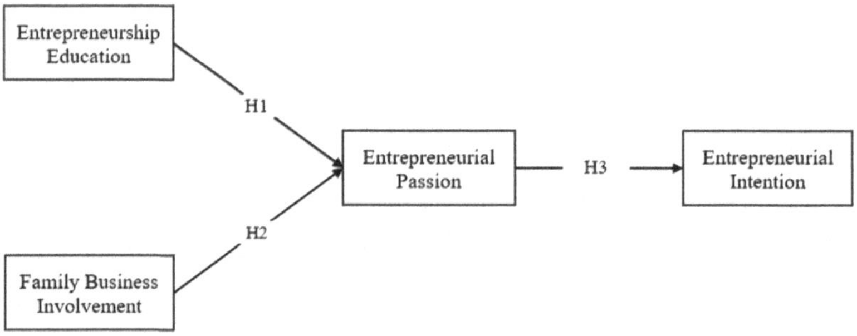

Fig. 1 Conceptual framework

3 Methodology

3.1 Sample

This study is part of a research project focusing on the entrepreneurial intention of Ho Chi Minh City Open University students. This study used a convenience sampling technique. The research subjects are Vietnamese students. Because the target data was pervasive enough to provide representative and reliable results, the study was conducted for four months (from 23/5/2023 to 12/9/2023). The online survey via the Google Forms platform included 596 students from 73 universities in Vietnam and 9 Vietnamese students from universities around the world.

The number of answers in Table 1 is relatively uniform, showing that the information obtained from the survey has little difference between factors.

Table 1 Demographic characteristics

Categories	Frequencies	Percentages (%)
Year		
First-year student	67	11.1
Second-year student	231	38.2
Third-year student	157	26.0
Fourth-year students or above	150	24.8
Type of university		
Public university	523	86.4
Private university	73	12.1
Study abroad	9	1.5
University		
Ho Chi Minh City Open University	107	17.7
University of Economics Ho Chi Minh City	104	17.2
Foreign Trade University	30	5.0
Ho Chi Minh University of Banking	26	4.3
University of Social Sciences and Humanities	23	3.8
Ho Chi Minh City International University	22	3.6
Ho Chi Minh City University of Technology and Education	18	3.0
Ho Chi Minh City University of Technology	15	2.5
Others	260	43.0

3.2 Measures

This study uses scales that have been tested in previous studies. University students were asked to respond to a questionnaire with 19 items totaling four scales, including the Entrepreneurship Education (EE) scale of 4 questions and the Entrepreneurial Intention (EI) scale of 5 questions, designed by the research of Voda et al. [12]. Family Business Involvement (FBI) includes 5 questions proposed by the research of Wang et al. [13], Entrepreneurial Passion (EP) scale includes 5 questions applied by the research of Karimi [14]. All factors are measured on a 5-point Likert scale in ascending (1 = strongly disagree, 2 = disagree, 3 = neutral, 4 = agree and 5 = strongly agree).

3.3 Data Analysis

Data from the online survey were recorded in Microsoft Excel via spreadsheet and analyzed using partial least squares structural equation modeling (PLS-SEM) in SmartPLS 4. When analyzing the data, Anderson and Gerbing's [15] two-step analysis procedure was applied, whereby the measurement model (validity and reliability) was implemented first and followed by the structure model (testing the relationship between variables) to produce final results using bootstrapping techniques with 5,000 samples [16].

4 Discussion

4.1 Assessment of Measurement Model

Scale reliability

This study used Cronbach's alpha (CA) and composite reliability (CR) measures to assess the scale's reliability.

Hair et al. [17] suggest that Cronbach's alpha greater than 0.7 is considered reliable. In this study, all variables were adequate in terms of reliability because all Cronbach's alpha coefficients were greater than 0.7.

According to Höck and Ringle [18], the composite reliability (CR) value is accepted as a value greater than 0.6. The composite reliability of all constructs exceeded the value of 0.6.

Convergent validity

This study tests convergent validity using the outer loadings and average variance extracted (AVE). After checking the validity of the outer loadings, all variables have outer loadings greater than 0.5 [19], indicating that the results are acceptable. A minimum AVE of 0.5 is necessary for a construct to have full convergent validity

Table 2 Convergent validity

Construct	CA	CR	Loadings	AVE
EE	0.959	0.97	0.933–0.951	0.891
EI	0.939	0.954	0.873–0.919	0.804
EP	0.892	0.92	0.818–0.849	0.698
FBI	0.964	0.972	0.925–0.950	0.874

Table 3 A Heterotrait-Monotrait Test (HTMT)

	EE	EI	EP	FBI
EE				
EI	0.347			
EP	0.387	0.621		
FBI	0.341	0.414	0.275	

[20]. Table 2 results show that all AVE values exceed 0.5, meeting the required threshold.

Discriminant validity

A creative approach for evaluating PLS-SEM's discriminant validity is the heterotrait-monotrait correlation ratio (HTMT). The HTMT ratio should be less than 0.85 [21]. According to the criteria, all values in Table 3 are less than or equal to 0.85. As a result, all variables are guaranteed about discriminant validity.

4.2 *Assessment of the Structural Model*

After evaluating the measurement model, the current study tested the structural model by a bootstrap analysis on 5000 replications to determine the significance of the coefficients [22]. R^2, Q^2, F^2, Path Coefficients, T-value, and P-value were taken to test, as suggested by Hair Jr et al. [16].

The level of predictive accuracy is measured by R^2 [16]. R^2 expresses the percentage variance of the dependent variables as explained by the independent variable. R^2 of entrepreneurial intention in this study is 0.323, which means that students' entrepreneurial passion causes 32.3% of the variance in entrepreneurial intention and indicates that the variable has a medium effect. Additionally, the R^2 of the entrepreneurial passion variable in this study is 0.15, proving that entrepreneurship education and family business involvement account for 15% of the variance in entrepreneurial passion.

Hair et al. [21] believe that the model has a predictive fit when the model has Q^2 greater than 0. Based on the results, the Q^2 values greater than 0, indicating that the model fits the prediction (Table 4).

Table 4 R Square and Q Square Analysis

Variables	R^2	Q^2
Entrepreneurial Intention	0.323	0.134
Entrepreneurial Passion	0.15	0.14

According to Cohen [23], F^2 values of 0.02, 0.15, and 0.35 are considered weak, medium, and strong effects, respectively. The results from Table 5 show that the F^2 values of the relationships in the model are all greater than 0.02, which proves that the level of influence is acceptable for the hypotheses. Among them, passion for entrepreneurship strongly impacts entrepreneurial intention because $F^2 = 0.475$.

We tested variance inflation factors (VIF) to determine redundancy. Table 5's findings demonstrate that there isn't a multicollinearity between the variables because VIF values range from 1.000 to 1.121, which are lower than the suggested threshold of 5 [24].

Hypothesis testing

According to Henseler et al. [25], the Path Coefficient values in the structural model show the strength of each independent variable. When the T-value > 1.65 and the P-value < 0.05, data are considered to be supported [25] (Fig. 2).

Table 5 Variance inflation factor (VIF) and F Square Analysis

Relationships	VIF	F^2
Entrepreneurship Education → Entrepreneurial Passion	1.121	0.099
Entrepreneurial passion → Entrepreneurial Intention	1.000	0.478
Family Business Involvement → Entrepreneurial Passion	1.121	0.025

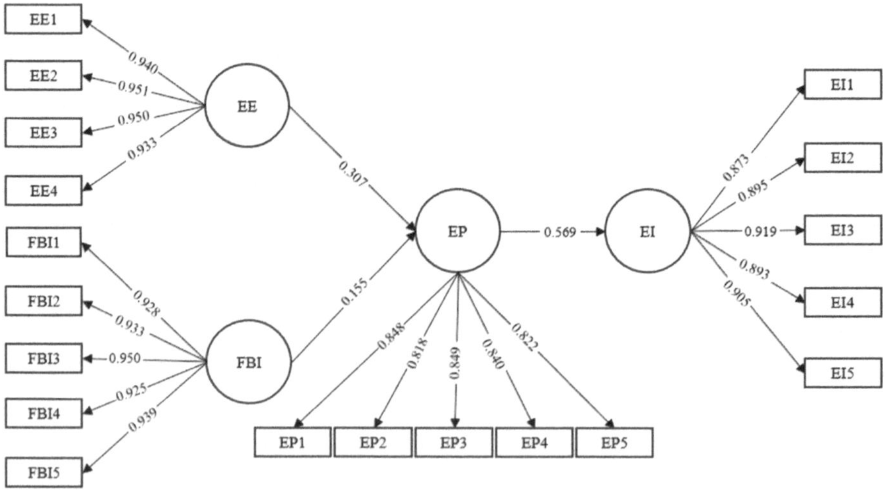

Fig. 2 SEM results

Table 6 The summarize of hypothesis testing

Hypothesis	β	T Value	P Value	Decision
EE → EP	0.307	6.895	0.000	Supported
FBI → EP	0.155	3.992	0.000	Supported
EP → EI	0.569	15.978	0.000	Supported

Regarding hypothesis H1, the results presented in Table 6 show that the direct impact of entrepreneurship education (EE) on entrepreneurial passion (EP) is statistically significant with Path Coefficients = 0.307, T Value = 6.895, and P Value = 0.000.

As for hypothesis H2, entrepreneurial passion (EP) is positively impacted by family business involvement (FBI), the hypothesis is statistically significant with Path coefficient, T-value, and P-value of 0.155, 3.992, and 0.000, respectively.

Same as hypotheses H1 and H2. According to Table 6's findings, hypothesis H3 is the most strongly supported and also statistically significant. The path coefficient, T-value, and P-value for the positive relationship between entrepreneurial passion (EP) and entrepreneurial intention (EI) are 0.569, 15.978, and 0.000, respectively.

5 Conclusions

Using the S–O-R model, the study inspected the indirect effects of entrepreneurial knowledge, including entrepreneurship education and family business involvement, on entrepreneurial intention through the intermediate variable of entrepreneurial passion. Although this model is relatively new in research on entrepreneurship, especially entrepreneurial intention, it has shown its effectiveness in exploring the relationships between the above factors. Therefore, the research contributes to diversifying theories in the field of entrepreneurship.

In response to research findings, entrepreneurship education dramatically impacts a person's entrepreneurial passion. This result is similar to Anwar et al. [26], who concluded that entrepreneurship education directly and indirectly stimulates entrepreneurial intention through entrepreneurial passion. As a result, support from the government and educators will help increase students' entrepreneurial passion and indirectly influence entrepreneurial intentions. In parallel, the government and educational institutions should work together to provide entrepreneurship programs to give students real experience in this field and increase their knowledge and entrepreneurial passion.

Additionally, the findings indicate that family business involvement has an impact directly on entrepreneurial passion and indirectly on entrepreneurial intention. This demonstrates that exposing students to their family's business can foster an entrepreneurial passion in the future. Then, these students develop stronger entrepreneurial intentions.

The findings also demonstrate that entrepreneurial passion is an emotional response factor in S–O-R influencing entrepreneurial intention. Promoting entrepreneurial passion will be the main factor that keeps people motivated to persevere through complex and challenging situations during the entrepreneurship process. As a result, governments and policymakers interested in fostering entrepreneurship should focus more on igniting entrepreneurial passion and develop sensible policies to support this crucial element, thereby helping to raise the rate of entrepreneurship entrepreneurs in the nation.

6 Limitations

Although research has had many results that fill the research gap, it still has certain limitations. The survey participants of this study were only students. Therefore, future research needs to diversify respondents to apply these results to other target groups. Next, it is necessary to compare the results of this study and that by Moses et al. [27]. Moses et al. [27] found that entrepreneurship education can increase students' entrepreneurial passion but reduce entrepreneurial intention. Therefore, the indirect effect of entrepreneurship education in influencing students' entrepreneurial intention needs to be further evaluated in future research.

References

1. Uddin, M.R., Bose, T.K.: Determinants of entrepreneurial intention of business students in Bangladesh. Intern. J. Busin. Manag. **7**(24), 128–137 (2012)
2. Teixeira, S.J., Casteleiro, C.M.L., Rodrigues, R.G., Guerra, M.D.: Entrepreneurial intentions and entrepreneurship in European countries. Intern. J. Innov. Sci. **10**(1), 22–42 (2018)
3. Miralles, F., Giones, F., Riverola, C.: Evaluating the impact of prior experience in entrepreneurial intention. Intern. Entrep. Manag. J. **12**, 791–813 (2016)
4. Mehrabian, A., Russell, J.A.: An approach to environmental psychology. MIT Press, Cambridge (1974)
5. Michl, T., Welpe, I.M., Spörrle, M., Picot, A.: The role of emotions and cognitions in the entrepreneurial process. In: Carlsrud, A.L., Brännback, M.E. (eds.) Understanding the entrepreneurial mind: Opening the black box, pp. 167–190. Springer, New York (2009)
6. Song, S., Yao, X., Wen, N.: What motivates Chinese consumers to avoid information about the COVID-19 pandemic?: The perspective of the stimulus-organism-response model. Inform. Proc. Manag. **58**(1), Article 102407 (2021)
7. Souitaris, V., Zerbinati, S., Al-Laham, A.: Do entrepreneurship programmes raise entrepreneurial intention of science and engineering students? The effect of learning, inspiration and resources. J. Bus. Ventur.Ventur. **22**(4), 566–591 (2007)
8. Wu, Y.L., Li, E.Y.: Marketing mix, customer value, and customer loyalty in social commerce: a stimulus-organism-response perspective. Internet Res. **28**(1), 74–104 (2018)
9. Fayolle, A., Liñán, F.: The future of research on entrepreneurial intentions. J. Bus. Res. **67**(5), 663–666 (2014)
10. Alcaraz, J.A.: Family influence on financial performance satisfaction in Mexican family businesses. Alliant International University, San Diego (2006)

11. Pittaway, L., Rodriguez-Falcon, E., Aiyegbayo, O., King, A.: The role of entrepreneurship clubs and societies in entrepreneurial learning. Int. Small Bus. J. **29**(1), 37–57 (2011)
12. Voda, A.I., Covatariu, D., Ghiuta, O.A.: Student's entrepreneurial intentions: role of entrepreneurial education and risk taken ability. Environ. Eng. Manag. J.Manag. J. **18**(7), 1527–1534 (2019)
13. Wang, D., Wang, L., Chen, L.: Unlocking the influence of family business exposure on entrepreneurial intentions. Intern. Entrep. Manag. J. **14**(2), 951–974 (2018)
14. Karimi, S.: The role of entrepreneurial passion in the formation of students' entrepreneurial intentions. Appl. Econ. **52**(3), 331–344 (2020)
15. Anderson, J.C., Gerbing, D.W.: Structural equation modeling in practice: A review and recommended two-step approach. Psychol. Bull. **103**(3), 411 (1988)
16. Hair, J., Jr., Hair, J.F., Jr., Hult, G.T.M., Ringle, C.M., Sarstedt, M.: A primer on partial least squares structural equation modeling (PLS-SEM), 2nd edn. SAGE Publications, Thousand Oaks (2021)
17. Hair, J.F., Hult, G.T.M., Ringle, C.M., Sarstedt, M., Thiele, K.O.: Mirror, mirror on the wall: a comparative evaluation of composite-based structural equation modeling methods. J. Acad. Mark. Sci. **45**(5), 616–632 (2017)
18. Höck, M., Ringle, C.M.: Local strategic networks in the software industry: An empirical analysis of the value continuum. Intern. J. Knowl. Manag. Stud. **4**(2), 132–151 (2006)
19. Hair, J.F., Jr., Black, W.C., Babin, B.J., Anderson, R.E.: Multivariate Data Analysis: A Global Perspective, 7th edn. Pearson Prentice Hall, New Jersey (2010)
20. Fornell, C., Larcker, D.F.: Evaluating structural equation models with unobservable variables and measurement error. J. Mark. Res. **18**(1), 39–50 (1981)
21. Hair, J.F., Ringle, C.M., Sarstedt, M.: PLS-SEM: indeed a silver bullet. J. Marketi. Theory Pract. **19**(2), 139–152 (2011)
22. Henseler, J., Ringle, C.M., Sinkovics, R.R.: The use of partial least squares path modeling in international marketing. In: Sinkovics, R.R., Ghauri, P.N. (eds.) New Challenges to International Marketing, vol. 20, pp. 277–320. Emerald Group Publishing Limited, Bingley (2009)
23. Cohen, J.: Statistical power analysis for the behavioral sciences, 2nd edn. Lawrence Erlbaum, Hillsdale (1988)
24. Brettel, M., Engelen, A., Müller, T., Schilke, O.: Distribution channel choice of new entrepreneurial ventures. Entrep. Theory Pract.. Theory Pract. **35**(4), 683–708 (2011)
25. Henseler, J., Ringle, C.M., Sarstedt, M.: A new criterion for assessing discriminant validity in variance-based structural equation modeling. J. Acad. Mark. Sci. **43**(1), 115–135 (2015)
26. Anwar, I., Ahmad, A., Saleem, I., Yasin, N.: Role of entrepreneurship education, passion and motivation in augmenting Omani students' entrepreneurial intention: A stimulus-organism-response approach. Intern. J. Manag. Educ. **21**(3), Article 100842 (2023)
27. Moses, C.L., Olokundun, M.A., Akinbode, M., Agboola, M., Inelo, F.: Entrepreneurship education and entrepreneurial intentions: the moderating role of passion. Soc. Sci. **11**(5), 645–653 (2016)

How Do Emotional Support and Emotional Exhaustion Affect the Relationship Between Incivility and Students' Subjective Well-Being?

Uyen Phuong Nguyen Le, Anh Tram Tuong Nguyen, Anh Van Nguyen, Van Khanh Huynh, Chi Thao Le Bui, and Anh Lan Thuy Nguyen

Abstract Incivility is increasingly receiving attention because of its increasing frequency, especially in educational environments. It is considered the leading cause of academic ineffectiveness, in addition to affecting the spiritual and psychological values of the individual. With the desire to understand the relationship between incivility and subjective well-being of college students in Vietnam through two mediating effects, including emotional exhaustion and emotional support, this study was conducted. The partial least squares structural equation modeling (PLS-SEM) was used to process the data set of 600 participants to produce specific figures. The results reveal that emotional exhaustion significantly mediates the relationship between incivility and subjective well-being, as does emotional support. However, the non-existence of a relationship between incivility and subjective well-being is a surprising result that emerged from this study, accompanied by arguments, explanations, and suggestions for universities. This study underscores the importance of addressing incivility in educational environments and fostering emotional support to mitigate emotional exhaustion and promote students' subjective well-being.

Keywords Emotional exhaustion · Emotional support · Higher students · Incivility · Subjective Well-being

---

U. P. N. Le (✉) · A. T. T. Nguyen · A. Van Nguyen · V. K. Huynh · C. T. Le Bui
Faculty of Advanced Studies, Ho Chi Minh City Open University, Ho Chi Minh City, Vietnam
e-mail: 2154011109uyen@ou.edu.vn

A. L. T. Nguyen
Faculty of Business Administration, Ho Chi Minh City Open University, Ho Chi Minh City, Vietnam

L. T. Tung et al. (eds.), *Disruptive Technology and Business Continuity*,
https://doi.org/10.1007/978-981-97-5452-6_18

1 Introduction

Related issues and the impact of schools on students have been reported in many countries [1]. Over the past ten years, researchers have increasingly begun to believe that incivility harms both the victim and the organization [2]. Behavioral science researchers have adopted a broader perspective and have expanded their work to include investigations related to the field of education. Unlike other anti-social behaviors, such as harassment or vandalism, incivility is often not a concern of the law [3]. Incivility is a joint organizational dysfunction [2]. Some examples of incivility in education include making rude comments, condescending, intentionally belittling others, and threatening or directing violence against individuals [4].

Incivility is common, and recent meta-analyses show it is negatively associated with psychological and physical health [5]. Furthermore, perceptions of incivility are also associated with emotional exhaustion [6–8]. Previous studies have shown evidence that emotional exhaustion is closely related to negative health outcomes and work performance [9]. Besides, burnout has become an essential factor affecting subjective well-being [10]. Recently, studies on people's subjective well-being worldwide have mainly focused on students. Subjective well-being is an individual's standard for assessing overall quality of life. It is a comprehensive index of critical responses to social functioning and adaptation, subjectivity, integrity, relative stability, and other characteristics. In some cases, subjective well-being can significantly impact an individual's health or longevity [11]. Students with lower subjective well-being often experience stress and mental exhaustion, leading to burnout, absenteeism, and academic decline [12, 13].

Although the above evidence has shown that incivility can negatively affect psychological health and well-being, this remains a major theoretical gap that needs to be addressed to help subjects. Students, in particular, and people in general, can identify psychological problems. Indeed, cross-cultural research shows that responses to incivility are influenced by cultural norms and values [14]. Because their need for emotional reinforcement remains unmet, they may feel helpless, distraught, and emotionally exhausted. Previous research has suggested that it is vital to consider the emotional experience triggered by incivility [15].

This study was conducted to understand the factors influencing incivility behavior on the subjective happiness of university students in the Vietnamese context. In addition, we aim to consider the factors of emotional exhaustion and emotional support as the mechanism connecting incivility behavior in the educational environment with students' subjective well-being.

2 Literature Review

2.1 The Concept

Incivility.

In the educational context of higher education, incivility refers to actions, attitudes, or speech that often aim to annoy, offend, belittle, disrupt harmony, and undermine respect in social interactions among people [16]. Incivility can manifest in various forms, from rude language and sarcasm to offensive behaviors and, in extreme cases, even violence. Within university-level education, incivility can occur in interactions between students and instructors, negatively impacting the teaching and learning processes. Common examples of incivility in this context include causing disruptions in the classroom, using cell phones during lectures, making disrespectful comments about instructors and fellow students, and more [17].

Emotional exhaustion

According to Maslach & Jackson (1981), burnout occurs in three forms: emotional exhaustion, increased depersonalization, and decreased personal accomplishments [10]. Among these, emotional exhaustion, which will be the focus of this study, is a state of emotional and psychological depletion due to prolonged exposure to an emotionally demanding environment. Individuals experiencing this state often feel overwhelmed by excessive negative feeling, depleting their internal resources and making them unable to do anything effectively [12, 18].

Emotional support.

Social support is one of the most common ways to enhance an individual's resilience. Social support involves positive help, encouragement, and caring from others, creating a sense of being nurtured and respected by individuals [19]. This support can be in the form of emotional support, which includes encouragement, attentive listening, understanding, and wholehearted sharing, coming from trusted relationships such as family, friends, teachers, colleagues, and more. It can help the recipients feel more comfortable expressing their emotions, reduce stress, and create favorable conditions for coping with challenging situations [20].

Subjective well-being.

According to Diener (2012), there are several approaches to subjective well-being (SWB) [21]. However, the widely accepted and popular approach divides subjective well-being into three main components: positive affect, negative affect, and life satisfaction. Within these components, positive affect represents the degree of positive emotions (such as joy and happiness in daily life), and negative affect reflects the level of negative emotions (like sadness, anxiety, and distress in daily life), which fall under the emotional SWB. Life satisfaction, on the other hand, represents an individual's overall evaluation of their life and belongs to cognitive SWB.

Subjective well-being is considered one of the vital aspects of human psychological well-being [11]. It pertains to an individual's perception of happiness, satisfaction, and overall mental state. It reflects temporary mood states and relates to long-term life satisfaction and a person's overall well-being.

2.2 Theoretical Basis

Transactional model of stress.

The model was initially proposed by psychologist Lazarus (1966) and later further developed by Lazarus & Folkman in a publication in 1984 [22, 23]. In psychology and sociology, this theory explains how individuals react to and cope with stress daily [12]. This model consists of components: stressor, appraisal, coping, and outcome, with "coping" being an important part of the interaction between individuals and their environment. In the study by Folkman et al. (1984), stress was specifically conceptualized as emotional exhaustion [23]. This research explains how individuals cope with incivility to measure the impact of emotional exhaustion on subjective well-being by applying this theory.

Conservation of Resources Theory (COR).

COR by Hobfoll (1989) explains the relationship between social support and job stress [24]. The fundamental principle of COR is that "people need to allocate their resources to protect against resource depletion, recover from losses, and gain resources" [25, p.73]. Resource depletion can lead individuals to be unable to complete tasks, and in psychology, an individual's resources are primarily their mental health. Therefore, emotional support from others or individuals can help reduce stress when encountering uncivil behavior, thereby maintaining subjective well-being more effectively [7].

2.3 Research Hypothesis

The mediating role of emotional support.

In the relationship between Incivility and SWB, this study predicts that Emotional Support plays a mediating factor influencing the impact of these two factors. As mentioned, emotional support refers to "actions of caring or empathetic listening toward others" [26, p.158]. Based on the principles of COR, an individual's happiness depends on the increase in resources, and stress depends on the loss of resources. When a stressful event occurs, individuals undergo an appraisal process in which they perceive the situation as threatening and demanding personal coping resources. Consequently, individuals seek new resources to replenish what has been lost [27]. However, psychological resources cannot be quickly replenished, so individuals who are not emotionally intelligent may exhibit a psychological defense mechanism in response to uncivil behavior. When faced with uncivil behavior, this coping mechanism can make individuals less receptive to emotional support, such as advice from friends, family, and university faculty. It is evident that when confronted with incivility, individuals may have a diminished perception of emotional support, leading to a decrease in their subjective well-being (SWB). On the other hand, individuals with high emotional intelligence tend to have a rich social network and more effective stress-coping strategies [27]. When they receive caring actions and encouragement from those around them, they are more likely to perceive uncivil behavior as manageable, increasing their subjective well-being [7].

H1: Emotional Support improves the relationship between Incivility and SWB as the role of a mediator.

The mediating role of emotional exhaustion.

In addition to Emotional Support, the impact of uncivil behavior on an individual's mental health is predicted to occur through a stress response mechanism by eliciting negative emotional reactions, affecting the individual's psychological and physical aspects. According to COR theory, individuals lose resources due to uncivil behavior from those around them, such as receiving disrespectful, intrusive, or mocking remarks. This leads to an increased intention to avoid, reluc-tance to engage inconversations, and a deterioration in their mental state. This means that even though uncivil behavior in an educational environment is not as severe as violence or bullying [28], over time, it can generate negative emotions and impact those who experience it [18]. Students may feel emotionally exhausted when they perceive helplessness and mental distress in response to uncivil behaviors, realizing that their emotional resources are insufficient to cope with stressors [9, 15]. Numerous prior studies have made findings on emotional ex-haustion's adverse effects on mental health by damaging personal resources and establishing negative links to subjective happiness [6, 12, 13, 18].

H2: Emotional Exhaustion decreases the relationship between Incivility and SWB as the role of a mediator.

Relationship between incivility and subjective well-being.

Previous research by Pearson & Porath (2005) showed that incivility had a negative impact on their performance and subjective well-being [29]. In addition, incivility was also found to have adverse effects on individual happiness and health. Those who were treated rudely often had psychological symptoms such as depression, anxiety, lack of concentration, and reduced motivation [29, 30].

Lata & Chaudhary (2020) argue that incivility is a serious issue many organizations face [31]. Rudeness can cause mental and physical health problems for those affected [28] and can reduce happiness [12]. Moreover, incivility can lead to increased absenteeism and decreased loyalty to society as well as personal happiness [8, 12]. Caza & Cortina (2007) assert that incivility violates the norms of respectful treatment and causes feelings of injustice [32]. This means those treated uncivilly may feel excluded from society as if they are not accepted or do not belong, damaging their positive self-perception.

H3: Incivility has a negative impact on Subjective Well-being.

3 Methodology

3.1 Participants

To test the model and hypotheses in the study, we surveyed students studying at universities in Vietnam. Through personal connections and permission from the university management department, we collected the gmail list of students. The survey sample was sent to students of universities via student gmail provided by the university management department. In the survey form, we explained the purpose of the study and committed that the participants were guaranteed confidentiality and anonymity for their answers and that all survey answer samples were under the system's management.

After filtering the survey samples, there were 600 valid responses. Among them, there were 276 male students (accounting for 46%), 324 female students (accounting for 54%); 207 students studying in the fields of Economics - Management (39.5%), 237 students studying Social Sciences and Humanities (26%) and 156 students in Natural Sciences and Engineering (accounting for 34.5%).

3.2 Measures

Four concepts are used in the research scale: Incivility, Emotional Exhaustion, Emotional Support, and Subjective Well Being. To analyze the impact of Incivility, Emotional Exhaustion, and Emotional Support on SWB, a survey method using a questionnaire based on the application of a 7-point Likert scale from "Strongly disagree" to "Strongly agree" was applied. After synthesizing and selecting the scales from previous studies, we used the definition of "Incivility" from the study by Cortina et al. (2001) consisting of 12 observed variables [30], the definition of "Emotional Exhaustion" measured from the study by Maslash & Jackson (1981) consisting of 7 observed variables [10], followed by "Emotional Support" with 5 observed variables from Baker & Kim (2020) [7], and finally "Subjective Well Being" measured from the study by Diener (1984) consisting of 5 observed variables [11].

3.3 Statistical Procedures

After collecting enough samples, the information obtained from the survey samples will be filtered and processed before entering data into the software for data analysis. The research team used the PLS-SEM method and SmartPLS4. The data was analyzed through descriptive statistics of the sample, scale reliability testing, and EFA analysis. Confirmatory factor analysis CFA and SEM model with observed variables were performed after meeting the sample size on SmartPLS [33]. The moderating effect was also performed separately with CFA and linear regression analyses on PLS-SEM.

4 Result and Discussion

4.1 Result

Measurement model assessment.

Issues for assessing the measurement model include data quality, reliability, convergent validity, and discriminant validity of the scale. The association level between variables is demonstrated through the outer loading scores, with values greater than or equal to 0,7, which were satisfied by the observed variables [34].

The scale's reliability is based on two key indices: Cronbach's Alpha and composite reliability. The analysis revealed that Cronbach's Alpha values for the constructs ranged from 0.827 to 0.928 (> 0.7). At the same time, the lowest composite reliability value was 0.879, and the highest was 0.938 (> 0.7), indicating that the observed variables meet the reliability criteria [34] (Table 1).

Furthermore, the value of AVE for each construct should be greater than 0.5 for the model to exhibit convergence. The average variance extracted (AVE) values are all greater than 0.5 (Table 2), with the lowest AVE value at 0.559 belonging to incivility and the highest at 0.660 for Emotional Exhaustion. This ensures that the scale meets the convergence criterion.

The examination of the discriminant validity of the scale indicates that all constructs meet this criterion, with the lowest square root of AVE larger than the highest correlation coefficient between pairs of concepts (Table 2). Additionally, the HTMT values for all constructs are below 0.90, signifying that distinctiveness exists between specific construct pairs [34] (Table 2).

Structural model assessment.

Hair et al. (2019) state that multicollinearity occurs when the variance inflation factor (VIF) values exceed 5 for latent variables [34]. In this study, all VIF values are below 5, with a maximum value of 2.987 and a minimum of 1.533 (Table 1), indicating the absence of multicollinearity.

Table 1 Cronbach's Alpha, composite reliability, outer loadings

	CA	CR	OT	VIF
Emotional exhaustion	0.914	0.931	0.774 – 0.846	1.989 - 2.941
Emotional support	0.827	0.879	0.716 – 0.825	1.533 - 2.266
Incivility	0.928	0.938	0.706 – 0.814	1.856 - 2.987
Subjective well-being	0.869	0.905	0.754 – 0.855	1.684 - 2.265

Table 2 Discriminant validity (Fornell-Larcker and HTMT ratio)

	AVE	Correlation			
		1	2	3	4
1. Emotional exhaustion	0.660	**0.813**	0.434	0.522	0.584
2. Emotional support	0.593	-0.380	**0.770**	0.428	0.662
3. Incivility	0.559	0.485	-0.377	**0.748**	0.430
4. Subjective well-being	0.656	-0.525	0.567	-0.392	**0.810**

Note AVE = Average Variance Extracted. The square root of AVE on the main diagonal is the Fornell-Larcker criterion (Bold numbers). Italic numbers are inter correlations; Nornal numbers are HTMT ratio

The R-squared (R^2) values indicate the accuracy of the model's predictions. According to Henseler et al. (2009), R^2 values can be used to assess the quality of the PLS structural model, where an R^2 more remarkable than 0.75 signifies a strong influence, values between 0.25 and 0.5 indicate a moderate influence, and values below 0.25 indicate a weak influence [35]. The study's results show that the R-squared values for Emotional Exhaustion are 0.235, Emotional Support is 0.142, and Subjective Well-being is 0.433, indicating that the model explains a moderate to slight variance (Table 4). The Q^2 values in Table 4 for Emotional Exhaustion (0.230), Emotional Support (0.136), and Subjective Well-being (0.150) are all greater than 0, demonstrating the model's predictive capability (Table 3).

The path coefficients are used to evaluate the structural model, with path coefficient values and R-squared (R^2) being significant at a 5% level (P values < 5%). The non-parametric bootstrap analysis was conducted with a sample size of 5000. The results of the data analysis show that out of the eight initial hypotheses, six meet the conditions to accept the hypothesis (P values < 0.05). These include hypotheses

Table 3 R squared, Q^2 predict

	R^2	Q^2 predict
Emotional exhaustion	0.235	0.230
Emotional support	0.142	0.136
Subjective well-being	0.438	0.150

Table 4 The results of testing the relationships between the structures in the model

Hypothesis	Relationship	Original Sample	STD	T-value	P value	Result
H1b	EE - > SWB	-0.331	0.038	8.704	0.000	Supported
H2b	ES - > SWB	0.413	0.036	11.322	0.000	Supported
H1a	INC - > EE	0.485	0.037	12.985	0.000	Supported
H2a	INC - > ES	-0.377	0.044	8.585	0.000	Supported
H3	INC - > SWB	-0.076	0.041	1.883	0.060	Rejected

H1a, H1b, H2a, and H2b. The remaining hypothesis, H3, has a P value > 0.05. Thus, it is not accepted (Table 4).

4.2 Discussion

This study was conducted to investigate the relationship between incivility and subjective well-being, as well as the mediating role of emotional exhaustion and emotional support among students in college. The results indicated that the mediator of emotional exhaustion on the relationship between incivility and subjective well-being was the strongest ($\beta = -0.161$). This is similar to the conclusions of Anjum et al. (2020) and Lee et al. (2020), demonstrating that findings on emotional exhaustion can adversely affect people's psychological health and well-being targets [9, 12]. Constant exposure to these stressors/misbehaviors depletes the target's social and emotional resources, culminating in emotional exhaustion. Furthermore, emotionally exhausted individuals experience decreased subjective well-being [18].

Besides, this study also tested the mediating relationship of emotional support between incivility and subjective well-being. The results of the study are supported by Baker & Kim (2020) ($\beta = -0.156$) [7]. Incivility can have immediate negative consequences for well-being, but intervention from others can counteract these effects by providing emotional reinforcement. Thus, emotional and mental reinforcement can serve as resources to cope with the threat of incivility. If victims do not receive any support, there can be a more significant negative impact.

The relationship between incivility and subjective well-being was rejected ($p = 0.060$). The results of Taheri et al. (2023) suggest that incivility is a psychological stressor that can challenge emotional and cognitive resources, leading to lower levels of subjective well-being [3]. Cortina et al.'s (2017) results also show that incivility in the workplace affects employee happiness [28]. However, the current results are an exciting finding in this study that incivility is not a factor that negatively impacts subjective well-being ($\beta = -0.076$). Our findings supported another mechanism: students' subjective well-being may be influenced by criteria other than incivility. These results highlight the vital role of educational administrators in preventing the spread of incivility and ensuring quality academic life for students.

5 Conclusion

This study made significant contributions to the field of SWB research by exploring the role of INC in creating SWB for individuals. The study results showed that INC influenced SWB through two mediating factors, ES and EE. This suggests that enhancing INC is an important strategy to improve the SWB of students.

We examined the relationship between incivility and emotional support of Vietnamese students in the educational environment. Heffernan & Bosetti (2021) found that 58% of students reported experiences of incivility in the learning environment, including disrupting, ostracizing, cursing peers in class, and being rude [17]. The results showed that the lack of civility and standards in the behavior of classmates and lecturers negatively affected emotional support. This can cause serious consequences for mental health, loss of motivation, stress, and loss of focus in learning [9, 12]. Therefore, educational organizations should strengthen measures to prevent and resolve incivility in the learning environment and create conditions for students to receive emotional support. This result is similar to Lee et al. (2020) in that emotional support greatly influences subjective well-being, playing an essential role in determining emotions [12].

Moreover, incivility is also related to emotional exhaustion, indicating that rudeness, such as being scolded and despised by peers, causes many negative consequences and depletes emotions [5]. This requires students to make more efforts to enhance their spirit and awareness to deal with these behaviors. Therefore, educational organizations should implement preventive and intervention measures to reduce incivility and enhance mental safety for students. However, this study also found that emotional support positively impacts subjective well-being, while emotional exhaustion has a negative impact, similar to previous studies [9, 12]. This means that students will feel happier and more satisfied when they receive care, encouragement, and assistance from classmates as well as lecturers.

One of the limitations of this study is that the survey sample only included university students in major cities of Vietnam.Thus, the generalizability and applicability to other populations and the different areas cannot be asserted. Moreover, research on incivility's impact on students' subjective well-being is still scarce compared to the work environment. Additionally, this study only used self-report measures, which may cause perceptual or confirmation bias.

Future studies could expand the survey sample to other types of businesses and use more objective measurement methods, such as observing behavior, interviewing or content analysis, to overcome these limitations. At the same time, extend the scope of research to the current adolescent subjects on the state of incivility.

References

1. Dolean, D.D., Lervag, A.: Variations of homework amount assigned in elementary school can impact academic achievement. J. Exp. Educ. **90**(2), 280–296 (2022)
2. Timming, A.R., Carpini, J.A., Hirst, T.M., Tian, A.W., Notebaert, L.: Experienced incivility undermines the positive effects of job autonomy on mental and physical health. Intern. J. Human Res. Manag. **35**(4), 1–24 (2023)
3. Taheri, F., Naderibeni, N., Mirzamani, A.: Subjective well-being in the relationship between workaholism and workplace incivility: the moderating role of gender. J. Organiz. Effect. People Perform **10**(1), 43–59 (2023)
4. Clark, C.M.: Fostering a culture of civility and respect in nursing. J. Nurs. Regul. **10**(1), 44–52 (2019)

5. Han, Y., Kim, Y., Hur, W.M.: The effects of perceived supervisor incivility on child-care workers' job performance: The mediating role of emotional exhaustion and intrinsic motivation. Curr. Psychol. **40**(4), 1979–1994 (2021)
6. Alola, U.V., Olugbade, O.A., Avci, T., Öztüren, A.: Customer incivility and employees' outcomes in the hotel: testing the mediating role of emotional exhaustion. Tourism Manag Persp **29**, 9–17 (2019)
7. Baker, M.A., Kim, K.: Dealing with customer incivility: The effects of managerial support on employee psychological well-being and quality-of-life. Int. J. Hosp. Manag. **87**, 102503 (2020)
8. Shin, Y., Hur, W.M., Hwang, H.: Impacts of customer incivility and abusive supervision on employee performance: a comparative study of the pre-and post-COVID-19 periods. Serv. Bus. **16**(2), 309–330 (2022)
9. Anjum, M.A., Liang, D., Durrani, D.K., Parvez, A.: Workplace mistreatment and emotional exhaustion: the interaction effects of self-compassion. Curr. Psychol. **154**, 1–12 (2020)
10. Maslach, C., Jackson, S.E.: The measurement of experienced burnout. J. Organ. Behav. **2**(2), 99–113 (1981)
11. Diener, E.: Subjective well-being. Psychol. Bull. **95**(3), 542–575 (1984)
12. Lee, Y.H.R., Richards, K.A., Washhburn, N.S.: Emotional intelligence, job satisfaction, emotional exhaustion, and subjective well-being in high school athletic directors. Psychol. Reports **123**(6), 2418–2440 (2020)
13. Kim, G., Yu, H., Ryu, E.: Social group membership, burnout, and subjective well-being in new nurses in the life transition period: a cross-sectional study. Nurs. Open **10**(5), 3295–3304 (2023)
14. Moon, C., Uskul, A.K., Weick, M.: Cultural differences in politeness as a function of status relations: comparing South Korean and British communicators. J. Theor. Soc. Psychol. **3**(3), 137–145 (2019)
15. Chen, Y., Li, S.: Relationship between workplace ostracism and unsafe behaviors: the mediating effect of psychological detachment and emotional exhaustion. Psychol. Rep. **123**(2), 488–516 (2020)
16. Berger, B.A.: Incivility. Am. J. Pharm. Educ. **64**(4), 445–450 (2000)
17. Heffernan, T., Bosetti, L.: Incivility: the new type of bullying in higher education. Camb. J. Educ. **51**(5), 641–652 (2021)
18. Koon, V.Y., Pun, P.Y.: The mediating role of emotional exhaustion and job satisfaction on the relationship between job demands and instigated workplace incivility. J. Appl. Behav. Sci. **54**(2), 187–207 (2018)
19. Taylor, S.E., Friedman, H.S.: Social support. In: Friedman, H.S., Silver, R.C. (eds.) Foundations of health psychology, pp. 145–171. Oxford University Press, New York (2006)
20. Mathieu, M., Eschleman, K.J., Cheng, D.: Meta-analytic and multiwave comparison of emotional support and instrumental support in the workplace. J. Occup. Health Psychol. **24**(3), 387–409 (2019)
21. Diener, E.: New findings and future directions for subjective well-being research. Am. Psychol. **67**(8), 590–597 (2012)
22. Lazarus, R.S.: Psychological stress and the coping process. McGrawHill, New York (1966)
23. Lazarus, R.S., Folkman, S.: Stress, appraisal, and coping. Springer publishing company, New York (1984)
24. Hobfoll, S.E.: Conservation of resources: a new attempt at conceptualizing stress. Am. Psychol. **44**(3), 513–524 (1989)
25. Hobfoll, S.E., Wells, J.D.: Conservation of resources, stress, and aging: Why do some slide and some spring? In: Lomranz, J. (ed.) Handbook of aging and mental health: an integrative approach, pp. 121–134. Springer Science & Business Media, New York (1998)
26. Fenlason, K.J., Beehr, T.A.: Social support and occupational stress: effects of talking to others. J. Organ. Behav. **15**(2), 157–175 (1994)
27. Cohen, S., Wills, T.A.: Stress, social support, and the buffering hypothesis. Psychol. Bull. **98**(2), 310–357 (1985)

28. Cortina, L.M., Kabat-Farr, D., Magley, V.J., Nelson, K.: Researching rudeness: the past, present, and future of the science of incivility. J. Occup. Health Psychol. **22**(3), 299–313 (2017)
29. Pearson, C.M., Porath, C.L.: On the nature, consequences and remedies of workplace incivility: no time for "nice"? Think again. Acad. Manag.Persp. **19**(1), 7–18 (2005)
30. Cortina, L.M., Magley, V.J., Williams, J.H., Langhout, R.D.: Incivility in the workplace: incidence and impact. J. Occup. Health Psychol. **6**(1), 64–80 (2001). https://doi.org/10.1037/1076-8998.6.1.64
31. Lata, M., Chaudhary, R.: Dark triad and instigated incivility: the moderating role of workplace spirituality. Personality Individ. Differ. **166**, 110090 (2020)
32. Caza, B.B., Cortina, L.M.: From insult to injury: explaining the impact of incivility. Basic Appl. Soc. Psychol. **29**(4), 335–350 (2007)
33. Hair, J.F., Black, W.C., Babin, B.J., Anderson, R.E., Tatham, R.L.: Multivariate data analysis. 10th edn. Pearson Education, New York (2010)
34. Hair, J.F., Risher, J.J., Sarstedt, M., Ringle, C.M.: When to use and how to report the results of PLS-SEM. Eur. Bus. Rev. **31**(1), 2–24 (2019)
35. Henseler, J., Ringle, C.M., Sinkovics, R.R.: The use of partial least squares path modeling in international marketing. In: Sinkovics, R.R., Ghauri, P.N. (Eds.) New challenges to international marketing, vol. 20, pp. 277–319. Emerald Group Publishing Limited, (2009)

How Does Acculturation Affect International Students' Choice to Study Abroad? Explanation and Comparison Based on a Relationship with Destination Country Image and Cross-Cultural Awareness

Tri Minh Cao, Anh Lan Thuy Nguyen, and Anh Quynh Duong Nguyen

Abstract Studying in a new country can be a great opportunity, an exciting adventure, but it also brings its own challenges, especially about acculture. This study examines factors affecting the choice of international students to study abroad, especially the roles of acculturation and cross-cultural awareness. This study was conducted on 434 international students studying in Vietnam, coming from different continents worldwide through online questionnaires. SmartPLS 4.0 software was selected for research to evaluate the measurement model and structural model. Through the structural model evaluation results, this study shows the impact of destination country image on acculturation and the choice to study abroad. It also identifies the mediating role of acculturation in the relationship between the destination country image and the choice to study abroad. However, the moderating role of cross-cultural awareness is rejected in the relationship between acculturation and the choice to study abroad. Academic and managerial implications are also suggested.

Keywords Acculturation · Choice to study abroad · Destination country image · Cross-cultural awareness · International students

1 Introduction

Studying in a new country can be a great opportunity and an exciting adventure. It provides students with countless opportunities to develop and cultivate their personal, but it also brings its own set of challenges. The reason for international students to

T. M. Cao (✉) · A. L. T. Nguyen · A. Q. D. Nguyen
Faculty of Business Administration, Ho Chi Minh City Open University, Ho Chi Minh City, Vietnam
e-mail: tri.cm@ou.edu.vn

L. T. Tung et al. (eds.), *Disruptive Technology and Business Continuity*,
https://doi.org/10.1007/978-981-97-5452-6_19

choose a country as a study abroad destination is not only dependent on objective factors such as the image, advantages and information of that country butalso depends on the individual's interaction, learning, culturally appropriate and intercultural competence, and ability to interact with society. In addition, social exposure has been studied extensively as a contributing factor to international students' ease of adaptation and integration [1].

Leaving home country to live abroad can be very difficult [2]. Students need to cope with the stresses of living away from home and adapting to new academic and social environments. When starting life in a new country, international students may encounter problems [3]. These problems can be adjusted in learning, sociocultural aspects, and students' psychology. Some international students find it easier to adapt or cope with the stressors associated when living and studying abroad [4]. Meanwhile, other students have difficulties in adjusting to new environment and psychological stress. This stress can come from many different reasons, but most of it comes from the background in the new country and the student's ability to adapt and integrate. Retention of international students depends on social inclusion ability, culture and integration with the university. Social inclusion is a significant variable for international students [5]. The characteristics of the host country, or destination country (culture, language and people) also contribute to several factors that promote students' motivation [6].

In recent years, the development momentum of international education is also considered to have a high potential for international students to choose Vietnam as a study-abroad destination. Therefore, increasing the competitive advantage, the ability to attract and the national recognition level for international students to study abroad should be goals for of national education not only for Vietnam but also for other. There are a lot of research studies on studying abroad. Approaching and adapting to culture is also a hotly-researched topic. Nevertheless, most of these studies are researched from the authors' perspective on understanding why domestic students choose to study overseas. There is no research on international students. More research is needed to develop more approaches, especially from the perspective of international students. This paper analyzes factors affecting the choice of Vietnam as a study-abroad destination for international students.

2 Theory and Framework

2.1 Destination Country Image and the Choice to Study Abroad of International Students

The image of a country is composed of a set of specific attributes associated with that country. In the current context of globalization and economic integration, most countries worldwide are competing to promote their country's image to many international friends [5]. From an international education perspective, attributes of a country, friendliness, cultural similarities, job opportunities, number of international students, scholarships, and length of study [7] are analyzed. They are motivating factors to push or motivate international students to choose this country as their study destination [7]. In addition, the country's reputation or economic characteristics, politics, and society play an important role in attracting international students to study [8]. Consistent with the push–pull theory of Mazzarol and Soutar (2002) [9], destination country image plays a vital role as a decisive factor in the consideration and selection of destination countries and programs courses offered [8, 10].

H1: Destination country image has a positive impact on the choice to study abroad of international students.

2.2 Destination Country Image and Acculturation of International Students

Acculturation focuses on the changes in immigrants after they join and settle in new countries. Zhou et al. (2008) [11] define acculturation as "the process of intercultural adaptation." This study's acculturation definition is based on Chien's (2013) [12] point of view "Acculturation is the adaptation of a person or group to living or experiencing another culture, based on relevant information."

Overseas students often have to experience and face various problems related to integration with the host country's environment [13]. Arthur (2017) [14] determined that international students need more support or help to adapt to society. When international students want to adapt quickly to a new culture, it is essential to communicate regularly with local people. Therefore, international students should develop a social network to help enhance the study abroad experience [4, 8], and it also deals with the cultural experience of learners in this country. When moving to an unfamiliar cultural environment, learners may feel more afraid, timid, and passive [15]. It is especially true in cases where the host country's culture is vastly different from the culture of their home country.

H2: Destination country image has a positive impact on acculturation of international students.

2.3 Acculturation and the Choice to Study Abroad of International Students

The adaptability and learning capacity of international students are closely related to the support from society [16]. Language barriers, diverse cultural norms, and time participation in social activities can become barriers to social interactions between local and international students [14]. Therefore, building an inclusive learning environment is extremely important for the capacity development of all students. The fact that international students have difficulty living in Vietnam can lead to cognitive stressors, influencing choice [8].

H3: Acculturation has a positive impact on international students' choice to study abroad.

2.4 *Moderating Role of Cross-Cultural Awareness on the Relationship of International Students' Acculturation and the Choice to Study Abroad*

Cross-cultural awareness is defined by Damen (1987) [17] as "the discovery and understanding of one's cultural behavior and thinking, as well as the patterns of others, and the discovery and understanding of behavior and conditioned thinking about one's own culture, as well as the stereotypes of others." In this context, it is how individuals perceive and interact with the culture of a host country they intend to choose. Some factors such as social communication, method of study, education style, teaching style in Vietnam, domestic faculty-foreign student relationship, and language can significantly influence their multicultural adaptation [5]. On the other hand, many students are concerned about making friends and fitting in. Building friendships with local students reduces loneliness and homesickness and increases satisfaction with international experiences [4].

H4: Cross-cultural awareness moderates the relationship between acculturation of international students and the choice to study abroad.

3 Methodology

The survey consists of two main parts. The first part of the questionnaire shows demographic factors such as gender and majors, etc. Questions related to destination country image, acculturation, cross-cultural awareness and the choice to study abroad belong to the second part of the survey questionnaire.

Wilkins et al., (2012) [18], Chien (2013) [12], and Chen (2007) [19] were selected as the scale of destination country image. Chen (2007) [19], Sheldon and Hilpert (2012) [20], and Chien (2013) [12] were selected for acculturation. Wilkins, Shams and Huisman (2013) [21], Li and Bray (2007) [22], Sheldon and Hilpert (2012) [20] were used to clarify cross-cultural awareness. Finally, Chen (2007) [19], Chen and Zimitat (2006) [23], and Chien (2013) [12] were selected to explain the choice to study abroad. The 5-point Likert scales have been adjusted and revised accordingly to the research context in Vietnam.

The survey was conducted for three months (from September to December 2022) on 434 international students in Vietnam which is a suitable size for PLS-SEM. The first phase of PLS-SEM is the evaluation of the measurement model and the second is the evaluation of the structural model [24]. Based on this instruction, this research continue to analyze the collected data to determine the relationships between variables, and verify the proposed hypotheses.

4 Results

Collected data contains 39.9% of male respondents and 60.1% of female. These 434 students come from 4 continents including Asia, Europe, Africa and America with 355, 39, 23 and 17 students respectively. Finally, it's about the field of study. With 48.8%, students majoring in Economics make up the largest number. Next is Social Sciences and Humanities with 26%. The Sciences of Technology—Engineering for 15.9% and the remaining 9.3% belong to the Medical Industry.

In the first phase of PLS-SEM, we check the scales' reliability and the data's validity, and then the scales' convergence. Cronbach's alpha values are all above 0.70, and all CR composite confidence values are more significant than 0.7 [24], ranging from 0.836 to 0.910. They prove the concepts in the model with high reliability. The convergence of the research concept is expressed through the AVE value showing high reliability and good fit. These values are all larger than the minimum threshold of 0.50, from 0.623. up to 0.630 [24]. In addition, the values of the Outer loadings coefficients of each research concept are above 0.708, so the reliability of these concepts is acceptable [24].

The discriminant validity of each structure concerning the other structures is more extensive than other coefficients in the same column, following the criteria of Fornell and Larcker (1981) [25]. Therefore, all scales have satisfied the discriminant validity (Table 2).

On the other hand, the VIF (Variance Inflation Factor) index is used to estimate the path coefficient based on the regression of each dependent variable and predictor. VIF values above 5 indicate a possible collinearity problem between predictive constructs. The results in Table 1 show that the VIF value ranges from 1,334 to 3,849, which is within the accepted threshold. Next, the explanatory power of R^2 is under 0.5 indicating that the model got to the weak level.

PLS-SEM is a non-parametric method [26], so bootstrapping method is used to prove the statistical significance of the research hypotheses. We use bootstrapping confidence interval ($N = 5000$) to test whether the reliability of the variable is significantly higher or lower than the recommended minimum threshold. In other words, bootstrapping applies to test the effects directly. From Table 3, the results show that except for the moderating relationship of cross-cultural awareness (H4) being rejected (p-values > 0.05), the remaining hypotheses all have p-values < 0.05 or mean statistical significance at the 95% level. Therefore, hypotheses H1, H2, H3, H4 are accepted.

Table 3 shows that the t-test P-value of the relationship between cross-cultural awareness and the choice to study abroad is $0.000 < 0.05$, showing that cross-cultural awareness impacts the choice to study abroad. The path coefficient $= 0.183 > 0$ shows

Table 1 Validity and Reliability Analysis, multicollinearity evaluation results, coefficient of determination R^2, predictive power Q^2

Research concept	Cronbach's alpha	Outer loadings		CR	AVE	VIF	R^2
		min	max				
Choice to study abroad	0.880	0.766	0.840	0.909	0.626	1.779–2.401	0.338
Acculturation	0.877	0.710	0.880	0.908	0.623	1.573–3.849	0.178
Cross-cultural awareness	0.707	0.760	0.813	0.836	0.630	1.334–1.448	
Destination country image	0.882	0.722	0.853	0.910	0.629	1.564–3.452	

Table 2 Discriminant validity—Fornell-Larcker

	Choice to study abroad	Acculturation	Cross-cultural awareness	Destination country image
Choice to study abroad	**0.791**			
Acculturation	0.473	**0.789**		
Cross-cultural awareness	0.295	0.178	**0.794**	

that cross-cultural awareness positively affects the choice to study abroad. That is, the higher the level of cross-cultural awareness, the more international students choose to study abroad. Besides, the t-test P-value of the relationship cross-cultural awareness x acculturation affecting the choice to study abroad is $0.965 > 0.05$, showing that this correlation is not significant and inconsistent with the author's original prediction. Thus, cross-cultural awareness has no role in moderating the relationship between acculturation to the choice to study abroad. Therefore, hypothesis H4 was rejected.

5 Discussion

With $\beta = 0.425$, destination country image significantly impacts international students' choices. Consistent with initial predictions, when there is a big difference between the culture of Vietnam and the student's home country, it is highly likely that they will not choose our country to study. The reason comes from the difficulties that cultural adaptation brings [27]. On the other hand, if cultural differences are minimal or there are significant similarities, international students tend to choose these countries to complete their intended study program. International students also appreciate not only cultural factors, but the aspect of geographical distance. In addition, studying abroad always requires financial resources many times larger than domestic [28]. It is consistent with the theory of Mazzarol and Soutar (2002) [9].

Table 3 Hypothesis analysis results and moderator analysis

Hypothesis	Relationship	Path coefficients	t-value	p-value	Results
H1	Destination country image - > Choice to study abroad	0.425	8.373	0.000	Accept
H2	Destination country image - > Acculturation	0.421	8.779	0.000	Accept
H3	Acculturation - > Choice to study abroad	0.317	6.957	0.000	Accept
H4	Cross-cultural awareness x Acculturation - > Choice to study abroad	-0.002	0.044	0.965	Rejected
Moderator analysis	***Cross-cultural awareness - > Choice to study abroad***	0.183	3.717	0.000	Accept
	Cross-cultural awareness x Acculturation - > Choice to study abroad	-0.002	0.044	0.965	Rejected

The integration of learners can be easily improved if they have a good perception of destination country image ($\beta = 0.421$). In addition, the data in Table 5 support the author's original hypothesis that acculturation plays a mediating role in the relationship between destination image and international students' choice to study abroad. To have good acculturation, the interaction of international students with Vietnamese citizens needs to be improved because friendship and good experience with the host country's culture greatly benefit them ($\beta = 0.317$). In addition, as discussed above, students who have had an experience of living abroad are less likely to have problems when studying abroad than others. Besides, students with excellent economic backgrounds often see studying abroad as a way of experience.

6 Conclusion

Based on the integrative theory of communication and cross-cultural adaptation [29] and the theoretical model Push–pull by Mazzarol and Soutar (2002) [9], this study examined the relationship between destination country image and international students' choice to study abroad. The mediating role of acculturation in the relationship between the destination country image and the choice to study abroad as well as the moderating role of cross-cultural awareness in the relationship between acculturation and the choice to study abroad were also tested.

The results show that the choice to study abroad is affected by destination country image, acculturation. The choice to study abroad is directly affected by the destination country image and indirectly through acculturation mediated. However, the hypothesis that cross-cultural awareness moderates the relationship between acculturation and the choice to study abroad has been rejected. Besides, the direct relationship between destination country image and the choice to study abroad produces better results, while destination country image affects the choice to study abroad through acculturation mediation has weaker results. Destination country image has a significant impact on acculturation and the choice to study abroad. In addition, Acculturation also has a significant impact on the choice to study abroad.

7 Implications

The reputation, positive image and awareness of destination country image need to be increasingly valued, attracting the international community's attention because this affects the country's competitiveness. Therefore, it is necessary to pay more attention to creating, promoting, enhancing the image and increasing the awareness of the country image among international students. In addition to the factors related to destination country image, it is necessary to consider how to help international students quickly and easily integrate into the environment in Vietnam. Helping students have sociability, feel close to the learning environment, and have an open mind to the new environment also helps speed up the integration process.

The results also show that acculturation is a factor with a positive effect, playing a mediating role in the relationship between destination country image and the choice to study abroad. When students choose to study abroad, they will always prepare themselves with a certain amount of knowledge and spirit to help them quickly integrate with the new country [30]. When these students equip themselves with a good spirit of inclusion, they can adapt no matter what country they are in. It can be explained that Vietnam is internationally known as a country with an open culture. The international students in this study can quickly adapt to Vietnam and have fewer problems with integration.

8 Future Research

This study has demonstrated the impact of destination country image, acculturation, cross-cultural awareness on the choice to study abroad. However, this model only stops at the point of view of objective prefixes, active factors have not been mentioned. Instead of continuing across continents as a whole, further studies should consider conducting the test on each group of continents and each geographical context. This paper is a cross-sectional study, in a given context, when the international students took the survey. In the future, international students may change their views, perspectives and comments. Studies should be carried out longitudinal and observed over a more extended period. From there, it is possible to consider the change in factors in choosing to study abroad. Further studies need to test the relationship between the prefixes instead of having a single impact on the dependent variable.

References

1. Szabó, Á., Papp, Z.Z., Luu, L.A.N.: Social contact configurations of international students at school and outside of school: Implications for acculturation orientations and psychological adjustment. Int. J. Intercult. Relat. **77**, 69–82 (2020). https://doi.org/10.1016/j.ijintrel.2020.05.001
2. Yang, Y., Zhang, Y., Sheldon, K.M.: Self-determined motivation for studying abroad predicts lower culture shock and greater well-being among international students: the mediating role of basic psychological needs satisfaction. Int. J. Intercult. Relat. **63**, 95–104 (2018). https://doi.org/10.1016/j.ijintrel.2017.10.005
3. Hendrickson, B., Rosen, D., Aune, R.K.: An analysis of friendship networks, social connectedness, homesickness, and satisfaction levels of international students. Int. J. Intercult. Relat. **35**(3), 281–295 (2011). https://doi.org/10.1016/j.ijintrel.2010.08.001
4. Mesidor, J.K., Sly, K.F.: Factors that contribute to the adjustment of international students. J. Intern. Stud. **6**(1), 262–282. https://doi.org/10.32674/jis.v6i1.569(2016)
5. Haverila, M.J., Haverila, K., McLaughlin, C.: Variables affecting the retention intentions of students in higher education institutions: a comparison between international and domestic students. J. Intern. Stud. **10**(2), 358–382. https://doi.org/10.32674/jis.v10i2.1849(2020)
6. Nghiêm-Phú, B., Nguyễn, T.H.: Impacts of perceived country image, institution image and self-image on students' intention to study abroad: a study in Hanoi, Vietnam. J. Market. Higher Educ. **30**(1), 26–44 (2020). https://doi.org/10.1080/08841241.2019.1658146
7. Nafari, J., Arab, A., Ghaffari, S.: Through the looking glass: analysis of factors influencing Iranian student's study abroad motivations and destination choice. SAGE Open **7**(2), 1–19 (2017). https://doi.org/10.1177/2158244017716711
8. Nghia, T.L.H.: Motivations for studying abroad and immigration intentions: the case of Vietnamese students. J. Intern. Stud. **9**(3), 758–776. https://doi.org/10.32674/jis.v0i0.731(2019)
9. Mazzarol, T., Soutar, G.N.: "Push-pull" factors influencing international student destination choice. Intern. J. Educ. Manag. **16**(2), 82–90 (2002). https://doi.org/10.1108/09513540210418403
10. Herrero, Á., Martín, H.S., García de los Salmones, M.D.M., Río Peña, A.D.: Influence of country and city images on students' perception of host universities and their satisfaction with the assigned destination for their exchange programmes. Place Brand. Public Diplom. **11**, 190-203. https://doi.org/10.1057/pb.2015.4(2015)
11. Zhou, Y., Jindal-Snape, D., Topping, K., Todman, J.: Theoretical models of culture shock and adaptation in international students in higher education. Stud. High. Educ. **33**(1), 63–75 (2008). https://doi.org/10.1080/03075070701794833
12. Chien, Y.Y.: Adjustment of international students in a UK university: Reasons for study abroad and subsequent academic and socio-cultural experiences. [PhD Thesis, University of Exeter, UK]. University of Exeter Repository (2013)
13. Gündüz, M., Alakbarov, N.: Analysis of social adjustment factors of international students in Turkey. J. Intern. Stud. **9**(4), 1155–1171. https://doi.org/10.32674/jis.v9i4.917(2019)

14. Arthur, N.: Supporting international students through strengthening their social resources. Stud. High. Educ. **42**(5), 887–894 (2017). https://doi.org/10.1080/03075079.2017.1293876
15. Yeh, E., Sharma, R., Jaiswal-Oliver, M., Wan, G.: Culturally responsive social emotional learning for international students: professional development for higher education. J. Intern. Stud. **12**(1), 19–41. https://doi.org/10.32674/jis.v12i1.2976(2022)
16. Zhang, J., Goodson, P.: Acculturation and psychosocial adjustment of Chinese international students: examining mediation and moderation effects. Int. J. Intercult. Relat. **35**(5), 614–627 (2011). https://doi.org/10.1016/j.ijintrel.2010.11.004
17. Damen, L.: Culture learning: the fifth dimension in the language classroom. Addison-Wesley (1987)
18. Wilkins, S., Balakrishnan, M.S., Huisman, J.: Student choice in higher education: motivations for choosing to study at an international branch campus. J. Stud. Int. Educ. **16**(5), 413–433 (2012). https://doi.org/10.1177/1028315311429002
19. Chen, L.H.: Choosing Canadian graduate schools from afar: east Asian students' perspectives. High. Educ. **54**(5), 759–781 (2007). https://doi.org/10.1007/s10734-006-9022-8
20. Sheldon, K.M., Hilpert, J.C.: The balanced measure of psychological needs (BMPN) scale: an alternative domain general measure of need satisfaction. Motiv. Emot. **36**, 439–451 (2012). https://doi.org/10.1007/s11031-012-9279-4
21. Wilkins, S., Shams, F., Huisman, J.: The decision-making and changing behavioural dynamics of potential higher education students: the impacts of increasing tuition fees in England. Educ. Stud. **39**(2), 125–141 (2013). https://doi.org/10.1080/03055698.2012.681360
22. Li, M., Bray, M.: Cross-border flows of students for higher education: push–pull factors and motivations of mainland Chinese students in Hong Kong and Macau. High. Educ. **53**, 791–818 (2007). https://doi.org/10.1007/s10734-005-5423-3
23. Chen, C.H., Zimitat, C.: Understanding Taiwanese students' decision-making factors regarding Australian international higher education. Intern. J. Educ. Manag. **20**(2), 91–100 (2006). https://doi.org/10.1108/09513540610646082
24. Hair, J.F., Risher, J.J., Sarstedt, M., Ringle, C.M.: When to use and how to report the results of PLS-SEM. Eur. Bus. Rev. **31**(1), 2–24 (2019). https://doi.org/10.1108/EBR-11-2018-0203
25. Fornell, C., Larcker, D.F.: Evaluating structural equation models with unobservable variables and measurement error. J. Mark. Res. **18**(1), 39–50 (1981). https://doi.org/10.1177/002224378101800104
26. Chin, W.W.: Commentary: issues and opinion on structural equation modeling. *MIS quarterly*, pp. vii-xvi (1998)
27. Shafaei, A., Razak, N.A.: Internationalisation of higher education: conceptualising the antecedents and outcomes of cross-cultural adaptation. Policy Fut. Educ. **14**(6), 701–720 (2016). https://doi.org/10.1177/1478210316645017
28. James-MacEachern, M., Yun, D.: Exploring factors influencing international students' decision to choose a higher education institution: a comparison between Chinese and other students. Int. J. Educ. Manag. **31**(3), 343–363 (2017). https://doi.org/10.1108/IJEM-11-2015-0158
29. Kim, Y.Y.: Becoming intercultural: an integrative theory of communication and cross-cultural adaptation. Sage Publishers (2001). https://doi.org/10.4135/9781452233253
30. Christofi, V., Thompson, C.L.: You cannot go home again: a phenomenological investigation of returning to the sojourn country after studying abroad. J. Couns. Dev. **85**(1), 53–63 (2007). https://doi.org/10.1002/j.1556-6678.2007.tb00444.x

Enhancing Student Satisfaction in Online Learning: An Empirical Study During the COVID-19 Pandemic

Nguyen Hoang Sinh and Hoang Thi Hoa

Abstract This research aimed to investigate the key determinants influencing the satisfaction of university students in Vietnam with online learning during the Covid-19 pandemic. Employing a mixed-method approach involving both qualitative and quantitative techniques, the study unfolded in two sequential phases: an initial exploratory phase and a subsequent comprehensive investigation. During the preliminary phase, data were collected through observations involving 100 students, in addition to two group discussions encompassing 20 students and four lecturers. These activities were designed to unveil the factors and variables that constitute the scales utilized in the study. The subsequent main research phase involved a survey method administered to 186 students, aimed at validating the scales and testing the research model. Specifically, multivariable linear regression analysis was employed to discern and quantify the factors impacting students' satisfaction with online learning. The findings of this study reveal five factors that influence student satisfaction, including Possession of personal electronic devices, Reliable access to internet connectivity, Effectiveness of online learning methods, Content suitability for online learning, and Instructor-student interaction. These insights not only provide a valuable framework for enhancing and innovating the quality of online learning for universities and education policymakers but also empower students to identify relevant factors and make necessary adjustments to enhance their online learning.

Keywords Satisfaction · Online learning · Covid-19 pandemic

1 Introduction

Online teaching and learning has become the preferred mode of instruction for numerous universities during the Covid-19 pandemic. It is also the solution that many countries worldwide employ when students cannot attend physical classes to ensure the continuity of their educational progress.

N. H. Sinh (✉) · H. T. Hoa
Ho Chi Minh City Open University, 97 Vo Van Tan, District 3, Ho Chi Minh City, Vietnam
e-mail: sinh.nh@ou.edu.vn

L. T. Tung et al. (eds.), *Disruptive Technology and Business Continuity*,
https://doi.org/10.1007/978-981-97-5452-6_20

According to a United Nations report published in August 2020, the Covid-19 pandemic has caused the most significant disruption to the education system in history, affecting nearly 1.6 billion individuals studying in 190 countries. The closure of schools and other educational institutions has impacted 94% of students globally, with this figure rising to 99% in low- and middle-income countries [1]. Furthermore, an analysis conducted by the International Labor Organization revealed that since the onset of the pandemic, over 70% of young people engaged in schooling or combining their studies with work have suffered adverse consequences due to the closure of schools, universities, and training centers [2, 3].

In response to the challenges posed by the Covid-19 pandemic, many countries have also embraced online teaching and learning. For instance, Afghanistan employs broadcast media (video and audio) to facilitate distance learning. Argentina adopted a broadcast media approach in April 2020, offering 14 h of content per day, catering to different audiences. In Australia, platforms such as LMS, Moodle, and Google Meet are utilized for online instruction. Bangladesh uses the state television network to deliver educational content from 9:30 am to 12:30 pm. Starting from February 2020, China implemented nationwide online learning initiatives [4]. In Vietnam, since March 2020, the Ministry of Education and Training has provided guidance to schools on selecting internet-based teaching tools, taking into account the specific needs and circumstances of each institution, with a particular emphasis on ensuring the quality of online instruction [5].

Despite these efforts, the question remains: Does online learning and training satisfy learners, and what are the factors influencing students' satisfaction with the quality of online education at universities? Surprisingly, no studies have yet addressed this issue in the context of Vietnam.

Given the likelihood that online teaching and learning will persist in the near future, even as the Covid-19 epidemic is expected to be controlled, the factors impacting student satisfaction with the quality of online education carry practical significance in assessing the efficacy of these instructional modes. This study seeks to elucidate the determinants affecting the satisfaction of students in Ho Chi Minh City regarding the quality of online learning. It not only offers a theoretical framework for assessing the effectiveness of online teaching and learning but also provides a foundation for universities, online education researchers, and educational policymakers to enhance and refine online instruction and learning services in the years ahead.

2 Literature Review

2.1 *Online Learning Quality*

In the current educational landscape, education is classified as a "service" because its recipients, namely students and parents, have the autonomy to select a service provider, such as universities, which they deem most suitable [6]. Consequently, the assessment of online education quality is contingent on the application of quality theory within the realm of online instruction.

Quality, as delineated by Juran and Gryna, is the degree to which a product or service conforms to the requirements and needs of the customer [7]. Feigenbaum's definition characterizes quality as the customer's judgment based on their real experiences with the product or service, juxtaposed against customer stipulations [8]. These stipulations may or may not be explicitly articulated, they can be conscious or tacit, and may vary from individual preferences to professional standards, continually evolving within a competitive market. In essence, the concept of service quality pertains to the perceptions formed by customers during the service provision process and the outcomes resulting from that process.

In the context of online education, various definitions exist. One author defines E-learning as a method of instruction facilitated through computers or smart devices interconnected via the internet. Within this framework, learners and instructors engage in direct communication through voice and video calls to exchange information, share learning materials, and resolve learners' challenges [9]. Another perspective characterizes E-learning as a mode of formal or informal education aimed at achieving robust learning objectives, emphasizing direct interactions between instructors and learners, as well as fostering a conducive learning environment through the integration of information technology and tradition. Yet another interpretation posits that E-learning entails the utilization of web and internet technologies in the learning process [10].

In line with the context of this study, the quality of online education is conceived as the level of quality perceived or measured in the context of learning and teaching, employing various tools and formats that leverage information technology and diverse media.

2.2 *Satisfaction*

Satisfaction encompasses various conceptualizations, such as the emotional or perceived response of customers to a service provider, rooted in the comparison between what they receive and their prior expectations [11]. Another perspective posits that satisfaction is determined by evaluating the results obtained from a service in relation to customer expectations [12].

However, in a study by Giese and Cote [13], satisfaction is defined as a succinct affective response with specific timing, intensity, and limited duration, addressing the fundamental aspects of product consumption. Similarly, satisfaction denotes a post-service/product usage emotional state for the customer [14]. In this context, this study gauges student satisfaction with online learning based on their perceptions of the online learning offerings provided by universities in Ho Chi Minh City during the Covid-19 pandemic.

2.3 SERVPERF Model

To assess online learning quality, this study employs the Service Performance (SERVPERF) model instead of the Service Quality (SERVQUAL) model, primarily due to the brevity of the questions comprising the scales, which reduces respondent time. Additionally, measuring expectations using the SERVQUAL model is challenging, despite its widespread use in general service quality studies [15].

The SERVPERF model posits that service quality is best represented by perceived quality, dispensing with the need for expected quality, and involves a weighted evaluation of five components. The components and observed variables of this SERVPERF model remain consistent with those of SERVQUAL, resulting in this measurement model being referred to as the perception model. Utilizing SERVPERF model scales to assess service quality helps alleviate some of the limitations associated with the SERVQUAL model's capacity to differentiate between customer satisfaction and attitude. Cornin and Taylor argue that service quality can be likened to "an attitude," asserting that "actual performance" rather than "expected performance" more effectively determines service quality [14]. Consequently, many service providers opt for the SERVPERF model as the preferred scale to expediently assess the quality of their services.

3 Methods

3.1 Research Design

The research methodology encompasses both qualitative and quantitative approaches, organized into two distinct phases: preliminary research and formal research (Fig. 1).

Preliminary research entails the use of observational techniques and group discussions to investigate the factors and variables that constitute the scales under consideration before progressing to the formal research phase.

The formal research phase involves employing a survey method to achieve the following objectives: (i) Assess the quality of the learning service and measure the

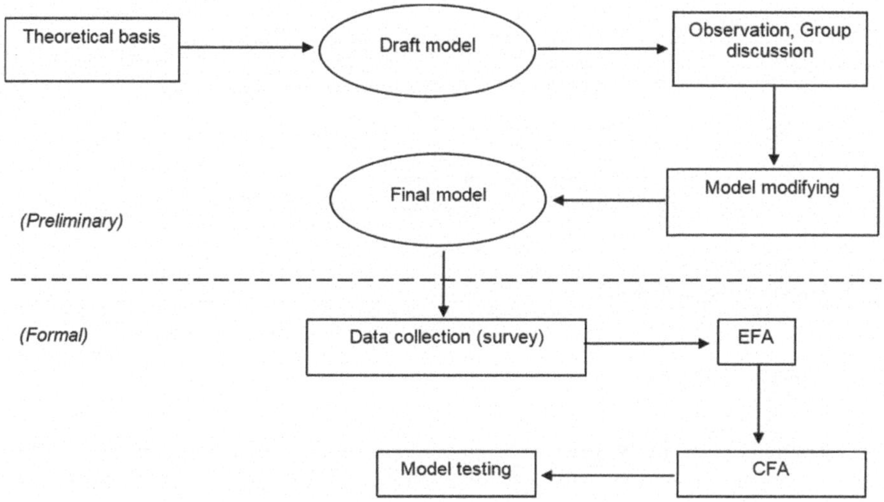

Fig. 1 Research process

level of satisfaction, (ii) evaluate the research model by applying exploratory factor analysis (EFA) and multivariable linear regression analysis, aimed at identifying and quantifying the factors that influence student satisfaction with online learning at universities in Ho Chi Minh City, Vietnam.

3.2 Research Model

The research methodology encompasses both qualitative and quantitative approaches, The preliminary research consists of two distinct steps: observations and discussions.

In the observation phase, which took place from February 25 to March 5, 2021, 100 students participating in online learning were observed. This stage led to the identification of eight factors that impact student satisfaction in online learning, including (i) Chapter training program, (ii) Lecturers, (iii) Study materials, (iv4) Facilities, (v) Online learning process and regulations, (vi) Study duration, (vii) Online learning methods, and (viii) Social knowledge.

Subsequently, two group discussions were conducted on March 10, 2021, involving 5 fourth-year students, 5 third-year students, 5 second-year students, 5 first-year students, and 4 university lecturers who were engaged in online teaching and learning. These discussions revolved around the eight factors that had emerged from the initial observations. Following the discussions, the research model was refined and developed by adjusting and incorporating relevant factors.

The formal research model was ultimately introduced, featuring five key factors (Fig. 2).

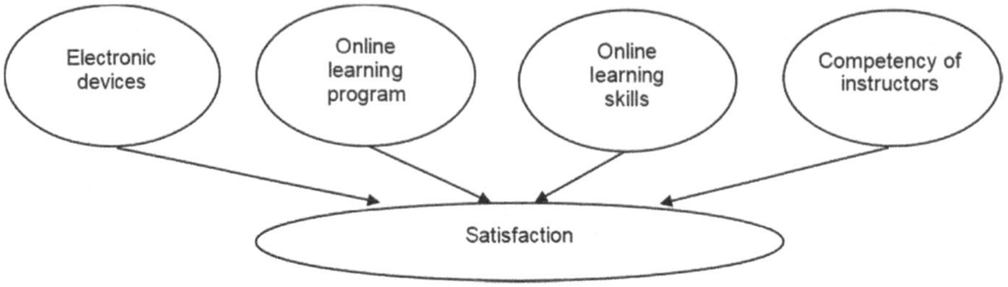

Fig. 2 Proposed research model

3.3 Measurements

The variables in this study were assessed using a 5-point Likert scale, with response options ranging from (1) "strongly disagree," (2) "disagree," (3) "neutral," (4) "agree," to (5) "strongly agree." A comprehensive list of the measurements for the 30 variables can be found in Table 1.

3.4 Participants

The formal research, involving a survey, was conducted during the period from March to April 2021. According to Hair et al. [16], the sample size for Exploratory Factor Analysis (EFA) should ideally be at least 100, with a recommended observation-to-variable ratio of 5:1. In this particular study, the model under examination comprised 29 independent variables and 1 dependent variable. Consequently, the minimum number of participants required would be 30×5, totaling 150. Notably, the study successfully gathered and analyzed 186 valid questionnaires out of a total of 300, ensuring a robust and statistically powerful sample size.

The participants in this research consisted of students from both private and state-owned universities in Ho Chi Minh City, including but not limited to Nguyen Tat Thanh University, Open University, University of Social Sciences and Humanities, Ton Duc Thang University, Law University, FPT University, University of Natural Sciences, Hong Bang International University, and Van Lang University.

4 Results and Discussion

The study utilized SPSS software for data analysis, yielding the following outcomes.

Table 1 Scales of independent and dependent variables

Factors	Encoding
Electronic devices	***YTVC***
1. Has its own smart electronic devices (smart phone, Ipad, laptop…)	YTVC1
2. Have its own desktop	YTVC2
3. Borrow equipment	YTVC3
4. No equipment	YTVC4
5. Devices with internet connection (or 3G, 4G)	YTVC5
6. Using the internet at home	YTVC6
7. Use 3G, 4G	YTVC7
8. No internet source (or 3G, 4G)	YTVC8
9. Have a quiet, comfortable place to study	YTVC9
Online learning program	***CTHO***
10. Clear curriculum goals	CTHO1
11. The right duration and the right level	CTHO2
12. Training program on schedule	CTHO3
13. Learning theory	CTHO4
14. Practical learning	CTHO5
15. Variety of content	CTHO6
Online learning skills	***KNHO***
16. Always attend school on time	KNHO1
17. Update class schedule regularly	KNHO2
18. Attend all classes	KNHO3
19. Follow all classroom rules	KNHO4
20. Health guarantee	KNHO5
21. Define learning goals	KNHO6
22. Build appropriate learning methods	KNHO7
Competency of instructors	***GVGV***
23. Ensure class time and study plan	GVGV1
24. Always ready to answer students' questions	GVGV2
25. During the lecture, there are videos and clips	GVGV3
26. Send documents to students in full	GVGV4
27. Good classroom control	GVGV5
28. Ask students to repeat what they have heard	GVGV6
29. There are many forms of student performance evaluation	GVGV7
Satisfaction	***Y***
30. Overall student satisfaction with the quality of online training	Y1

4.1 Measurement Model

The study conducted separate Exploratory Factor Analysis (EFA) procedures for independent variables (X) and dependent variables (Y). The coexistence of the dependent and independent variables within the same EFA analysis led to a strong correlation between these variables. This robust correlation made it challenging to distinctly identify the structure of observed variables for the dependent variable in EFA, leading to an unsecured scale structure, characterized by a disordered rotation matrix [16, 18]. Furthermore, the model employed in this study is relatively straightforward, with clearly defined variable roles. It incorporates a limited number of dependent variables in contrast to a higher number of independent variables, many of which influence the outcomes of the dependent variable.

Reliability of the Measurement. The reliability assessment of the independent variables revealed that all factors exhibited Cronbach's Alpha coefficients exceeding 0.8, and the observed variables were correlated with the total variable at levels greater than 0.3. Consequently, all 29 variables were deemed suitable for inclusion in the exploratory factor analysis. Moreover, the reliability examination of the dependent variable established that the factor possessed a Cronbach's Alpha coefficient exceeding 0.7, and it displayed a p-value of 0.000, which is less than 0.05. Hence, the data's appropriateness was confirmed (Table 2).

Exploratory Factor Analysis. Cronbach's Alpha coefficients were observed to range between 0.8 and 1.0, indicating good measurement quality. However, the initial KMO and Bartlet's test, conducted with 29 observed independent variables, resulted in the elimination of six variables. In accordance with the criteria outlined by Nguyen [17], Peterson [18], and Slater [19], variables were excluded if their variable-total correlation coefficient fell below 0.3. The discarded variables were as follows: YTVC4—No equipment to study, YTVC9—Having a quiet and comfortable place to study, KNHO5—Ensuring health, KNHO6—Developing appropriate learning methods, CTHO3—Training program on schedule, and GVGV5—Classroom control is good.

Table 2 Reliability of independent and dependent variables

Factors	Number of observation variables	Cronbach's Alpha
Independent variables		
Electronic devices (YTVC)	9	0.809
Online learning program (CTHO)	6	0.852
Online learning skills (KNHO)	7	0.867
Competency of instructors (GVGV)	7	0.815
Dependent variable		
Satisfaction (Y)	1	0.709

With the remaining 23 observed variables, post-exploratory factor analysis, five new factors emerged, each influencing the level of student satisfaction with the quality of online training during the Covid-19 period.

Consequently, Factor X1 encompasses three closely correlated variables pertaining to students' personal equipment for online learning (YTVC1, YTVC2, YTVC3), thus earning the name "Having own electronic devices." Factor X2 comprises variables related to the types of online connections available for student learning (YTVC5, YTVC6, YTVC7) and is aptly labeled "Stable internet or 3G, 4G." The third factor encompasses five observed variables tied to online learning content (KNHO1, KNHO2, KNHO3, KNHO4, KNHO7), denoted as "Content suitable for online learning (X3)." Factor X4 encompasses six observed variables focused on the teaching dynamics between lecturers and students (GVGV1, GVGV2, GVGV3, GVGV4, GVGV6, GVGV7), earning the name "Lecturers interact well with students while lecturing." The final factor encompasses six observed variables (CTHO1, CTHO2, CTHO4, CTHO5, CTHO6, YTVC8) and is aptly labeled "Online learning method (X5)."

4.2 Research Model

Linear Regression Analysis. The results of the regression analysis reveal that the adjusted R^2 coefficient is 0.575, indicating that 57.5% of the variance in satisfaction with the quality of online learning can be accounted for by the five factors incorporated into the model. The remaining 42.5% is attributed to unexamined factors. The Sig.F coefficient, with a value of 0.00, is significantly smaller than the significance level $\alpha = 5\%$, thus affirming the statistical significance of the regression model. This implies that the independent variables indeed exert an influence on the dependent variable. A Durbin–Watson value of 1.762 demonstrates the absence of correlation between residuals, and hence, the model adheres to the assumption of error independence. Consequently, all variables encompassed within the model are statistically significant (Table 3).

In terms of significance, the Beta coefficients indicate the following order from highest to lowest importance: (X2) Having own electronic devices, (X1) Stable

Table 3 Results of linear regression analysis

Factors	B coefficient	Beta coefficient
Constant	0.152	
Have own electronic devices (X1)	0.324	0.533
Have stable internet or 3G, 4G (X2)	0.295	0.543
Content suitable for online learning (X3)	0.116	0.210
Lecturers interact well with students while lecturing (X4)	0.075	0.149
Online learning methods (X5)	0.153	0.267

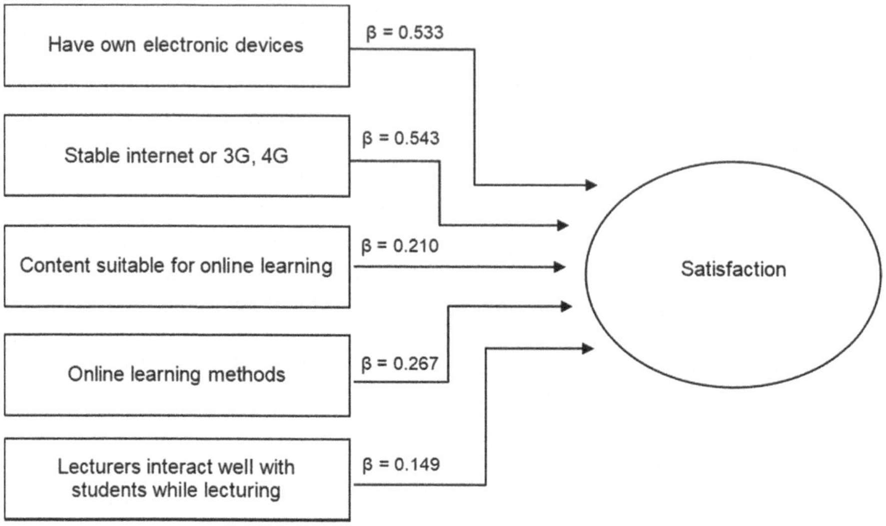

Fig. 3 Modified research model

internet or 3G, 4G, (X5) Online learning methods, (X3) Content suitable for online learning, and (X4) Lecturers interact well with students while lecturing.

Modified Research Model. The research model for student satisfaction with online learning is modified as follows (Fig. 3).

5 Conclusion and Implications

5.1 Conclusion

The primary aim of this study was to investigate the factors influencing student satisfaction with online learning in the context of the Covid-19 pandemic in Ho Chi Minh City. The study has successfully identified and delineated five significant factors, namely: (i) Owning electronic devices ($\beta = 0.533$), (ii) Access to stable internet or 3G, 4G ($\beta = 0.543$), (iii) Availability of appropriate content suitable for online learning ($\beta = 0.210$), (iv) Effective online learning methods ($\beta = 0.267$), and (v) Quality of lecturer-student interaction during online instruction ($\beta = 0.149$).

This research contributes to both theoretical and practical aspects. Theoretically, it furnishes a model that elucidates the factors influencing student satisfaction with online learning in Ho Chi Minh City, encompassing the unique challenges posed by the Covid-19 pandemic. In a practical context, the findings offer valuable guidance for researchers, educational institutions, policy-makers, and students. Consequently, the recommendations can be tailored to the evolving landscape of online learning methods, influenced by the ongoing impact of Covid-19 and the ever-changing educational requirements.

5.2 *Implications*

For Educational Institutions. *Tailoring Program Design:* Educational institutions should ensure that program designs are suitable for each subject. This necessitates the development of policies that encourage instructors to create online training materials distinct from those used in face-to-face teaching. Furthermore, institutions should facilitate training programs and the exchange of experiences among lecturers engaged in online learning.

Guidelines and Facility Investment: To support students effectively, educational institutions should provide clear instructions on the online learning process, the requisite skills, and essential elements. Additionally, they should allocate resources for investments in new facilities specifically designed for online training.

For Lecturers. *Embracing Innovative Online Teaching:* Lecturers must be willing to adopt new online teaching methods and gain a deep understanding of technology devices, applications, and effective teaching techniques in the online environment. It is important to maintain a student-centered approach while increasing interactions and implementing assessment methods suitable for online learning.

For Students. *Defining Learning Goals:* Students should take the initiative to clearly define their learning goals and invest time in acquiring the skills necessary for successful online learning. Active engagement with instructors, including seeking help when needed, is crucial for a productive online learning experience.

References

1. United Nations. https://www.un.org/development/desa/dspd/wp-content/uploads/sites/22/2020/08/sg_policy_brief_covid-19_and_education_august_2020.pdf (2020)
2. International Labor Organization. https://www.ilo.org/global/about-the-ilo/newsroom/news/WCMS_753060/lang--en/index.htm (2020)
3. International Labor Organization. https://www.ilo.org/global/topics/youth-employment/publications/WCMS_753026/lang--en/index.htm (2020)
4. World Bank. https://www.worldbank.org/en/topic/edutech/brief/how-countries-are-using-edtech-to-support-remote-learning-during-the-covid-19-pandemic (2020)
5. Vietnam Ministry of Education and Training . https://moet.gov.vn/tintuc/Pages/phong-chong-nCoV.aspx?ItemID=6550 (2020)
6. Pham Thi Lien: Chất lượng dịch vụ đào tạo và sự hài lòng của người học: Trường hợp Trường Đại học Kinh tế, Đại học Quốc gia Hà Nội. Tạp chí Khoa học ĐHQGHN: Kinh tế và Kinh doanh **32**(4), 81–89 (2016)
7. Juran, J.M., Gryna, F.M.: Juran's quality control handbook. McGraw-Hill, New York (1988)
8. Feigenbaum, A.V.: Total quality control. McGraw-Hill, New York (1991)
9. Kieu Anh. https://khoahocphattrien.vn/khoa-hoc/be-mat-duong-pho-gop-phan-gay-o-nhiem-khong-khi/20200910090824939p1c160.htm (2020)

10. Thach Thi Tuyen. https://repository.vnu.edu.vn/bitstream/VNU_123/11701/1/OER-Book%2812%29.pdf (2020)
11. Oliver, R.L.: Customer satisfaction with service. Handbook of services marketing and management, 247–254 (2000)
12. Kotler, P., Armstrong, G.: Principles of Marketing. Pearson Prentice Hall (2012)
13. Giese, J.L., Cote, J.A.: Defining consumer satisfaction. Academy of Marketing Science Review, pp. 1–22 (2000)
14. Cronin, J.J., Jr., Taylor, S.A.: Measuring service quality: a reexamination and extension. J. Mark. **56**(3), 55–68 (1992)
15. Babakus, E., Boller, G.W.: An empirical assessment of the SERVQUAL scale. J. Busin. Res., 253–268 (1992)
16. Hair, J.F., Black, W.C., Babin, B.J., Anderson, R.E.: Multivariate data analysis, 7th edn. Pearson-Prentice Hall, Upper Saddle River, NJ (2010)
17. Nguyen, S.H.: Using an experiment and a survey to examine guilt and shame separately via the distinct emotional arousals of guilt versus shame under moderating effects, part II: the case of personal cultural orientation. Business. Sage Publications, Sage Research Methods (2024)
18. Peterson, R.A.: A meta-analysis of Cronbach's coefficient alpha. J. Cons. Res. **21**, 381–391 (1994)
19. Slater, S.: Issues in conducting marketing strategy research. J. Strat. **5**, 147–151 (1995)

The Relationship Between Public Debt and Economic Growth: A Note from Developing Countries

Le Thanh Tung and Tran Le Nguyen

Abstract The impact of sovereign debt on economic development varies across many studies and concerns many countries. This issue is especially crucial for policymakers in developing nations seeking to improve their economic status. This paper explores data from 25 developing nations from 1980 to 2015 to examine the relationship between public debt and economic growth. Unlike previous research, one model is constructed with three groups of samples: lower-middle-income nations, upper-middle-income nations, and overall sample, to compare the effects of debt level on the economic development of each country group. In the overall sample, the outcomes show a negative correlation between sovereign debt and economic development. However, in the sub-samples, the results are contradictory. Government debt has a positive correlation with economic growth in the lower-middle-income nations, but a negative relationship in the upper-middle-income group. The empirical evidence indicates that the income level of a nation influences the relationship between national debt and economic development. Hence, governments need to exercise caution when making policies for economic growth, considering the income levels of different countries.

Keywords Public debt · Economic growth · Sustainable development

L. T. Tung (✉)
Faculty of Economics and Public Management, Ho Chi Minh City Open University, Ho Chi Minh City, Vietnam
e-mail: tung.lt@ou.edu.vn

T. L. Nguyen
Tomas Bata University in Zlin—TBU, Zlin, Czech Republic

Ho Chi Minh University of Banking—HUB, Ho Chi Minh, Vietnam

L. T. Tung et al. (eds.), *Disruptive Technology and Business Continuity*,
https://doi.org/10.1007/978-981-97-5452-6_21

1 Introduction

Public debt is the cumulative sum of funds owed by a government to both foreign lenders and its populace [1]. It constitutes a vital element of a nation's fiscal strategy and significantly influences the economic terrain over both immediate and extended periods. The accumulation of public debt occurs when a government borrows funds to finance its expenditures or when its expenses exceed its revenues. Governments typically incur public debt for various reasons, such as funding infrastructure projects, addressing budget deficits, responding to economic downturns, or covering other essential expenses [2]. While moderate levels of public debt are considered a normal and sometimes necessary part of economic management, excessively high levels can have profound implications for the overall health of an economy.

The impact of public debt on the economy is a subject of extensive study and debate among economists [3]. In the short run, public debt, if used judiciously, can be a tool for stimulating economic growth by boosting aggregate demand. However, concerns arise when public debt reaches elevated levels, as it may lead to adverse consequences in the long term [4]. The long-term effects of public debt are often associated with its potential to crowd out private investment, increase interest rates, and create challenges for sustained economic growth. High levels of public debt can limit a government's flexibility to respond to future economic shocks and may lead to higher taxes or inflation, both of which can hinder private sector activities. Moreover, public debt can influence a country's creditworthiness, impacting its ability to borrow at favorable terms. Excessive public debt may result in credit rating downgrades, making it more expensive for the government to service its debt and potentially leading to a debt crisis.

While economic growth is generally viewed positively, it is important to consider its sustainability and inclusivity [5]. Growth that is environmentally sustainable, socially inclusive, and resilient to economic shocks is often a more desirable and holistic goal. Striking the right balance between promoting economic growth and addressing challenges such as income inequality, environmental degradation, and social disparities is a complex task that requires careful policy consideration and implementation.

Governments play a crucial role in influencing economic growth through the formulation and implementation of fiscal and monetary policies. Fiscal policies, involving government spending and taxation, can impact overall demand and investment. Monetary policies, controlled by central banks, influence interest rates and money supply, affecting borrowing costs and investment decisions. Understanding the dynamics of public debt and economic growth is crucial for policymakers, as they involve finding a delicate balance between utilizing debt to stimulate economic activity and avoiding the negative consequences associated with unsustainable debt levels and sustainable economic growth. Effective management of public debt requires careful consideration of economic conditions, fiscal policies, and the long-term implications for both the government and the broader economy.

2 Literature Review

Economic growth stands as a cornerstone concept in economics, denoting the expansion of a nation's production and consumption of goods and services across time. It is a key indicator of a nation's prosperity and is closely monitored by policymakers, economists, and the public alike. The gauge for economic growth commonly relies on the elevation of a nation's gross generated within its territorial confines. Sustained economic development is indispensable for enhancing the quality of living standards, alleviating poverty, and fostering overall societal well-being. It provides nations with the means to invest in public services, amenities, and other critical areas, contributing to an enhanced quality of life for its citizens. Economic growth can take various forms, including extensive growth, which involves increasing the quantity of inputs like labor and capital, and intensive growth, which emphasizes improvements in productivity and technological innovation. Additionally, inclusive growth focuses on ensuring that the advantages of economic development are distributed across different segments of the population, reducing income inequality.

A study analyzing the consequences of trade liberalization in five transitional economies from 1993 to 2016 is conducted by [6]. Utilizing panel estimation techniques, the study found a consistent correlation between inflation, trade liberalization, economic and financial development, labor force, and innovation. Long-term elasticities indicated a significantly positive effect of trade liberalization on economic development. Additionally, panel tests revealed bidirectional causality between economic development and cost increases, and unidirectional causality from economic growth to trade openness and financial progress in the short-term. These results recommend that trade liberalization significantly contributes to the advancement and progress of these developing economies.

The outcome of external national debt on the economic development of Morocco spanning from 1988 to 2016 is investigated in [7]. Employing the ARDL bound testing method for econometric analysis, the research reveals a consistently negative and statistically significant influence of elevated public debt on economic development, evident in both the short and long run. Notably, the study indicates that this negative impact is more prominent over the short term rather the long term. The outcomes are consistent with prior research findings, supporting the notion that external debt can harm economic growth.

The correlation between trade liberalization and economic development by examining two aspects of economies' collaboration in international commerce: product diversity and range of exports is examined in the paper of [8]. Analyzing a panel of 169 nations ranging from 1988 to 2014 and leveraging a generalized method of moments estimator, the study reveals that nations exporting top-notch quality and introducing innovative product selections tend to experience swifter economic growth. Notably, a non-linear trend emerges, indicating that the impact of trade liberalization on development might be unfavorable for nations specializing in low-grade merchandise. Furthermore, a non-monotonic connection is observed between the assortment of exports, export proportion, and expansion, recommending that economies may undergo accelerated growth once they attain a certain threshold in the diversity of their exports.

In the study conducted by [2], examines how debt threshold impacts economic development in Africa, employing both static and dynamic panel threshold regression methods. The results suggest that the identified liabilities boundary is influenced by both the selected approximation method and the incorporation of growth restriction factors. Nonlinearities in the correlation between debt and growth are evident, with low levels of debt being considered neutral or even beneficial to growth, whereas consistently high debt levels are consistently found to impede growth in all examined scenarios. This study emphasizes the need for careful consideration when suggesting a precise debt threshold, highlighting its susceptibility to variations in modeling approaches and the inclusion of growth control factors. While the analysis identifies nonlinearities in the debt-growth relationship, the paper suggests that further research is essential to offer specific policy recommendations.

The connection between trade liberalization and economic development in Cote d'Ivoire from 1965 to 2014 is explored by [9], in which addressing the potential limitations in previous studies by incorporating capital assets and manpower in the analysis. Using the bounds testing for autoregressive distributed lag for co-movement and the Toda and Yamamoto-Granger causality examination, the study finds that trade liberalization positively contributes to economic development over the short and long run. Further, the results underscore a positive and robust complementary relationship between trade liberalization and capital statistics in fostering economic progress.

The influence of sovereign debt on economic development in industrialized nations from 1946 to 2009 is found in the econometric methods of [10]. The findings reveal a significant and inverse affiliation between national debt and economic expansion in these high-income economies. According to the study, the growth rate of real GDP remains unaffected a sharp downturn until the fiscal leverage exceeds 220%. The elasticity analysis indicates that a 1% raise in public debt/GDP above 120% is linked to a 1.13% drop in the growth rate of real GDP. The adverse impact of national debt becomes particularly pronounced when the debt burden surpasses 220%. The paper suggests a reconsideration of austerity policies and advocates for new tactics in debt supervision for developed nations, reflecting upon both economic and fiscal well-being.

The widespread assumption of uniform effects of sovereign debt on economic development across nations is discovered by [11]. Instead, the study argues for significant cross-country heterogeneity in this relationship. Three different economic clusters can be identified: Continental (Core EU members), Nordic (Scandinavian), and Liberal (Anglo-Saxon) clusters. The scholars posit that varying level of unpredictability at the equivalent extent of government debt contribute to this observed heterogeneity. Observational findings endorse this assertion, suggesting that mainland countries tend to experience more pronounced growth-reducing impacts from public debt compared to Liberal countries, where public debt appears to have neutral or potentially positive effects on growth. Northern European countries exhibit an irregular association, with adverse effects of debt emerging at a liability threshold hovering at about 60% of GDP.

Again, the significant influence of public debt on the economy, particularly focusing on its long-term effects is explored by [3]. The research highlights that, in the short run, public debt arising from deficit financing is viewed as a stimulant for aggregate demand and output. However, the conventional perspective suggests that, in the long term, elevated public debt may have negative repercussions on economic growth through various channels.

Moreover, a mechanism variable approach to examine the causal-and-effect connection between public debt and economic growth in a subset of OECD nations is employed in the model of [1]. The conclusions align with available studies that have identified an opposite relationship between indebtedness and economic expansion. However, the paper argues that this link dissipates after addressing endogeneity. The study conducts various robustness tests, demonstrating that the results remain unaffected by weak instrument issues and are consistent even when relaxation of exclusion restrictions is considered. The crucial conclusion drawn is that there is no absence of proof supporting a cause-and-effect relationship of government debt on economic expansion. This finding holds significance, particularly given that the commonly observed inverse correlation between debt and development is sometimes used to justify policies assuming a detrimental influence of causality of liabilities and GDP growth.

The substantial impact of public debt on the economy, with a specific emphasis on its long-term consequences is examined in the paper of [12]. It highlights that in the short run, public debt, arising from deficit financing, is perceived as a driver for aggregate demand and output. However, the conventional perspective indicates that over the long term, elevated public debt may have adverse effects on economic growth through multiple channels.

In conclusion, the diverse studies reviewed provide valuable insights into the complex relationship between public debt and economic growth across different regions and periods. Collectively, these studies underscore the multifaceted nature of the relationship between trade openness and economic growth; and the complexity of the debt-growth relationship, emphasizing the need for nuanced policy considerations that account for regional and temporal variations. The findings contribute valuable insights to ongoing discussions on effective debt management and its implications for sustained economic growth.

3 Methodology and Data

3.1 Econometric Methodology

Based on previous research, several variables fall within the category of global capital factors, including inbound investment, remittance income, international liabilities, and foreign aid. Nevertheless, due to the extensive existing literature on foreign direct investment, it will be excluded from our mathematical model. The residual

Table 1 Definition and measure of the variables

Variable	Definition and measure	Source
GR	GDP per capita growth (annual %)	World Bank
INV	Gross capital formation (% of GDP)	World Bank
DEBT	Central government debt (% of GDP)	IMF
INF	Inflation, GDP deflator (annual %)	World Bank
OPEN	Export + Import (% of GDP)	World Bank

Source World Bank (2023); IMF (2023)

three factors will be incorporated into the poverty analysis as overseas capital variables. Additionally, given the significant role of cross-border commerce in poverty reduction, this variable will also be included in the model to assess its impact on poverty in growth markets. Global trade will be represented by the international trade factor. The analytical framework is structured as follows:

$$GR_{i,t} = \beta_0 + \beta_1 INV_{i,t} + \beta_2 DEBT_{i,t} + \beta_3 INF_{i,t} + \beta_4 OPEN_{i,t} + \delta_{i,t} \quad (1)$$

where: GR is calculated by the growth of GDP per capita, INV is denoted by domestic investment, DEBT is the value of central government debt, INF is based GDP deflator, OPEN presents the international trade of the economy and δ is the error term. In the function, t denotes periods, and I present the cross-sectional units. Table 1 shows the definition and measure of the variables.

Table 2 A statistical summary of the variables

Sample	Variable	Max	Min	Mean	Std. Dev	Obs
Lower-middle income economies (13 countries)	GR	22.770	-29.834	2.2793	4.9603	413
	INV	42.875	1.7289	22.988	7.3311	386
	DEBT	279.49	3.7729	50.161	32.610	397
	INF	125.27	-1.7103	9.5402	10.856	372
	OPEN	178.76	9.1056	69.573	34.366	411
Upper-middle-income economies (12 countries)	GR	33.030	-40.746	2.6637	6.5770	372
	INV	70.229	-0.6908	28.141	9.5212	365
	DEBT	219.73	3.6734	47.266	29.866	362
	INF	3373.4	-23.822	32.083	225.47	373
	OPEN	375.37	14.144	102.30	47.093	398
Full panel (25 economies)	GR	33.030	-40.746	2.4615	5.7824	785
	INV	70.229	-0.6908	25.492	8.8447	751
	DEBT	279.49	3.6734	48.780	31.344	759
	INF	3373.4	-23.822	20.826	160.01	745
	OPEN	375.37	9.1056	85.677	44.239	809

Source: Authors calculate from the research data

The paper applies two methods including the Ordinary Least Squares (OLS) for the estimation of Eq. 1 and the graphical method for investigating the database. To deeply analyze, the methods will undergo estimation using various models and will be compared with others to obtain the optimal outcome while elucidating the precise relationships between variables. The estimation process comprises of two primary steps.

Initially, the Ordinary Least Squares (OLS) technique is utilized with two models: the Fixed Effects Model (FEM) and the Random Effects Model (REM). Subsequently, the Hausman test is employed to determine whether the Fixed Effects or Random Effects model is more suitable. If the null hypothesis is rejected (p-value is smaller than 0.05), the evidence implies that the Random effects are biased, and the Fixed effects are chosen. Second, the graphical method is used to analyze the database. Finally, we compare the estimated result and graphical results for concluding the study's findings.

3.2 Data Source

The research uses annual data from 1980 to 2015 from 25 developing and emerging countries in the Asia–Pacific region. The data concerning the growth rate of GDP per capita, investment, and inflation are directly obtained from the World Bank's World Development Indicators database. Trade openness data is derived by dividing the sum of export and import values by the GDP for the corresponding period. Public debt information is sourced from the International Monetary Fund (IMF). Country classifications are based on criteria provided by the World Bank, where income groups are distinguished using thresholds adjusted for inflation over time. As per the World Bank's classification as of July 2022, lower-middle-income economies have a Gross National Income (GNI) per capita ranging between \$1086 and \$4255, while upper-middle-income economies have a GNI per capita between \$4256 and \$13,205 (World Bank, 2022).

The upper-middle-income group includes Armenia, Azerbaijan, Fiji, Iran, Jordan, Kazakhstan, Sri Lanka, Maldives, Mongolia, Malaysia, Thailand, and Tonga (12 countries). The lower-middle-income countries are Bangladesh, Indonesia, India, Kyrgyz Republic, Lao PDR, Philippines, Papua New Guinea, Pakistan, West Bank and Gaza, Vanuatu, Solomon Islands, Vietnam, and Yemen (13 countries). The fast description of the key variables is shown in the below table.

4 Regression Result

4.1 The Lower-Middle-Income Economies

Analyzing Table 3 reveals interesting insights into the research findings. The Hausman test confirms that FEM is better than REM in all estimated results. In Models 1, 3, and 4, Investment shows no significant effect, but in Models 2 and 5, it emerges as highly significant at the 5% level. This inconsistency highlights the sensitivity of the relationship between investment and economic growth to the chosen econometric model, suggesting that the nuances of this connection are contingent on specific analytical methodologies.

Notably, Model 5 stands out as the only one where the study observes a substantial effect of Inflation and Investment at the 5% level. This finding could signal that the impact of inflation on economic growth may be more pronounced when certain factors are considered, as captured by the specific characteristics of Model 5. The contrasting results across models underscore the importance of robustness checks and sensitivity analyses to ensure the reliability of research conclusions.

Public debt's impact on economic growth is identified in Model 3 (Fixed effects model—FEM) at the 5% significance level, while the most robust effect is observed in Model 5 (Random effects model—REM) at the 5% significance level. The diversity in results observed among different models indicates that the connection between public debt and economic growth is intricate and susceptible to the statistical methodologies employed. Policymakers and researchers should exercise caution when drawing conclusions based on a single model, emphasizing the need for a comprehensive

Table 3 The lower-middle-income economies

Variable	Model 1		Model 2		Model 3		Model 4		Model 5	
	FEM	REM	FEM	REM	FEM	REM	FEM	REM	FEM	REM
Const	3.07* [5.80]	2.64* [4.22]	-2.65* [-2.21]	-3.90* [-3.77]	3.85* [7.45]	3.35* [5.25]	-1.333 [-1.05]	0.476 [0.43]	0.69 [0.50]	-2.26* [-2.30]
INV			0.219* [5.42]	0.24* [7.05]					0.13* [3.51]	0.21* [7.39]
DEBT	-0.01 [-1.22]	-0.01 [-0.45]	0.01 [0.004]	0.01 [1.500]	-0.02* [-1.82]	-0.01 [-0.83]	0.01 [0.11]	0.01 [0.13]	-0.01 [-0.68]	0.03* [2.99]
INF					-0.028 [-1.50]	-0.029 [-1.58]			-0.09* [-3.34]	-0.09* [-3.58]
OPEN							0.05* [3.71]	0.025* [2.32]	-0.01 [-0.05]	-0.01* [-2.16]
R^2	0.01	0.01	0.10	0.12	0.20	0.01	0.16	0.01	0.32	0.18
Obs	376	376	342	342	336	336	365	365	303	303
Hausman test	3.7469 (0.0529)		6.2104 (0.0448)		7.5523 (0.0229)		12.7478 (0.0017)		24.3492 (0.0001)	

Notes The t-statistics are in parentheses below the coefficients; * significant at 5%

examination of various methodologies to capture the multifaceted nature of this relationship.

Interestingly, Models 1, 2, and 4 do not provide substantial evidence of public debt's impact. This lack of consistent findings across models raises questions about the robustness of the relationship between public debt and economic growth in this study. It prompts a closer examination of potential factors contributing to this discrepancy, such as data limitations, model specifications, or other unaccounted variables.

Moreover, Openness demonstrates a significant influence on economic growth at the 5% significance level in Model 4, and it achieves a 5% significance level in Model 5. These nuanced findings suggest that the relationship between openness and economic growth is contingent on the econometric approach. The variations in significance levels across models emphasize the importance of considering different methodological approaches when assessing the impact of these variables on economic growth in developing countries. Policymakers and researchers should acknowledge the complexity of these relationships and approach their analyses with a nuanced understanding of the diverse factors at play.

4.2 The Upper-Middle-Income Economies

Delving into the insights provided by Table 4 enriches our understanding of the research outcomes. However, the Hausman test suggests that REM is better than FEM in regressions. In Models 1, 3, and 4, Investment appears to have no discernible effect, but its significance is notably established at the 5% level in Models 2 and 5. This inconsistency reinforces the notion that the relationship between investment and economic growth is contingent on the specific modeling choices made, underlining the importance of methodological considerations in interpreting these results.

Within Models 3 and 5, the study reveals a substantial effect of Inflation at the 5% level, indicating the importance of considering inflation dynamics in the economic growth equation. The recognition of inflation as a significant factor underscores the complex nature of economic environments in developing countries, where inflationary pressures can significantly influence overall economic performance. Policymakers should take note of these nuanced findings when crafting monetary and fiscal policies to ensure sustainable and inclusive economic growth.

A consistent and noteworthy finding is the significant impact of public debt on economic growth, consistently observed at the 1% significance level across all models. This robust and pervasive influence suggests that public debt plays a crucial role in shaping the economic growth trajectory of the examined developing countries. Policymakers must navigate this intricate relationship carefully, weighing the benefits of utilizing public debt for developmental purposes against the potential risks of overleveraging.

Furthermore, the role of Openness in influencing economic growth comes to the forefront, with a significant impact observed at the 5% significance level in Model

Table 4 The upper-middle-income economies

Variable	Model 1		Model 2		Model 3		Model 4		Model 5	
	FEM	REM	FEM	REM	FEM	REM	FEM	REM	FEM	REM
Const	5.63* [6.41]	5.53* [6.17]	-0.33 [-0.20]	0.22 [0.13]	6.25* [7.62]	6.23* [7.02]	2.34 [1.45]	3.24* [2.30]	-0.26 [0.12]	0.40 [0.02]
INV			0.18* [4.09]	0.17* [4.01]					0.13* [3.15]	0.13* [3.19]
DEBT	-0.05* [-2.95]	-0.05* [-0.45]	-0.03* [-1.86]	-0.03* [-2.27]	-0.06* [-3.52]	-0.05* [-3.82]	-0.05* [-2.80]	-0.05* [-3.33]	-0.04* [-2.39]	0.04* [-2.90]
INF					-0.02 [-6.71]	-0.02* [-6.60]			-0.02* [-6.12]	-0.02* [-6.06]
OPEN							0.03* [2.24]	0.02* [2.19]	0.02 [1.48]	0.02 [1.51]
R^2	0.15	0.03	0.19	0.07	0.26	0.14	0.16	0.04	0.29	0.18
Obs	339	339	321	321	338	338	339	339	320	320
Hausman test	0.3418 (0.5588)		0.8797 (0.6441)		2.8273 (0.2432)		0.7746 (0.6789)		0.5842 (0.3584)	

Notes The t-statistics are in parentheses below the coefficients; * significant at 5%

Table 5 The full panel of developing countries

Variable	Model 1		Model 2		Model 3		Model 4		Model 5	
	FEM	REM	FEM	REM	FEM	REM	FEM	REM	FEM	REM
Const	3.96* [8.52]	3.99* [7.17]	-1.71 [-1.71]	-1.76 [-1.83]	4.97* [1.03]	4.81* [8.77]	0.35* [0.34]	1.64* [1.85]	0.02 [0.16]	0.07 [0.06]
INV			0.20* [6.60]	0.21* [7.17]					0.12* [4.43]	0.14* [5.26]
DEBT	-0.02* [-2.66]	-0.02* [-2.54]	-0.01 [-1.81]	-0.01* [-1.17]	-0.04* [-3.96]	-0.03* [-3.73]	-0.01* [-1.74]	-0.02* [-2.11]	-0.03* [-2.76]	-0.02* [-2.69]
INF					-0.02* [-7.90]	-0.02* [-7.69]			-0.02* [-7.52]	-0.01* [-7.35]
OPEN							0.04* [3.86]	0.02* [3.14]	0.01 [1.34]	0.01 [1.13]
R^2	0.13	0.01	0.20	0.08	0.24	0.10	0.16	0.02	0.29	0.15
Obs	715	715	663	663	672	672	704	704	623	623
Hausman test	0.7873 (0.3749)		0.2244 (0.8938)		8.9487 (0.0114)		5.7039 (0.0577)		6.1069 (0.1913)	

Notes The t-statistics are in parentheses below the coefficients; * significant at 5%

4. This underscores the relevance of international trade and economic openness in fostering economic development. As developing nations increasingly integrate into the global economy, the findings suggest that policies promoting trade and openness can be vital drivers of economic growth.

The nuanced dynamics revealed in Table 3 underscore the intricate interplay between key economic variables, highlighting the need for a comprehensive and multifaceted approach when formulating policies. The consistency of findings across various models enhances the reliability of the conclusions, reinforcing the importance of considering a range of factors to gain a holistic understanding of the complex relationship between public debt, investment, inflation, openness, and economic growth in developing nations. Policymakers and researchers alike should heed these insights to inform evidence-based decision-making and to address the unique challenges faced by developing economies.

4.3 The Full Panel of Developing Economies

The broader examination across all developing countries reaffirms and extends the observed patterns within the upper-middle-income country group. The Hausman test suggests that FEM is better than REM in models 3 and 4. However, it confirms that REM is better than REM in models 1, 2, and 5). The consistent alignment of outcomes underscores a substantial impact of public debt on economic growth, robustly significant at the 5% level across all models. This persistent finding across diverse developing nations highlights the universal relevance of public debt dynamics in shaping economic trajectories.

The impact of Investment, however, remains selective, manifesting solely in Models 2 and 5. This selective influence suggests nuanced relationships that may be contingent on specific economic circumstances or policy contexts. In contrast, the significance of Openness persists in Model 4 at the 5% level, emphasizing the enduring role of international trade and economic openness in influencing economic growth.

The trend line depicted in Figs. 1b and 1c illustrates a downward slope, indicating a negative impact of public debt on economic growth in both upper income developing countries and the entire sample. However, it exhibits an upward slope in lower income developing countries, suggesting a positive effect of public debt on economic growth in this category.

Intriguingly, Fig. 1a reveals an upward slope in lower-income developing countries, implying a positive correlation between public debt and economic growth within this category. This intriguing dichotomy suggests that the relationship between public debt and economic growth may vary based on income levels, necessitating a nuanced approach in policy formulation tailored to the specific economic context of each category.

This heightened slope depicted in Fig. 1b, following the trajectory observed in Fig. 1c, signifies a more pronounced negative relationship between public debt and economic growth across most countries. The graphical representation in Fig. 1b and 1c enhances the narrative, depicting a downward slope indicative of a negative correlation between public debt and economic growth in both upper-middle-income developing countries and the overall sample. While the inverse correlation persists in

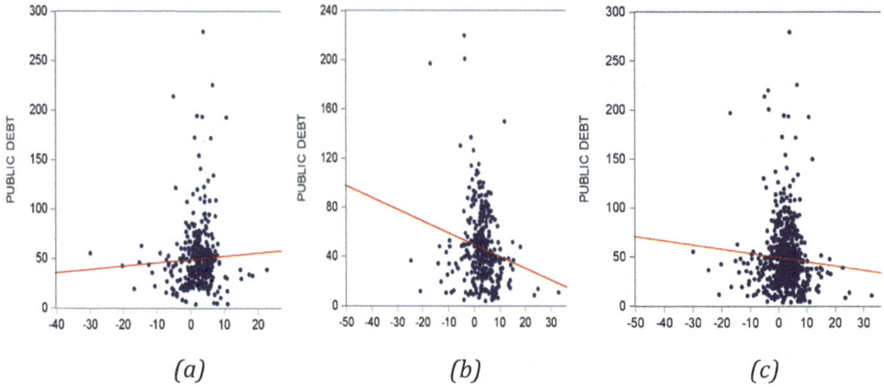

Fig. 1 The relationship between public debt and economic growth in the lower-middle-income group (**a**), upper-middle-income group (**b**), and full sample (**c**)

nearly all nations, the strength of this association appears less robust when compared to high-income countries. This suggests that, although public debt tends to impact economic growth adversely in various economies, the degree of correlation is notably less pronounced in contexts with lower income levels.

The contrast becomes particularly evident when examining lower-income countries, where an intriguing pattern emerges. Here, a clear inverse relationship prevails, indicating that as income levels decrease, the ratio of public debt also diminishes. This nuanced observation challenges the conventional wisdom surrounding public debt and economic growth, suggesting that the dynamics between these variables may be intricately linked to the specific economic conditions prevalent in lower-income nations.

The divergent trends showcased in Fig. 1c underscore the complexity of the relationship between public debt and economic growth, emphasizing the necessity for nuanced policy considerations tailored to the unique circumstances of each income group. This nuanced perspective becomes crucial for policymakers aiming to navigate the intricate interplay between public debt and economic growth in diverse economic landscapes.

5 Conclusion and Policy Implications

The results of the research project indicate that an increase in public debt leads to a decrease in economic growth in high-income countries, but an increase in public debt contributes to improved economic growth in lower to middle-income countries. Thus, the study suggests that public debt may not be inherently detrimental to countries; rather, its impact depends on the level of development. Based on the results, the study provides some policy implications. It suggests that the impact of public debt on economic growth varies across different income levels, necessitating tailored approaches for policymakers.

In lower-middle-income countries, public debt is seen as a potential tool to spur economic growth. These nations may lack sufficient financial resources for critical infrastructure development, social programs, and other key investments. Public debt, when managed prudently, can provide the necessary capital to fund these initiatives, fostering economic development, job creation, and poverty reduction. Policymakers in such countries may view borrowing as a strategic means to address developmental gaps and kickstart their economies.

However, a cautionary note arises when considering upper-middle-income countries. At this stage of economic development, these nations might already have achieved a certain level of infrastructure and social development. Excessive reliance on public debt in these contexts may lead to diminishing returns and pose risks to economic stability. Policymakers in upper-middle-income countries need to be cautious about accumulating too much debt, as it could potentially hinder further growth and leave the economy vulnerable to financial shocks.

The result highlights the importance of a balanced and context-specific approach to public debt management. Policymakers must carefully assess their country's economic conditions, debt capacity, and the potential impact of borrowing on long-term sustainability. Effective fiscal policies should be crafted to align with the unique challenges and opportunities present in each income group. Additionally, the research emphasizes the need for continuous monitoring and adjustment of debt management strategies as countries progress through different income brackets to ensure sustained and inclusive economic growth.

References

1. Panizza, U., Presbitero, A.F.: Public debt and economic growth: Is there a causal effect? J. Macroecon. **41**, 21–41 (2014)
2. Ndoricimpa, A.: Threshold effects of debt on economic growth in Africa. Afr. Dev. Rev. **29**(3), 471–484 (2017)
3. Woo, J., Kumar, M.S.: Public debt and growth. Economica **82**(328), 705–739 (2015)
4. Augustine, B., Rafi, O.P.C.M.: Public debt—economic growth nexus in emerging and developing economies: exploring nonlinearity. Financ. Res. Lett. **52**, 103540 (2023)
5. Tung, L.T., Hoang, L.: N: impact of R&D expenditure on economic growth: evidence from emerging economies. J. Sci. Technol. Policy Manag. **15**(3), 636–654 (2024)
6. Raghutla, C.: The effect of trade openness on economic growth: some empirical evidence from emerging market economies. J. Public Aff. **20**(3), e2081 (2020)
7. Nor-Eddine, O., Driss, C.: External public debt and economic growth in Morocco: assessment and Impacts. Intern. J. Econ. Sci. **8**(2), 80–95 (2019)
8. Huchet-Bourdon, M., Le Mouël, C., Vijil, M.: The relationship between trade openness and economic growth: some new insights on the openness measurement issue. World Economy **41**(1), 59–76 (2018)
9. Keho, Y.: The impact of trade openness on economic growth: the case of Cote d'Ivoire. Cogent Econ. Fina. **5**(1), 1332820 (2017)
10. Serrão, A.: Impact of public debt on economic growth in advanced economies. Intern. J. Manag. Stud. Res. **4**(2), 70–77 (2016)

11. Ahlborn, M., Schweickert, R.: public debt and economic growth – Economic Systems Matter, Working paper (2016)
12. Azam, M., Emirullah, C., Prabhakar, A.C., Qayyum Khan, A.: The role of external debt in economic growth of Indonesia—a blessing or burden? World Appl. Sci. J. **25**(8), 1150–1157 (2013)
13. IMF.: Data. https://www.imf.org/en/Data, last accessed 2023/12/26 (2023)
14. World Bank.: Data. https://data.worldbank.org/indicator, last accessed 2023/10/11 (2023)
15. World Bank.: New World Bank country classifications by income level: 2022–2023, last accessed 2023/11/05 (2022)

Diversity and Bank Performance in Transition Economies: The Mediating Role of State Ownership

Doan Ngan Ha, Duong Dang Khoa, and Pham Ha

Abstract This study examines the effect of diversification on commercial banks' performance in Vietnam, a transitional economy. The diversification of commercial banks in Vietnam has problems due to the size of the economy and the macro-strategies that focus on state-owner involvement in business. By employing data from 37 Vietnamese commercial banks, the endogeneity problem is controlled; the study finds that diversification negatively affects bank performance. Interestingly, the existence of state ownership is evidence that banks should reduce their efforts to boost their performance. Moreover, the robustness shows that liquidity changes its effects on bank performance in terms of the involvement of state-owners. The findings can be evidence to policymakers to make a transparent and competitive banking sector in Vietnam.

Keywords Diversification · Mediating role of state ownership · Performance · Transition economies

1 Introduction

Previous studies show that government-owned banks are less efficient [1], and this statement also argues state ownership is costly to banks in transition economies [2]. As the transition towards market-oriented economies, financial liberalization was performed from the 1990s, but in some countries, the state-owned banks remained dominant players and were defined as the key supporters of state-owned enterprises

D. N. Ha · D. D. Khoa
Faculty of Finance and Banking, Ton Duc Thang University, Ho Chi Minh City, Vietnam
e-mail: doannganha@tdtu.edu.vn

D. D. Khoa
e-mail: duongdangkhoa@tdtu.edu.vn

P. Ha (✉)
Ho Chi Minh City Open University, Ho Chi Minh City, Vietnam
e-mail: ha.p@ou.edu.vn

L. T. Tung et al. (eds.), *Disruptive Technology and Business Continuity*,
https://doi.org/10.1007/978-981-97-5452-6_22

with cheaper funding [3]. In 2007, Vietnam implemented a reform program for the banking sector. It reduced the state ownership proportions in commercial banks and supported the privatization process of state-owned banks. Still, state ownership in commercial banks plays an important role in supporting them in obtaining cheap funding from the government and the central bank.

Commercial banks are defined as the bridge to connect the depositors and creditors in the economy, which means their main income comes from the interest income; diversification is discussed as the method to reduce bank risk-taking and to increase bank efficiency and performance. Vietnam was recognized as an emerging market, and transitioning to a market-oriented economy created more opportunities for the private sector to set up new businesses. In parallel, the credit demand soared when the financial market slowly developed. Commercial banks are less motivated to diversify their services when they are the key players in the market, and the net interest margin (NIM) tends to be larger in this market.

As a transitional country, the financial market in Vietnam has recently developed, and the banking system plays a critical role in the economy. The government would like to interfere and be deeply involved in banking management. As a result, this trend has different impacts due to the government's policy and the restructuring of banks. A typical example is that the banking sector needs various changes in supervision and administration after the financial crisis of 2007–2008. It affects not only developed nations but also developing countries and emerging economies based on previous findings, such as Ho and Vo [4], Duho et al. [5], and Adu [6]. Therefore, establishing an effective banking system is a prerequisite to stabilizing the financial market and promoting economic development.

Besides, Vietnam embarked on participating in and becoming the World Trade Organization's membership 150th in 2006. Therefore, the Vietnamese market took various steps towards the liberalization and reform of the formal financial sector under Decision No. 1577/QD-NHNN dated August 9, 2006. As a result, the year 2010, total assets and profit of the banking system in 2010 grew 10 and 20 times compared with 2001, respectively. However, a considerable increase faced various problems, for example, a high bad debt ratio of 2.16%. In 2016, the banking system in Vietnam embarked on applying Basel II. Complying with Basel II's strict requirements guarantees that banks may operate securely and follow the developing markets' global standards. By doing this—credit, market, and potential operational risks could be reduced. Capital was an important obstacle for commercial banks in fulfilling requirements and following Basel II guidelines.

The study discusses the effects of income diversification and ownership on bank performance, focusing on the net interest margin to capture the main business of the commercial banking sector in Vietnam. Since the primary income of commercial banks in Vietnam is from the lending business, income diversification can influence the bank's net interest margin. From that aspect, the study is different from previous studies in that we explain the mediating role of state ownership in association with income diversification and liquidity on bank net interest margin. State ownership in banks is controversial, with different results, but the findings of this study show that the mediating role of ownership has a negative influence on net interest margin.

The rest of this study is structured as follows. Session 2 defines the literature review. Section 3 is the research methodology. The empirical is Sect. 4, and the last section is the conclusion.

2 Literature Review

Bank diversification theory is derived from diversification theory in the financial sector and a strategic approach based on cost–benefit analysis. There is an argument that diversification reduces risk concentration and, therefore, the possibility of financial distress.

Deng and Elyasiani [31] analyze the diversification characteristics of US banks from 1994 to 2005 and find that larger institutional ownership positively affects diversification leading to lower risk. Abedifar et al. [7] also investigated US banks and modeled the link between non-interest income sources and credit risk—they found no strong link between the two outside of banks. Smaller participation in fiduciary activities tends to reduce credit risk. Elsa et al. [8] find that diversification increases the profitability of banks and, thus, their market value. Sawada [9] reports positive evidence that revenue diversification increases the market value of banks but has no significant mitigating effect on banking risk in Japan.

The impact of state ownership on bank performance can be broadly divided into three categories. The first category investigates the effects of state ownership by looking at the financial and economic trends occurring in various nations. The second classification looks at the impact of state ownership concerning potential distinctions between the lending practices of state banks and private banks. In the third category, researchers investigate how a specific event, such as presidential elections, affects state banks' performance or behavior compared to private banks. If the objectives of multiple shareholders are not aligned, state ownership may impact bank performance. Numerous empirical studies have investigated the impact of state ownership in the banking sector. To examine the links between the size of state ownership and the degree of banking development, Barth et al. [10] gathered data on several nations. The authors asserted that government ownership has a detrimental effect on the performance of several commercial enterprises, including banks, non-banks, and securities markets, and that state ownership of banks is more closely related to poorly run capital markets, which has a detrimental effect on long-term growth.

State ownership tends to concentrate on emerging economies or developing countries. State ownership is worthless because of political interference and weakened managerial incentives compared to foreign and private banks. It can be seen that previous empirical research illustrated that state-owned banks showed lower financial performance due to worthless corporate governance and high levels of risk based on Kim and Lee [11] in Korea and China. On the other hand, these results contradicted the work in which some researchers found a positive relation between state ownership and bank performance. Ownership structure is one of the most powerful tools that affects banks' performance. When the government has supported commercial banks, they could easily approach capital and central banks [12].

Banks exist as a bridge to the gap between depositors and borrowers. Bank income could be recorded from various sources, such as interest, fees, commission, etc. Although lending is risky and competitive among commercial banks, the problem is how banks could diversify their earnings. This is a typical example of banks' inflow that can not only depend on traditional products, for example, deposits and loans. In addition, diverse income could minimize risk by limiting risky decisions. Therefore, diversification is a positive aspect of bank performance based on studies by Nisar et al. [13] in South Asia from 2000 to 2014 and Mateev and Bachvarov [14] in the MENA region.

Whereas management expertise and government policy have become banks' drawbacks, diversified income pressures senior managers and affects bank performance. It could be proved through different results, such as Stiroh and Rumble [15] and Lepetit et al. [16] with the negative aspect and Nguyen et al. [17], Meslier et al. [18] in the opposite view.

It is hard to diversify capital in transition economies, which is why the economy tends to belong to bank services. Thus, Vietnamese commercial banks concentrated on traditional products despite diversification activity.

Indeed, diversification activity has been a significant trend in banking management, but the recent research on the determination of bank net interest margins has not adequately demonstrated the consequences of diversification. As a result, the primary aim of the present result is to explore how the diversification income of banks affects the determinants of net interest margins, for example, Vietnamese commercial banks.

3 Research Methodology

3.1 Data Selection

We collected data from audited consolidated financial statements and annual reports of 37 Vietnamese commercial banks from 2010 to 2020 since the Vietnam Central Bank applied a restructuring program to make sure that all domestic commercial banks can reach a minimum regulatory capital (or the equity of bank) by 3,000 billion Vietnam dongs or 162.3 million USD approximately (the exchange rate USD/VND was 18,479.1 in 2010). The data was selected from the full financial statements, including the balance sheet, income statement, cash flow statement, and financial statement explanation. We obtain the inflation variable from the General Statistics Office of Vietnam since the central bank applies its monetary policy to support the government in controlling inflation and in supporting the development of the economy, so the effects of inflation on net interest margin are recognized as a critical component, we define it as the macro factor on bank performance.

3.2 Variable Definitions

Bank performance: Almarzoqi and Nacuer [19] indicate that net interest margins (NIMs) are recognized as the intermediation efficiency since it is derived from the difference between interest income and interest expense (or we define it as the net interest income as Lepetit et al. [16], Nguyen et al. [20], Ho and Vo [4]). The economy and business in Vietnam relied on bank credits, and NIM can be recognized as the main source of income for banks in Vietnam.

Bank's income diversification: The bank's traditional income focuses mainly on the net interest income. To diversify its profitable activities, it will provide other services and products that rely on the fees and other benefits from nontraditional activities. Based on Stiroh and Rumble [15], Brighi and Venturelli [21], Chiorazzo et al. [22], Ferreira et al. [23], Mercieca et al. [24], the study constructs bank's income diversification by the adjusted Hirshmann-Herfindahl Index (HHI) to measure the bank's income diversification levels (the diversification index). This variable ranges from 0.0 to 0.5; the highest level is 0.5, which explains the full diversification of bank income and vice versa.

Liquidity ratio: Duho et al. [5] and Meng et al. [25] discuss that bank liquidity is a proxy for liquidity risk; banks will take more risk if they focus on their traditional products and fewer incentives to generate non-interest income since they can benefit from the ability of cash and cash equivalent to providing credit products to the economy and business. This ratio is used by Duho et al. [5] and Meng et al. [25].

Equity ratio: according to the restructuring program of the Vietnam Central Bank, all commercial banks need to raise their equity to ensure that they can reduce the risk-taking in their main business from deposit and credit products from 2010. Following Ho and Vo [4], Meng et al. [25], and Nguyen et al. [20], we define the equity ratio as a proxy to measure the bank's capacity to provide credit products to the economy.

Bank size: DeYoung and Rice [26], Duho et al. [5], Meng et al. [25], Mercieca et al. [24], Nguyen et al. [20] define the logarithm of total assets as the bank size, this variable is to measure the bank scale and if this scale is increasing, this implies that banks have more power to deal with their customers and they can increase their NIM to maximize their profitability.

State Ownership: Barth et al. [10] and Figueira (2006) study takes the proportion of state ownership in banks to measure the involvement of the state/government in bank performance.

The establishment of banks: to measure the experience of banks and their expansion, we take the gap between the operating year and the establishment of banks. Besides that, inflation is recognized as a proxy for macroeconomic factors that directly affect the decisions of bank executives regarding the deposit and lending rates of banks.

To measure the bank performance, we follow Lee et al. [11] and Phan et al. (2022) to construct the estimation model as:

$$Y_{i,t} = \beta_0 + \beta_1 Y_{i,t-1} + \beta Z_{i,t} + \beta_3 W_t + \varepsilon_{i,t} \tag{1}$$

Table 1 Variable definitions

Variables	Definition	Measurement	Expected sign
NIM	Net interest margin	$\frac{Netinterestincome}{Totalearningasset}$	
DII	Diversification Index	$1 - \left(\left(\frac{noninterestincome}{Totalincomes}\right)^2 + \left(\frac{interestincome}{Totalincomes}\right)^2\right)$	-
LIQUID	Liquidity ratio	$\frac{Liquidassets}{Totalassets}$	-
EQTA	Equity ratio	$\frac{Totalequity}{Totalassets}$	+
SIZE	Bank size	Log (total assets)	+
OWN	Proportion of State ownership	$\frac{Stateownersshares}{Totalshares}$	-
AGE	Duration of establishment	Number of years of establishment	+
INF	Inflation	Yearly inflation	+

Source Compile by authors

where: $Y_{i,t}$: bank performance (net interest margin), $Y_{i,t-1}$ is the lagged bank performance, $Z_{i,t}$: set of bank specified variables as shown in Table 1- including diversification index (DII), liquidity ratio (LIQUID), Equity ratio (EQTA), bank size (SIZE), Proportion of State ownership (OWN) and Duration of establishment (AGE), W_t: yearly inflation (INF).

3.3 Estimation Strategies

Arellano and Bover [27] and Blundell and Bond [28] proposed the system generalized method of moments (GMM) estimator to solve problems with distinct GMMs. There are several advantages to using system GMM estimates. First, the differences were not correlated even though the extent of the independent variables essentially correlated with bank-specific fixed effects. Second, pseudo-time variables can be included to control for time-specific effects and to eliminate cross-dependencies in data and banks. Finally, in the case of unbalanced dashboard data, Roodman [29] points out that it is better to use system GMM and avoid differential GMM estimates. However, System GMM also has two weaknesses. First, the two-step GMM performs estimates of standard errors that tend to be biased. To solve this problem, Wind Meijer [30] used finite pattern correction for a two-step covariance matrix. Roodman [29] showed that this resolution makes two-step GMM estimation more efficient than one-step by specifically using the system GMM regression method. The Hansen Index [32] tests the validity of instrument variables.

Based on the estimation model (1), we will run simultaneously the bank-specific variables to measure the impacts of state-ownership and diversification index on bank performance and the interaction of both variables. To do the robustness test,

Table 2 Descriptive statistics

Variable	OBS	Mean	SD	Min	Max
NIM	329	0.0301328	0.0138106	-0.0066007	0.0945348
DII	329	0.2958837	0.12355	0.000381	0.4999909
EQTA	329	0.0912779	0.0422159	0.0140535	0.2750346
LIQUID	329	0.5592578	0.1294981	0.2223948	0.8074811
SIZE	329	18.51708	1.192851	15.86618	21.17241
OWN	329	0.164947	0.3022949	0	1
INF	329	0.0588561	0.0481186	0.006312	0.1867773
AGE	329	23.61094	11.62763	0	63

Source:Results calculated by the authors

we add the duration of the establishment to capture the bank experience; besides that- we develop the interaction between state ownership and other variables, such as liquidity ratio and the size of the bank, to measure the risk-taking in the presence of state ownership.

4 Experimental Findings

Table 2 lists the descriptive statistics, and Table 3 shows the correlation between the dependent variable and other independent variables.

Table 2 shows that the NIM means is roundly 3%, and the maximum spread is 9.45%, the highest spreads were recorded after the liquidity problem at the beginning of the study period. And the negative spreads are from a bailed-out bank by the central bank.

Standard errors in parentheses. *** $p < 0.01$, ** $p < 0.05$, * $p < 0.1$

The results in Table 4 illustrate that Vietnamese banks have less motivation to diversify their income resources, and state ownership negatively affects bank performance; this evidence is also proven by the positive effects of liquidity ratio on bank performance. The moderating role of state ownership takes banks to pay more attention to traditional products to increase their interest income instead of forcing banks to find other incomes from non-traditional services and products. The robustness test in Table 5 shows that the moderating role in the interaction between state ownership with bank size and liquidity ratio changes the impacts of liquidity and bank size on performance.

Standard errors in parentheses. *** $p < 0.01$, ** $p < 0.05$, * $p < 0.1$

Table 3 Correlation matrix

	NIM	DII	EQTA	LIQUD	SIZE	OWN	INF	AGE
NIM	1.0000							
DII	-0.1956	1.0000						
EQTA	0.3508	-0.0331	1.0000					
LIQUID	0.2533	0.0377	-0.1672	1.0000				
SIZE	0.0095	0.2704	-0.6575	0.3968	1.0000			
OWN	0.0339	0.1651	-0.2536	0.3661	0.5777	1.0000		
INF	0.1946	-0.2038	0.1997	-0.3234	-0.2417	0.0064	1.0000	
AGE	0.1078	0.1833	-0.1900	0.4272	0.4938	0.4587	-0.1301	1.0000

Source Results calculated by the authors

Table 4 Estimation results

VARIABLES	MODEL 1	MODEL 2	MODEL 3	MODEL 4
L.NIM	0.267***	0.559***	0.472***	0.484***
	(0.030)	(0.031)	(0.034)	(0.030)
OWN	-0.019***		-0.012***	
	(0.002)		(0.002)	
LIQUID	0.030***	0.020***	0.019***	0.020***
	(0.004)	(0.001)	(0.002)	(0.003)
EQTA	0.263***	0.122***	0.168***	0.167***
	(0.022)	(0.028)	(0.025)	(0.024)
SIZE	0.008***	0.004***	0.006***	0.006***
	(0.001)	(0.001)	(0.001)	(0.001)
INF	0.095***	0.062***	0.061***	0.057***
	(0.009)	(0.005)	(0.008)	(0.007)
OWN*DII		-0.030***		-0.037***
		(0.005)		(0.007)
DII			-0.025***	-0.023***
			(0.001)	(0.001)
Const	-0.166***	-0.090***	-0.112***	-0.114***
	(0.012)	(0.015)	(0.014)	(0.014)
Observation	279	279	279	279
Number of Banks	36	36	36	36
AR (1)	0.0869	0.00996	0.0300	0.0335
AR (2)	0.192	0.0539	0.242	0.202
Hansen test	0.233	0.992	0.990	0.988

Table 5 Robustness test

VARIABLES	MODEL 5	MODEL 6	MODEL 7	MODEL 8
L.NIM	0.497***	0.497***	0.402***	0.463***
	(0.074)	(0.074)	(0.023)	(0.069)
AGE	0.001***	0.001***	0.000	0.002***
	(0.000)	(0.000)	(0.000)	(0.000)
DII	-0.090***	-0.090***		-0.146***
	(0.013)	(0.013)		(0.012)
LIQUID	0.048***	0.048***		
	(0.012)	(0.012)		
EQTA	0.028	0.028	0.278***	0.151***
	(0.036)	(0.036)	(0.019)	(0.050)
OWN*SIZE	-0.002***	-0.002***		
	(0.000)	(0.000)		
INF	0.100***	0.100***	0.039***	0.117***
	(0.009)	(0.009)	(0.007)	(0.014)
OWN*LIQUID			-0.006	-0.080***
			(0.004)	(0.010)
SIZE			0.006***	0.008***
			(0.001)	(0.002)
Const	-0.013	-0.013	-0.127***	-0.149***
	(0.009)	(0.009)	(0.014)	(0.038)
Observation	279	279	279	279
Number of Banks	36	36	36	36
AR (1)	0.00559	0.00559	0.194	0.00121
AR (2)	0.685	0.685	0.260	0.680
Hansen test	0.463	0.463	0.214	0.250

5 Conclusion

The study investigates the diversity of bank income and the state ownership on the bank performance, which employs the net interest margin as a proxy due to the large income of Vietnamese banks on the traditional products as an intermediation role. The results state that banks continue to have their main income from traditional products, and the presence of state ownership is not expected to support banks' development. Even though all banks do not cover state ownership, the involvement of state ownership is a barrier to making the banking sector more transparent and competitive.

Author contribution statement:

Doan Ngan Ha (doannganha@tdtu.edu.vn) conceived, designed, and performed the experiments.

Duong Dang Khoa (duongdangkhoa@tdtu.edu.vn) performed the experiments.

Pham Ha (ha.p@ou.edu.vn) wrote the first and final drafts of the manuscript.

Acknowledgements We also thank anonymous reviewers for their constructive feedback, which helps us revise our manuscript. This study was supported by Ton Duc Thang University and Ho Chi Minh City Open University.

Ethics Statement This study does not involve animals or humans.

Data Availability Statement: The data used to support the findings of this study are available from the corresponding author upon request.

Conflict of Interest Statement: None of the authors have a conflict of interest to disclose.

References

1. Bonin, J.P., Hasan, I., Wachtel, P.: Privatization matters: bank efficiency in transition countries. NYU Working Paper No. S-FI-04–04, (March 2004). Available at SSRN: https://ssrn.com/abstract=1297739, last accessed 2023/09/05
2. Sherif, K., Borish, M., Gross, A.: State-owned Banks in the Transition: Origins, Evolution, and Policy Responses, World Bank Publications - Books, The World Bank Group, number 14851 (2003)
3. Le, P.T., Harvie, C., Arjomandi, A., Borthwick, J.: Financial liberalisation, bank ownership type and performance in a transition economy: the case of Vietnam. Pacific-Basin Fin. J. **57**, 101182–1–101182–17 (2019)
4. Ho, T., Vo, Q.: The relationship between market power and income diversity with ownership structure as a moderator–a study of Vietnamese commercial banks. Asian J. Econ. Busin. Account. **10**(3), 1–16 (2019). https://doi.org/10.9734/ajeba/2019/v10i330106
5. Duho, K.C.T., Onumah, J.M., Asare, E.T.: Determinants and convergence of income diversification in Ghanaian banks. J. Res. Emerg. Mark. **2**(2), 34–47 (2020). https://doi.org/10.30585/jrems.v2i2.499
6. Adu, D.A.: How do board and ownership characteristics affect bank risk-taking? New evidence from sub-Saharan Africa. J. Banking Regul., 1–25 (2023). https://doi.org/10.1057/s41261-023-00226-7
7. Abedifar, P., Molyneux, P., Tarazi, A.: Non-interest income and bank lending. J. Bank. Finance **87**, 411–426 (2018)
8. Elsas, R., Hackethal, A., Holzhäuser, M.: The anatomy of bank diversification. J. Bank. Fina. **34**, 1274–1287 (2010)
9. Sawada, M.: How does the stock market value bank diversification? Empirical evidence from Japanese banks. Pac. Basin Financ. J. **25**, 40–61 (2013)
10. Barth, M.E., Beaver, W.H., Landsman, W.R.: The relevance of the value relevance literature for financial accounting standard setting: another view. J. Account. Econ. **31**(1–3), 77–104 (2001)
11. Lee, J.Y., Kim, D.: Bank performance and its determinants in Korea. Jpn. World Econ. **27**, 83–94 (2013). https://doi.org/10.1016/j.japwor.2013.05.001

12. Nassar, K.B., Edder Martinez, E., Pineda, A.: Determinants of Banks' Net Interest Margins in Honduras. IMF working paper WP/14/163. (2014). https://www.imf.org/external/pubs/ft/wp/2014/wp14163.pdf, last accessed 2023/09/15
13. Nisar, S., Peng, P., Wang, S., Ashraf, A.N.: The impact of revenue diversification on bank profitability and stability: empirical evidence from South Asian Countries. Intern. J. Finan. Stud. **6** (2), 40 (2018). https://doi.org/10.3390/ijfs6020040
14. Mateev, M., Bachvarov, P.: Regulation, ownership and bank performance in the MENA region: evidence for Islamic and conventional banks. Emerg. Markets Rev. Elsevier 47(C) (2021)
15. Stiroh, K.J., Rumble, A.: The dark side of diversification: the case of US financial holding companies. J. Bank. Finance **30**(8), 2131–2161 (2006). https://doi.org/10.1016/j.jbankfin.2005.04.030
16. Lepetit, L., Nys, E., Rous, P., Tarazi, A.: The expansion of services in European banking: implications for loan pricing and interest margins. J. Bank. Fin. **32**(11), 2325–2335 (2008). https://doi.org/10.1016/j.jbankfin.2007.09.025
17. Nguyen, M., Perera, S., Skully, M.: Bank market power and revenue diversification: evidence from selected ASEAN countries. J. Asian Econ. **23**, 1–31 (2012). https://doi.org/10.2139/ssrn.1949548
18. Meslier, C., Tacneng, R., Tarazi, A.: Is bank income diversification beneficial? Evidence from an emerging economy. J. Int. Finan. Markets. Inst. Money **31**, 97–126 (2014)
19. Almarzoqi, R., Naceur, S.B.: Determinants of bank interest margins in the Caucasus and Central Asia, IMF working paper no. WP/15/87 (2015) https://www.imf.org/external/pubs/ft/wp/2015/wp1587.pdf, last accessed 2016/11/21
20. Nguyen, M., Perera, S., Skully, M.: Bank market power, ownership, regional presence and revenue diversification: evidence from Africa. Emerg. Mark. Rev. **27**, 36–62 (2016). https://doi.org/10.1016/j.ememar.2016.03.001
21. Brighi, P., Venturelli, V.: How functional and geographic diversification affect bank profitability during the crisis. Financ. Res. Lett. **16**, 1–10 (2016). https://doi.org/10.1016/j.frl.2015.10.020
22. Chiorazzo, V., Milani, C., Salvini, F.: Income diversification and bank performance. J. Fin. Serv. Res. **33**(3), 181–203 (2008). https://doi.org/10.1007/s10693-008-0029-4
23. Ferreira, J.H.L., Zanini, F., Alves, T.W.: Bank revenue diversification: its impact on risk and return in Brazilian banks. Revista Contabilidade Finanças **30**(79), 91–106 (2019). https://doi.org/10.1590/1808-057x201805810
24. Mercieca, S., Schaeck, K., Wolfe, S.: Small European banks: benefits from diversification? J. Bank. Finance **31**(7), 1975–1998 (2007). https://doi.org/10.1016/j.jbankfin.2007.01.004
25. Meng, X., Cavoli, T., Deng, X.: Determinants of income diversification: evidence from Chinese banks. Appl. Econ. Taylor Francis Group **50**(17), 1934–1951 (2018). https://doi.org/10.1080/00036846.2017.1383594
26. DeYoung, R., Rice, T.: Non-interest income and financial performance at US commercial banks. Finan. Rev. **39**(1), 101–127 (2004). https://doi.org/10.1111/j.0732-8516.2004.00069.x
27. Arellano, M., Bover, O.: Another look at the instrumental variable estimation of error-components models. J. Econom. **68**, 29–35 (1995)
28. Blundell, R., Bond, S.: Initial conditions and moment restrictions in dynamic panel data models. J. Economet. **87**, 115–143 (1998)
29. Rood man, D.: How to do xtabond2: An introduction to difference and system GMM in Stata. Stata J. **9**(1), 86–136 (2009)
30. Meijer, F.W.: A finite sample correction for the variance of linear efficient twostep GMM estimators. J. Economet. **126**, 25–51 (2005)
31. Deng, S., Elyasiani, E.: Geographic diversification, bank holding company value, and risk. J. Money, Credit, Bank. **40**(6), 1217–1238 (2008)
32. Hansen, L.P.: Large sample properties of generalized method of moments estimators. Economet. J. Economet. Soc., 1029–1054 (1982)

Trading Strategies in the Ho Chi Minh Stock Exchange

Thach H. Pham and Thi Minh Hue Phan

Abstract This study examines the efficacy of stock selection techniques by analyzing the impact of several factors on stock returns. The evaluation of strategies' effectiveness is conducted through the utilization of both non-parametric and parametric tests. The non-parametric test employs a t-test, while the parametric test utilizes alpha, which represents the intercept of the chosen risk factor model. The research conducted revealed that both long and arbitrage strategies exhibit favorable returns and good alphas within the context of the Ho Chi Minh Stock Exchange (HSX). The outperformance of the market is observed when purchasing small-size stocks with high Value-at-Risk, as evidenced by the performance of the SHVaR portfolio. This specific strategy yields the greatest return, roughly 2.38% on a monthly basis, surpassing other methods. This suggests that the efficiency of the HSX may be suboptimal, and the solutions proposed in this paper are expected to assist investors in achieving favorable returns. The findings of this paper provide valuable practical implications. Initially, policymakers have the capacity to employ risk factors as a means of assessing the efficacy of the market. Furthermore, investors have the ability to choose stocks for their portfolios by considering the connection between stock returns and their respective qualities.

Keywords Asset pricing · Portfolio performance · Stock market · Stock selection · Trading strategies

1 Introduction

Numerous variables have been developed in order to elucidate the variations in stock returns [1, 2]. Nevertheless, it is worth noting that several factor models have been examined primarily within the United States, reflecting a tendency towards home bias, or in developed markets outside of the United States, indicating a foreign bias

T. H. Pham (✉) · T. M. H. Phan
Ho Chi Minh City Open University, 35-37 Ho Hao Hon Street, District 1, Ho Chi Minh City, Vietnam
e-mail: thach.ph@ou.edu.vn; lncs@springer.com

L. T. Tung et al. (eds.), *Disruptive Technology and Business Continuity*,
https://doi.org/10.1007/978-981-97-5452-6_23

[3]. Hence, it might be argued that these models may not be suitable for implementation in developing nations due to the disparities in market systems. According to Jacobs and Müller [4], and Mclean and Pontiff [5], it has been observed that the diminishing significance of some parameters might be attributed to their publishing.

Lo and MacKinlay [6] express skepticism regarding the notion that variables in asset pricing models are just a result of data snooping. In order to address this issue, Aziz and Ansari [7] utilize information from several marketplaces and sample periods to support their findings. Hanauer and Lauterbach [3] recommended employing developing market samples in empirical asset pricing research to mitigate the influence of "home bias" and "foreign bias". Therefore, the utilization of data from the HSX to evaluate factor models is regarded as an out-of-sample examination in literature.

This study examines several stock selection methods, including static beta, dynamic beta, company size, company value, momentum, illiquidity, Value-at-Risk (VaR), and conditional Value-at-Risk (CVaR), in order to identify profitable returns and propose effective trading techniques. This facilitates the utilization of market data by investors to develop equilibrium models and implement these methods in their trading activity inside the HSX, hence yielding enhanced profits. The technique proposed in this study has the potential for use in other markets.

2 Theoretical Basis

Patterns in stock returns have been identified by researchers. According to Harvey [2], a substantial number of financial anomalies, over 400, have been identified and documented. The various categories of assets are commonly referred to as styles, and the distribution of funds among these styles is known as style investing [8]. Hence, comprehending the determinants of stock returns can assist investors in making informed decisions when selecting equities for their investment portfolios.

According to Sharpe [9], a positive correlation exists between anticipated returns and systematic risk, as measured by static beta. However, some studies have indicated that there exists no significant correlation between static beta and stock returns [10, 11]. Engle [12] introduced a method known as dynamic conditional correlation (DCC) inside the framework of the GARCH model. This strategy aims to augment the impact of static beta by capturing time-varying correlations across assets, so generating dynamic betas.

It is evident that there exists an inverse relationship between the firm size and their corresponding returns, whereby larger stocks tend to exhibit lower returns compared to smaller equities. The phenomenon being referred to is commonly known as a size anomaly or size effect within the field of finance. The influence of business size may be attributed to several factors, such as information risk [13], financial distress risk [14], or illiquidity risk (Amihud 2002).

Numerous studies have demonstrated that value equities exhibit superior long-term returns compared to growth stocks [3]. According to Fama and French [11,

15], equities exhibiting a high book-to-market ratio tend to provide greater returns compared to stocks with a low book-to-market ratio. This discrepancy in returns may be attributed to the higher level of risk associated with stocks possessing a higher book-to-market ratio.

Rational investors hold the belief that the gains derived from engaging in momentum investing serve as compensation for assuming elevated levels of risk. The present methodology incorporates the concept of momentum as a kind of systematic risk, which is elucidated by risk-based models [16]. The significance of the momentum effect has been seen in both emerging and developed markets, as indicated by the studies conducted by Singh and Walia [17], and Wang et al. [18].

The phenomenon of illiquidity premiums has been posited as a potential explanation for variations in stock returns across different stocks, as discussed in the works of Amihud (2002) and Amihud et al. [25]. Previous empirical research has demonstrated a robust positive correlation between stock returns and illiquidity, as evidenced by studies conducted by Amihud et al. [25] and Chen et al. [26].

3 Methodology

The study examines several stock picks derived from factors such as company size, firm value, momentum, VaR, CVaR, illiquidity, CAPM beta, and DCC beta. Stocks are categorized based on two characteristics. The initial variable that has been arranged in a sorted manner is size, with the firm size median serving as the dividing point. The additional sorted variable represents another attribute, such as firm value, momentum, VaR, CVaR, illiquidity, CAPM beta, and DCC beta. These attributes are divided into two groups based on their 30th and 70th percentiles. Consequently, a total of six portfolios are constructed for each of the following factors: Size-Value, Size-Momentum, Size-VaR, Size-CVaR, Size-Illiquidity, Size-CAPM beta, and Size-DCC beta. The performance of strategies is evaluated by a non-parametric test using a t-test and a parametric test using alpha (the intercept of the selected risk factor model). If the alpha of a strategy is positive, that strategy outperforms the market, and investors can apply it for their trading. If the alpha of a strategy is negative, that strategy underperforms the market, investors can reject it. If the alpha is zero, the return of a strategy is predicted by the market. Details are as follows:

3.1 Variables

The estimation of static beta is conducted by the use of ordinary least squares (OLS) regression across a time period spanning 24 to 36 months, inclusively. The logarithmic returns of equities and the market, namely the VN-index, are being examined.

$$Ln\left(1+R_{i,t}\right)=\alpha_{i,t}+\beta_{i,t}^{CAPM}Ln\left(1+R_{m,t}\right)+\varepsilon_{i,t} \tag{1}$$

The current research employs historical excess monthly returns to calculate the dynamic conditional correlation (DCC) betas for individual companies and the market (VN-index) by utilizing the DCC GARCH model proposed by Engle [12].

The company size variable represents the natural logarithm of the market value, whereas the firm value variable corresponds to the natural logarithm of the book-to-market ratio of stocks. The determination of a stock's book value occurs at the conclusion of the preceding year in December, whereas the market value is derived from the most recent monthly market value during the current year.

$$Size_{i,t}=Ln\left(MV_{i,t-1}\right) \tag{2}$$

$$\mathrm{BTM_{i,t}}=\frac{\mathrm{BV_{i,t-1}}}{\mathrm{MV_{i,t-1}}} \tag{3}$$

$$\mathrm{Value_{i,t}}=\mathrm{Ln}\left(\mathrm{BTM_{i,t}}\right) \tag{4}$$

The calculation of stock momentum involves multiplying the gross returns seen in the 11 months preceding the current month, except the current month itself (referred to as month t). This exclusion is done to distinguish the medium-term momentum from the short-term momentum's reversal impact, as explained by Bali et al. [19].

$$Mom_{i,t}=100\left[\prod_{t-11}^{t-1}\left(R_{i,t}+1\right)-1\right] \tag{5}$$

The calculation of Value at Risk (VaR) employs a time frame ranging from 24 to 36 months, inclusively, and a confidence level of 95 percent. Initially, the calculation of the 5th percentile of the monthly return r_(i,t) (namely, the lower tail representing negative values) is conducted in the subsequent manner:

$$P\left(R_{i,t}<r_{i,t}\right)=5\% \tag{6}$$

3.2 The Downside Risk is Measured by Multiplying the Monthly Value at Risk (VaR) by -1, as Suggested by Bali and Cakici (2004) and Further Supported by Bali Et Al. (2007):

$$VaR_{i,t}=-r_{i,t} \tag{7}$$

Conditional Value at Risk (CVaR) refers to the expected value of losses that exceed the Value at Risk (VaR). CVaR, like VaR, is multiplied by a negative factor of 1. The formula for computing Conditional Value at Risk (CVaR) is as follows:

$$CVaR_{i,t} = -E\left[R_{i,t}|R_{i,t} < r_{i,t}\right] \tag{8}$$

According to Amihud (2002), the monthly illiquidity of a stock may be determined by calculating the ratio of the total absolute value of daily returns to the daily dollar volume traded in the security. This calculation should be averaged across the trading days in each month. The present study addresses the issue of illiquidity by employing the logarithmic form as a means to mitigate the skewness observed in the dataset.

$$\text{Illiq}_{\text{i,t}} = \text{Ln}\left[\frac{1}{\text{D}}\sum_{1}^{\text{D}}\frac{|\text{R}_{\text{i,d}}|}{\text{Vold}_{\text{i,d}}}\right] \tag{9}$$

The MKT represents the performance of the market portfolio, whereas the VN-index (Eikon item HCMNVNE) is a value-weighted index. The Capital Asset Pricing Model (CAPM) utilizes the Market Risk Premium (MKT) as a component in multifactor models to elucidate the reasons behind the phenomenon of average stock returns above the risk-free rate, as discussed by Fama and French in their seminal work in 1993. The SMB (Small Minus Big) and CMA (Conservative Minus Aggressive) factors were introduced by Fama and French in their works published in 1993 and 2015, respectively. These factors represent the size-mimicking and investment-mimicking portfolios, as proposed by Fama and French.

$$\text{MKT}_{\text{t}} = \text{R}_{\text{VNI,t}} - \text{R}_{\text{f}} \tag{10}$$

$$\text{SMB}_t = S_t - B_t \tag{11}$$

$$\text{CMA}_t = Conservative_t - Aggressive_t \tag{12}$$

3.3 *Portfolio Assessments*

Nonparametric and parametric approaches are employed to evaluate the efficacy of long and arbitrage strategies on portfolio returns. The nonparametric approach employs a t-test. The parametric approach employs alpha values, which represent the intercepts of regression models that analyze the returns of long and arbitrage strategies in relation to the returns of the MKT, SMB, and CMA components. T-tests are commonly employed to assess the efficacy of various methods by examining excess returns or returns of arbitrage portfolios. These studies involve both single-sort and double-sort methodologies. The use of the Newey and West (1987) approach is utilized to address the issue of heteroscedasticity in time series analysis. The performance of excess returns of long strategies (R_L-R_F) and the zero-investment returns of arbitrage strategies (R_Z) is benchmarked with the three-factor model as follows:

$$R_L - R_F = \alpha + \beta_{MKT} MKT + \beta_{SMB} SMB + \beta_{CMA} CMA + \epsilon \tag{13}$$

$$R_Z = \alpha + \beta_{MKT} MKT + \beta_{SMB} SMB + \beta_{CMA} CMA + \epsilon \tag{14}$$

3.4 Data

The dataset comprises the stock returns and business characteristics of the 100 biggest non-financial equities listed on the HSX. The data spans a period of 108 months, from January 2011 to December 2019. To ensure the integrity and comparability of our sample, we have opted to remove financial enterprises such as banks, securities firms, insurance companies, and real estate investment entities. This decision is based on the fact that these stocks typically exhibit higher leverage and possess distinct characteristics in terms of their business operations, which may introduce confounding factors when analyzing non-financial equities. Furthermore, the time frame of 2011–2019 has been chosen to mitigate the adverse impact of the worldwide financial crisis that occurred in 2007–2008.

4 Results and Discussion

The returns of the arbitrage techniques that are based on CAPM beta exhibit no significant deviation from zero, as seen in Table 6. Nevertheless, it is seen that the act of purchasing medium-DCC beta companies and then selling low-DCC beta stocks within the large size group (BMDCC-BLDCC) results in a notably favorable return, as indicated in Table 7. Therefore, it may be argued that dynamic beta is a more suitable measure of systematic risk compared to static beta when it comes to elucidating stock returns.

Purchasing stocks of smaller sizes and subsequently selling stocks of larger sizes has been observed to yield significantly positive returns in various scenarios. These scenarios include the acquisition of small-size stocks and the sale of big-size stocks within the medium-value group (SM–BM) as indicated in Table 1, within the up-momentum group (SU–BU) as shown in Table 2, within the high-VaR group

(SHVaR–BHVaR) as presented in Table 3, within the high-CVaR group (SHCVaR–BHCVaR) as outlined in Table 4, and within both the high-illiquid group (SHIlliq–BHIlliq) and medium-illiquid group (SMIlliq–BMIlliq) as depicted in Table 5. This finding provides evidence of the existence of a negative relationship between the size of a corporation and its stock returns.

There is an expectation that the firm value exhibits a positive correlation with its stock returns. This correlation is substantiated by the fact that purchasing medium-value stocks and selling low-value stocks within the small size group (SM-SL) (as shown in Table 1) result in a notably positive rate of return.

There is an expected positive correlation between momentum and stock performance. This correlation is substantiated by the fact that purchasing stocks with upward momentum and selling companies with downward momentum in the small-size group (SU–SD) (as shown in Table 2), as well as buying stocks with neutral velocity and selling stocks with downward momentum in the big-size group (BN–BD) (also shown in Table 2), result in notably favorable returns.

Table 3 provides evidence in favor of the positive relationship between Value at Risk (VaR) and stock returns, as supported by previous research conducted by Aziz and Ansari (2017), Chen et al. [27], and Iqbal and Azher [20]. However, Table 4 contradicts the notion of a negative connection between Conditional Value at Risk

Table 1 Size–value portfolios and strategies (Jan 2011 – Dec 2019)

Panel A: Monthly Returns (%)			
Size Value	Small (S)	Big (B)	S–B
High (H)	1.443*	1.239	0.203
Medium (M)	1.610***	0.519	1.091***
Low (L)	0.440	0.747	− 0.307
H–L	1.003	0.492	*Trading Strategies* *Long strategies* *Arbitrage (firm size)* *Arbitrage (firm value)*
H–M	− 0.167	0.720	
M–L	1.170*	− 0.227	
Panel B: Monthly Alphas (%)			
Size Value	Small (S)	Big (B)	S–B
High (H)	0.828**	1.045*	− 0.216
Medium (M)	1.190***	0.464	0.726***
Low (L)	0.112	0.839***	− 0.728
H–L	0.717	0.205	*Notes: The standard errors are robust using the method developed by Newey and West (1987)*
H–M	− 0.362	0.581	
M–L	1.079*	− 0.375	

Table 2 Size–momentum portfolios and strategies (Jan 2011 – Dec 2019)

Panel A: Monthly Returns (%)			
Size Momentum	Small (S)	Big (B)	S–B
Up (U)	1.941***	0.766	1.174*
Neutral (N)	1.366***	0.582	0.783
Down (D)	0.792	− 0.244	1.036*
U–D	1.149*	1.011	*Trading Strategies* *Long strategies* *Arbitrage (firm size)* *Arbitrage (momentum)*
U–N	0.575	0.184	
N–D	0.574	0.827*	
Panel B: Monthly Alphas (%)			
Size Momentum	Small (S)	Big (B)	S–B
Up (U)	1.599***	0.872*	0.727
Neutral (N)	0.967***	0.580	0.387
Down (D)	0.163	− 0.340	0.503
U–D	1.436**	1.212*	*Notes: The standard errors are robust using the method developed by Newey and West (1987)*
U–N	0.633	0.293	
N–D	0.803	0.920**	

(CVaR) and stock returns, suggested by Ling and Cao [28], and Tokpavi and Vaucher [29].

Likewise, the results challenge the notion of a positive relationship between stock returns and illiquidity, suggested by Amihud (2002), Amihud et al. [25], Chen et al. [27], and Gunathilaka et al. [30]. The findings indicate that the profits of arbitrage techniques are statistically insignificant (Table 5).

5 Conclusion and Implications

In summary, the analysis revealed that both long and arbitrage strategies exhibit favorable returns and good alphas. The strategy of purchasing small-size companies in the high Value-at-Risk (SHVaR portfolio) has been shown to exhibit superior performance relative to the market. Specifically, this approach yields the best return, around 2.38% on a monthly basis, as indicated in Table 3, when compared to alternative methods. This suggests that the efficiency of the HSX is questionable, and the solutions proposed in this paper are intended to assist investors in achieving favorable returns. The findings of this paper provide valuable practical implications. Initially, policymakers have the capacity to employ risk factors as a means of assessing the efficacy of the market. Furthermore, investors have the ability to choose stocks for

Table 3 Size–VaR Portfolios and Strategies (Jan 2011 – Dec 2019)

Panel A: Monthly Returns (%)

Size VaR	Small (S)	Big (B)	S–B
High (HVaR)	2.382**	0.028	2.355***
Medium (MVaR)	0.617	0.859	– 0.242
Low (LVaR)	0.929**	0.610	0.319
HVaR–LVaR	1.453*	– 0.582	*Trading Strategies*
HVaR–MVaR	1.765***	– 0.832	*Long strategies* *Arbitrage (firm size)*
MVaR–LVaR	– 0.312	0.250	*Arbitrage (VaR)*

Panel B: Monthly Alphas (%)

Size VaR	Small (S)	Big (B)	S–B
High (HVaR)	1.716***	– 0.16	1.876***
Medium (MVaR)	0.234	0.855**	– 0.621**
Low (LVaR)	0.633**	0.752*	– 0.119
HVaR–LVaR	1.083*	– 0.912	*Notes: The standard errors are robust using the method developed by Newey & West (1987)*
HVaR–MVaR	1.482***	– 1.015*	
MVaR–LVaR	– 0.399	0.103	

their portfolios by considering the connection between stock returns and their respective qualities. Lastly, investors have the option to choose the most suitable risk model in order to assess if their investment methods yield superior returns compared to the market's necessary returns.

5.1 Author Declarations

6 Competing Interests

There is NO conflict of interest in relation to this study.

Table 4 Size–CVaR portfolios and strategies (Jan 2011 – Dec 2019)

Panel A: Monthly Returns (%)

Size CVaR	Small (S)	Big (B)	S–B
High (HCVaR)	2.067**	0.050	2.017***
Medium (MCVaR)	1.044	0.418	0.626
Low (LCVaR)	0.844*	1.089*	− 0.244
LCVaR–HCVaR	− 1.223	1.038	*Trading Strategies* *Long strategies* *Arbitrage (firm size)* *Arbitrage (CVaR)*
MCVaR–HCVaR	− 1.024**	0.367	
LCVaR–MCVaR	− 0.199	0.671	

Panel B: Monthly Alphas (%)

Size CVaR	Small (S)	Big (B)	S–B
High (HCVaR)	1.413***	− 0.042	1.454***
Medium (MCVaR)	0.685*	0.418	0.267
Low (LCVaR)	0.468	1.172***	− 0.704*
LCVaR–HCVaR	− 0.944*	1.214**	*Notes: The standard errors are robust using the method developed by Newey & West (1987)*
MCVaR–HCVaR	-0.727*	0.46	
LCVaR–MCVaR	-0.217	0.754*	

Table 5 Size–illiquidity portfolios and strategies (Jan 2011 – Dec 2019)

Panel A: Monthly Returns (%)			
Size Illiquidity	Small (S)	Big (B)	S–B
High (HIlliq)	1.539***	0.049	1.490***
Medium (MIlliq)	1.390*	0.661	0.729*
Low (LIlliq)	0.667	0.752	− 0.085
HIlliq–LIlliq	0.871	− 0.703	*Trading Strategies* *Long strategies* *Arbitrage (firm size)* *Arbitrage (illiquidity)*
HIlliq–MIlliq	0.149	− 0.612	
MIlliq–LIlliq	0.722	− 0.092	
Panel B: Monthly Alphas (%)			
Size Illiquidity	Small (S)	Big (B)	S–B
High (HIlliq)	1.038***	0.038	1**
Medium (MIlliq)	0.961**	0.528	0.433
Low (LIlliq)	− 0.165	0.824***	− 0.989
HIlliq–LIlliq	1.203	− 0.786*	*Notes: The standard errors are robust using the method developed by Newey & West (1987)*
HIlliq–MIlliq	0.077	− 0.49	
MIlliq–LIlliq	1.126	− 0.296	

Table 6 Size–CAPM beta portfolios and strategies (Jan 2011 – Dec 2019)

Panel A: Monthly Returns (%)			
Size CAPM Beta	Small (S)	Big (B)	S–B
High (HCAPM)	1.501	0.480	1.021
Medium (MCAPM)	1.018	0.725	0.293
Low (LCAPM)	1.611***	0.546	1.065
HCAPM–LCAPM	– 0.110	– 0.066	*Trading Strategies* *Long strategies* *Arbitrage (firm size)* *Arbitrage (CAPM beta)*
HCAPM–MCAPM	0.483	– 0.245	
MCAPM–LCAPM	– 0.593	0.179	
Panel B: Monthly Alphas (%)			
Size CAPM Beta	Small (S)	Big (B)	S–B
High (HCAPM)	0.896*	0.361	0.535
Medium (MCAPM)	0.577	0.722	– 0.144
Low (LCAPM)	1.138***	0.642	0.496
HCAPM–LCAPM	– 0.242	– 0.281	*Notes: The standard errors are robust using the method developed by Newey & West (1987)*
HCAPM–MCAPM	0.319	– 0.361	
MCAPM–LCAPM	– 0.561	0.08	

Table 7 Size–DCC Beta Portfolios and Strategies (Jan 2011 – Dec 2019)

Panel A: Monthly Returns (%)			
Size DCC Beta	Small (S)	Big (B)	S–B
High (HDCC)	1.447	0.428	1.019
Medium (MDCC)	1.053	1.125**	– 0.073
Low (LDCC)	1.417***	0.013	1.404***
HDCC–LDCC	0.030	0.415	*Trading Strategies* *Long strategies* *Arbitrage (firm size)* *Arbitrage (DCC beta)*
HDCC–MDCC	0.394	– 0.697	
MDCC–LDCC	– 0.364	1.112**	
Panel B: Monthly Alphas (%)			
Size DCC Beta	Small (S)	Big (B)	S–B
High (HDCC)	– 0.08	0.821	0.406*
Medium (MDCC)	– 0.416	0.696*	1.254**
Low (LDCC)	0.558	0.952**	– 0.055
HDCC–LDCC	– 1.007**	– 0.131	*Notes: The standard errors are robust using the method developed by Newey & West (1987)*
HDCC–MDCC	0.461	0.126	
MDCC–LDCC	– 0.848*	– 0.257	

Data Availability Research data will be made available upon reasonable request.

References

1. Cochrane, J.H.: Presidential address: discount rates. J. Financ. **66**, 1047–1108 (2011)
2. Harvey, C.R., Liu, Y.: A Census of the Factor Zoo (SSRN Scholarly Paper No. ID 3341728). Rochester, NY: Social Science Research Network (2019)
3. Hanauer, M.X., Lauterbach, J.G.: The cross-section of emerging market stock returns. Emerg. Mark. Rev. **38**, 265–286 (2019)
4. Jacobs, H., Müller, S.: Anomalies across the globe: once public, no longer existent? J. Financ. Econ. **135**, 213–230 (2020)
5. Mclean, R.D., Pontiff, J.: Does academic research destroy stock return predictability? J. Fin. **71**, 5–32 (2016)
6. Lo, A.W., MacKinlay, A.: Data-snooping biases in tests of financial asset pricing models. Rev. Finan. Stud. **3**, 431–467 (1990)
7. Aziz, T., Ansari, V.A.: Value-at-risk and stock returns: evidence from India. Int. J. Emerg. Mark. **12**, 384–399 (2017)
8. Barberis, N., Shleifer, A.: Style investing. J. Financ. Econ. **68**, 161–199 (2003)

9. Sharpe, W.F.: Capital asset prices: a theory of market equilibrium under conditions of risk. J. Financ. **19**, 425–442 (1964)
10. Bali, T.G., Engle, R.F., Tang, Y.: Dynamic conditional beta is alive and well in the cross section of daily stock returns. Manage. Sci. **63**, 3760–3779 (2017)
11. Fama, E.F., French, K.R.: The cross-section of expected stock returns. J. Financ. **47**, 427–465 (1992)
12. Engle, R.F.: Dynamic conditional correlation: a simple class of multivariate generalized autoregressive conditional heteroskedasticity models. J. Busin. Econ. Stat. **20**, 339–350 (2002)
13. Banz, R.W.: The relationship between return and market value of common stocks. J. Financ. Econ. **9**, 3–18 (1981)
14. Hwang, Y.-S., Min, H.-G., McDonald, J.A., Kim, H., Kim, B.-H.: Using the credit spread as an option-risk factor: size and value effects in CAPM. J. Bank. Finance **34**, 2995–3009 (2010)
15. Fama, E.F., French, K.R.: Size and book-to-market factors in earnings and returns. J. Financ. **50**, 131–155 (1995)
16. Li, J.: Explaining momentum and value simultaneously. Manage. Sci.. Sci. **64**, 4239–4260 (2018)
17. Singh, S., Walia, N.: Time-series and cross-sectional momentum in Indian stock market. Copernican J. Finan. Account. **9**, 161–176 (2021)
18. Wang, F., Yan, X. (Sterling), Zheng, L.: Time-series and cross-sectional momentum in anomaly returns. Eur. Fin. Manag. **27**, 736–771 (2021)
19. Bali, T.G., Engle, R.F., Murray, S.: Empirical asset pricing: the cross-section of stock returns. New York: John Wiley & Sons, Incorporated (2016)
20. Iqbal, J., Azher, S.: Value-at-risk and expected stock returns: evidence from Pakistan. Lahore J. Econ. **19**, 71–100 (2014)
21. Abad, P., Benito, S., López, C.: A comprehensive review of value at risk methodologies. Spanish Rev. Finan. Econ. **12**, 15–32 (2014)
22. Unbreen, A., Sohail, M.T.: Asset pricing with higher co-moments and CVaR: evidence from Pakistan stock exchange. Int. J. Econ. Financ. Issues **10**, 243–255 (2020)
23. Artzner, P., Delbaen, F., Eber, J.-M., Heath, D.: Coherent measures of risk. Math. Financ. **9**, 203–228 (1999)
24. Uryasev, S.: Conditional value-at-risk: optimization algorithms and applications. *Proceedings of the IEEE/IAFE/INFORMS 2000 Conference on Computational Intelligence for Financial Engineering (CIFEr) (Cat. No.00TH8520)*, 49–57 (2000)
25. Amihud, Y., Hameed, A., Kang, W., Zhang, H.: The illiquidity premium: international evidence. J. Financ. Econ. **117**, 350–368 (2015)
26. Chen, C.-C., Tai, C.-L., Cho, Y.-C.: Market illiquidity premium on stock returns: an empirical study of Taiwan stock markets. Asian Econ. Finan. Rev. **9**, 778–788 (2019)
27. Chen, D.-H., Chen, C.-D., Wu, S.-C.: VaR and the cross-section of expected stock returns: an emerging market evidence. J. Bus. Econ. Manag. **15**, 441–459 (2014)
28. Ling, A., Cao, Z.: Two-side CVaRs and cross-sectional expected stock returns: evidence from the Chinese stock market (SSRN Scholarly Paper No. ID 3468275). Rochester, NY: Social Science Research Network (2020)
29. Tokpavi, S., Vaucher, B.: Conditional value-at-risk: an alternative measure for low-risk strategies? SSRN Elect. J. (2012)
30. Gunathilaka, C., Jais, M., Balia, S.S.X.: Illiquidity, investor sentiment and stock returns: evidence from Malaysia. Intern. J. Econ. Finan. Iss. Mersin, **7**, 478–487 (2015)
31. Amihud, Y.: X: Illiquidity and stock returns: cross-section and time-series effects. J. Finan. Mark. **5**, 31–56 (2014)
32. Bali, T.G., Gokcan, S., Liang, B.: Value at risk and the cross-section of hedge fund returns. J. Bank. Finance **31**, 1135–1166 (2007)
33. Fama, E.F., French, K.R.: Common risk factors in the returns on stocks and bonds. J. Financ. Econ. **33**, 3–56 (1993)

34. Fama, E.F., French, K.R.: A five-factor asset pricing model. J. Financ. Econ. **116**, 1–22 (2015)
35. Newey, W., West, K.: A simple, positive semi-definite, heteroskedasticity and autocorrelation consistent covariance matrix. Econometrica **55**, 703–708 (1987)
36. Tian, D., Cai, Z., Fang, Y.: Econometric modeling of risk measures: a selective review of the recent literature. Appl. Mathem. -A J. Chinese Univ. **34**, 205–228 (2019)

SPRINGER NATURE

GPSR Compliance

The European Union's (EU) General Product Safety Regulation (GPSR) is a set of rules that requires consumer products to be safe and our obligations to ensure this.

If you have any concerns about our products, you can contact us on ProductSafety@springernature.com

In case Publisher is established outside the EU, the EU authorized representative is:

Springer Nature Customer Service Center GmbH
Europaplatz 3
69115 Heidelberg, Germany

The manufacturer's authorised representative in the EU is Springer Nature Customer Service Centre GmbH, Europaplatz 3, 69115 Heidelberg, Germany. If you have any concerns regarding our products, please contact ProductSafety@springernature.com

Printed and bound by CPI Group (UK) Ltd, Croydon, CR0 4YY
01/10/2026
02225859-0007